Sherlock's *Map of* CALGARY

S0-BXM-722

PAGE KEY

CITY OF CALGARY KEY MAP . . . . Page 1
DISTRICTS & SUBDIVISIONS . . . . Pages 3-4
CALGARY CITY MAPS . . . . Maps 1-98
RURAL MAPS . . . . Maps 99-115
FEATURES INDEX . . . . Pages 116-119
STREET INDEX . . . . Pages 120-141
RURAL AREA KEY MAP . . . . Page 142
MAP LEGEND . . . . Back Cover

RURAL MAPS

Airdrie	Map 113	Heritage Pointe	Map 115
Banff	Map 21	High River	Map 109
Beiseker	Map 111	Irricana	Map 111
Black Diamond	Map 106	Langdon	Map 88
Bragg Creek	Map 33	Okotoks	Map 107
Canmore	Map 101	Redwood Meadows	Map 33
Chestermere	Map 80	Springbank	Map 99
Cochrane	Map 103	Strathmore	Map 112
Crossfield	Map 8	Turner Valley	Map 105
Elbow Valley	Map 115		

STREET ABBREVIATIONS

AL	Alley	KEY	Key
AV	Avenue	LD	Landing
BY	Bay	LN	Lane
BEND	Bend	LK	Link
BLVD	Boulevard	LOOP	Loop
CASTLE	Castle	MR	Manor
CTR	Centre	MDWS	Meadows
CIR	Circle	MS	Mews
CL	Close	MT	Mount
CM	Common	PR	Parade
CT	Court	PK	Park
CV	Cove	PS	Passage
CR	Crescent	PH	Path
CREST	Crest	PL	Place
CROSS	Crossing	PT	Point
DR	Drive	RDG	Ridge
EST	Estates	RS	Rise
GDN	Gardens	RD	Road
GT	Gate	ROW	Row
GLEN	Glen	SQ.	Square
GN	Green	ST.	Street
GV	Grove	TER	Terrace
HAVEN	Haven	TR	Trail
HE.	Heath	VW.	View
HTS	Heights	VL	Villa or Villas
HWY	Highway	VILLAGE	Village
HL	Hill	WK.	Walk
ISLAND	Island	WY	Way

NOTE TO READERS

The publishers wish to acknowledge their appreciation for the advice and information given by the various public and private organizations who have contributed to this directory. While considerable care has been taken to ensure the accuracy of this book the publisher does not accept responsibility for any errors or omissions.

The boundaries and land use indicated on the maps are intended as a guide only. For accurate legal descriptions contact the City of Calgary or other appropriate authority.

REVISIONS

Many good map amendments are the result of information sent from readers. Please send your map suggestions to Sherlock Publishing Ltd.

Produced by:
SHERLOCK PUBLISHING LTD.
205 - 355 Centre St N
Langdon, AB T0J 1X2
Tel: (403) 291-1001
www.sherlockmaps.com

CALGARY *District Index*

District Name	Map Page
ABBEYDALE	54
ACADIA	75
AIRWAYS INDUSTRIAL PARK	42
ALBERT PARK	52
ALTADORE	58
ALYTH INDUSTRIAL	60
APPLEWOOD PARK	54
ARBOUR LAKE	11
ASPEN WOODS	45
BANFF TRAIL	38
BANKVIEW	58
BAYVIEW	73
BEAVERDAM	28
BEDDINGTON	15
BEL-AIRE	67
BONNYBROOK	60
BOWNESS	36
BRAESIDE	74
BRENTWOOD	38
BRIAR HILL	48
BRIDGELAND	51
BRIDLEWOOD	89
BRITANNIA	59
BURNS INDUSTRIAL PARK	68
CALGARY INTERNATIONAL AIRPORT	18
CAMBRIAN HEIGHTS	39
CANYON MEADOWS	82
CAPITOL HILL	39
CASTLERIDGE	31
CEDARBRAE	73
CFB CURRIE	58
CFB LINCOLN PARK	66
CHAPPARRAL	93
CHINOOK PARK	67
CHRISTIE PARK	46
CITADEL	12
CLIFF BUNGALOW	59
COACH HILL	46
COLLINGWOOD	39
CONNAUGHT	49
COPPERFIELD	98
CORAL SPRINGS	32
COUGAR RIDGE	35
COUNTRY HILLS	15
COUNTRY HILLS VILLAGE	5
COVENTRY HILLS	6
CRANSTON	96
CRESCENT HEIGHTS	50
CRESTMONT	34
DALHOUSIE	25
DEER RIDGE	84
DEER RUN	84
DEERFOOT INDUSTRIAL PARK	29
DIAMOND COVE	84
DISCOVERY RIDGE	55
DOUGLAS GLEN	76
DOUGLASDALE BUSINESS PARK	85
DOUGLASDALE ESTATES	85
DOVER	61
DOWNTOWN	50
DOWNTOWN EAST VILLAGE	50
DOWNTOWN WEST END	49
DUFFERIN INDUSTRIAL	78
EAGLE RIDGE	66
EAST FAIRVIEW INDUSTRIAL	68
EAST SHEPARD INDUSTRIAL	77
EASTFIELD BUSINESS PARK	62
EAU CLAIRE	50
EDGEMONT	13
ELBOW PARK	59
ELBOYA	59
ELLISTON PARK	63
ERIN WOODS	62
ERLTON	59
EVANSTON	4
EVERGREEN	89
EVERGREEN ESTATES	82
FAIRVIEW	67
FAIRVIEW INDUSTRIAL	67
FALCONRIDGE	32

District Name	Map Page
FONDA	53
FOOTHILLS INDUSTRIAL PARK	70
FOOTHILLS INDUSTRIAL SOUTH	77
FOREST HEIGHTS	53
FOREST LAWN	62
FRANKLIN INDUSTRIAL PARK	52
FREEPORT BUSINESS PARK	17
GLAMORGAN	57
GLENBROOK	57
GLENDALE	57
GREAT PLAINS	71
GREENVIEW	28
GREENVIEW INDUSTRIAL	41
GREENWOOD	35
HAMPTONS	13
HANSON RANCH	4
HARVEST HILLS	16
HARVEST HILLS BUSINESS PARK	16
HAWKWOOD	12
HAYSBORO	74
HAYSBORO INDUSTRIAL	74
HIDDEN VALLEY	13
HIGHFIELD	60
HIGHLAND PARK	40
HIGHLAND PARK INDUSTRIAL	40
HIGHWOOD	40
HILLHURST	49
HORIZON INDUSTRIAL PARK	42
HOUNSFIELD HEIGHTS	48
HUNTINGTON HILLS	27
INGLEWOOD	51
KELVIN GROVE	67
KILLARNEY	57
KINGSLAND	67
LAKE BONAVISTA	83
LAKEVIEW	65
LINCOLN PARK	57
MACEWAN	14
MANCHESTER	67
MANCHESTER INDUSTRIAL NORTH	60
MANCHESTER INDUSTRIAL SOUTH	67
MAPLE RIDGE	75
MARLBOROUGH	53
MARLBOROUGH PARK	53
MARTINDALE	31
MAYFAIR	67
MAYLAND HEIGHTS	52
MAYLAND INDUSTRIAL PARK	52
McCALL INDUSTRIAL PARK	41
McKENZIE LAKE	95
McKENZIE TOWNE	97
MEADOWLARK PARK	67
MERIDIAN INDUSTRIAL PARK	52
MIDNAPORE	91
MILLRISE	90
MISSION	59
MONTEREY PARK	44
MONTGOMERY	37
MOUNT PLEASANT	40
MOUNT ROYAL	59
MOUNTAIN PARK	95
MOUNTVIEW	40
NEW BRIGHTON	97
NORTH AIRWAYS	42
NORTH GLENMORE PARK	66
NORTH HAVEN	39
NORTH HAVEN UPPER	27
OAKRIDGE	73
OGDEN	69
OGDEN INDUSTRIAL PARK	69
PALLISER	73
PANORAMA HILLS	5
PARKDALE	47
PARKHILL	59
PARKLAND	92
PATTERSON	46
PEGASUS INDUSTRIAL PARK	30
PENBROOKE	53
PINERIDGE	44
PLEASANT HEIGHTS	39

District Name	Map Page
POINT McKAY	47
PUMP HILL	74
QUEENSLAND	84
RADISSON HEIGHTS	52
RAMSAY	51
RANCHLANDS	24
RENFREW	51
RICHMOND	58
RICHMOND HILL	57
RIDEAU PARK	59
RIVERBEND	76
RIVERDALE	59
RIVERVIEW	68
ROCKY RIDGE	9
ROSEDALE	49
ROSEMONT	39
ROSSCARROCK	47
ROXBORO	59
ROYAL OAK	10
RUNDLE	43
RUTLAND PARK	57
SADDLE RIDGE	19
SADDLE RIDGE INDUSTRIAL	31
ST ANDREWS HEIGHTS	48
SANDSTONE	15
SCARBORO	48
SCENIC ACRES	23
SHAGANAPPI	47
SHAWNEE SLOPES	82
SHAWNESSY	90
SHEPARD INDUSTRIAL	77
SIGNAL HILL	56
SILVER SPRINGS	24
SKYLINE INDUSTRIAL PARK	29
SOMERSET	90
SOUTH AIRWAYS	42
SOUTH CALGARY	58
SOUTHBEND BUSINESS PARK	86
SOUTHVIEW	61
SOUTHWOOD	74
SPRINGBANK HILL	55
SPRUCE CLIFF	47
SPY HILL	1
STANLEY PARK	59
STARFIELD INDUSTRIAL	71
STONEY INDUSTRIAL PARK	7
STRATHCONA PARK	46
SUNALTA	49
SUNDANCE	91
SUNNYSIDE	50
SUNRIDGE BUSINESS PARK	42
SYMONS VALLEY	3
TARADALE	32
TEMPLE	44
THE SLOPES	55
THORNCLIFFE	28
TSUU T'INA NATION	65
TUSCANY	22
TUXEDO PARK	40
UNIVERSITY HEIGHTS	38
UNIVERSITY OF CALGARY	38
UNIVERSITY RESEARCH PARK	38
VALLEY RIDGE	34
VALLEYFIELD	61
VARSITY ACRES	37
VARSITY ESTATES	25
VARSITY VILLAGE	37
VICTORIA PARK	50
VISTA HEIGHTS	41
WEST HILLHURST	48
WEST SPRINGS	45
WESTGATE	47
WESTWINDS BUSINESS PARK	31
WHITEHORN	43
WILDWOOD	47
WILLOW PARK	75
WINDSOR PARK	67
WINSTON HEIGHTS	40
WOODBINE	81
WOODLANDS	81

Page 3

Sherlock's
CALGARY
District Map

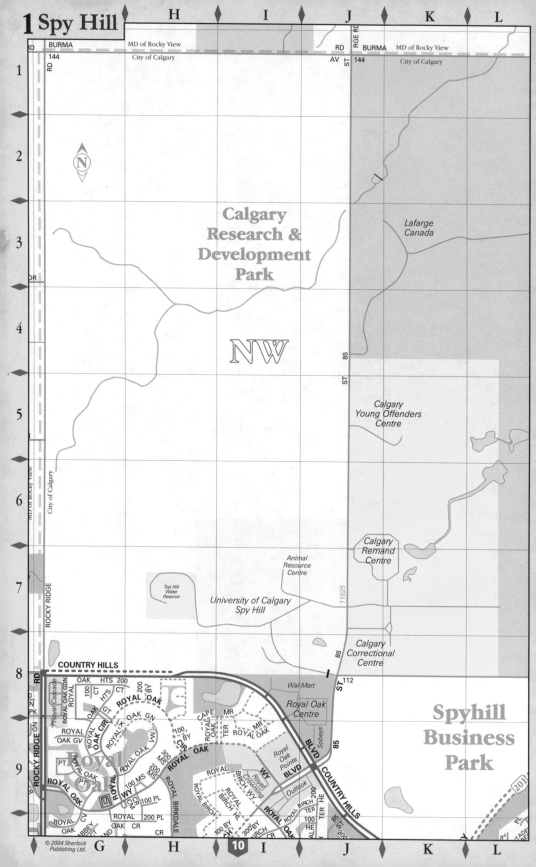

H I J K L

RD BURMA
144
RD 144 AV ST
MD of Rocky View
City of Calgary
RGE RD
BURMA
MD of Rocky View
City of Calgary

1

N

2

Lafarge
Canada

**Calgary
Research &
Development
Park**

3

DR

4

𝕹𝖂

85 ST

Calgary
Young Offenders
Centre

5

MD of Rocky View
City of Calgary
City of Calgary

6

Calgary
Remand
Centre

ROCKY RIDGE

Top Hill
Water
Resevoir

11625

Animal
Resource
Centre

7

University of Calgary
Spy Hill

85

Calgary
Correctional
Centre

RD
COUNTRY HILLS

8

OAK HTS 200
OAK GDN
ROYAL 100
OAK HTS
ROYAL GT
OAK CR
ROYAL OAK
ROYAL OAK GN
OAK LK VW
ST 112
Wal-Mart

**Spyhill
Business
Park**

Royal Oak
Centre

ROCKY RIDGE GN

**Royal
Oak**

ROYAL
OAK GV
ROYAL OAK WY
CAPE
OAK
MR
TER
ROYAL OAK
MR
ROYAL OAK
Sobeys

100 BY
CR
ROYAL OAK
Royal
Oak
Pointe
BLVD

201

9

PT
ROYAL OAK PT
100 MS
300 MS
200 MS
ROYAL OAK
ROYAL OAK WY
ROYAL OAK
ROYAL OAK
ROYAL
BIRKDALE
ROYAL BIRCH
Royal
Crowning
WY
ROYAL OAK
Outlook
BLVD
ROYAL OAK
COUNTRY HILLS
85 ST
HE

ROYAL
OAK CV
ABBEY
100 PL
ROYAL
OAK CR
200 PL
ROYAL
BIRCH
100 BY
300 BY
ROYAL
BIRCH
CR
ROYAL BIRCH
HE
TER
HE
100 HE

G H I J K L

10

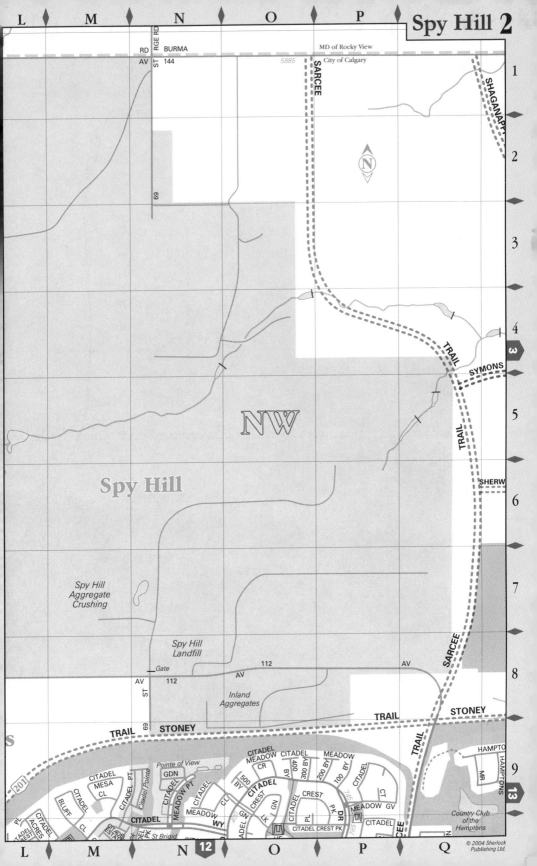

L   M   N   O   P

RGE RD
RD
BURMA   MD of Rocky View
AV   144   5885   City of Calgary

1

SHAGANAPP

SARCEE

69

2

3

N

TRAIL

4

3

NW   SYMONS

5

TRAIL

Spy Hill   SHERW

6

Spy Hill
Aggregate
Crushing

7

Spy Hill
Landfill   SARCEE

Gate   112   AV   AV
AV   112   8
ST   Inland
Aggregates   TRAIL   STONEY

TRAIL   STONEY   TRAIL

69   HAMPTO

201   Pointe of View   CITADEL   HAMPTONS
CITADEL   GDN   MEADOW   CITADEL   MEADOW   MR
MESA   CR   400   300   200   100   9
CITADEL   CL   500   BY   BY   BY   BY   CT   13
BLUFF   MEADOW PT   CITADEL   CITADEL   GN   MEADOW GV
CITADEL   CREST   LK   GN   CITADEL   Country Club
CITADEL   MEADOW   GN   CITADEL   CREST   of the Hamptons
ACRES   WY   CITADEL   CREST   DR   CITADEL
CREST   St Brigid   CITADEL CREST PK   CEE

CITADEL

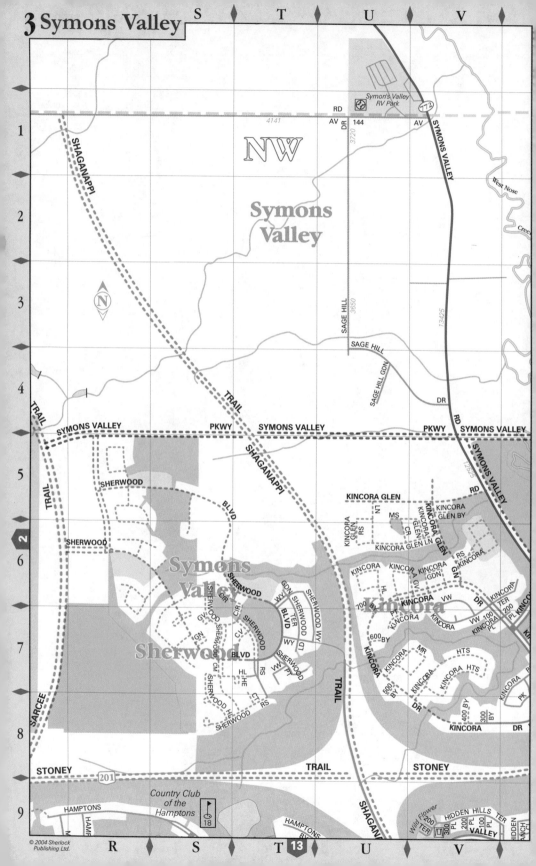

S   T   U   V

1

NW

Symons
Valley

2

3

N

4

5

2

6

Symons
Valley

Sherwood

7

8

9

Country Club
of the
Hamptons

18

SHAGANAPPI

TRAIL

SYMONS VALLEY

SYMONS VALLEY

West Nose
Creek

Symon's Valley
RV Park

772

RD

AV 144

DR

4141

3720

AV

SAGE HILL

3650

SAGE HILL

SAGE HILL GDN

DR

RD

13425

12825

SYMONS VALLEY

PKWY

SYMONS VALLEY

PKWY

SYMONS VALLEY

TRAIL

SYMONS VALLEY

SHERWOOD

SHERWOOD

BLVD

KINCORA GLEN

KINCORA GLEN BY

KINCORA
GLEN
RS

KINCORA GLEN MS

KINCORA
GLEN
CR

KINCORA GLEN LN

KINCORA GLEN

RS

GN

SHERWOOD

SHERWOOD
GV

SHERWOOD
GN

SHERWOOD
CIR

SHERWOOD
GDN

SHERWOOD
WY

SHERWOOD

SHERWOOD
TER

SHERWOOD WY

SHERWOOD
BLVD

SHERWOOD
CT

SHERWOOD
PT

SHERWOOD
BLVD

SHERWOOD
CV

SHERWOOD
WY

SHERWOOD
RS

SHERWOOD
VW

SHERWOOD
HL

SHERWOOD
HE

SHERWOOD
CT

SHERWOOD
CM

SHERWOOD
RS

SHERWOOD
HL

SHERWOOD

KINCORA

KINCORA
GV

KINCORA
GDN

KINCORA
GN

KINCORA

KINCORA

KINCORA

HL
PT

700

KINCORA

KINCORA
VW

KINCORA
DR

TER

KINCORA
PL

200

100

KINCORA
PL

600
BY

KINCORA
MR

KINCORA
HTS

KINCORA
HTS

500
BY

KINCORA

KINCORA
DR

400 BY

300
BY

KINCORA
PK

KINCORA
DR

KINCORA

TRAIL

SARCEE

TRAIL

STONEY

201

STONEY

TRAIL

STONEY

SHAGANA

HAMPTONS

HAMP

HAMPTONS
BV

Wild Flower
TER

HIDDEN HILLS TER

200

300

PL

200

PL

100

PL

VALLEY

HIDDEN

© 2004 Sherlock
Publishing Ltd.

R   S   T   13   U   V

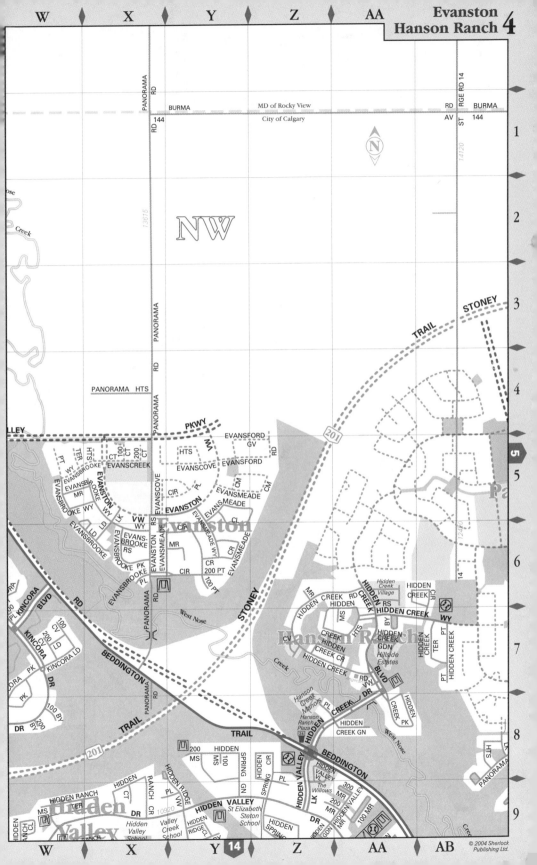

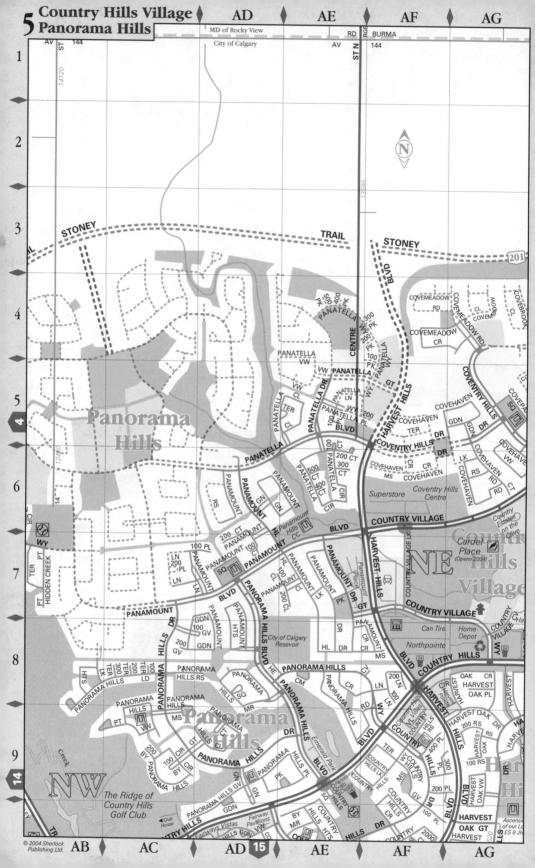

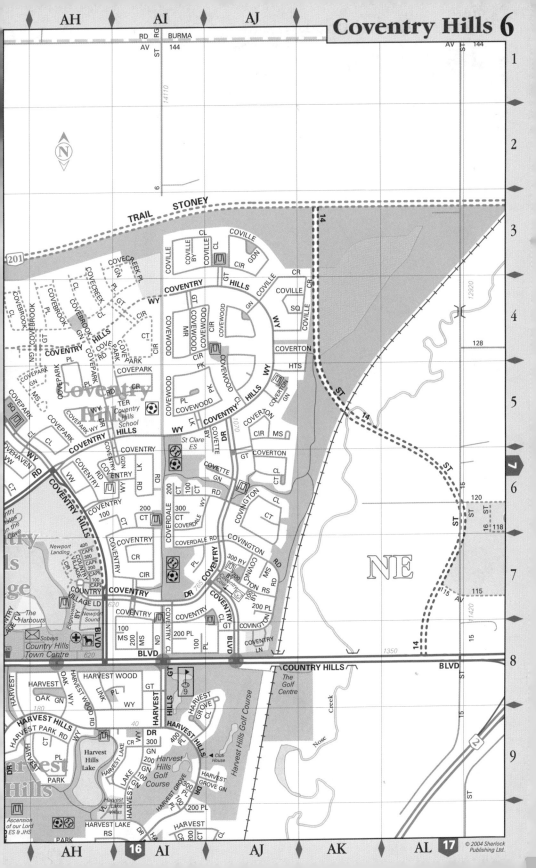

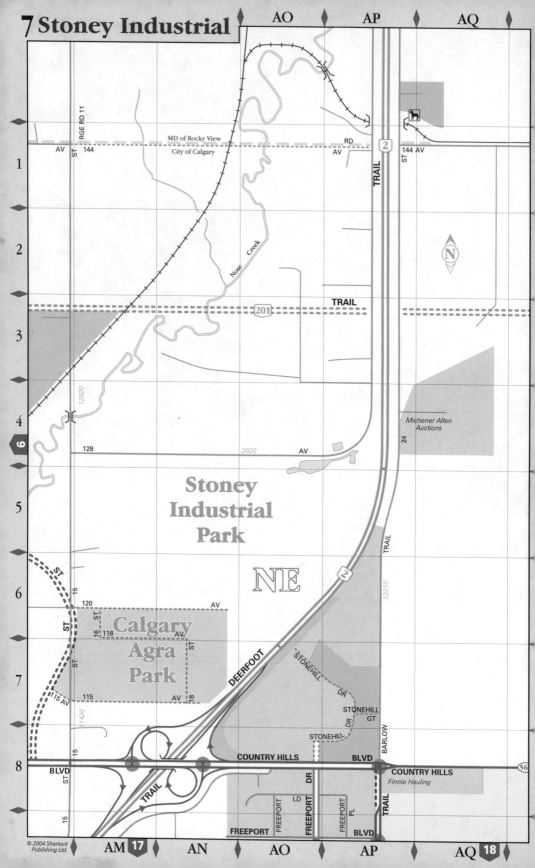

AO   AP   AQ

AV   ST   RGE RD 11   144

MD of Rocky View
City of Calgary

RD
AV

144 AV

TRAIL

2

1

Nose   Creek

N

2

TRAIL

201

3

12920

4

6

128

2020   AV

24

Michener Allen
Auctions

Stoney
Industrial
Park

5

NE

2

12210

TRAIL

ST

15

6

120   AV
ST
16   ST   118   AV
ST

Calgary
Agra
Park

ST

ST

7

115 AV   115   AV
18

11420

DEERFOOT

STONEHILL

DR

STONEHILL
GT

STONEHILL
DR

STONEHILL

BARLOW

15

COUNTRY HILLS   BLVD

TRAIL

8

BLVD
ST

COUNTRY HILLS
Finnie Hauling

56

TRAIL

15

DR
FREEPORT

FREEPORT
LD

FREEPORT
PL

TRAIL

FREEPORT   BLVD

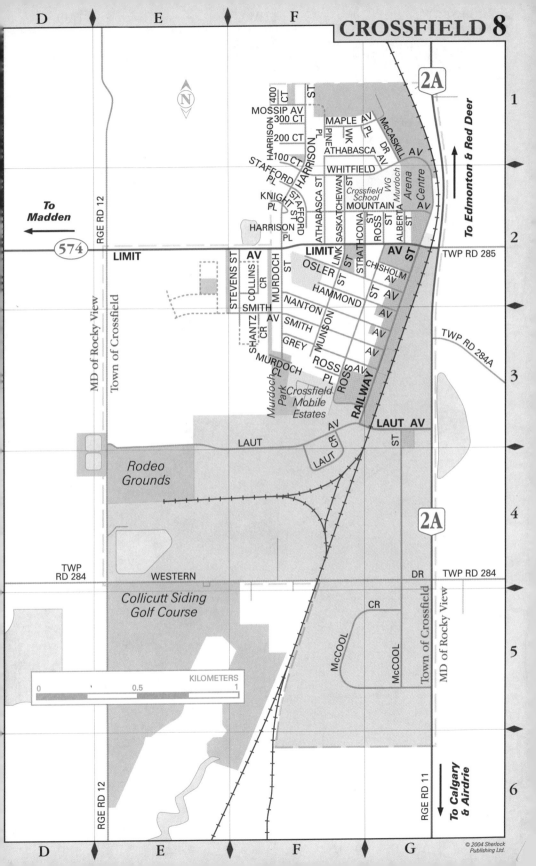

D   E   F

2A

1

To Edmonton & Red Deer

MOSSIP AV
400 CT
300 CT
200 CT
100 CT
MAPLE AV
McCASKILL DR
ATHABASCA AV
WHITFIELD
Crossfield School
Arena Centre
Murdoch WG
MOUNTAIN
HARRISON
STAFFORD PL
STAFFORD
KNIGHT PL
HARRISON PL
PINE PL
MK
ATHABASCA ST
SASKATCHEWAN ST
STRATHCONA ST
ROSS ST
ALBERTA ST

To Madden

574

RGE RD 12

MD of Rocky View
Town of Crossfield

LIMIT

2

LIMIT
AV

AV ST

TWP RD 285

STEVENS ST
COLLINS CR
MURDOCH ST
SMITH CR
SHANTZ CR
OSLER
HAMMOND
NANTON
SMITH
GREY
LINK ST
MUNSON
ROSS PL
CHISHOLM AV
AV
AV
AV
AV
AV
AV
ROSS AV
RAILWAY ST

3

MURDOCH CL
Murdoch Park
Crossfield Mobile Estates

TWP RD 284A

LAUT AV
LAUT CR
LAUT AV
ST

4

Rodeo Grounds

2A

TWP RD 284

WESTERN

Collicutt Siding Golf Course

DR
TWP RD 284

McCOOL CR
McCOOL

Town of Crossfield
MD of Rocky View

5

KILOMETERS
0   0.5   1

RGE RD 12

RGE RD 11

To Calgary & Airdrie

6

D   E   F   G

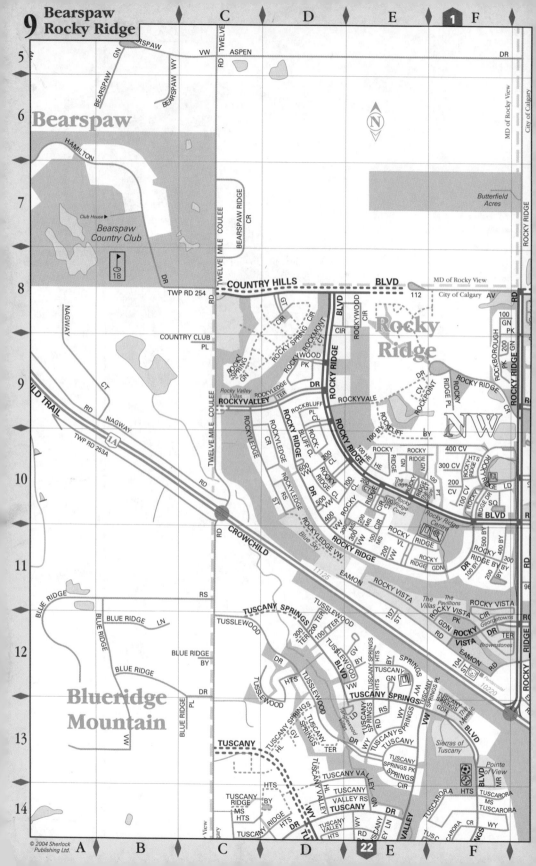

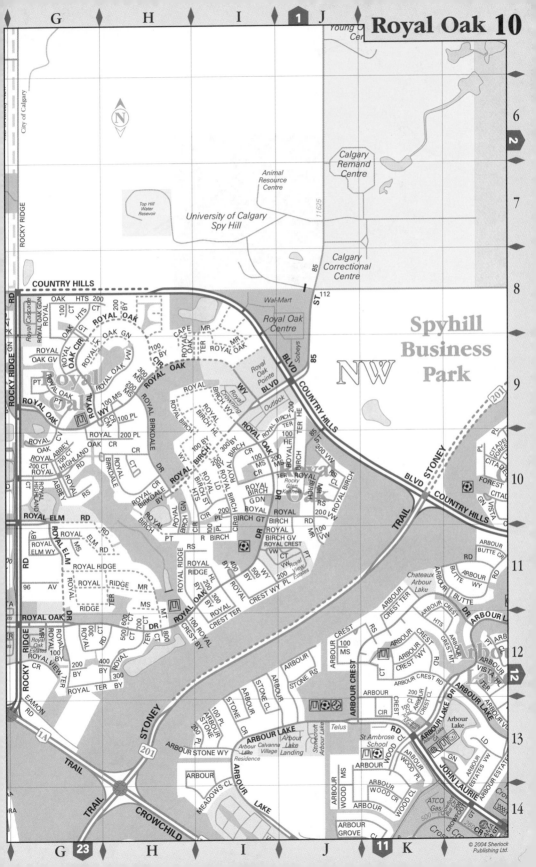

G   H   I   **1**   J

6

2

7

8

9

10

11

12

12

13

14

City of Calgary

N

Top Hill Water Resevoir

Animal Resource Centre

University of Calgary Spy Hill

Young O Cen

Calgary Remand Centre

Calgary Correctional Centre

COUNTRY HILLS

Wal-Mart

Royal Oak Centre

Royal Oak Pointe

Spyhill Business Park

NW

ROCKY RIDGE GN

RD

Royal Cascade

OAK HTS 200
100 CT
ROYAL OAK GDN
ROYAL
OAK CT
OAK CIR
ROYAL OAK
CAPE
MR
ROYAL OAK
MR
TER
ROYAL OAK
100
CR
CR
ROYAL OAK GV
ROYAL
ROYAL OAK GV
PT
Royal Oak
ROYAL
OAK ABBEY
HIGHLAND RD
ROYAL
OAK CR
100 PL
200 PL
Royal Crowning WY
ROYAL BIRCH HL
BIRCH
ROYAL BIRCH
100 BY
ROYAL BIRCH ST
ROYAL BIRCH
Outlook
BLVD
Royal Oak Pointe
BLVD
COUNTRY HILLS
85 ST
112
85 ST
Sobeys
Stoney
BLVD
TRAIL
COUNTRY HILLS
201

Royal Oak

ROYAL OAK DR

ROYAL ELM RD

ROYAL ELM WY
ROYAL ELM RD
ROYAL RIDGE
ROYAL RIDGE MR
ROYAL RIDGE
96 AV

ROYAL OAK DR

ROCKY RIDGE
Royal Oak Estates
ROYAL VIEW TER
ROYAL TER BY

STONEY
201
TRAIL
CROWCHILD
TRAIL

ARBOUR LAKE

ARBOUR CREST

ARBOUR CREST RS
ARBOUR CREST
ARBOUR CREST WY
ARBOUR CREST RD
ARBOUR CREST CL

ARBOUR STONE RS
ARBOUR STONE CR
ARBOUR STONE WY

ARBOUR LAKE
Arbour Lake Residence
Calvanna Village
Arbour Lake Landing

St Ambrose School

ARBOUR WOOD MS
ARBOUR WOOD
ARBOUR WOOD CR
ARBOUR WOOD CL
ARBOUR WOOD PL

ARBOUR GROVE

JOHN LAURIE

ARBOUR LAKE DR

Arbour Lake

ARBOUR BUTTE CR
ARBOUR BUTTE DR

G   **23**   H   I   J   **11**   K

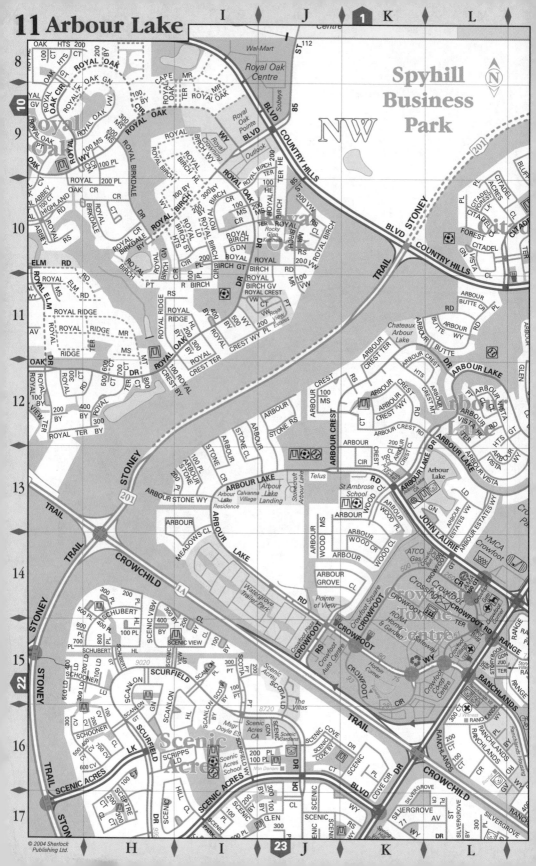

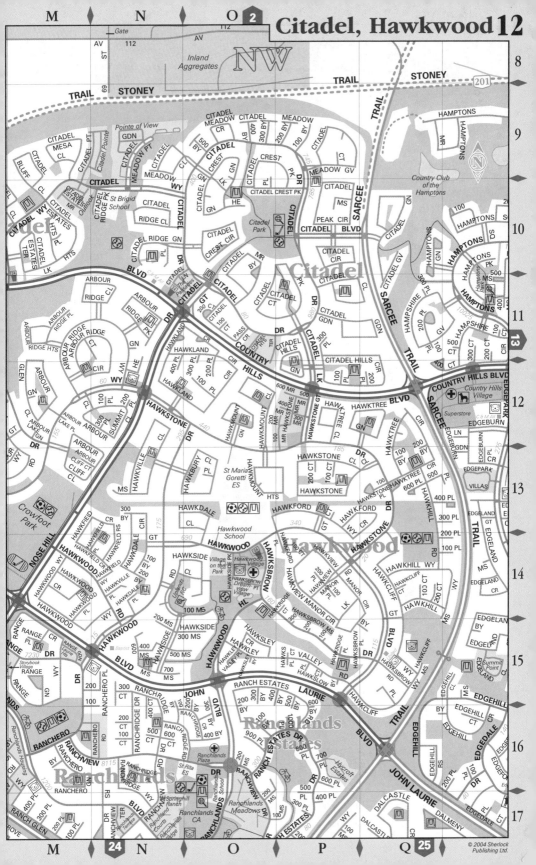

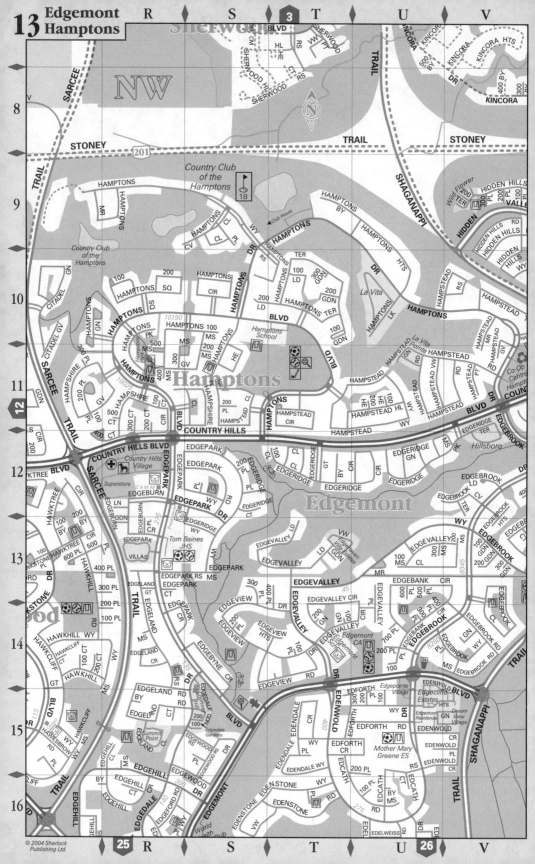

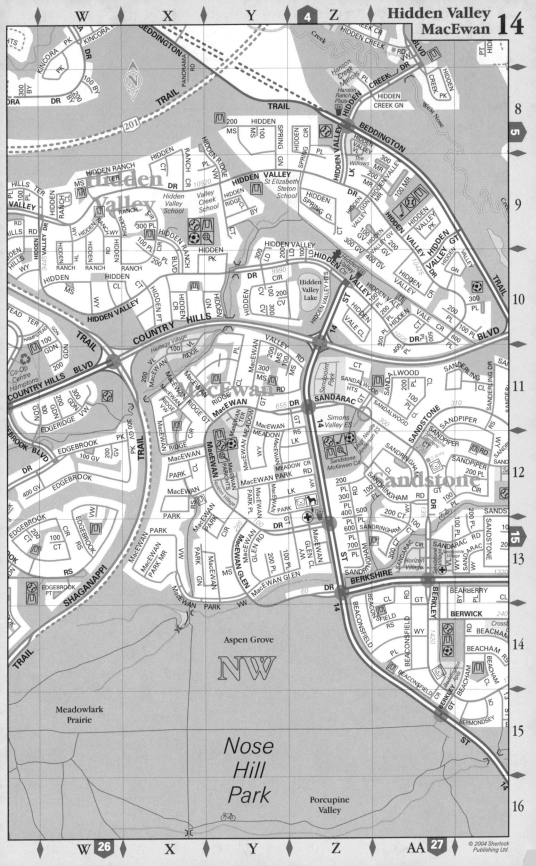

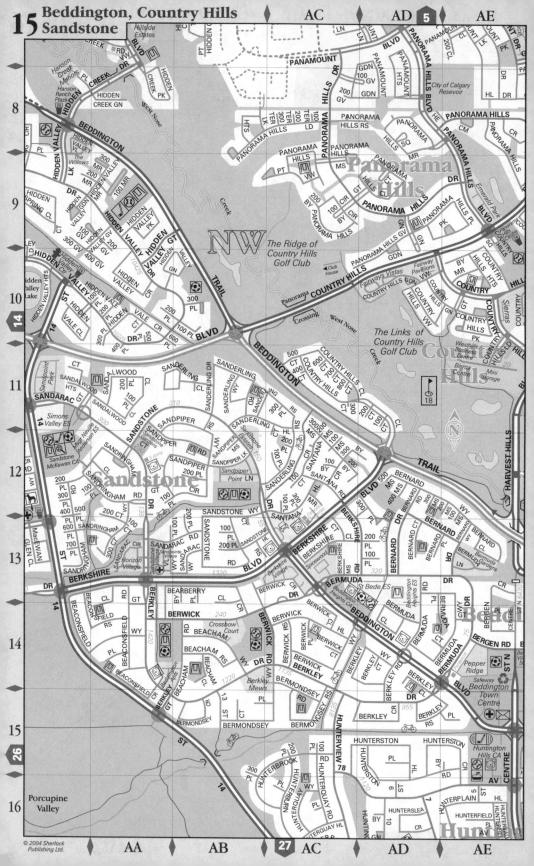

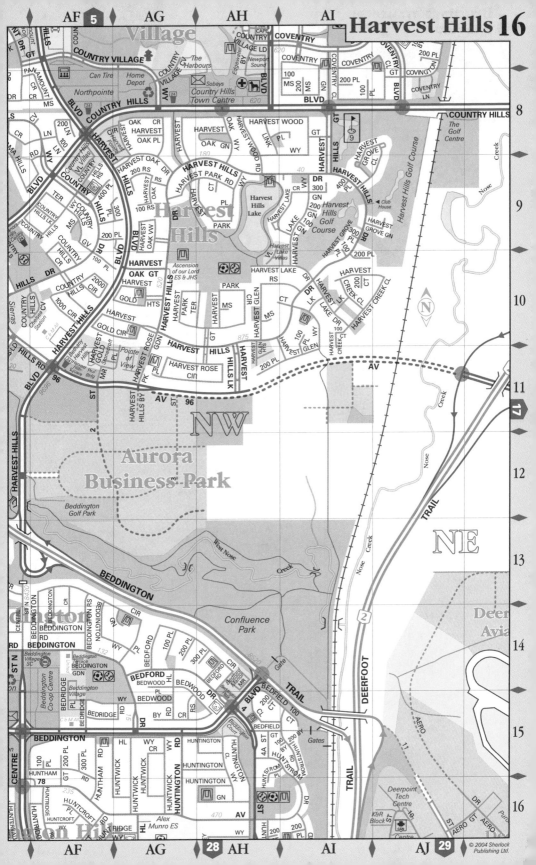

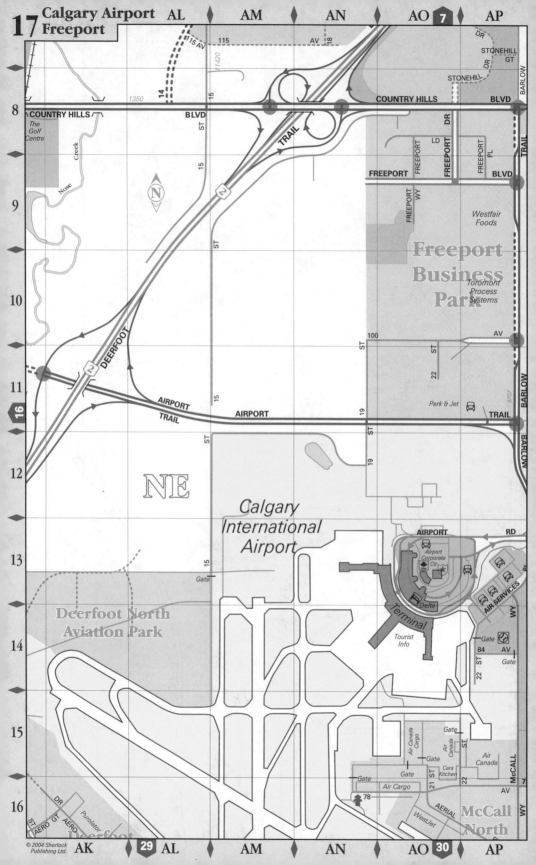

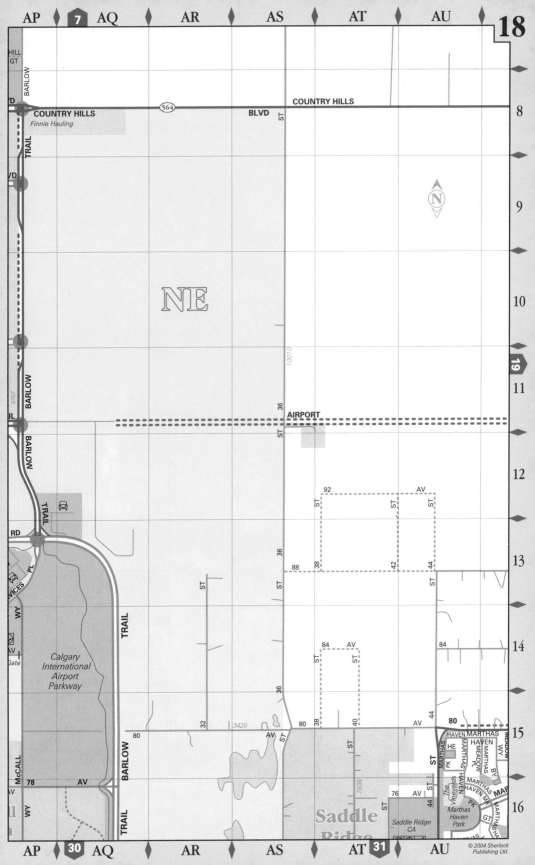

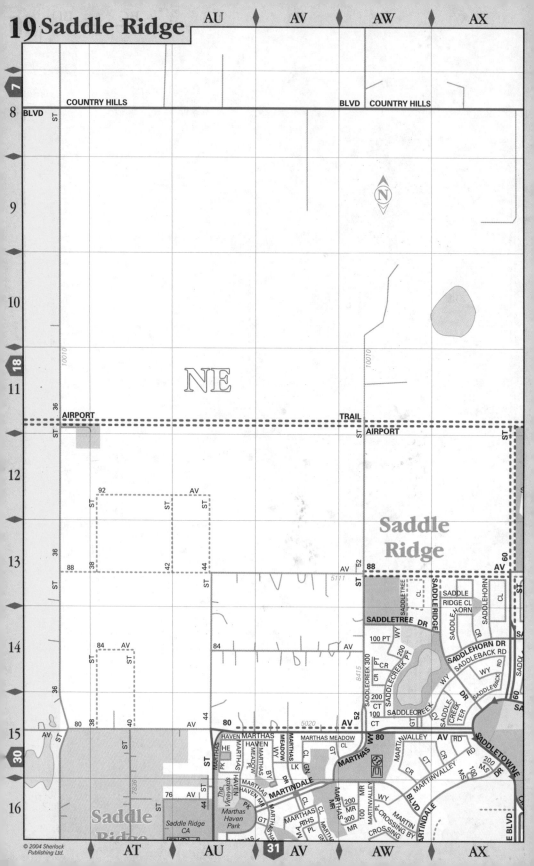

AU AV AW AX

7

COUNTRY HILLS

8 BLVD
ST
BLVD COUNTRY HILLS

18

NE

11

36
ST
10010

AIRPORT
ST
TRAIL
ST
AIRPORT
ST

12

92 AV
ST
ST
ST

13
36
88
38
42
44
ST
AV 52
88
AV
60
ST

Saddle
Ridge

SADDLETREE
CL
SADDLERIDGE
SADDLEHORN
CL
SADDLE
RIDGE CL
HORN
SADDLETREE DR

14
84 AV
ST
ST
84
AV
100 PT
WY
200 PT
SADDLEHORN DR
SADDLEBACK RD
WY

36
ST
8415
SADDLECREEK 300
PT
CR
200 PT
CR
SADDLE
CREEK
TER
SADDLEBACK
DR
SADDLEBACK RD
60
ST
SA

15
36
ST
80
38
40
ST
ST
44
AV
80
AV
5020
AV 52
100
CT
200
CT
SADDLECREEK
CV
GT
MARTINVALLEY AV
RD
SADDLETOWNE DR

30
AV
ST

Saddle
Ridge

HAVEN
MARTHAS
HE
PK
MARTHAS
HAVEN
MEADOW
WY
MARTHAS MEADOW
CL
MARTHAS WY
80
MARTINVALLEY
CR
CR
RD
100
MS

16
76 AV
ST
ST
44
ST
The
spielway
Marthas
Haven
Park
Saddle Ridge
CA
MARTHAS
HAVEN
PK
GT
MARTHAS
HAVEN
MR
MARTINDALE
MARTHAS
HAVEN
PL
MARTHAS
RIHS
PL
MARTHAS
CL
200
MR
300
MR
100
MR
MARTINVALLEY
PL
MARTIN
CROSSING BY
CROSSING
MARTINDALE BLVD
E BLVD

© 2004 Sherlock
Publishing Ltd.

AT AU **31** AV AW AX

8

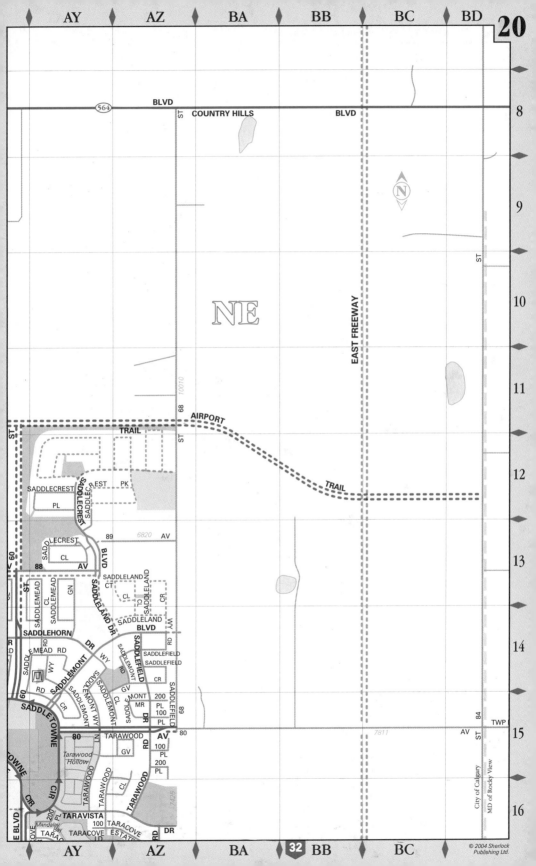

BLVD
564
COUNTRY HILLS　　ST　　BLVD

9

N

NE

EAST FREEWAY

ST

10

11

10010

68
ST
AIRPORT
TRAIL

12

TRAIL

SADDLECREST
EST　　PK
SADDLECREST
PL
SADDLE
BLVD
89　　6820　　AV

13

SADDLECREST
SADDLE
CL
AV
88　　BLVD
SADDLELAND
ST　　CT
CL　　SADDLELAND
SADDLELAND
CR
60

SADDLEMEAD
CL　　GN
SADDLEMEAD
SADDLEHORN　　WY
RD　　BLVD
DR　　SADDLELAND DR

14

SADDLEMEAD RD
RD
CL　　RD　　WY
SADDLEFIELD
SADDLEFIELD
SADDLEMONT
RD
GV
SADDLEMONT WY
CR
60
RD　　CR
SADDLEMONT
CL
MONT　　200
MR　　PL
SADDLETOWNE
DR　　100
PL
80　　SADDLEFIELD
69
84
TWP
SADDLEFIELD

80　　TARAWOOD　　AV　　7811　　AV　　ST　　15
100

TOWNE
N
RD
GV
Tarawood
Hollow
TARAWOOD
PL
200
TARAWOOD
PL

CIR
CL
TARAWOOD

City of Calgary
MD of Rocky View

16

E BLVD
200
TARAVISTA
PL
COVE
Mandalay
Bay
TARACOVE
100
TARACOVE
ESTATE
17425
TARA
RD　　DR

© 2004 Sherlock
Publishing Ltd.

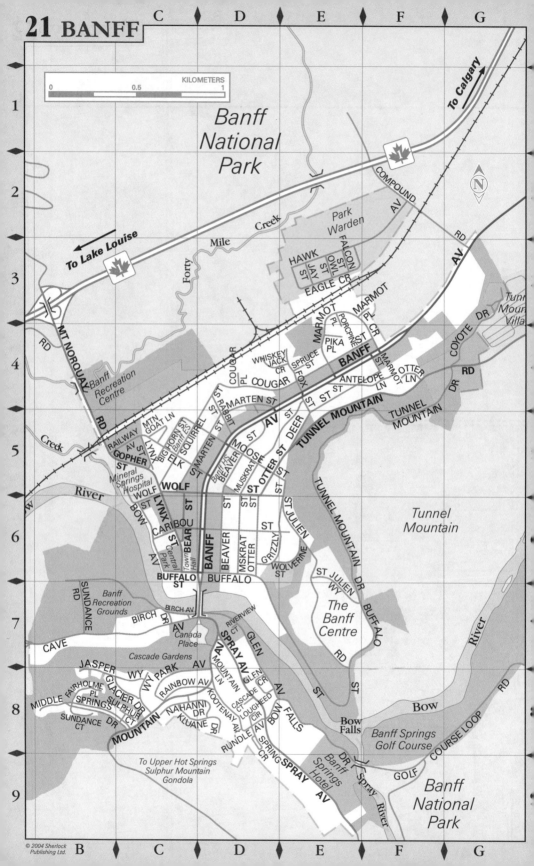

21 BANFF

KILOMETERS
0   0.5   1

Banff National Park

To Calgary

COMPOUND AV

To Lake Louise

Mile
Forty
Creek

Park Warden

HAWK ST
FALCON ST
OWL ST
JAY ST
EAGLE CR

MARMOT PL
PORCPNE PL
MARMOT CR
PIKA PL
PORCPNE ST

COYOTE DR

Tunnel Mour Villa

MT NORQUAY RD

RD

Banff Recreation Centre

Creek
River

WHISKEY JACK CR
SPRUCE ST
FOX ST
COUGAR PL
COUGAR

BANFF AV

MARTEN ST
ANTELOPE ST

MARMOT LN
OTTER LN

BANFF AV

RD

TUNNEL MOUNTAIN

TUNNEL MOUNTAIN

RAILWAY AV
MTN GOAT LN
BIG HORN ST
Banff's
SQUIRREL ST
RABBIT ST
MARTEN ST
MOOSE ST
Banff's BEAVER ST
MUSKRAT ST
DEER ST
OTTER ST
TUNNEL MOUNTAIN

GOPHER ST
LYNX AV
ELK ST
WOLF ST
WOLF ST

Mineral Springs Hospital

LYNX ST
BOW ST
CARIBOU ST
BEAR ST
BANFF ST
BEAVER ST
MSKRAT ST
OTTER ST
GRIZZLY ST
WOLVERINE ST
ST JULIEN ST
ST JULIEN WY

Central Park
Town Hall

Tunnel Mountain
TUNNEL MOUNTAIN DR
BUFFALO RD

BUFFALO ST
BUFFALO
AV

SUNDANCE RD
Banff Recreation Grounds

BIRCH DR
BIRCH AV
AV
Canada Place
RIVERVIEW CT

SPRAY AV
GLEN AV
MOUNTAIN LN
GLEN CR

The Banff Centre

ST JULIEN WY
ST

Bow River

CAVE
JASPER WY
FAIRHOLME PL
GLACIER DR
SULPHUR CT
MIDDLE SPRINGS DR
SUNDANCE CT
MOUNTAIN AV

PARK AV
RAINBOW AV
NAHANNI DR
KOOTENAY AV
KLUANE DR
CASCADE CR
LOUGHEED CIR
RUNDLE AV
BOW AV
AV FALLS
SPRING CR
SPRAY AV

Cascade Gardens

Bow Falls
Banff
Bow

Banff Springs Golf Course

GOLF COURSE LOOP

To Upper Hot Springs Sulphur Mountain Gondola

Spray River
Banff Springs Hotel
SPRAY DR
GOLF

Banff National Park

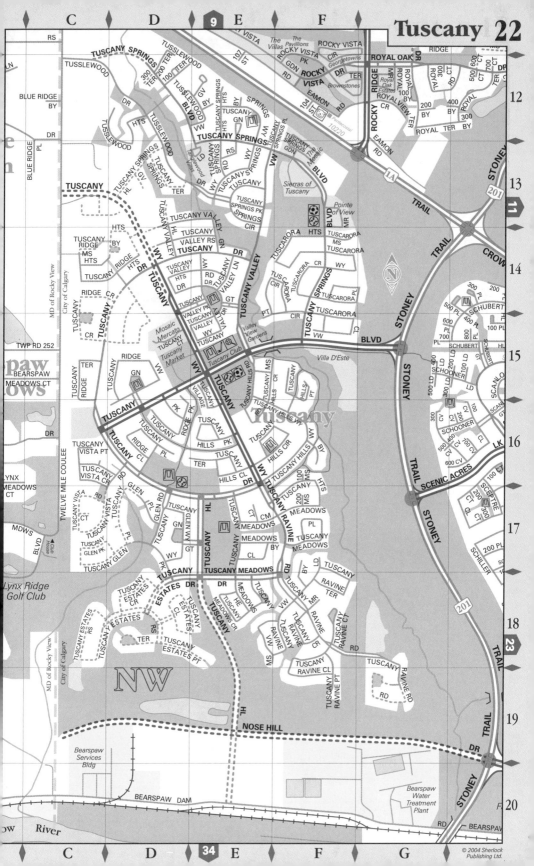

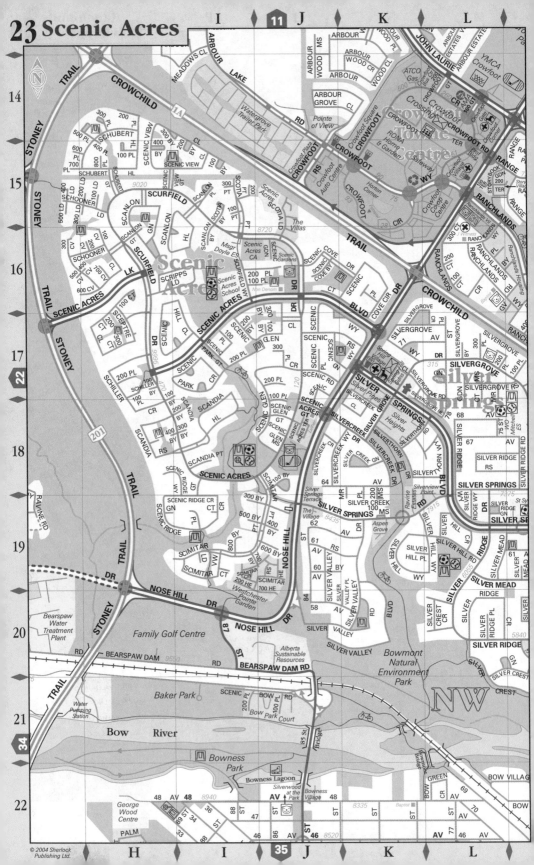

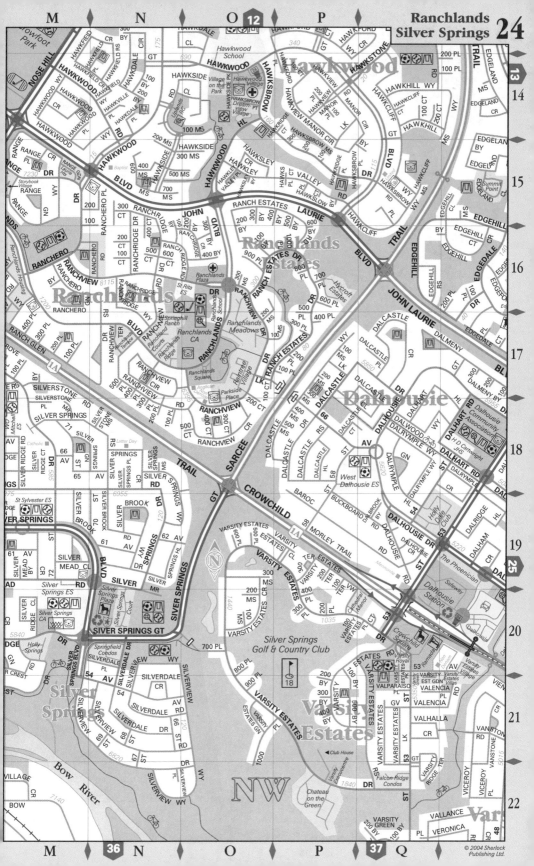

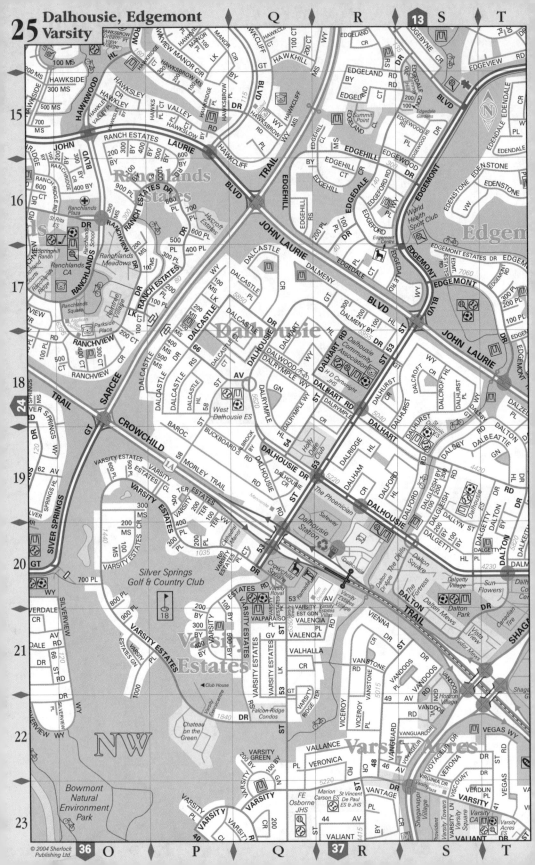

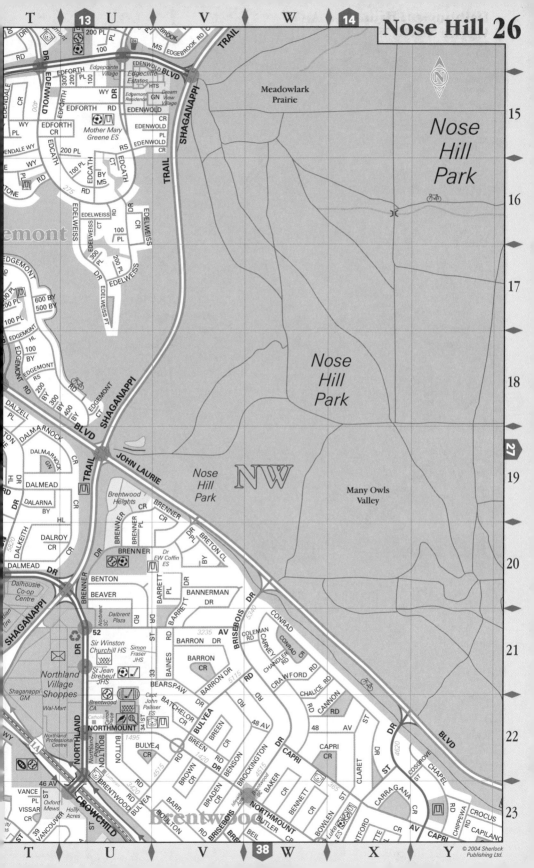

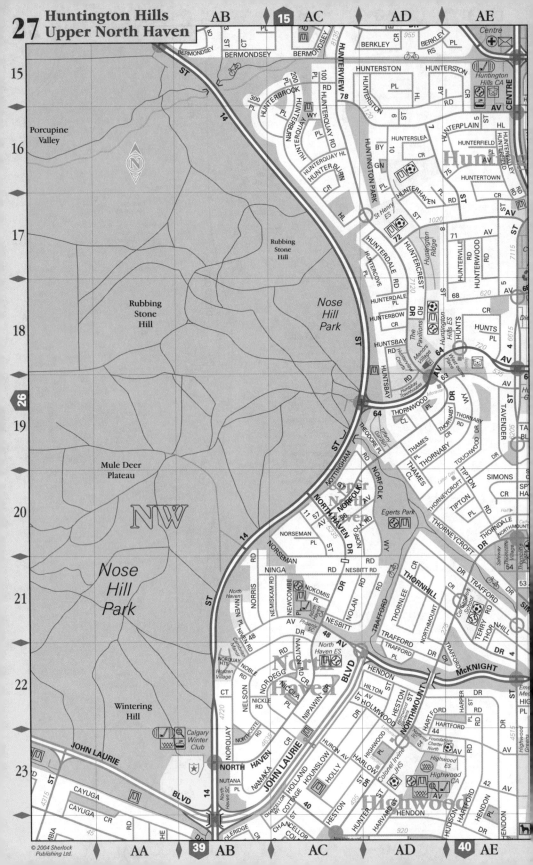

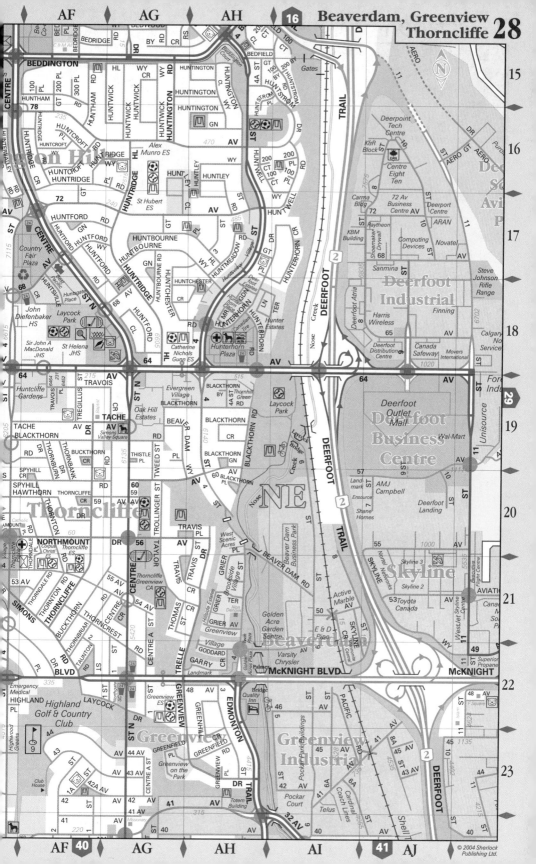

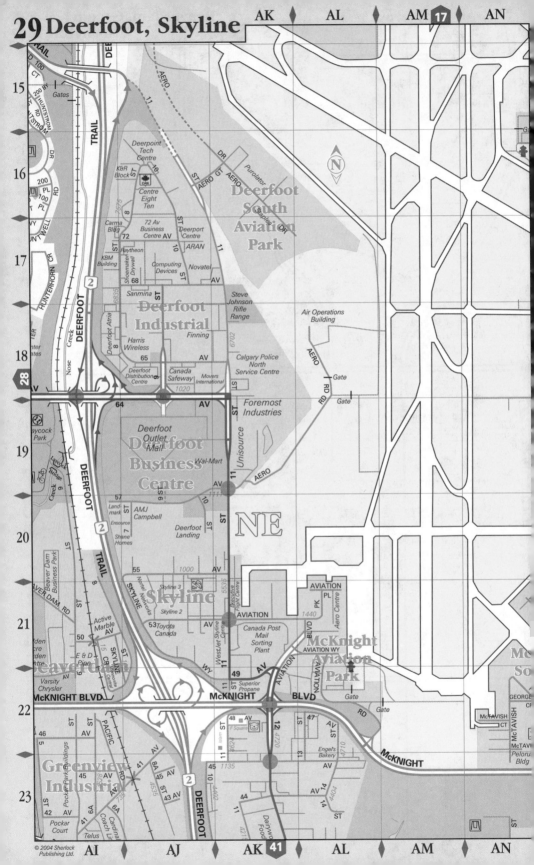

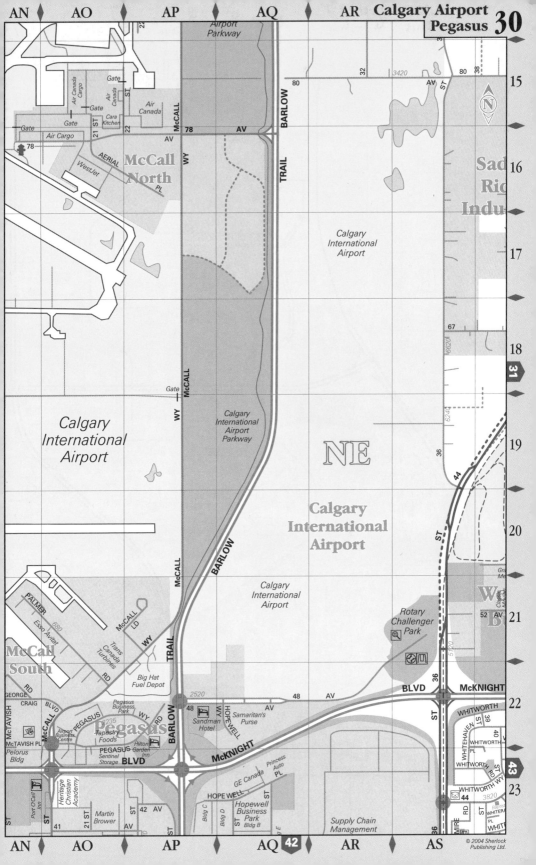

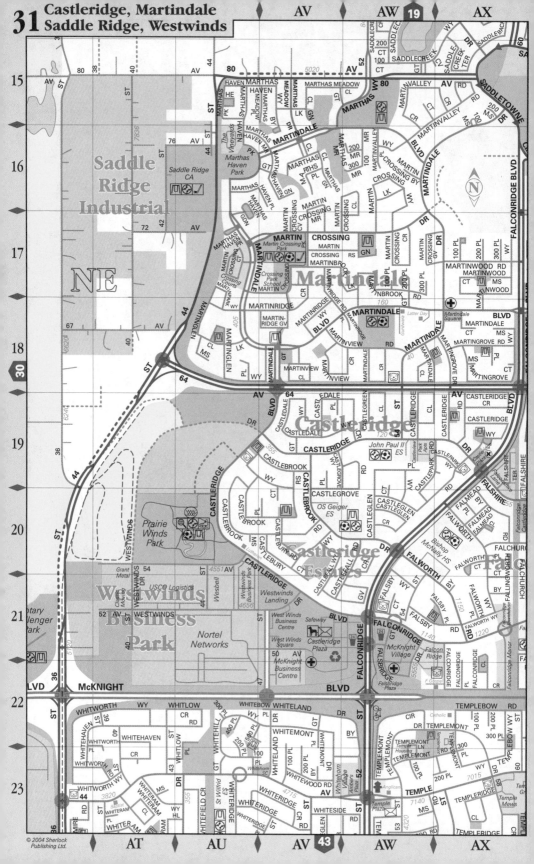

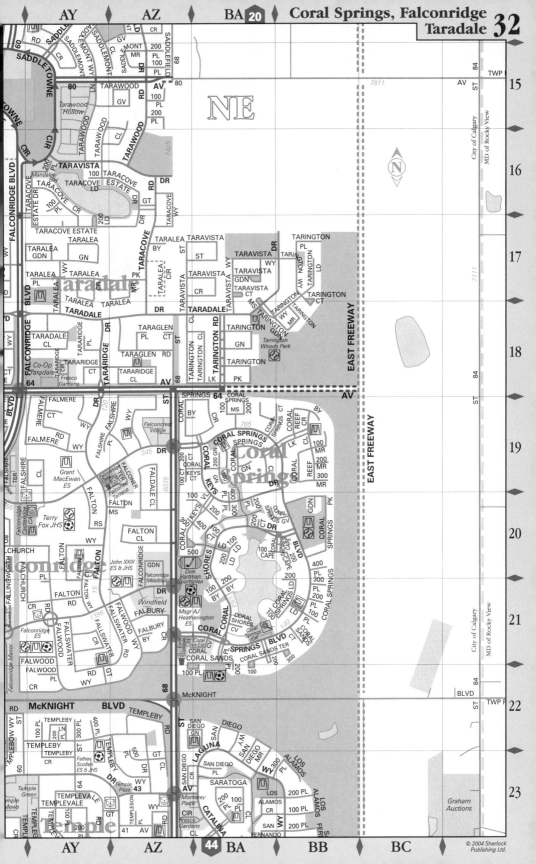

NE

N

EAST FREEWAY

City of Calgary

MD of Rocky View

15
16
17
18
19
20
21
22
23

SADDLETOWNE

SADDLEMONT WY

TARAWOOD

Tarawood Hollow

TARAWOOD RD

TARAVISTA DR

Mandalay Bay

TARACOVE ESTATE DR

TARACOVE LD

TARACOVE CR

TARACOVE ESTATE

TARACOVE DR

TARACOVE WY

TARALEA GDN

TARALEA GN

TARALEA WY

TARALEA PK

TARALEA BLVD

Taradale

TARALEA

TARALEA

TARALEA DR

TARADALE

FALCONRIDGE BLVD

TARAVISTA BY

TARAVISTA ST

TARAVISTA ST

TARAVISTA CR

TARAVISTA WY

TARAVISTA GDN

TARAVISTA CT

TARADALE

TARINGTON

TARINGTON PL

TARINGTON LD

TARINGTON

TARINGTON CT

TARINGTON WY

TARINGTON MR

TARINGTON GDN

TARINGTON

TARINGTON GN

Tarrington Woods Park

TARINGTON

TARINGTON PK

TARADALE DR

TARADALE CL

TARARIDGE DR

TARARIDGE PL

TARARIDGE CT

TARARIDGE CL

Co-Op Taradale

Fresco Gardens

TARAGLEN PL

TARAGLEN CT

TARAGLEN RD

TARINGTON CL

TARINGTON ST

TARINGTON RD

AV

64

68

FALSHIRE

FALMERE CT

FALMERE RD

FALMERE WY

FALSHIRE WY

FALSHIRE

FALCONER

Falconridge Terrace

FALDALE CL

Grant MacEwan ES

FALTON

FALTON MS

FALTON RS

FALTON CL

Terry Fox JHS

Falconridge Castleridge CA

CHURCH

FALTON PL

FALTON

John XXIII ES & JHS

FALTON RD

Falconridge Meadows

FALTON GDN

FALTON DR

Windfield

FALBURY

Falconridge ES

FALWOOD

FALLSWATER WY

FALLSWATER RD

FALWOOD CR

FALWOOD PL

FALWOOD RD

FALWOOD WY

FALLSWATER CR

FALBURY BY

FALBURY GT

CORAL SPRINGS BY

CORAL SPRINGS

Coral Springs MS

CORAL SPRINGS

Falconcrest Village

CORAL KEYS CT

CORAL KEYS

CORAL GN

CORAL

CORAL

CORAL LK

CORAL REEF CT

CORAL REEF

Coral Springs

CORAL SPRINGS GV

CORAL SPRINGS PK

CORAL SPRINGS GDN

CORAL SHORES CAPE

CORAL CAPE

CORAL SHORES LD

CORAL SHORES BLVD

CORAL SPRINGS

CORAL SPRINGS BLVD

CORAL SPRINGS LD

CORAL SANDS

Don Hartman Sportsplex

Msgr AJ Heatherington ES

CORAL SHORES CV

Coral Springs CA

CORAL SPRINGS BLVD

CORAL SANDS

CORAL SANDS TER

CORAL SANDS

McKNIGHT BLVD

TEMPLEBY

TEMPLEBY

TEMPLEBY

TEMPLEBY CR

Father Scollen ES & JHS

TEMPLESON

TEMPLEVALE

TEMPLEVALE

Temple Green

Temple Plaza

Temple Mews

SAN DIEGO GN

SAN DIEGO

SAN DIEGO

SAN DIEGO WY

SAN DIEGO MR

SAN DIEGO PL

LAGUNA

SARATOGA

LOS ALAMOS

LOS ALAMOS CR

LOS ALAMOS PL

Monterey Place

CATALINA

CIR

Fresco Gardens

SAN FERNANDO

SAN WY

Graham Auctions

© 2004 Sherlock
Publishing Ltd.

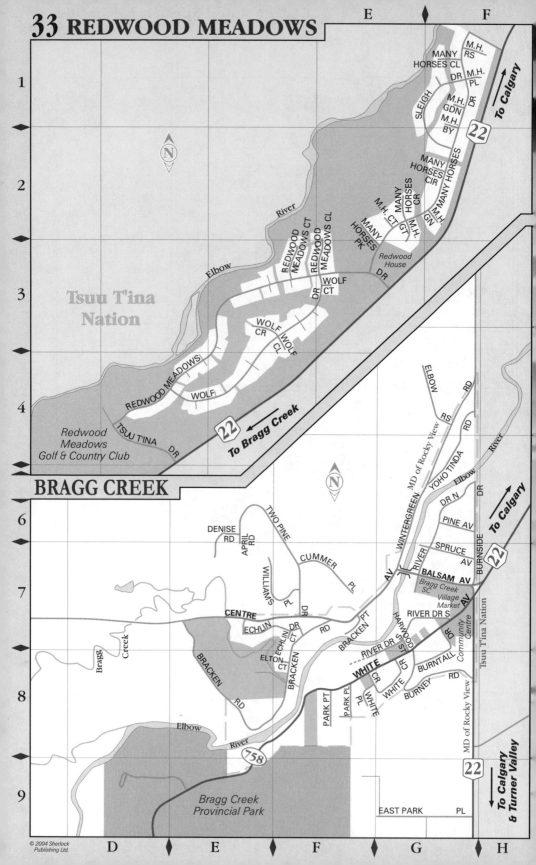

E   F

1

To Calgary

M.H.
RS
MANY
HORSES CL
DR   M.H.
PL
SLEIGH   M.H.
GDN   DR
M.H.
BY

22

2

MANY
HORSES
CIR

MANY
HORSES
CR   MANY HORSES DR

M.H.
CT   GT   M.H.   M.H.
GN

River

MANY
HORSES
PK

Redwood
House   DR

REDWOOD
MEADOWS CT

REDWOOD
MEADOWS CL

Tsuu T'ina
Nation

3

Elbow

DR   WOLF
CT

WOLF   WOLF
CR   CL

REDWOOD MEADOWS

WOLF

4

TSUU T'INA   DR

22   To Bragg Creek

Redwood
Meadows
Golf & Country Club

BRAGG CREEK

N

6

DENISE
RD   APRIL
RD   TWO PINE   ELBOW   RD

WINTERGREEN   RS
RD

MD of Rocky View   YOHO TINDA

Elbow   DR   River   To Calgary

CUMMER   DR N   PINE AV   22

WILLIAMS   PL   SPRUCE
AV

7

CENTRE   PL   DR   RD   AV   River   BALSAM AV   AV   BURNSIDE

ECHLIN   DR   BRACKEN   PT   Bragg Creek
Village
Market

Bragg Creek
SC

RIVER DR S   Community
Centre

Tsuu T'ina Nation

ELTON   ECHLIN
CT   RD   HARWOOD   DR

BRACKEN   CR   WHITE   RIVER DR ST   BURNTALL

8

BRACKEN
RD   PARK PT   PARK PL   WHITE
CR   WHITE   BURNEY   RD

MD of Rocky View

Bragg   Creek

WHITE   PL

Elbow   River   758

22

9

Bragg Creek
Provincial Park   EAST PARK   PL   To Calgary
& Turner Valley

D   E   F   G   H

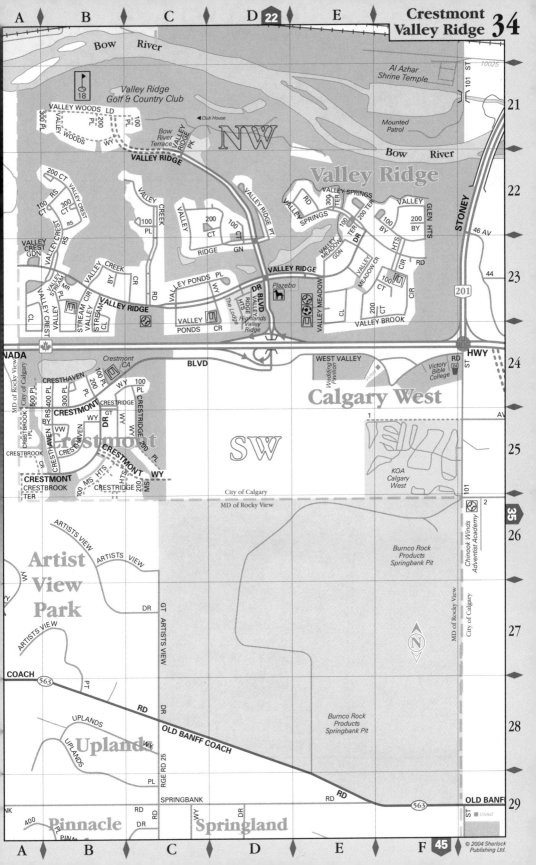

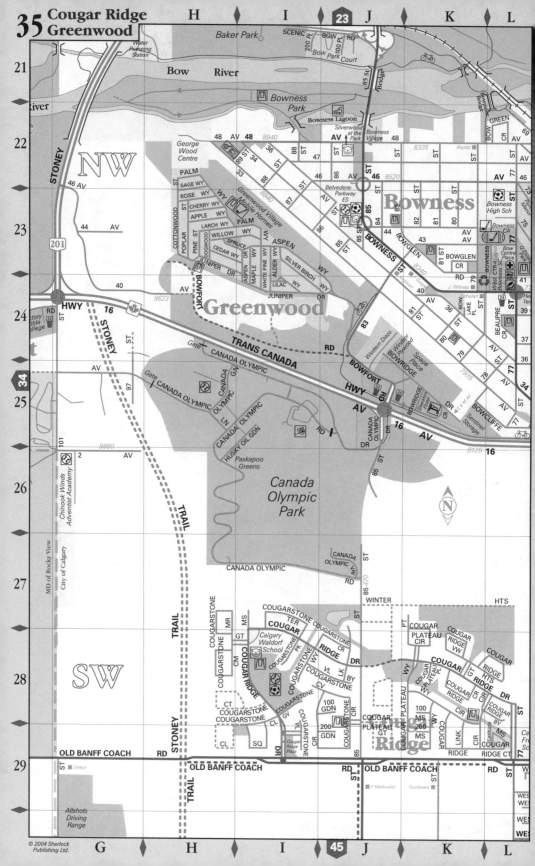

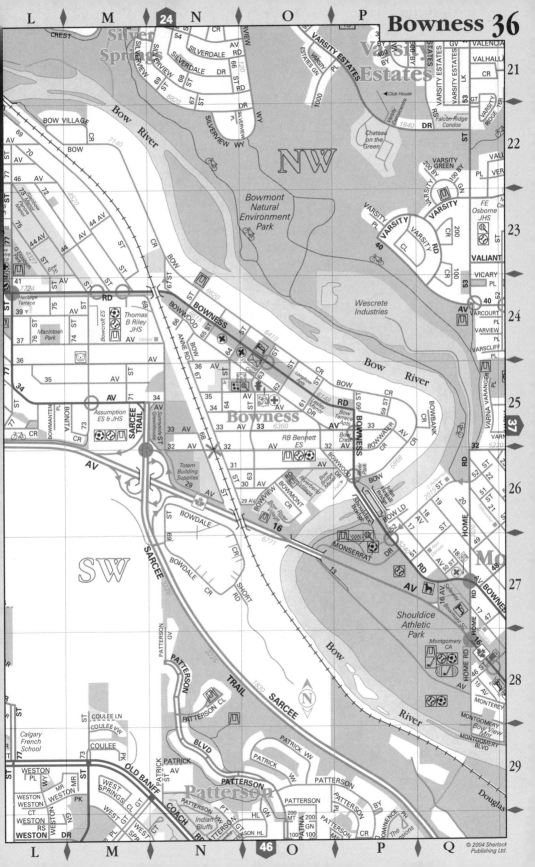

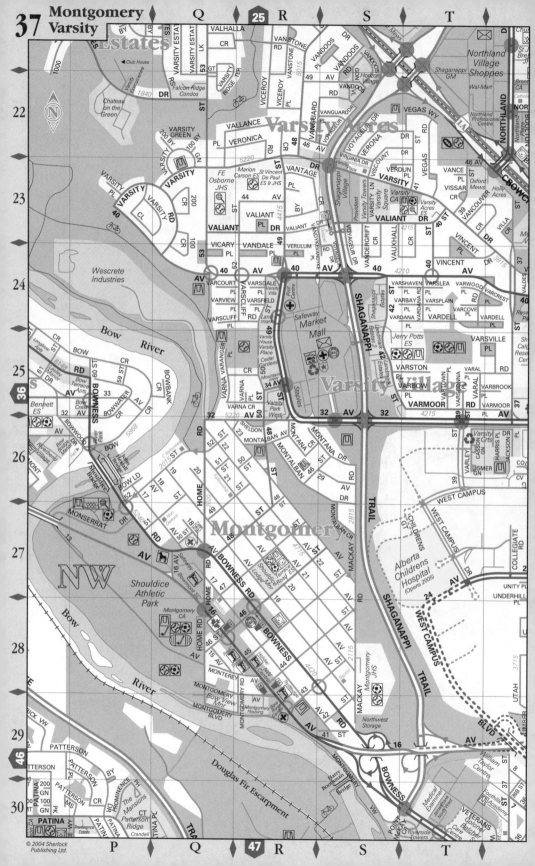

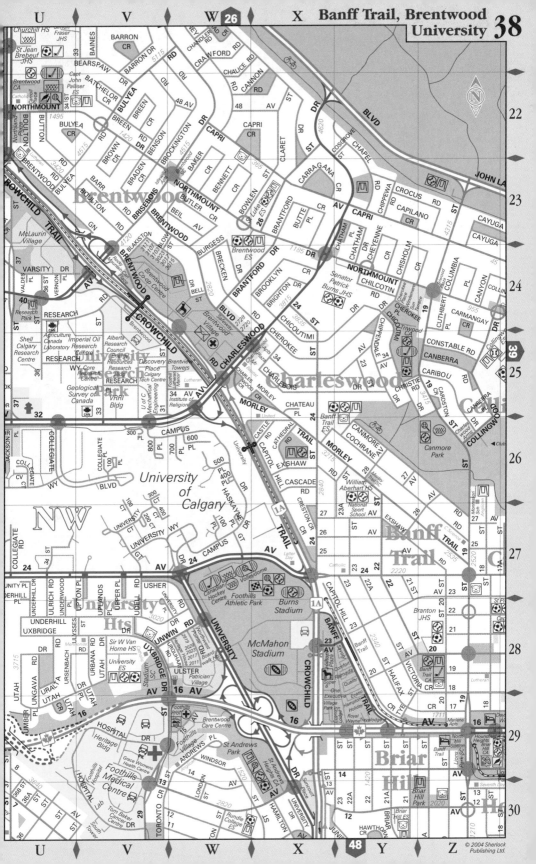

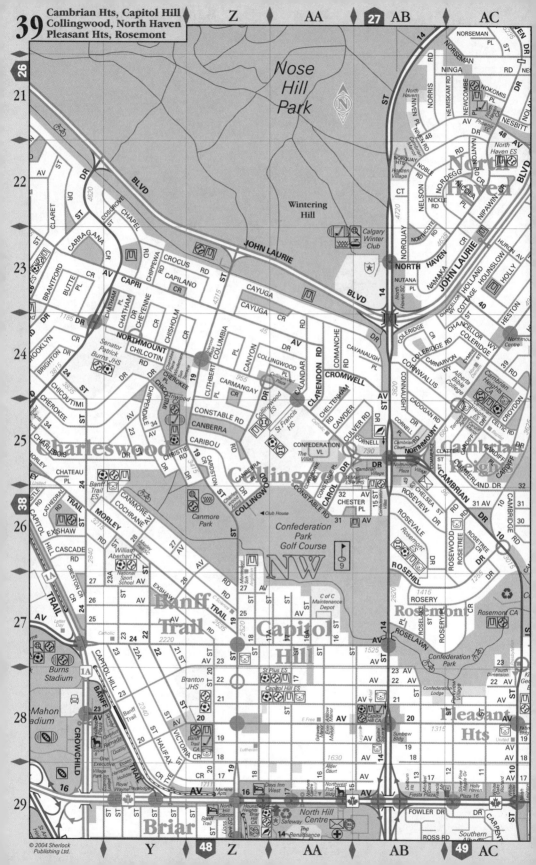

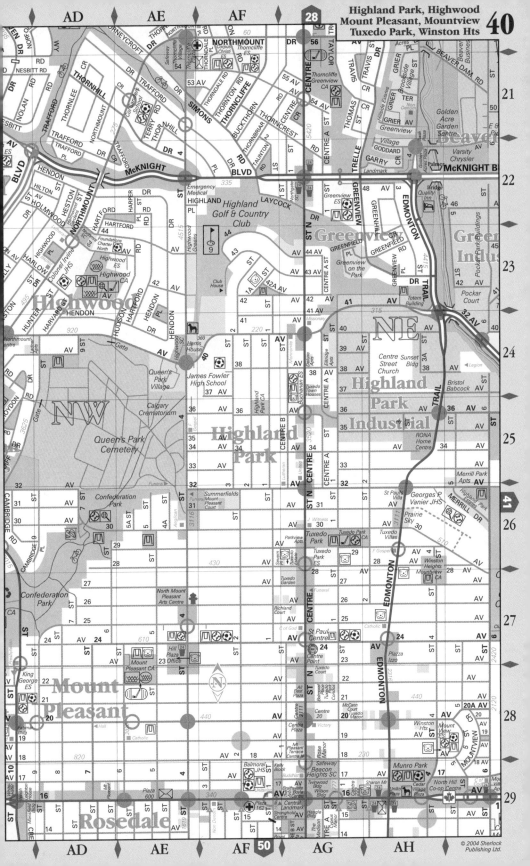

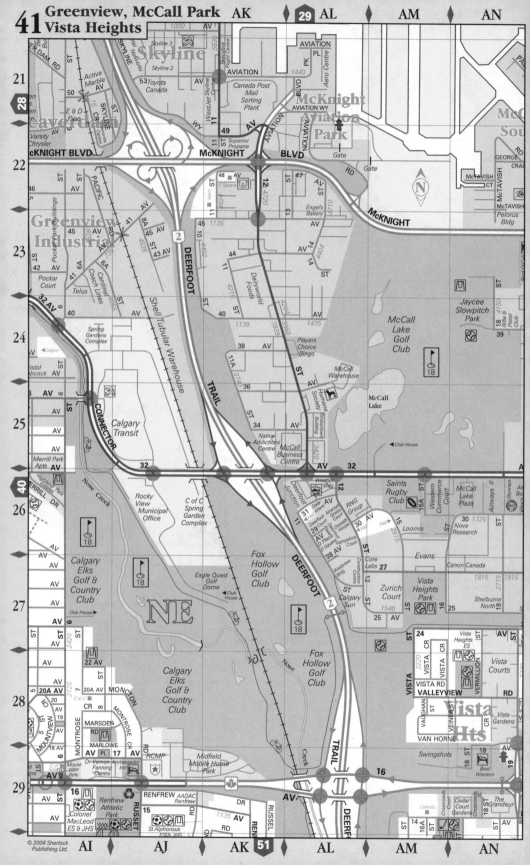

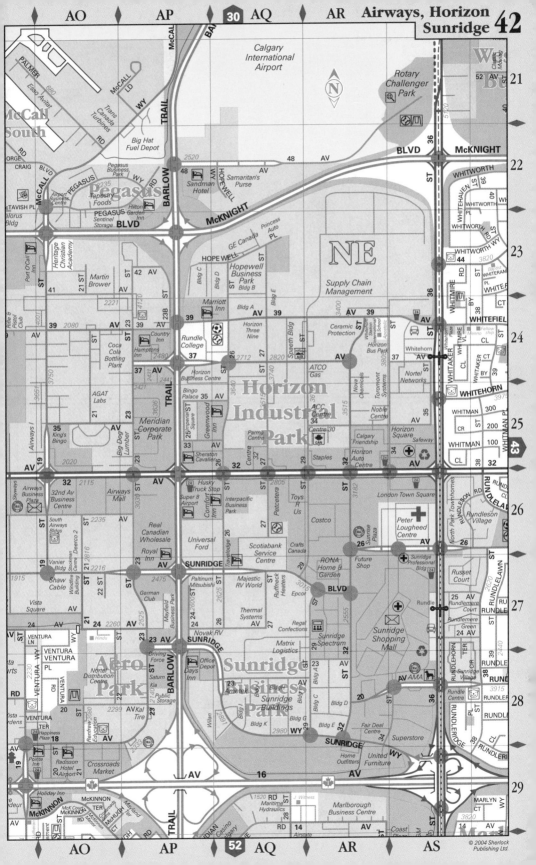

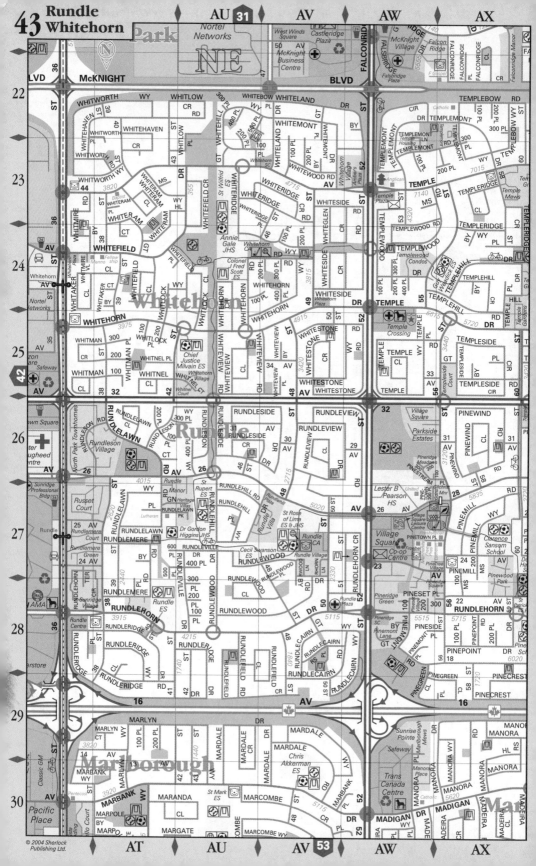

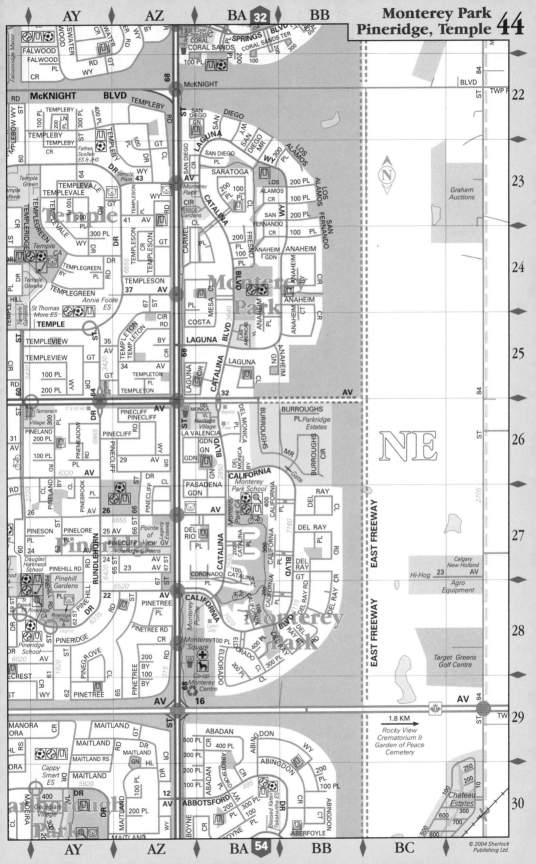

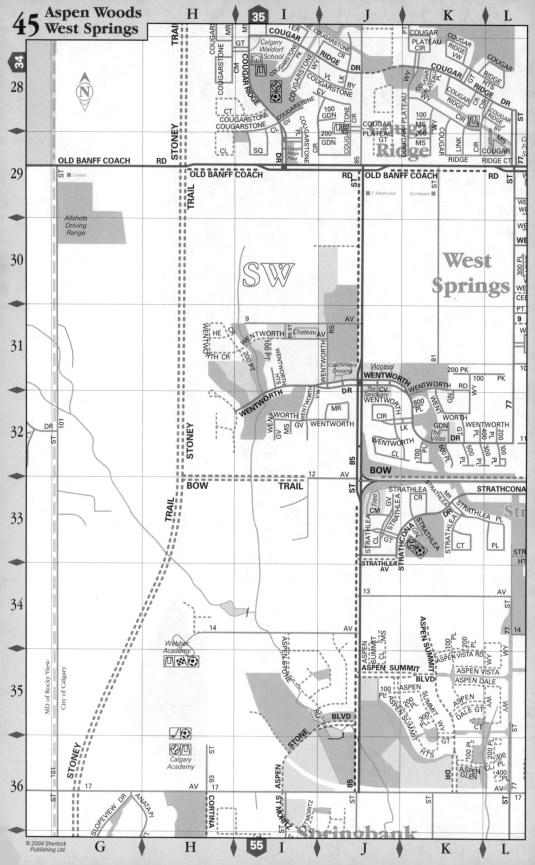

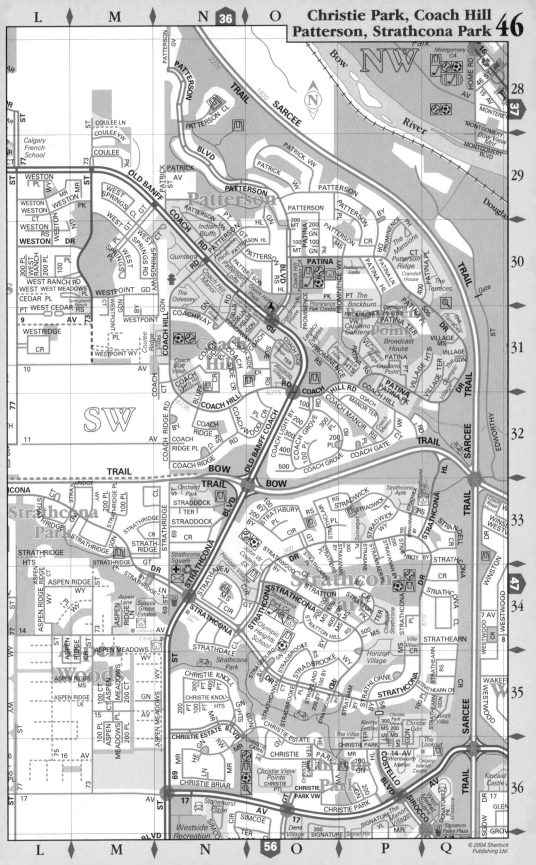

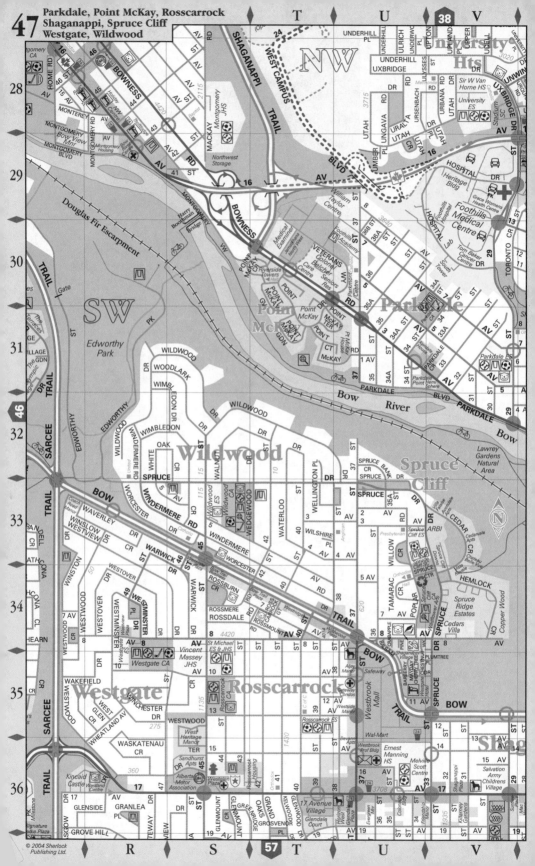

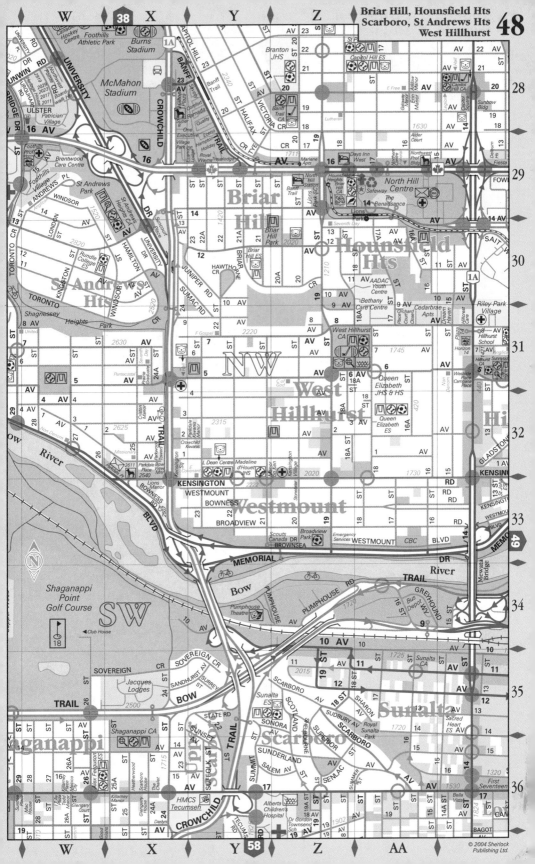

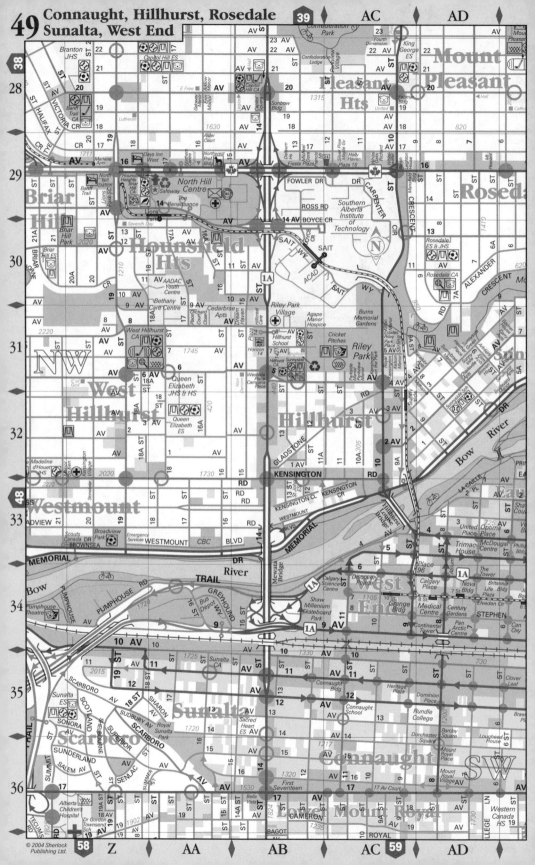

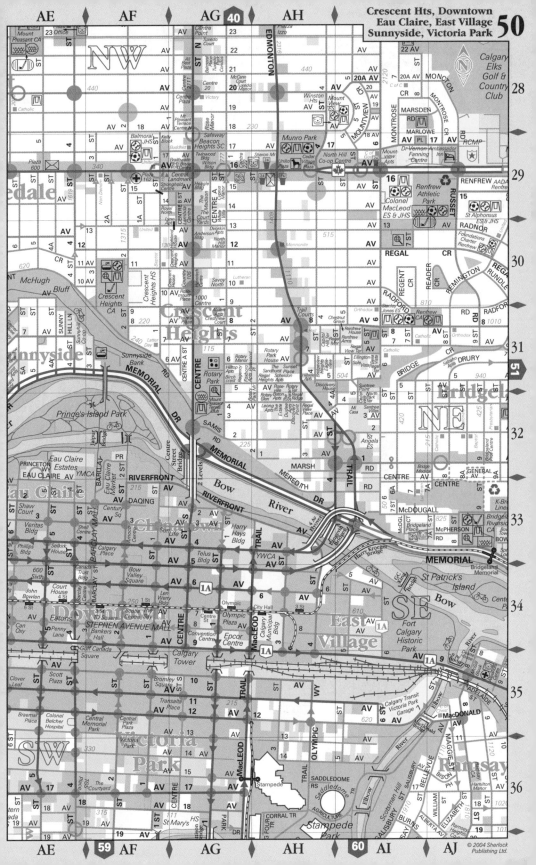

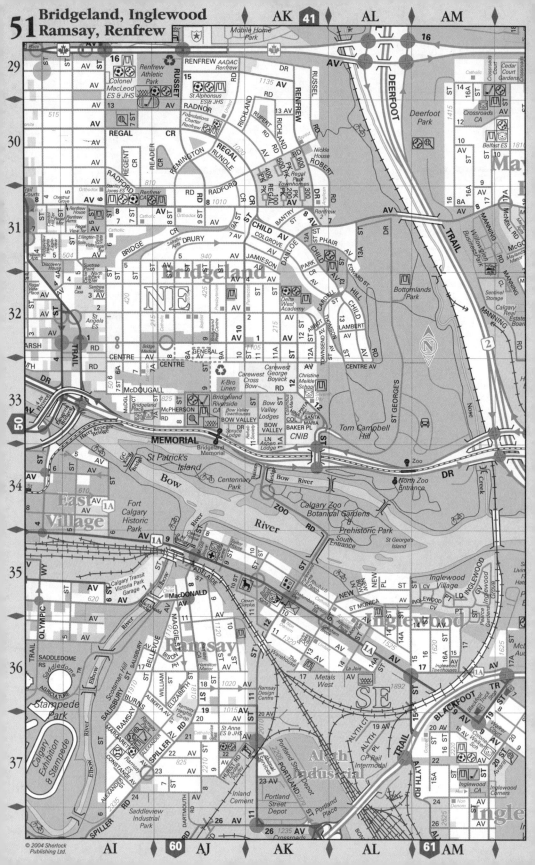

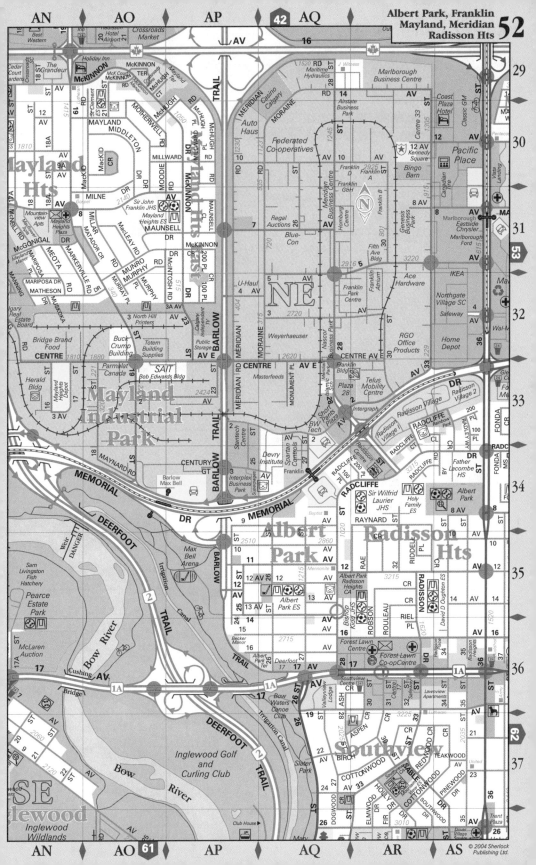

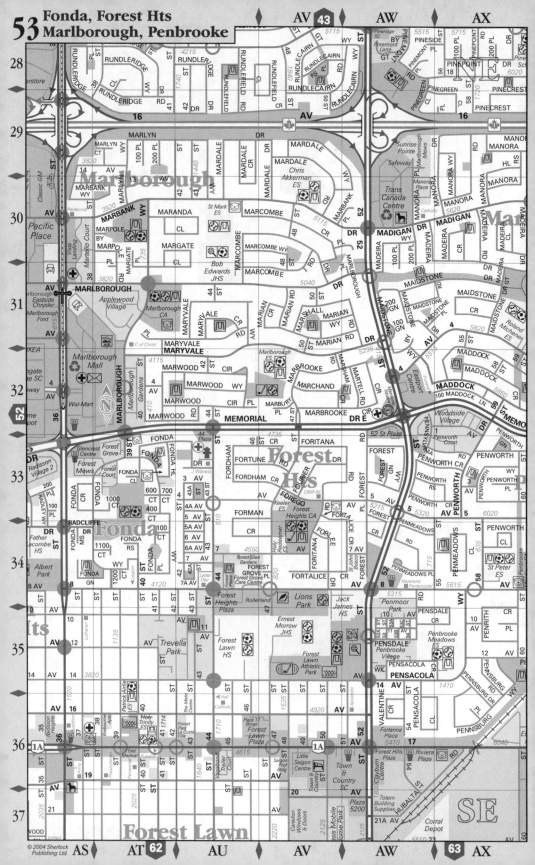

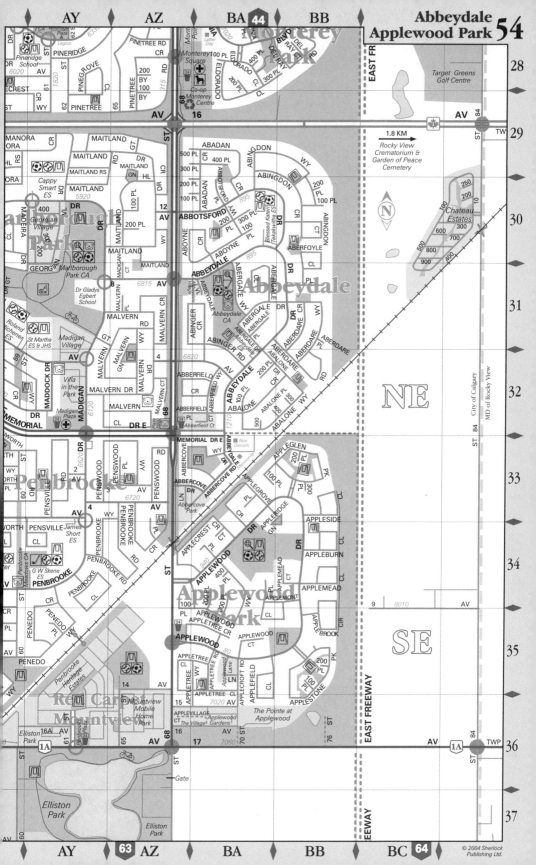

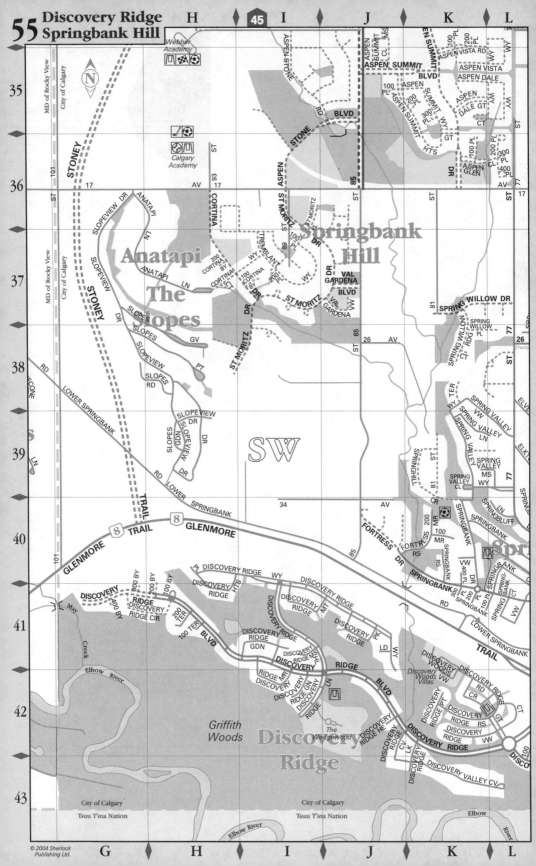

G   H   I   J   K   L

45

35

36

37

38

39

40

41

42

43

MD of Rocky View
City of Calgary

STONEY

101

17

MD of Rocky View
City of Calgary

STONEY

101

Webber Academy

Calgary Academy

SLOPEVIEW DR
ANATAPI

SLOPEVIEW DR

Anatapi

ANATAPI LN

The Slopes

SLOPES

SLOPES

SLOPEVIEW DR

SLOPES RD

GV

PT

SLOPEVIEW DR

SLOPES NDG

SLOPEVIEW DR

SLOPES

LOWER SPRINGBANK RD

LOWER SPRINGBANK RD

TRAIL

8 TRAIL

8 GLENMORE

GLENMORE

101

GLENMORE TRAIL

CORTINA
ST

93 ST

17 AV

CORTINA

CORTINA BY
200

CORTINA BY
CT

100 CORTINA

ST MORITZ

ST MORITZ DR

TREMBLANT

98 PL

ST MORITZ

ST MORITZ DR

200 PL

ASPEN STONE RD

ASPEN STONE BLVD

STONE BLVD

ASPEN ST

85 ST

Springbank Hill

DR
VAL GARDENA BLVD

VAL GARDENA

DR

ST

85 ST   26 AV

34

SW

85 ST

FORTRESS DR

FORTRESS RS

200
MR

100
MR

ASPEN SUMMIT

ASPEN SUMMIT BLVD

ASPEN SUMMIT WY

100 PL
200 PL
300 PL

ASPEN SUMMIT

ASPEN SUMMIT

HTS

DR

ASPEN VISTA RD

ASPEN VISTA

ASPEN DALE

ASPEN DALE GT

ASPEN DALE CT

GT

ASPEN GLEN

100 PL
200 PL
300 PL
400 PL

AV

ST

77

17

81

SPRING WILLOW DR

SPRING WILLOW RDG

SPRING WILLOW PL

SPRING WILLOW CT

77

26

81 ST

SPRINGHILL

WY

SPRING VALLEY VW

SPRING VALLEY

SPRING VALLEY LN

SPRING VALLEY

SPRING VALLEY MS WY

77

SPRING VALLEY CL

SPRING VALLEY CR

ELV

ELK

81 ST

200 RS

SPRINGBLUFF

SPRINGBANK

SPRINGBANK

SPRINGBANK

SPRINGBANK
400 PL

Spr

Spr

SPRINGBANK DR

200 PL

SPRINGBANK

SPRING BANK VW

SPRING BANK CT

LOWER SPRINGBANK TRAIL

RD

DISCOVERY RIDGE WY

DISCOVERY RIDGE

DISCOVERY RIDGE HTS

DISCOVERY RIDGE

DISCOVERY RIDGE

DISCOVERY RIDGE MT

DISCOVERY RIDGE PK

DISCOVERY RIDGE WY

LD

600 BY

200 BY

100 BY

DISCOVERY RIDGE

DISCOVERY RIDGE CIR

400 BY

200 TER

100 TER

BLVD

DISCOVERY RIDGE GDN

DISCOVERY RIDGE MS

DISCOVERY **RIDGE**

RIDGE MR

DISCOVERY RIDGE GN

DISCOVERY RIDGE

DISCOVERY RIDGE LN

BLVD

May

Creek

Elbow   River

Griffith Woods

Discovery Ridge

The Wedgewood

DISCOVERY RIDGE HE

DISCOVERY RIDGE

DISCOVERY RIDGE CV

DISCOVERY RIDGE LK

DISCOVERY RIDGE

DISCOVERY

Discovery Woods Villas

DISCOVERY WOODS VW

DISCOVERY RIDGE

DISCOVERY RIDGE RD

DISCOVERY RIDGE PT

DISCOVERY RIDGE RS

DISCOVERY RIDGE VW

RD

CR

GT

DISCOVERY RIDGE

DISCOVERY VALLEY CV

DISCO

City of Calgary

City of Calgary

Tsuu T'ina Nation

Tsuu T'ina Nation

Elbow River

Elbow   River

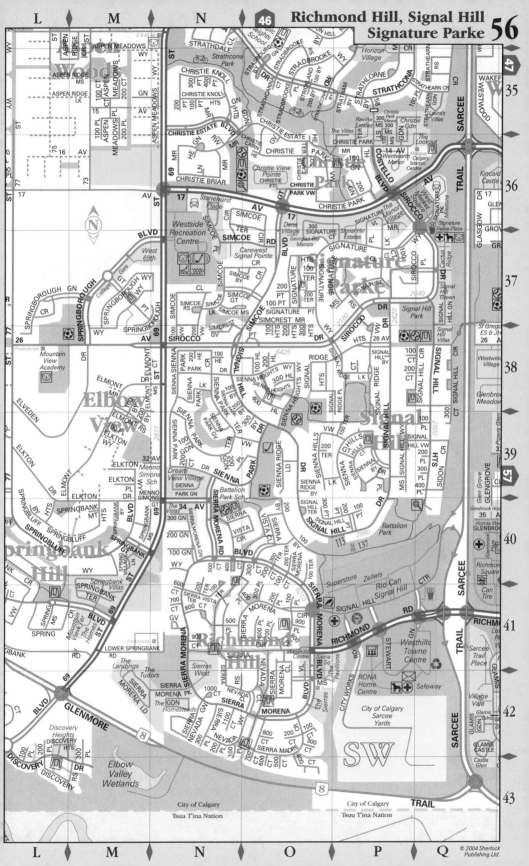

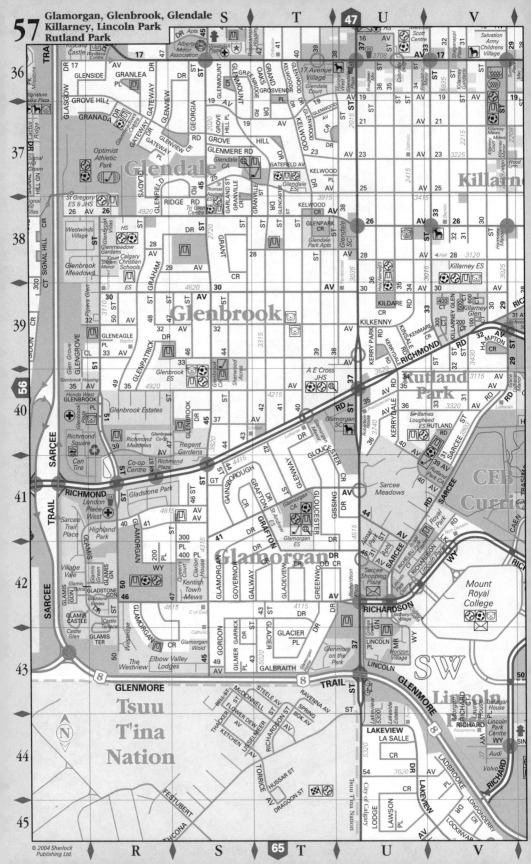

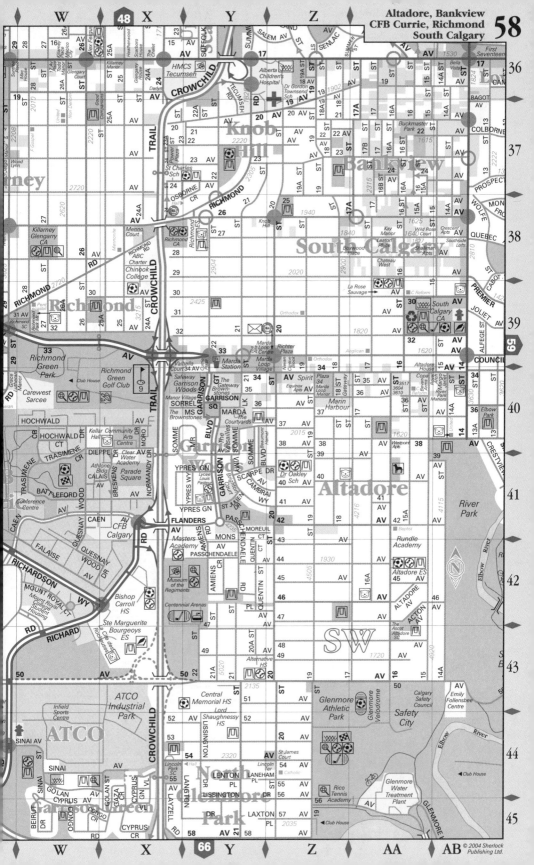

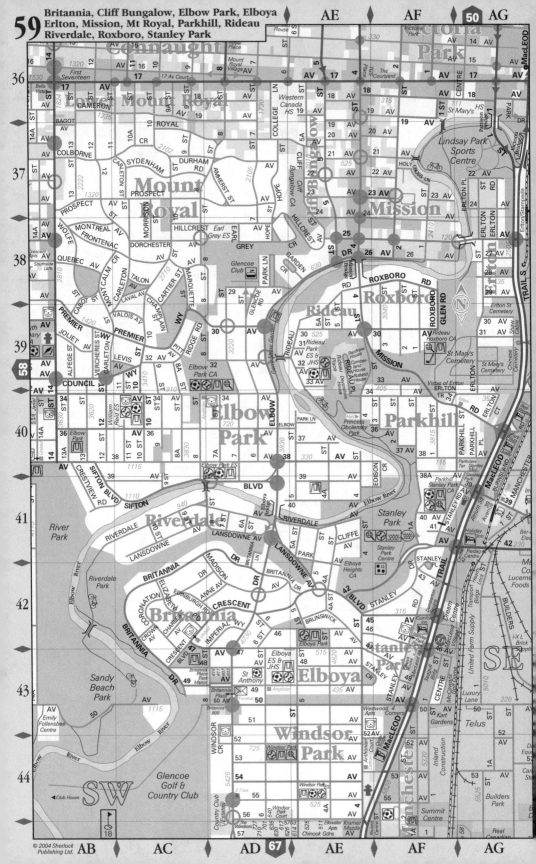

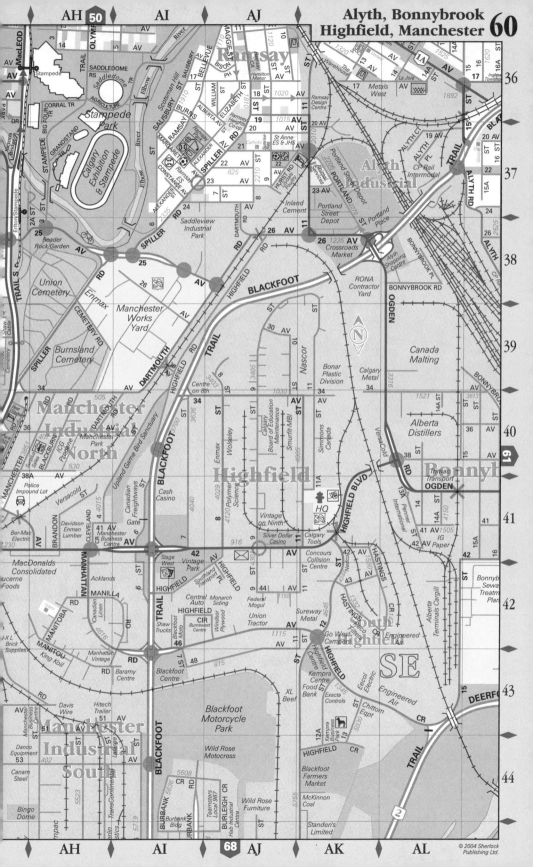

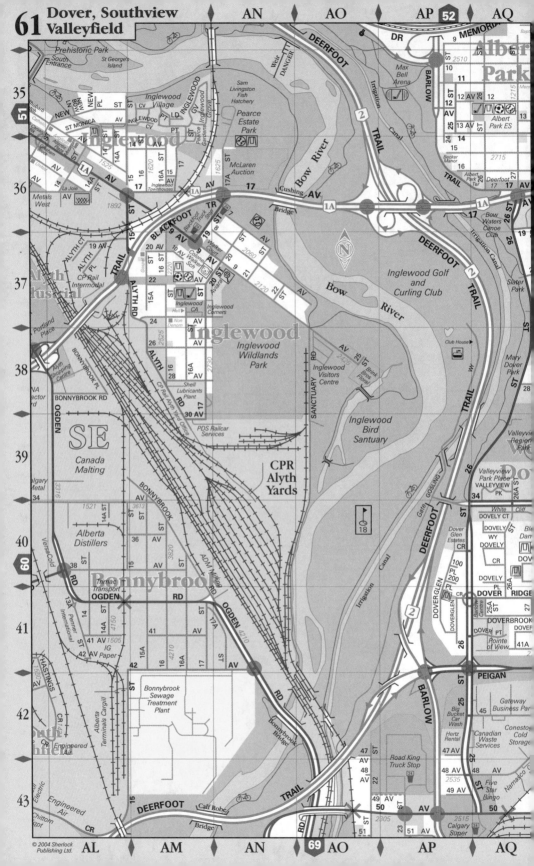

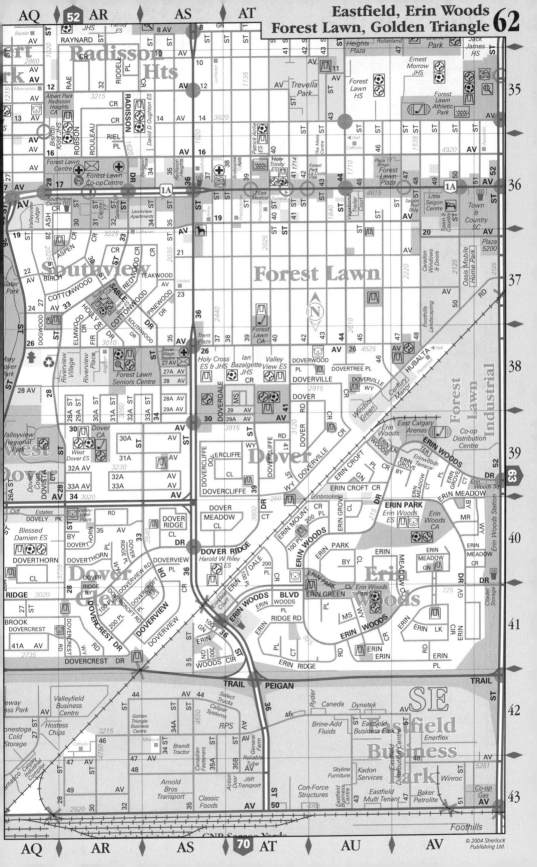

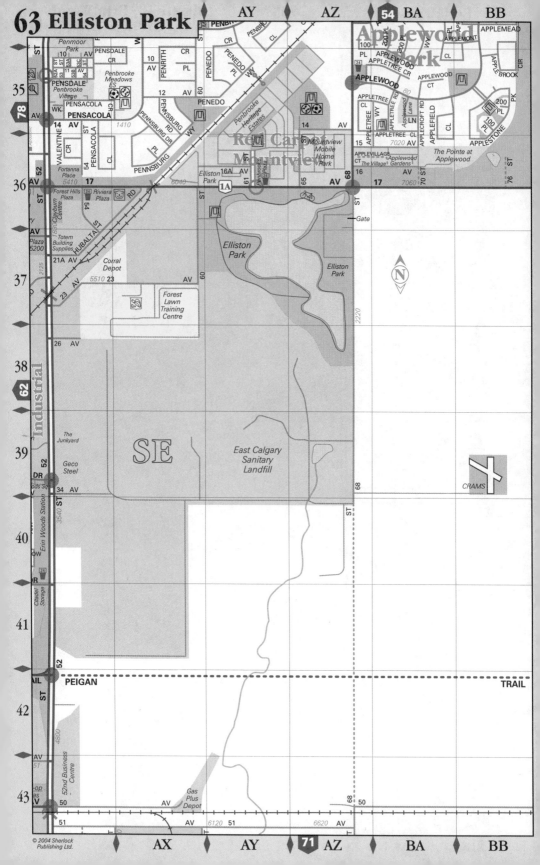

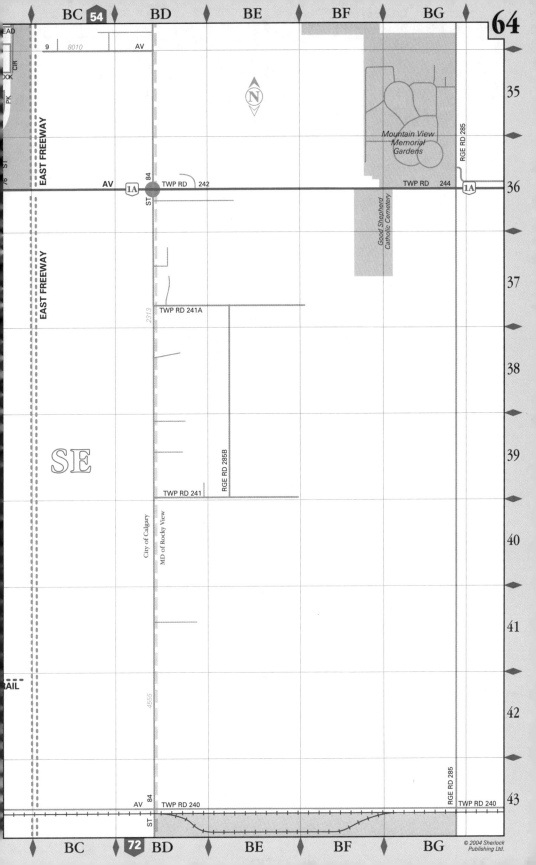

9 | 8010 AV

CIR

PK

76 ST

EAST FREEWAY

35

Mountain View Memorial Gardens

RGE RD 285

AV 1A 84 ST TWP RD 242 TWP RD 244 1A 36

EAST FREEWAY

Good Shepherd Catholic Cemetery

37

2313

TWP RD 241A

38

39

RGE RD 285B

TWP RD 241

SE

City of Calgary
MD of Rocky View

40

41

4555

RAIL

42

RGE RD 285

AV 84 ST TWP RD 240 TWP RD 240 43

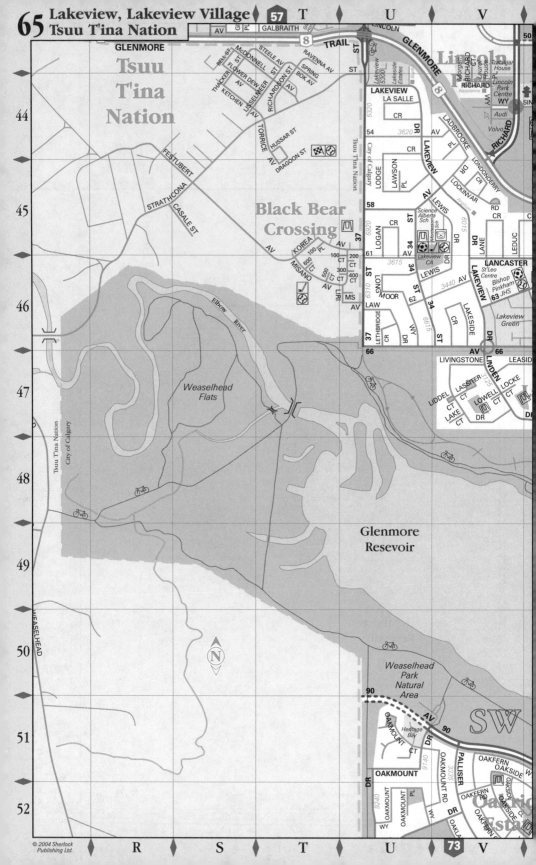

T   U   V

57

50

GLENMORE

Tsuu
T'ina
Nation

LINCOLN

GLENMORE

8

Lincoln
PK

Trafalgar
House

RICHARD

Nazarrenne

Lincoln
Park
Centre
WY

Audi

SIN

Volvo

TRAIL

GALBRAITH

AV

McDONNELL

STEELE AV

RAVENNA AV

SPRING

BELL ST

THACKER

FLOWER DEW

ASSELMEER

KETCHEN

RICHARDSON ST

BOK AV

AV

LAKEVIEW

LA SALLE

CR

LADBROOKE

LONDONDERRY

RICHARD

LAKEVIEW

44

54

3620

LODGE

LAWSON

CR

PL

AV

LOCKINVAR

RD

CR

LEDUC

TORRICE

HUSSAR ST

DRAGOON ST

AV

Tsuu T'ina Nation

City of Calgary

Black Bear
Crossing

45

FESTUBERT

STRATHCONA

CASALE ST

37

AV

AV

KOREA

MISANO

100

200

300

400

500

600

CT
CT
CT
CT
CT
CT
CT
CT

PL

LIRI

MS

AV

LEWIS

Science
Alberta
Sch

Montessori
Sch

Lakeview
CA

58

5920

LOGAN

CR

ST

34

LEWIS

LANE

LANCASTER

St Leo
Centre

Bishop
Pinkham
JHS

61

3615

34

63

6015

DR

LAKEVIEW

Elbow River

46

LAW

6310

LONG

ST

62

MOOR

34

WY

LAKESIDE

CR

Lakeview
Green

LETHBRIDGE

CR

6615

ST

DR

37

66

66

AV

LAKEVIEW

LIVINGSTONE

LEASIDE

LIDDEL

LASSITER

LOWELL

LOCKE

47

*Weaselhead
Flats*

LAKE

CT

DR

CT

CT

DR

3125

48

Tsuu T'ina Nation

City of Calgary

Glenmore
Resevoir

49

WEASELHEAD

50

N

*Weaselhead
Park
Natural
Area*

90

AV

90

SW

51

90

OAKMOUNT

DR

*Heritage
Bay*

CT

PALLISER

OAKFERN

OAKSIDE

52

OAKMOUNT

DR

9240

OAKMOUNT

PL

OAKMOUNT

WY

OAKMOUNT RD

3335

DR

OAKFERN

OAKLA

Oak...
ista

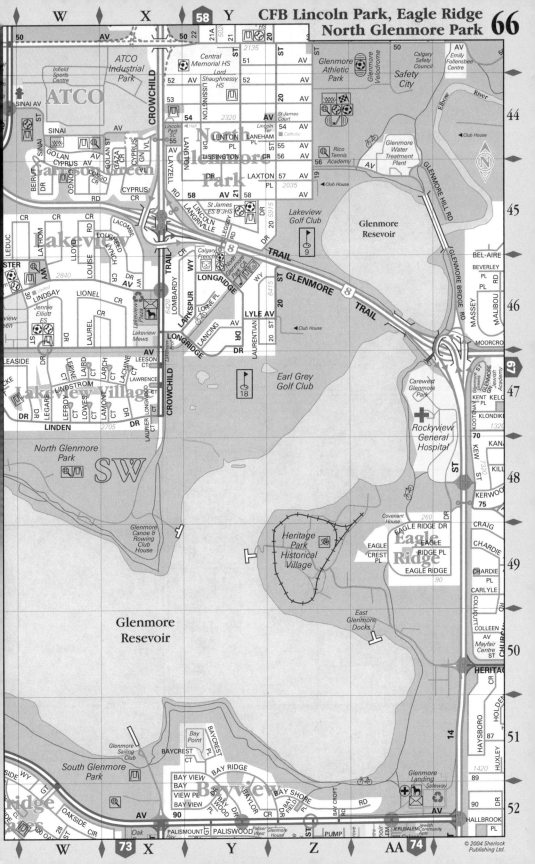

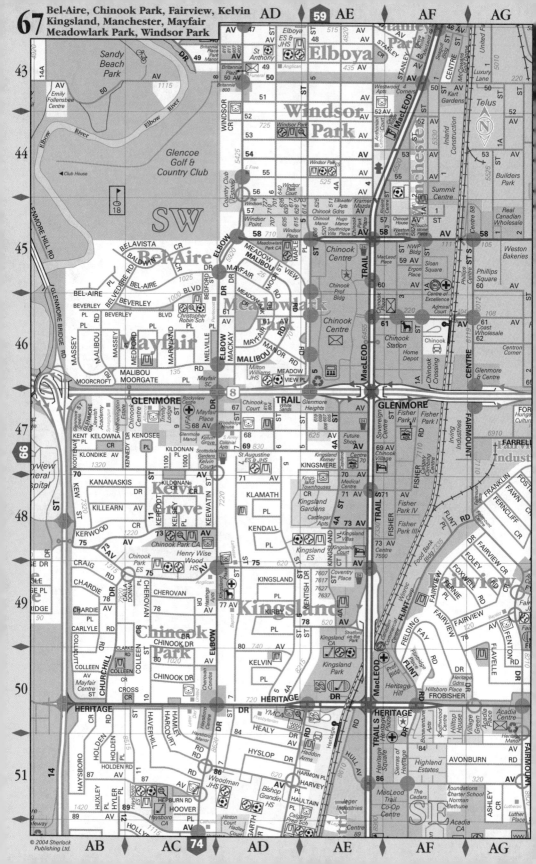

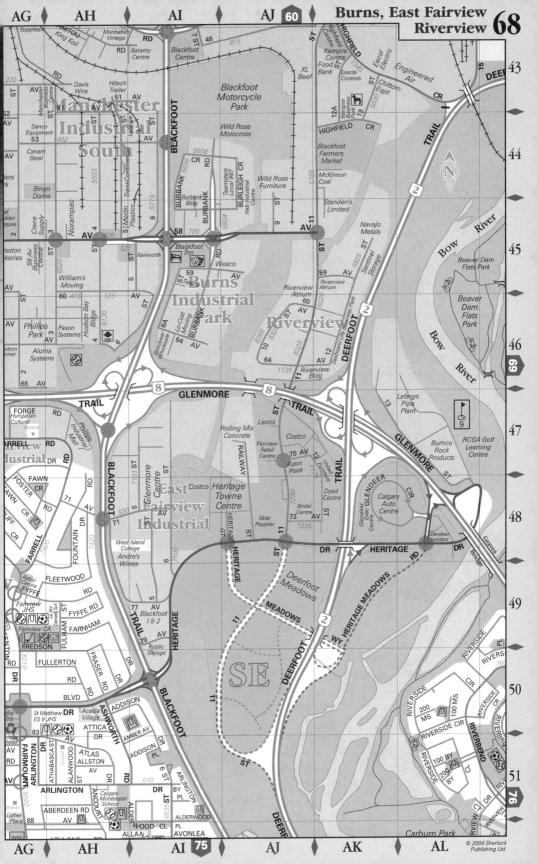

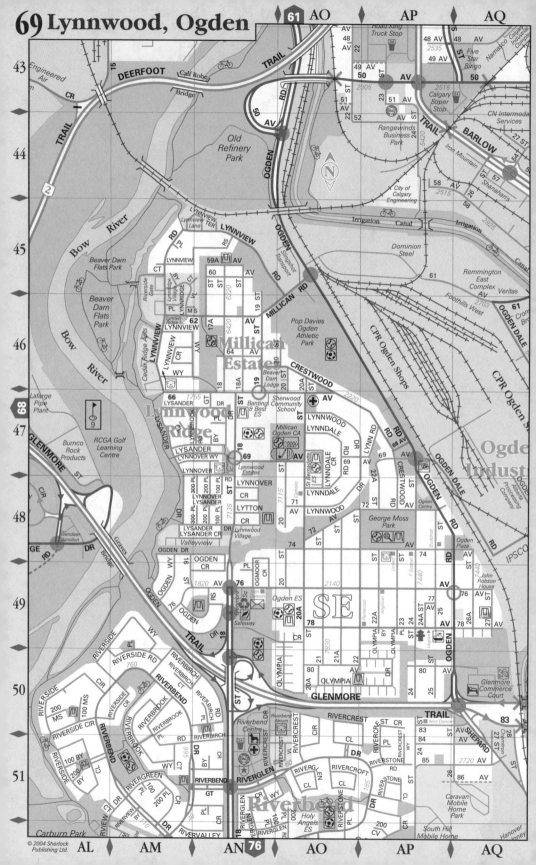

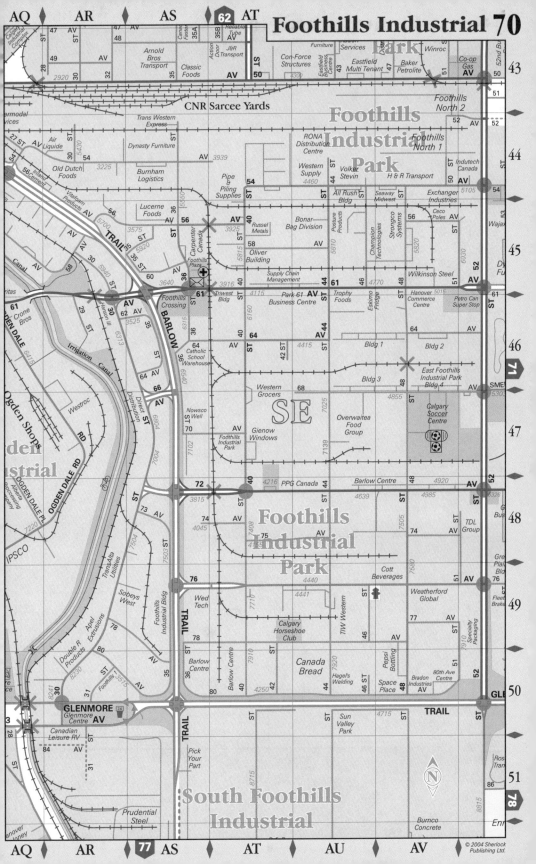

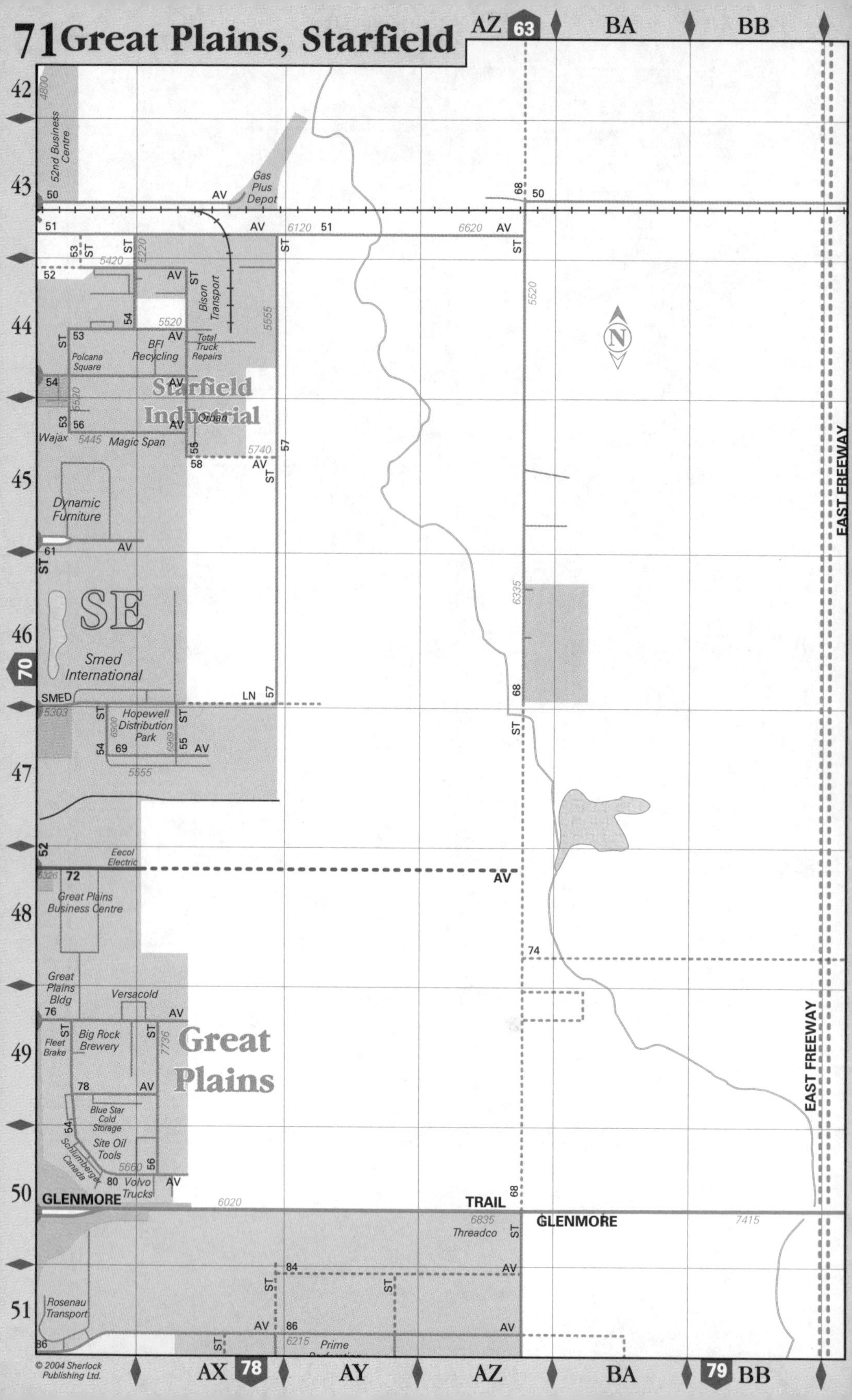

AZ **63** BA BB

42
4600

52nd Business Centre

50 43
Gas Plus Depot
AV
68 50
6120 51 6620 AV
51 AV ST ST
53 ST ST 5220
52 5420 AV
Bison Transport

54 5520 AV 5555
44 53 Total Truck Repairs
ST BFI Recycling AV
Polcana Square
54 AV
Starfield Industrial
5520
53 56
Wajax 5445 Magic Span
Orban 57 5740
58 AV
45 ST

Dynamic Furniture

61 AV
ST

SE

70 46
Smed International
LN 57
SMED
5303 ST ST 6335
54 69 55 AV
47 5555

52
Eecol Electric
6326 **72** AV
48 Great Plains Business Centre

74
Great Plains Bldg
76 Versacold AV
49 Fleet Brake Big Rock Brewery ST
7736 **Great Plains**
78 AV
Blue Star Cold Storage
54 Site Oil Tools
56
5660 80 Valvo Trucks AV
50 **GLENMORE** 6020 **TRAIL** 68 **GLENMORE** 7415
6835 Threadco
84 AV
ST ST
51 Rosenau Transport
AV 86 AV
86 ST 6215 Prime

N

EAST FREEWAY

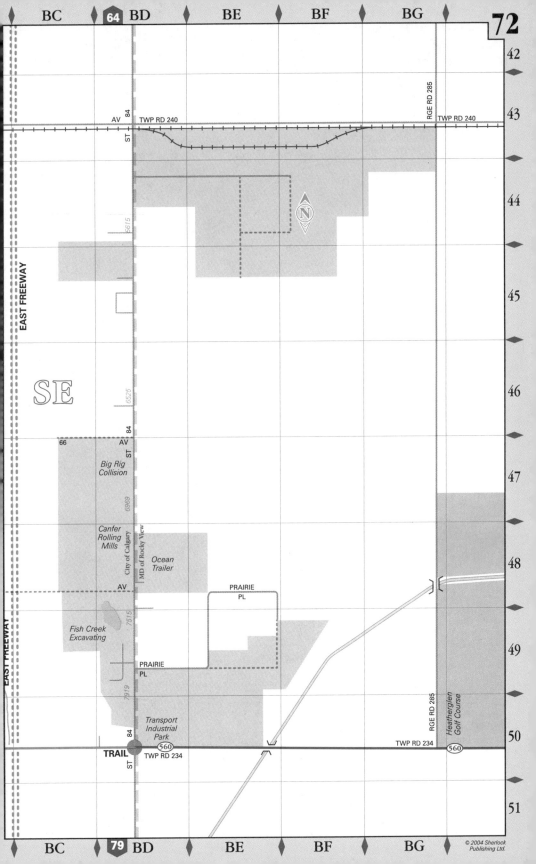

RGE RD 285

TWP RD 240

AV 84

TWP RD 240

ST

44

N

6675

45

EAST FREEWAY

SE

6525

46

84

AV

66

ST

Big Rig Collision

47

6969

Canfer Rolling Mills

City of Calgary

MD of Rocky View

Ocean Trailer

PRAIRIE PL

48

AV

7515

Fish Creek Excavating

PRAIRIE PL

49

PRAIRIE PL

RGE RD 285

Heatherglen Golf Course

7919

EAST FREEWAY

Transport Industrial Park

50

84

560

TWP RD 234

ST

TRAIL

TWP RD 234

560

51

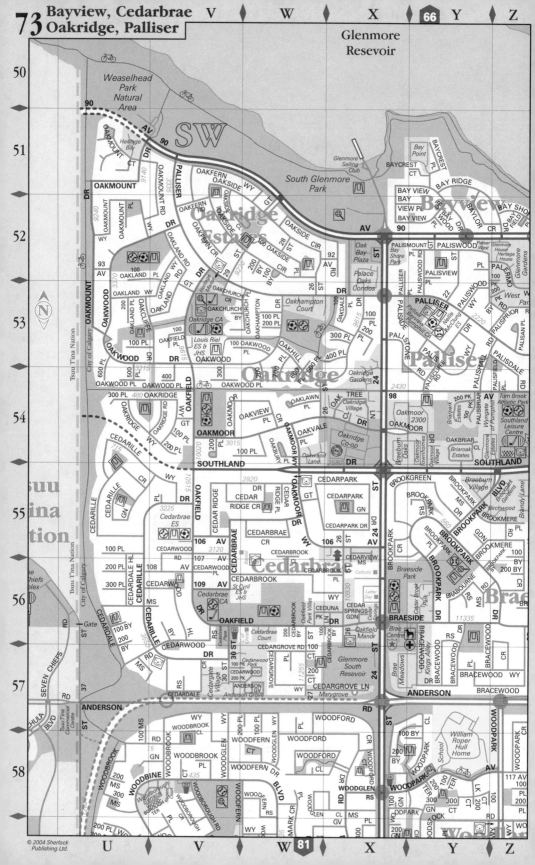

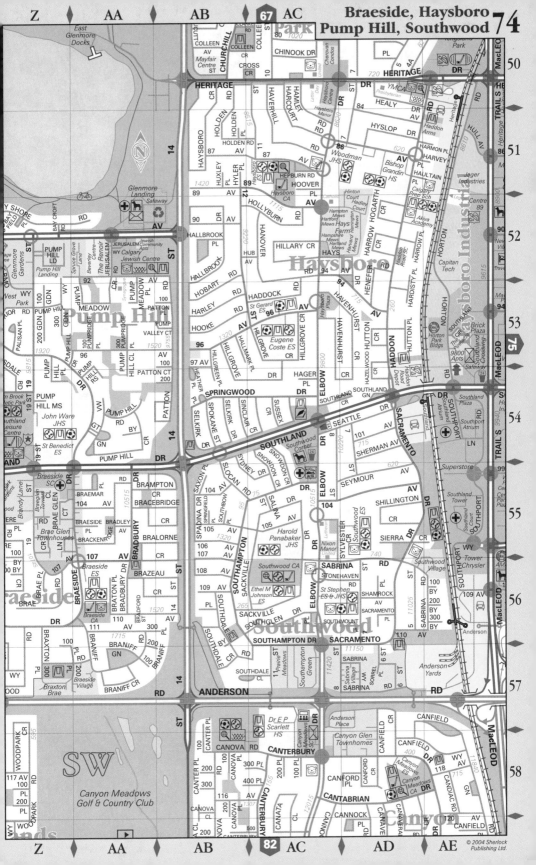

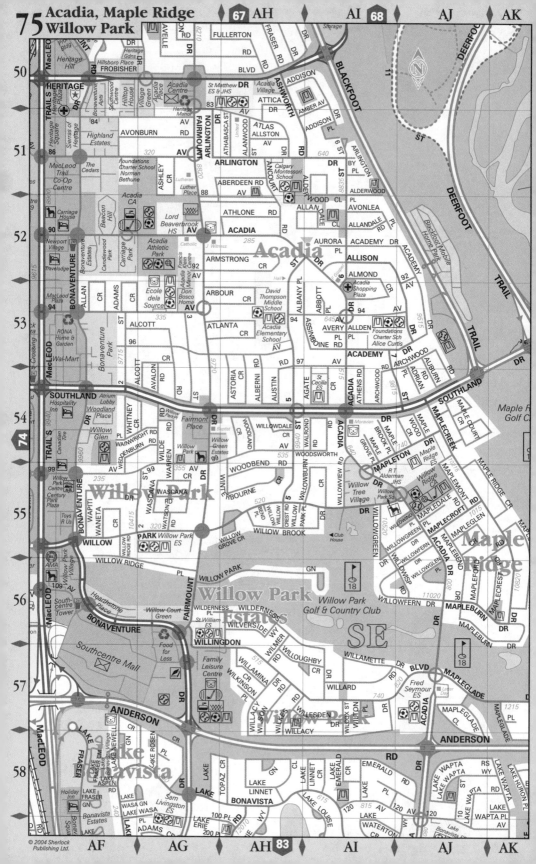

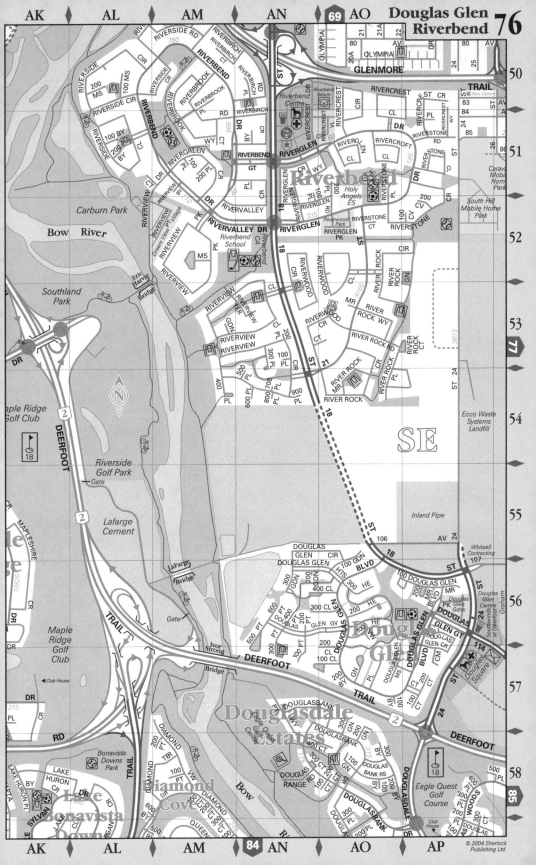

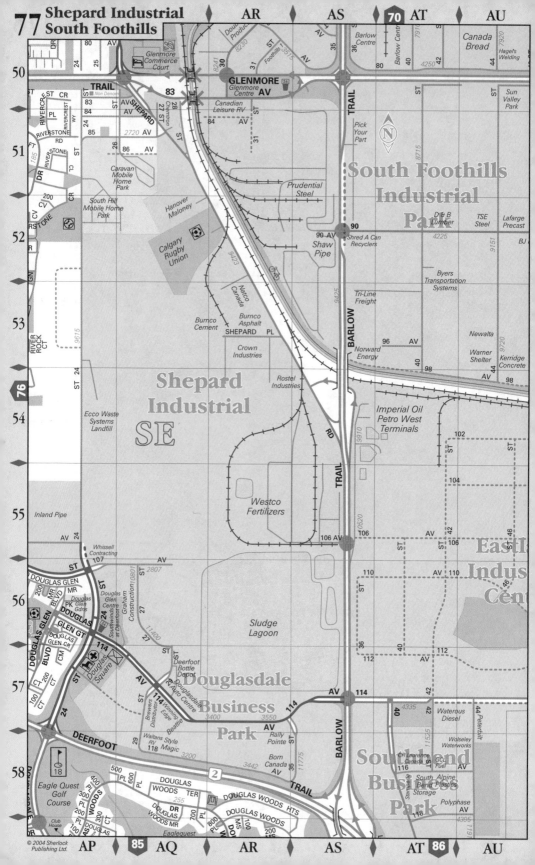

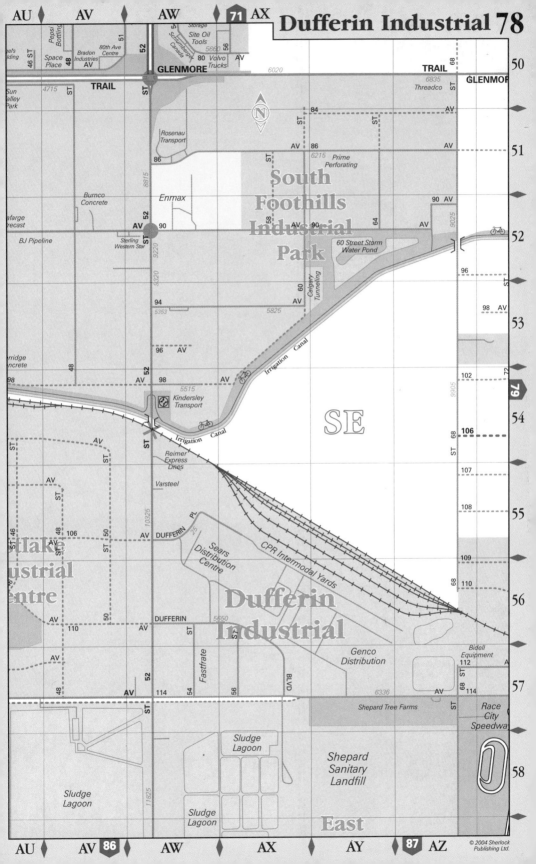

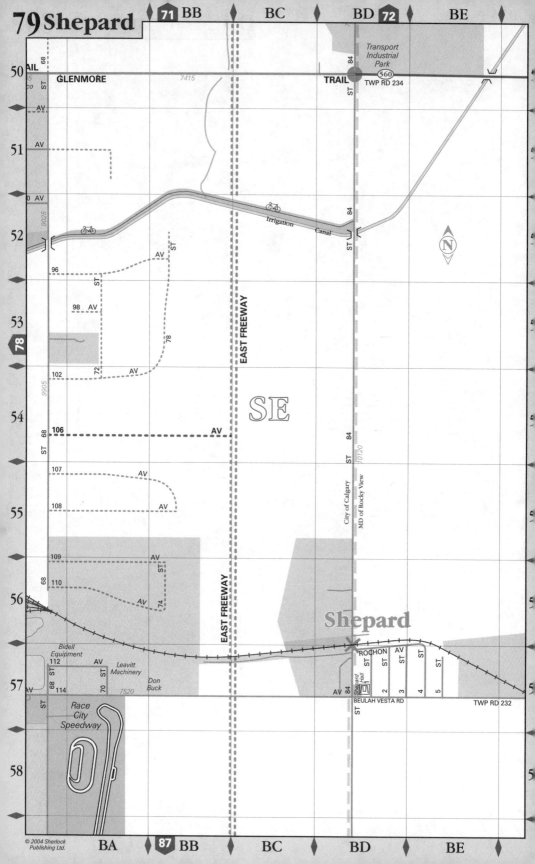

Transport
Industrial
Park

84

GLENMORE | TRAIL | ST
560
TWP RD 234

AIL 68
15
co ST
AV
51 AV

0 AV
9025
Irrigation   Canal
84
52 ST

96 ST
AV ST
98 AV

N

78
78

102
9905
72 AV

SE

106 AV
68 ST
84 ST

107 AV
City of Calgary
MD of Rocky View
70120

108 AV

109 AV
ST
68 110
74 AV

EAST FREEWAY

EAST FREEWAY

Shepard

Bidell
Equipment
112 AV ST
Leavitt
Machinery
68 ST 70 ST
114
Don
Buck
7520

ROCHON AV
ST ST ST ST ST
2 3 4 5
AV 84 ST
Shepard
Hall
BEULAH VESTA RD
TWP RD 232

AV ST
Race
City
Speedway

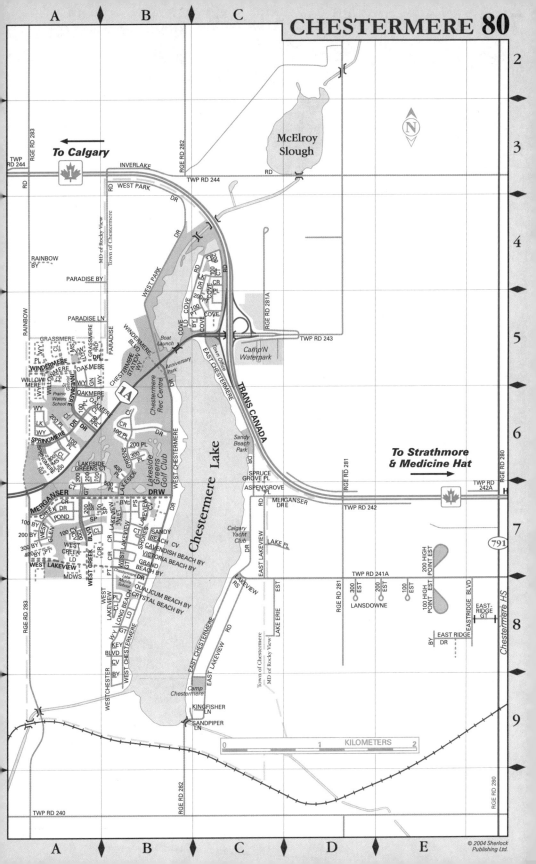

To Calgary

McElroy
Slough

N

To Strathmore
& Medicine Hat

TWP RD 244

RGE RD 283

TWP RD 244

INVERLAKE

WEST PARK

RGE RD 282

RD

TWP RD 243

RGE RD 281A

Camp 'N
Waterpark

Boat
Launch

Anniversary
Park

Chestermere
Rec Centre

RAINBOW
BY

PARADISE BY

PARADISE LN

RAINBOW

GRASSMERE

WINDERMERE

WILLOWMERE

OAKMERE

SPRINGMERE

PARADISE

Prairie
Waters
School

Town Office
EAST CHESTERMERE

WEST PARK

WINDERMERE BLVD
WINDERMERE WY

CHESTERMERE STATION WY

WEST CHESTERMERE

COVE

COVE

COVE

COVE

Chestermere Lake

Sandy Beach
Park

SPRUCE
GROVE PL

ASPEN GROVE
PL

MERGANSER
DR E

TRANS CANADA

RGE RD 281

RGE RD 281

TWP RD 242

TWP RD 242A

RGE RD 280

791

H

Lakeside
Greens
Golf Club

Lakeside
Greens Ct

WEST CHESTERMERE

MERGANSER

WEST CREEK

WEST CREEK

WEST LAKEVIEW

WEST LAKEVIEW

WEST CHESTERMERE

POND

CREEK DR

GLEN

MDWS

Chestermere
Lake Middle
School

Sandy
Beach CV

CAVENDISH BEACH BY

VICTORIA BEACH BY

GRAND
BEACH BY

QUALICUM BEACH BY

CRYSTAL BEACH BY

KEY
BLVD

CV

WESTCHESTER

BY

LONG BEACH

SHORES

LAKEVIEW

INLET

PS

SP

Calgary
Yacht
Club

LAKE PL

LAKEVIEW

EAST CHESTERMERE

LAKE ERIE

LAKE EST

EST

LAKEVIEW
RD

LAKEVIEW
RS

EAST LAKEVIEW
RD

200 HIGH
POINT EST

100 HIGH
POINT EST

300
EST

200
EST

100
EST

LANSDOWNE

TWP RD 241A

EASTRIDGE BLVD

EAST
RIDGE
GT

BY

EAST RIDGE
DR

Chestermere HS

RGE RD 283

TWP RD 240

RGE RD 282

Town of Chestermere
MD of Rocky View

Camp
Chestermere

KINGFISHER LN

SANDPIPER
LN

MD of Rocky View

Town of Chestermere

0   1   2
KILOMETERS

RGE RD 280

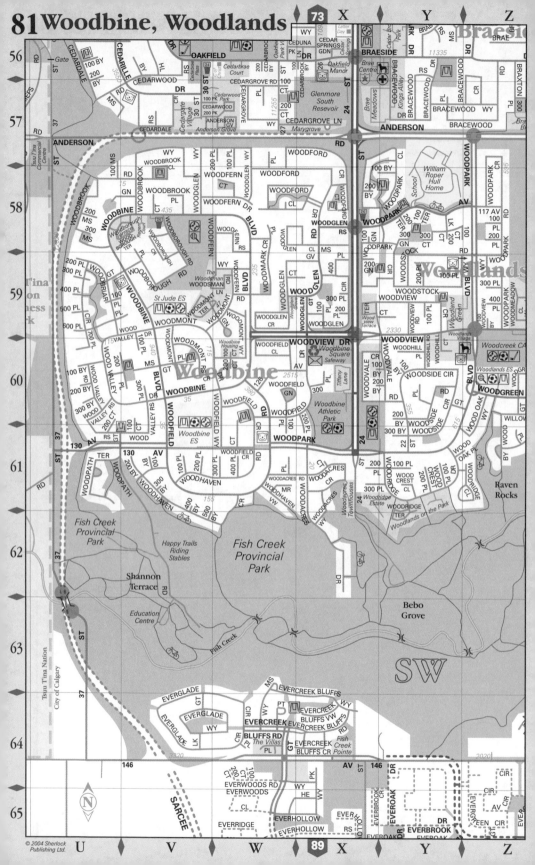

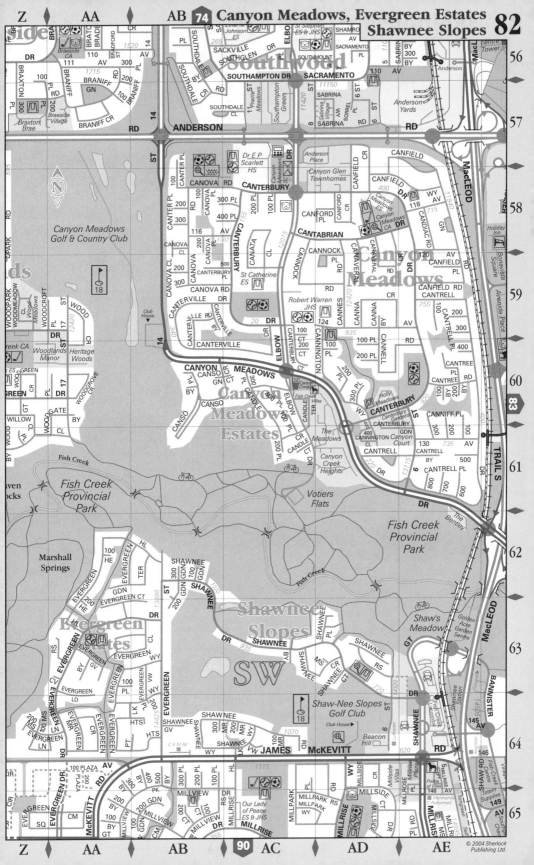

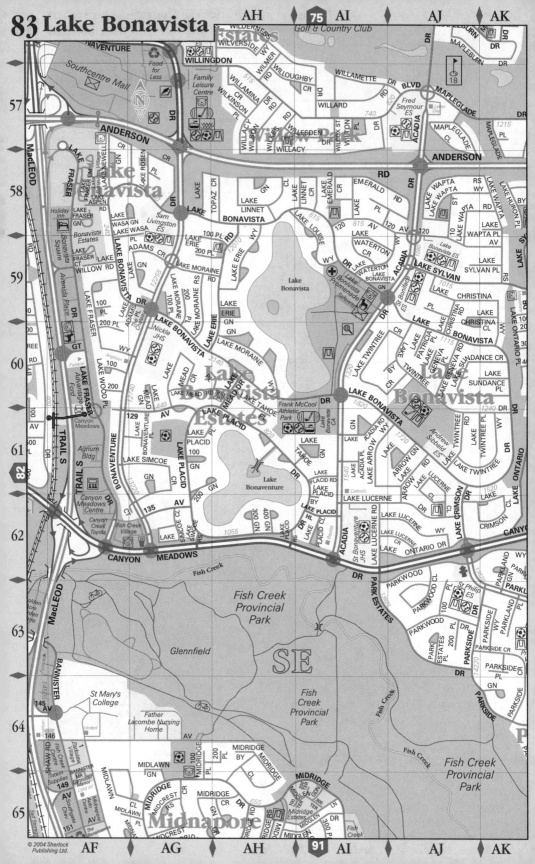

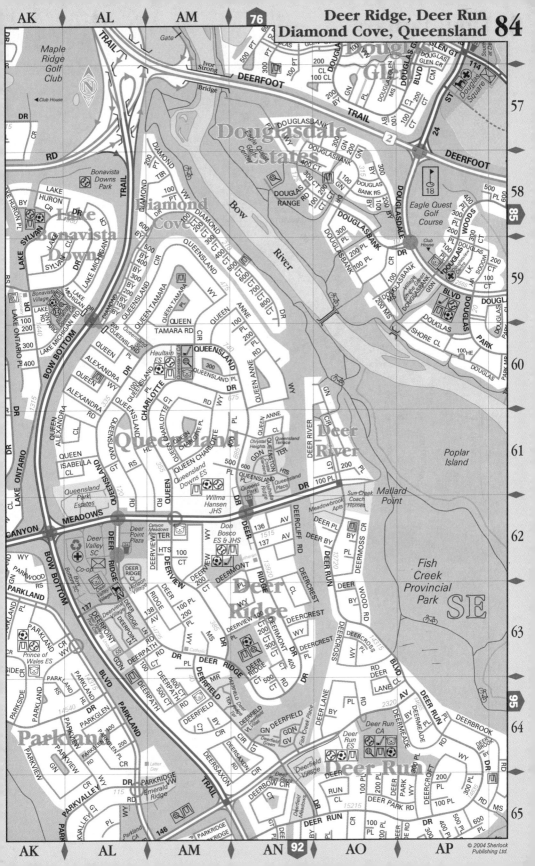

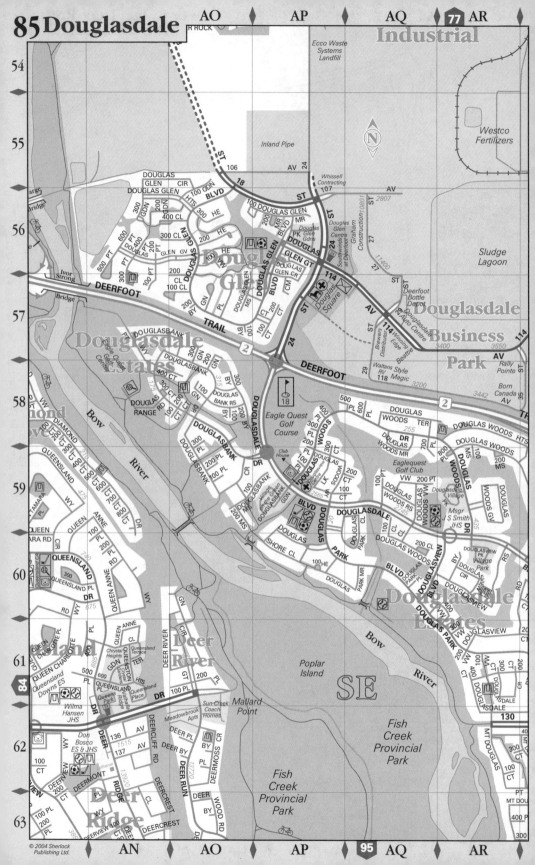

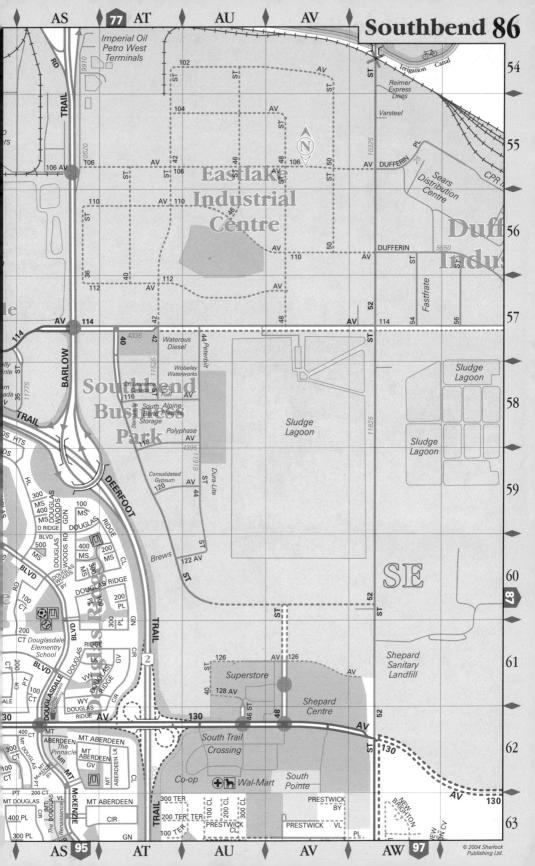

AS 77 AT AU AV

Imperial Oil
Petro West
Terminals

RD

TRAIL

9910

10520

Irrigation
Canal

Reimer
Express
Lines

Varsteel

10325

54

102 ST

104 ST

AV

106 AV

106

106

AV

42 ST

46 ST

48 ST

50 ST

DUFFERIN

PL

25

Sears
Distribution
Centre

CPR

**Eastlake
Industrial
Centre**

N

55

110

110

AV

110

AV

**Duff
Indus**

56

36

40

42 ST

46 ST

50

DUFFERIN

5650

ST

116 ST

112

112

AV

AV

52 ST

AV

Fasttrate

54 ST

56

57

AV 114

114

AV

48 ST

AV 114

54

56

114

BARLOW

40

4335

42

11525

Waterous
Diesel

44 Peterbilt

Sludge
Lagoon

11825

TRAIL

WOODS HTS

WOODS

11775

**Southbend
Bus
Park**

Stampede

116

Wolseley
Waterworks

CR Laurence
Canada

GCL
Fuel

AV

South Alpine
Bend Plastics
Storage

Polyphase

AV

Sludge
Lagoon

Sludge
Lagoon

58

59

118

4395

11919

Consolidated
Gypsum

120

AV

Dura-Lite ST

44

ST

DEERFOOT

RIDGE

GDN

300
MS

400
MS

100
MS

DOUGLAS

RIDGE

DOUGLAS
WOODS RD

D RIDGE

BLVD

500
MS

400
MS

200
MS

DOUGLAS
WOODS

CL

200
MS

300
PL

Brews

122 AV

ST

SE

60

87

HL

BLVD

DOUGLAS
WOODS
CT

100
CT

200
PL

PL

200
PL

GN

TRAIL

52 ST

Shepard
Sanitary
Landfill

61

200
CT

*Douglasdale
Elementry
School*

CIR

RIDGE

LK

GV

2

126

126 AV

126

AV

Superstore

128 AV

40 ST

46 ST

48 ST

BLVD

DOUGLAS

VW

DOUGLASDALE

WY

DOUGLAS
RIDGE

CIR

AV 130

*Shepard
Centre*

52 ST

62

30

400
CT

MT
ABERDEEN

MT
ABERDEEN

100
CT

*The
Pinnacle*

MT
ABERDEEN
GV

CL

*South Trail
Crossing*

130

AV 130

300
CT

100
CT

MT DOUGLAS MR

MT

MT
ABERDEEN LK

MT

Co-op

Wal-Mart

*South
Pointe*

NEW
BRIGHTON

NEW
CV

63

PT

200 CT

MT DOUGLAS

McKENZIE

MT ABERDEEN

CIR

GN

400
PL

300
PL

The
Douglas
Renaissance

VL

300 TER

200 TER TER

TRAIL

100 TER

100 CL

200 CL

300 CL

PRESTWICK
CL

*PRESTWICK
BY*

PRESTWICK VL

PL

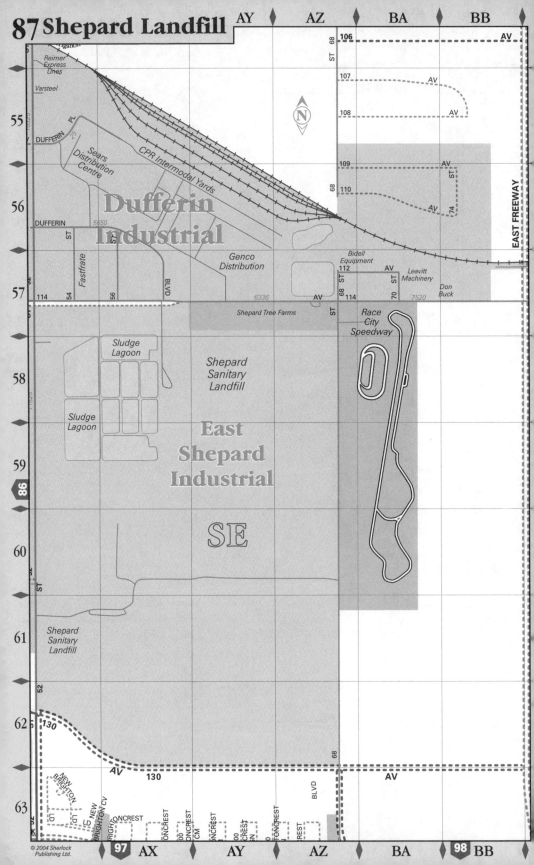

AY   AZ   BA   BB

55

56

57

58

59

86

60

61

62

63

Reimer Express Lines

Varsteel

DUFFERIN PL

Sears Distribution Centre

CPR Intermodal Yards

Dufferin Industrial

DUFFERIN ST

5650

Fastfrate

114   54   56

BLVD

Genco Distribution

6336

AV

Shepard Tree Farms

Bidell Equipment

112   114

Leavitt Machinery

Don Buck

7520

N

68 ST

106   AV

107   AV

108   AV

109   AV

68

110   AV

74 ST

EAST FREEWAY

68 ST

70 ST

AV

Race City Speedway

Sludge Lagoon

Shepard Sanitary Landfill

Sludge Lagoon

East Shepard Industrial

SE

ST

Shepard Sanitary Landfill

52

130

NEW BRIGHTON CV

NEW BRIGHTON

AV   130

68

BLVD

AV

ONCREST
ONCREST CM
ONCREST
CREST
N
ONCREST
CREST

97   AX   AY   AZ   BA   98 BB

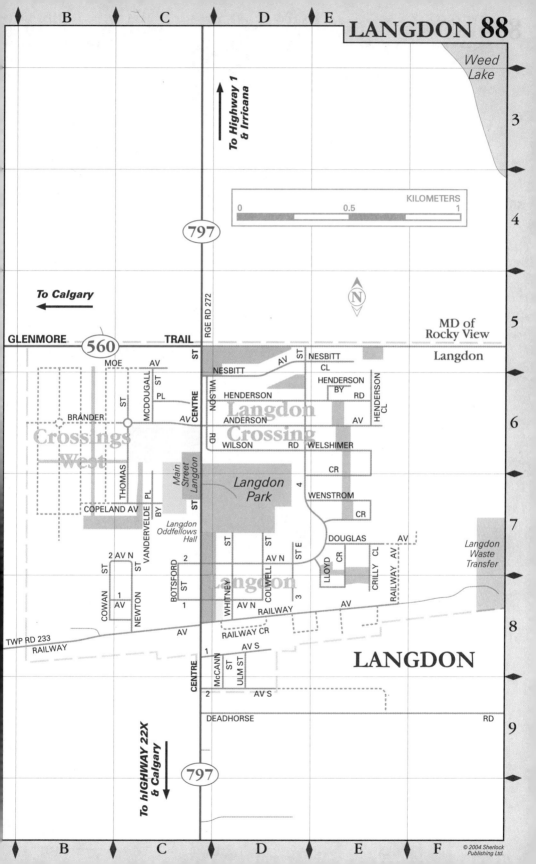

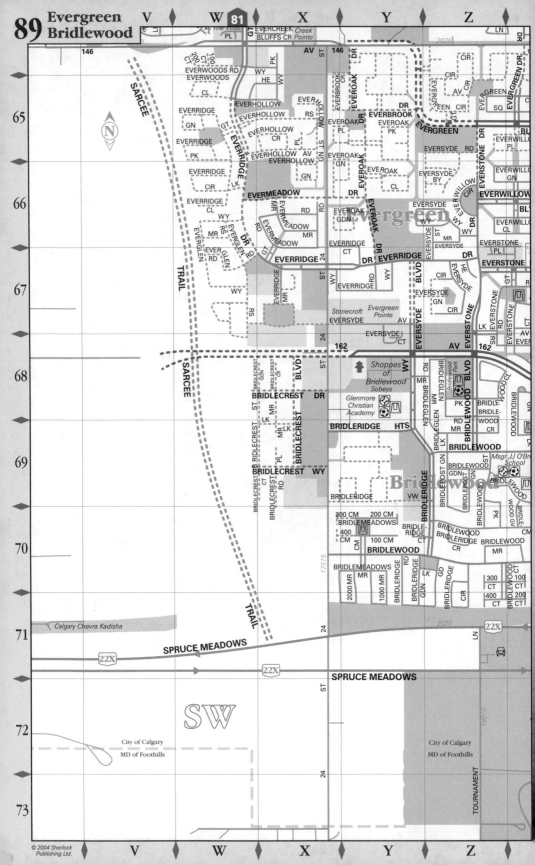

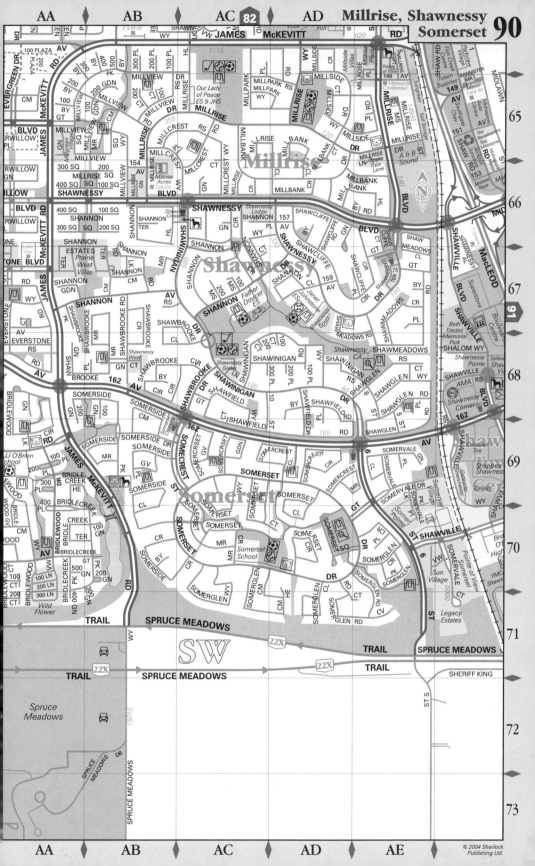

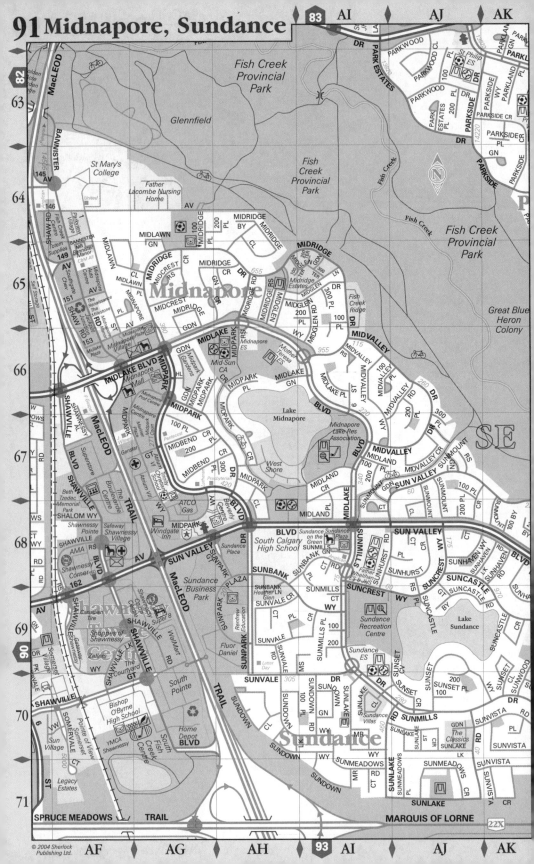

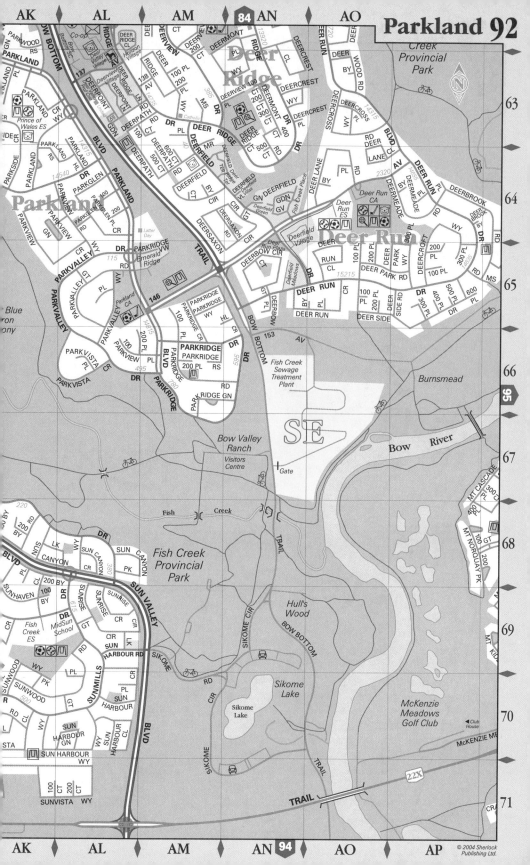

AI   91   AJ   AK   AL

71

72

73

74

75

76

77

78

79

SUNDOWN

SUNLAKE

MR   RD
CT

SUNMEADOWS

SUNMEADOWS PL

SUNMEADOWS CR

SUNVISTA

SUNVISTA CR

100 CT   200 CT

SUNVISTA WY

SUNLAKE

MARQUIS OF LORNE   22X

SHERIFF KING 18846

PL

RD

2A

N

MacLEOD

TRAIL

2A

210

210

AV W

210

AV W

210

Pine

Creek

Pine

Creek

Pine

Creek

194

2A

AV

DAWES RD

City of Calgary
MD of Foothills

City of Calgary
MD of Foothills

SE

CHAPARRAL BLVD

CHAPARRAL

Village CHAPARRAL

CHAPARRAL BLVD

200 PL
100 PL

CHAPALINA WY

CHAPALINA MR

CHAPALINA CR

CHAPALINA

PARK CR

CHAPALINA CL

CHAPARRAL

CHAPARRAL DR

CIR

TER

BY

VL

HE

CL

GV

AG

CHAPARRAL

CHAPARRAL

CM

CHAPARRAL

CHAPARRAL PK

CHAPARRAL

MR

CV

PT

Chaparral
Pointe

CHAPARRAL ST

CHAPARRAL

200 CT

CR 100
CT

PL

100

PL 100

300 PL

GN RD
PL

200
RD

CHAPARRAL WY

CHAPARRAL

CHAPARRAL

WY LK

CHAPARRAL

RD

MS

Chaparral Corner

Lake
Chaparral
Park

Lake
Chaparral

CHAPALA

CR
BY

CR
CT

CHAPALA DR

CHAPMAN

CHAPALA DR

CHAPMAN WY

TER
RD

CHAPMAN
HE

CHAPALA

CHAPALA CL

CHAPALA
CL

CHAPALA DR

CHAPALA

CL

RD

SQ

CHAPALINA
GN

CHAPALINA TER

CHAPALINA
HE

CHAPALINA HTS

CHAPARRAL

CHAPARRAL DR

LK
RS

GT

CHAPALA
TER

CHAPALA GV

CHAPALA

CHAPALA

CHAPALA WY

LD

CHAPMAN
CIR

CHAPMAN MS

CHAPMAN

PL
CHAPMAN CL

CH   DR

CHAPALA BLVD

CHAPALA WY
CT
CL

Pine Creek
Cemetery

Pine Creek
RV Campgound

71

TRAIL

22X

CRANLEIGH CRANLEIGH
PK
GN
CRANLEIGH
100 BY
DR
CRANLEIGH
CL
CRANSTON PL
CRANLEIGH

Gate

CRANLEIGH
MR
CM

CRAN LEIGH
CRANLEIGH
MS

72

CRANLEIGH
HTS
MR

CRAN LEIGH
CT

CRANLEIGH
GDN

CRA

Bow

CRANLEIGH

CRANSTON

River

GT

100 CHAPARRAL
RIDGE
CHAPARRAL
RIDGE

CRANLEIGH WY AM

200 100
PL PL

CRANLEIGH
WY

100 BY
CHAPARRAL RIDGE CIR

100
PL

200

CHAPARRAL
WY

73

96

CHAPARRAL
RIDGE DR
LK

CRANLEIGH
VW

200
VW

CRANLEIGH
WY

1
CR

CHAPARRAL
RIDGE

SE

200
PT

CIR

CHAPARRAL
RIDGE CIR

300
PT

N

74

CHAPARRAL
BLVD

75

194
RD

BFI Waste Systems
Sanitary Landfill

DAWES

AV

Gate
RD

Dawes Pit

City of Calgary
MD of Foothills

76

77

78

W

ne
eek
etery

79

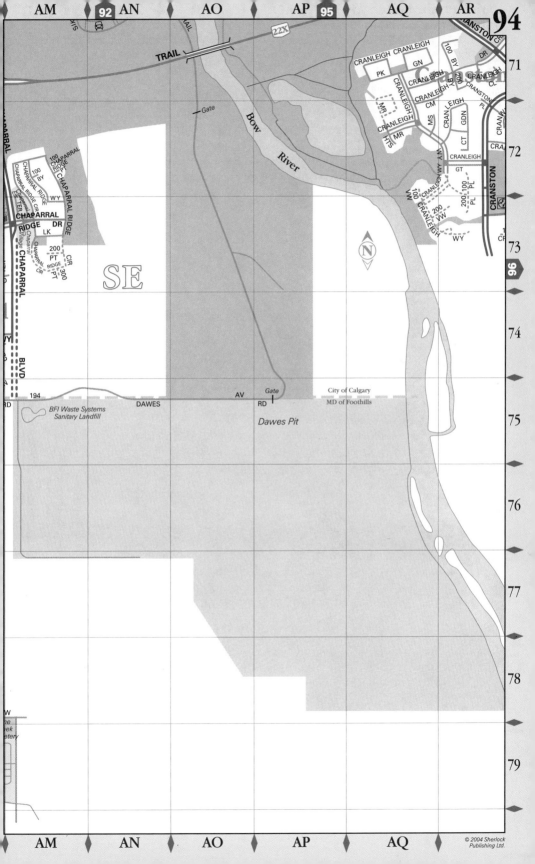

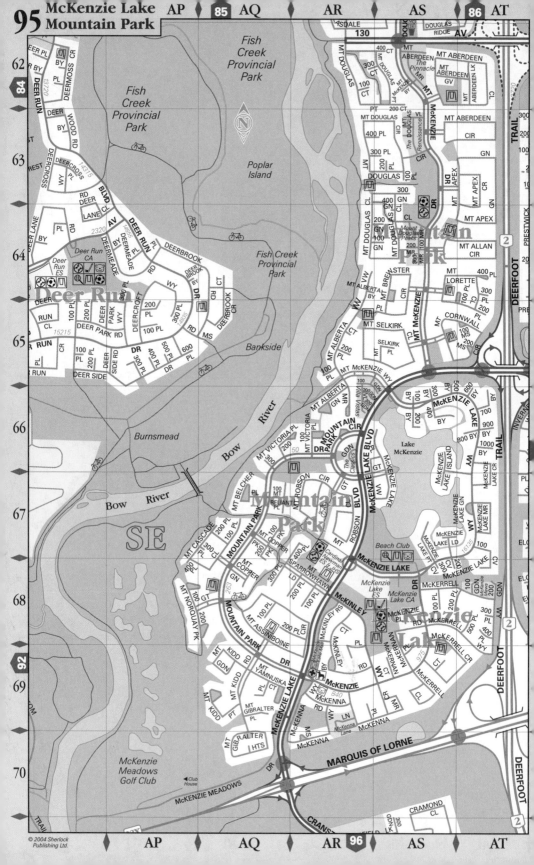

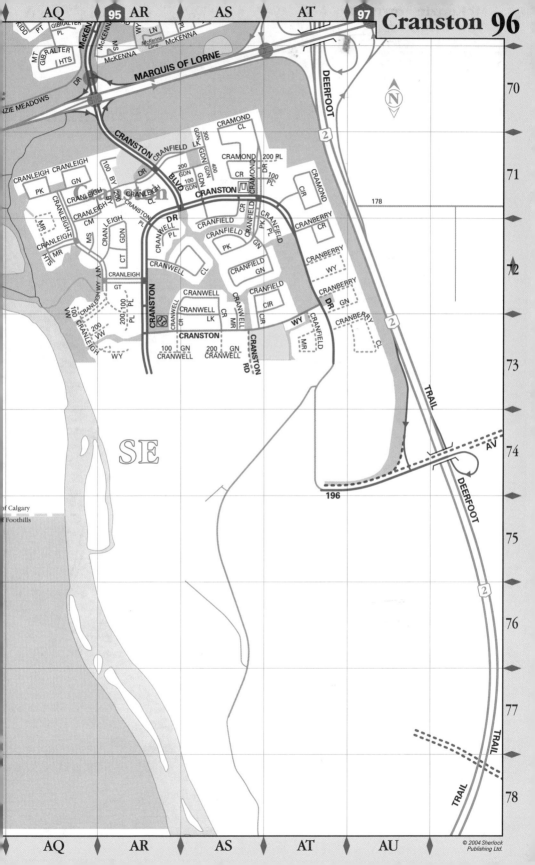

AQ AR AS AT

95 97

MT GIBRALTER PL
GIBRALTER HTS
KIDD PT
PL

McKENNA
McKenna Lane
McKENNA
LN
McKENNA

DR

MARQUIS OF LORNE

DEERFOOT

N

NZIE MEADOWS

2

CRANSTON

CRANFIELD

CRAMOND
CL

300 GDN LK
200 GDN
400 GDN
100 GDN

CRAMOND
CR

200 PL

CRAMOND
PL

100 PL

CRAMOND
CIR

CRANLEIGH
GN
CRANLEIGH
PK

100 BY
200 DR

CRANLEIGH
CM

CRANLEIGH
CL

CRANSTON
PL

CRANSTON

DR

CRANSTON

Cranston

BLVD

CRANLEIGH

CRANFIELD
PL

CRANFIELD
GN

CRANBERRY
CR

178

CRANFIELD
CIR

PK

CRANBERRY
CR

CRANLEIGH
MR

CRANLEIGH
MS

CM

GDN

CT

CRANLEIGH
WY

GT

CRAN-LEIGH

CRANWELL
PL

CRANFIELD
PK

CRANFIELD
GN

CRANFIELD
CL

CRANBERRY
WY

2

CRANLEIGH
HTS
MR

CRANLEIGH
MR

CRANWELL
CL

CRANFIELD
GN

CRANBERRY
GN

CRANLEIGH WY

CRANSTON
PL

100 PL
200 PL

CRANWELL
CR

CRANWELL

CRANWELL
LK

CRANFIELD
CR MR

CRANFIELD
CIR

CRANBERRY
DR

WY

2

100
VW
200
VW

200
CRANLEIGH

CRANSTON

100 GN
CRANWELL

200 GN
CRANWELL

CRANSTON
RD

CRANFIELD
MR

CRANBERRY
CL

WY

TRAIL

SE

AV

196

74

DEERFOOT

of Calgary
f Foothills

75

2

76

77

TRAIL

TRAIL

78

70
71
72
73

AQ AR AS AT AU

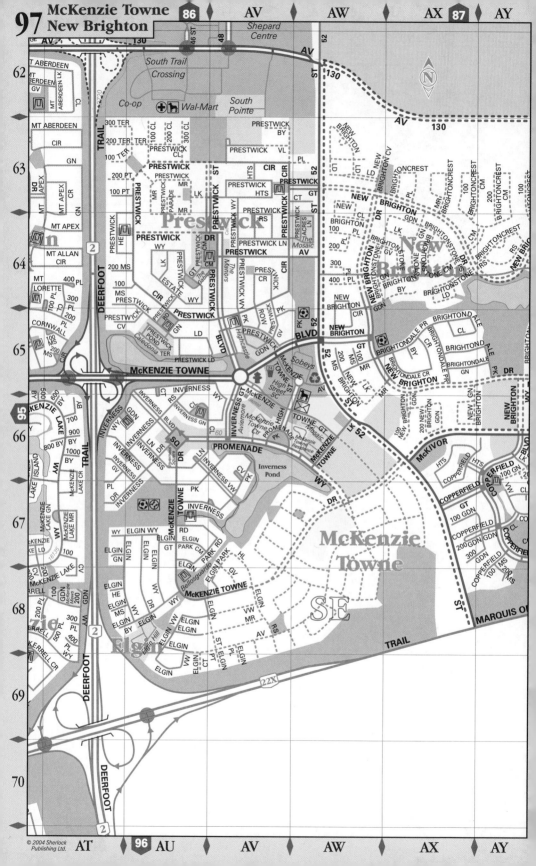

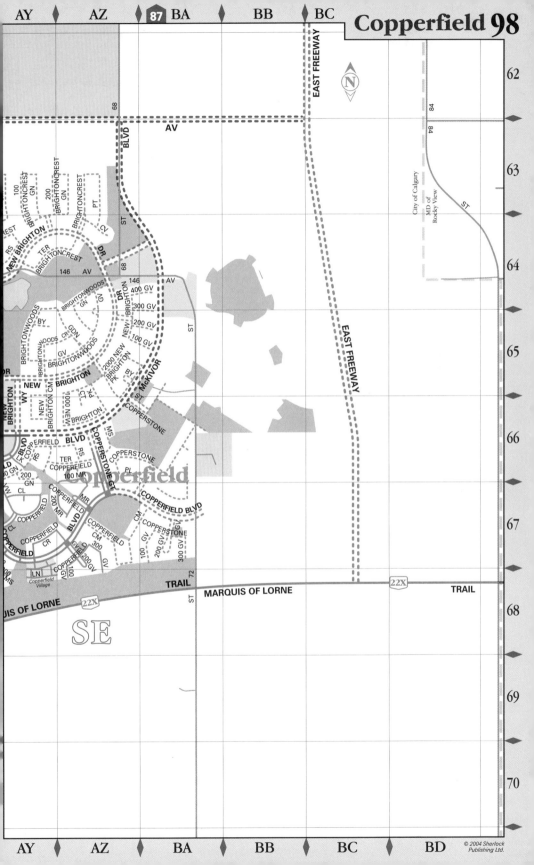

62

N

63

City of Calgary
MD of
Rocky View

64

65

66

67

68

69

70

84
84
ST

EAST FREEWAY

EAST FREEWAY

NEW BRIGHTON
BRIGHTONCREST
100 GN
200 GN
BRIGHTONCREST
PT
CV
ST
DR
68
BLVD
AV
146 AV
68
146 AV
400 GV
300 GV
200 GV
100 GV
DR
NEW BRIGHTON
ST
BRIGHTONWOODS
GN
GV
BY
CR
GDN
BRIGHTONWOODS
GV
BRIGHTONWOODS
TER
BRIGHTONCREST
RS
2000 NEW
BRIGHTON
PK
BY
1000 NEW
BRIGHTON
CT
PK
BRIGHTON
McIVOR
ST
COPPERSTONE
NEW BRIGHTON
NEW BRIGHTON CM
WY
BRIGHTON
COPPERSTONE
MS
COPPERFIELD
BLVD
BLVD
RS
TER
COPPERFIELD GT
COPPERSTONE
PL
COPPERSTONE
200 GN
100 GN
GN
CL
200 MR
100 MR
MR
COPPERFIELD
CM
COPPERSTONE
GV
Copperfield
COPPERFIELD BLVD
CL
COPPERFIELD
BLVD
COPPERFIELD
CM
100 GV
200 GV
300 GV
GV
CR
200 MR
CL
COPPERFIELD
100
LN
Copperfield
Village
ST
72
TRAIL
22X
MARQUIS OF LORNE
22X
TRAIL
QUIS OF LORNE
SE

© 2004 Sherlock
Publishing Ltd.

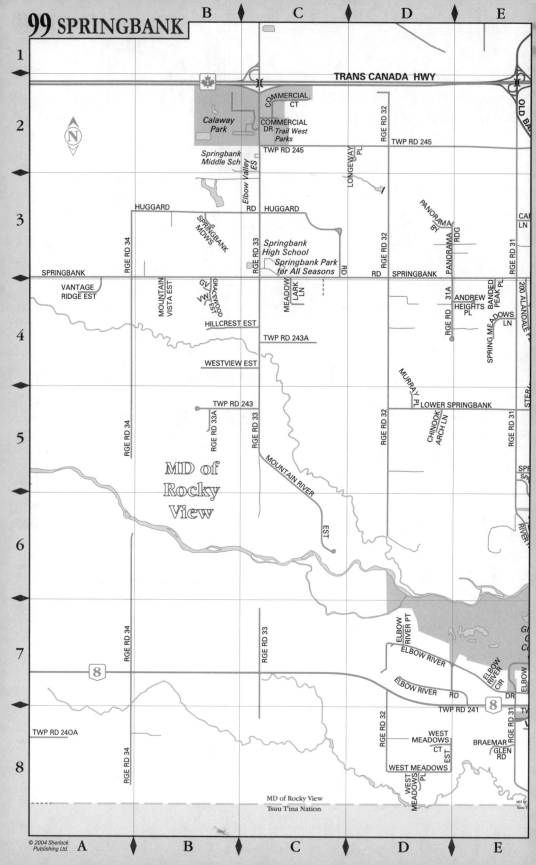

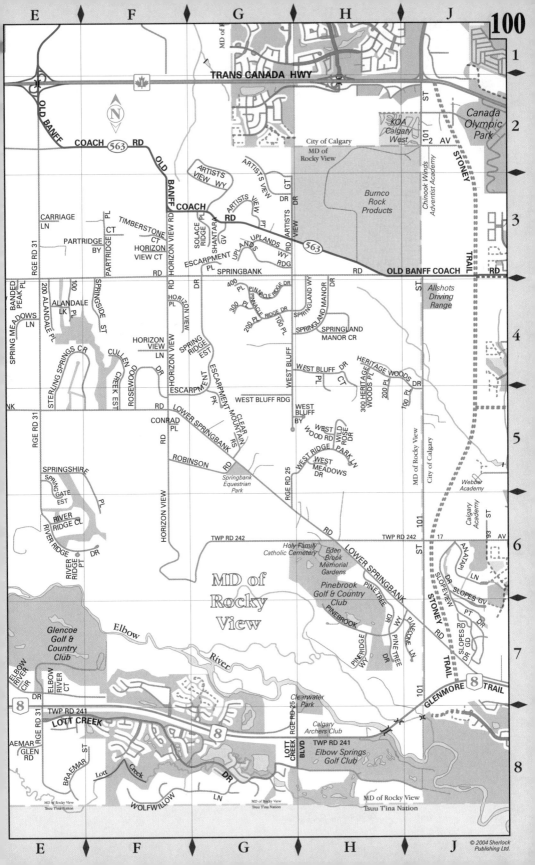

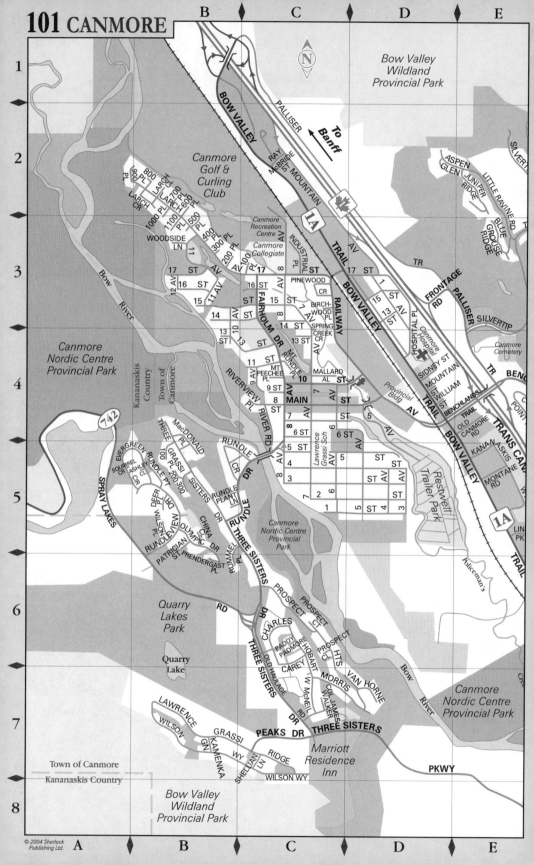

101 CANMORE

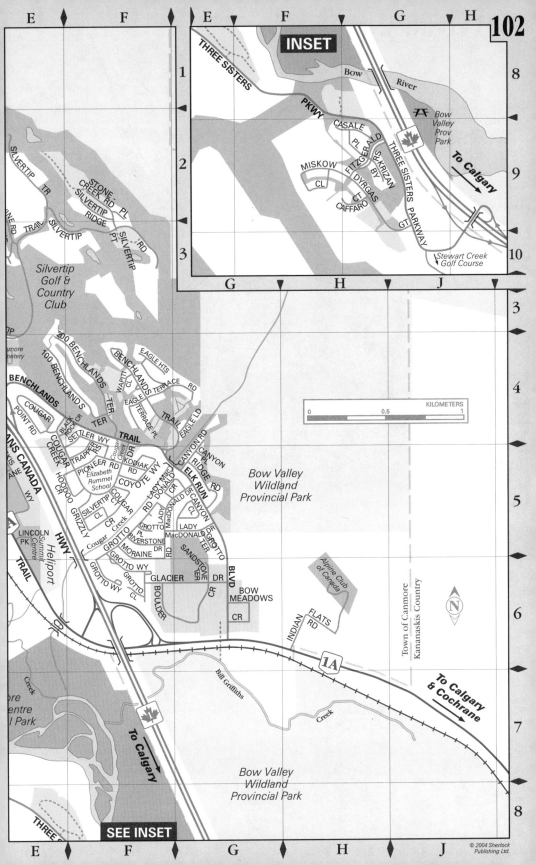

INSET

E F G H

THREE SISTERS

Bow River

PKWY

CASALE

Bow Valley Prov Park

MISKOW

CL

FITZGERALD

PL

DYRGAS

S. KRIZAN

BY

THREE SISTERS PARKWAY

To Calgary

CAFFARO

CT

GT

Stewart Creek Golf Course

SILVERTIP TR

STONE CREEK RD PL

SILVERTIP

ONE RD

SILVERTIP RIDGE

SILVERTIP PT

RD

SILVERTIP

TRAIL

Silvertip Golf & Country Club

TIP

anmore Cemetery

200 BENCHLANDS TER

100 BENCHLANDS

BENCHLANDS TER

EAGLE HTS

WAPITI CL

EAGLE TERRACE RD

EAGLE TERRACE PL

BENCHLANDS

TRAIL

BENCHLANDS

TER

EAGLE TERRACE

TRAIL

EAGLE LD

COUGAR CREEK

POINT RD

SETTLER WY

TRAPPER RS

BLACK ROCK CR

Cougar Creek

CANYON RIDGE RD

EAGLE RIDGE

CANYON RD

Bow Valley Wildland Provincial Park

0   0.5   1

KILOMETERS

TRANS CANADA

AVIS LANE

WY

HOODOO

PIONEER RD

Elizabeth Rummel School

SILVERTIP CL

GRIZZLY

COYOTE

KODIAK RD

COUGAR CR

Cougar Creek

LADY MacDONALD CR

RD

KODIAK

GROTTO PL

Riverstone DR

LADY MacDONALD

MacDONALD DR

CANYON CL

ELK RUN

LADY MacDONALD TER

CANYON DR

RD

LINCOLN PK

Summit Centre

HWY

Heliport

GRIZZLY

GROTTO

MORAINE

GROTTO WY

GROTTO WY

GROTTO CL

GLACIER DR

SANDSTONE TER

GROTTO

BOULDER CR

BLVD

BOW MEADOWS CR

Alpine Club of Canada

INDIAN

FLATS RD

Town of Canmore Kananaskis Country

N

TRANS CANADA TRAIL

To Calgary

ore entre l Park

Bill Griffiths

1A

Creek

To Calgary & Cochrane

Creek

Bow Valley Wildland Provincial Park

THREE S

SEE INSET

E F G H J

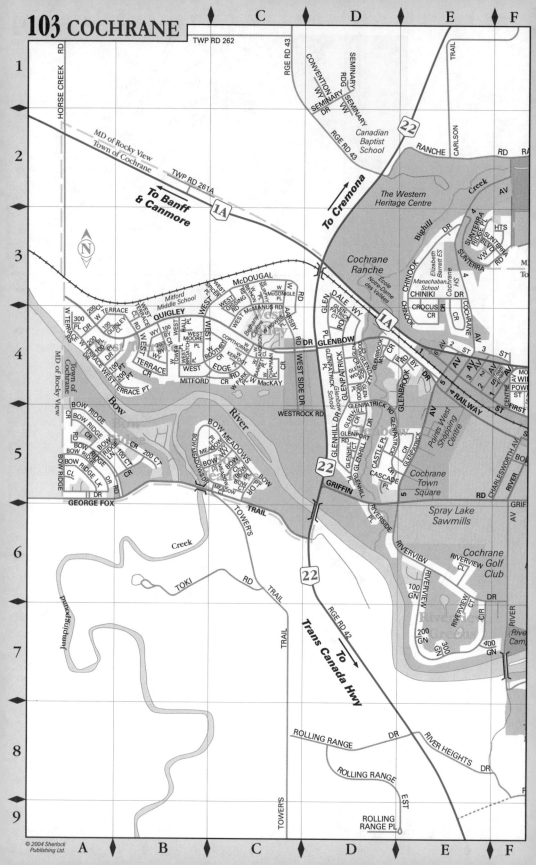

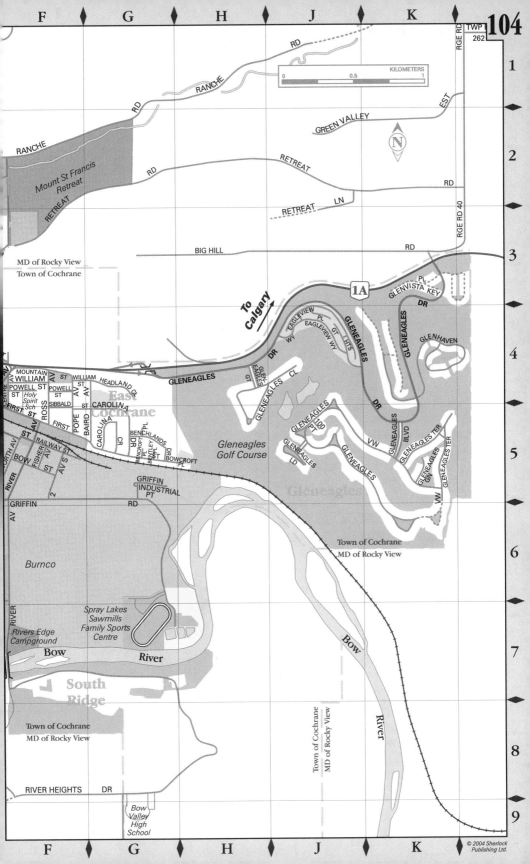

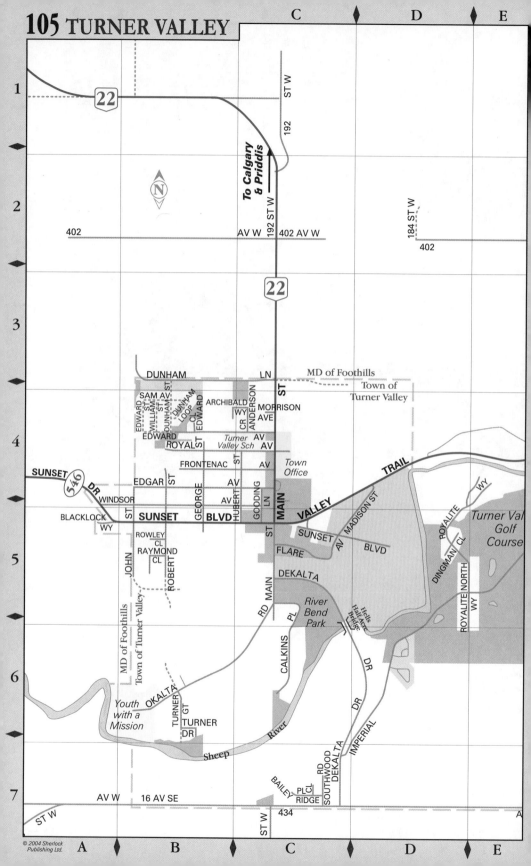

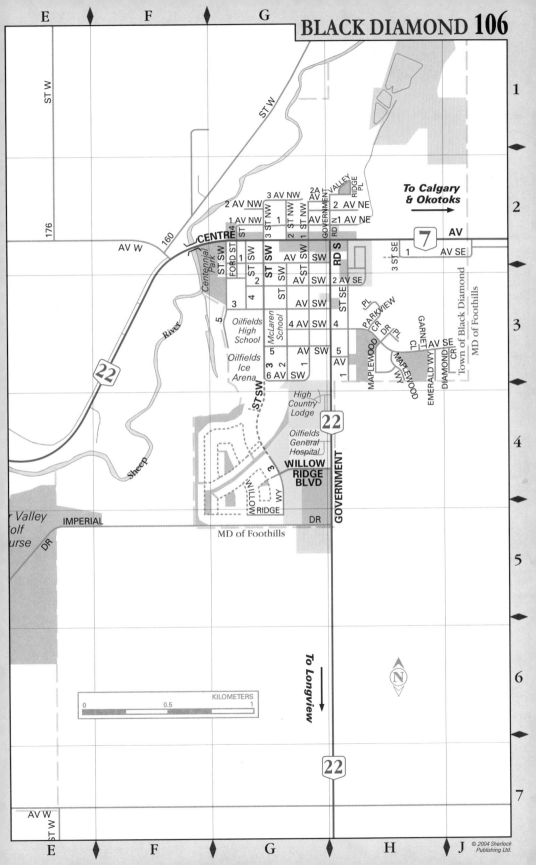

E   F   G

1

2A AV
2 AV NW   3 AV NW   VALLEY   RIDGE PL
2 AV NW   ST NW   GOVERNMENT   2 AV NE

To Calgary & Okotoks

2

1 AV NW   3 ST NW   2 ST NW   1 ST NW   N 1 AV NE

ST W

176

160

AV W   **CENTRE**   ST   3 ST SW   2 ST   1 ST   GOVERNMENT RD S   **7**   **AV**

Centennial Park   FORD ST   ST SW   1   **ST SW**   AV SW   SW   3 ST SE   1 AV SE

River

ST SW   ST SW   4   ST SW   2 ST   AV SW   SW   2 AV SE

3   AV SW   SW   ST SE

5   *Oilfields High School*   *McLaren School*   4 AV SW   4   PARKVIEW   GARNET   AV SE   Town of Black Diamond   MD of Foothills

5   5   AV SW   MAPLEWOOD CR   DR PL   DIAMOND CR

Oilfields Ice Arena   3   2   1   AV   EMERALD WY   MAPLEWOOD WY

22   6 AV   SW   1

ST SW

3

High Country Lodge

22

Oilfields General Hospital

WILLOW   3   **WILLOW RIDGE BLVD**   GOVERNMENT

WY   RIDGE   **To Longview**

4

Sheep

r Valley olf urse   DR   IMPERIAL   DR   MD of Foothills   DR

5

KILOMETERS
0   0.5   1

6

N

22

7

AV W

ST W   E   F   G   H   J

© 2004 Sherlock Publishing Ltd.

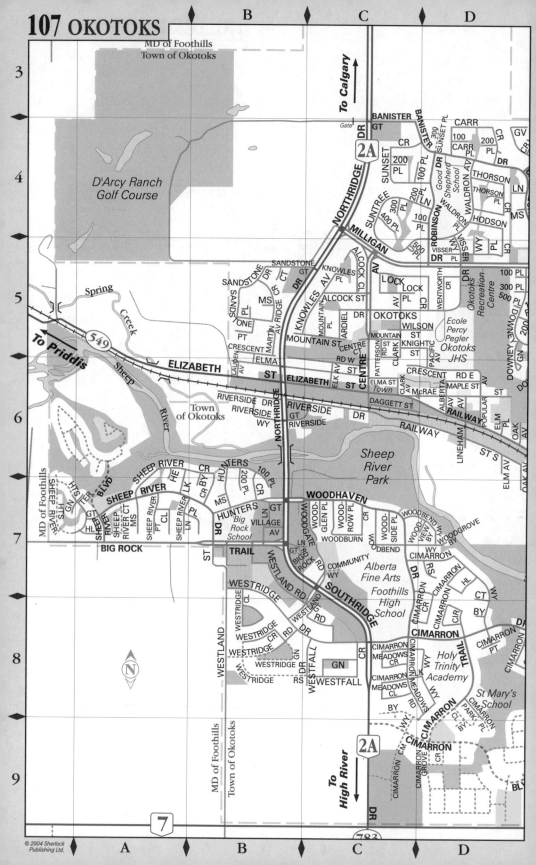

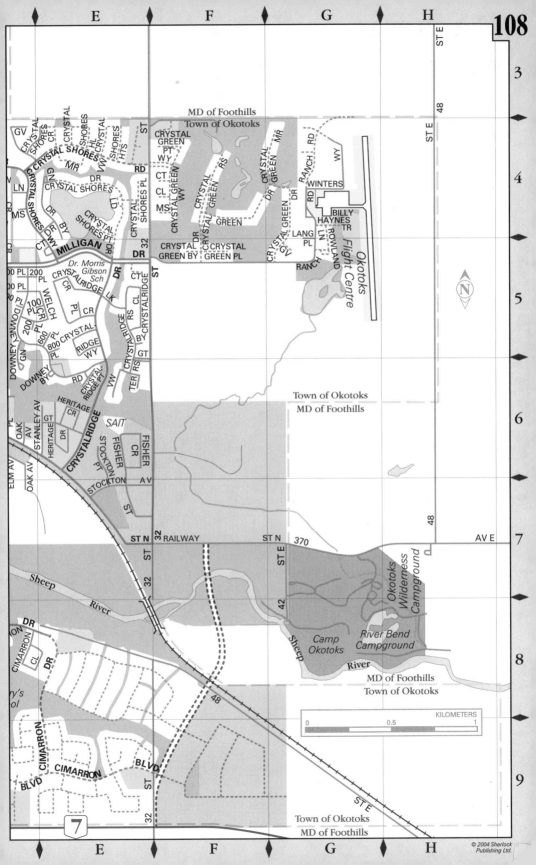

E · F · G · H

3

ST E

48 ST E

4

MD of Foothills
Town of Okotoks

CRYSTAL SHORES
CRYSTAL SHORES RD
CRYSTAL SHORES HTS
CRYSTAL SHORES HL
CRYSTAL SHORES VW
GV
GN
LN
MR
DR
MS
CRYSTAL SHORES DR
CRYSTAL SHORES BY
CRYSTAL SHORES PT
CRYSTAL SHORES CT
CRYSTAL SHORES DWY
CRYSTAL SHORES LD
MILLIGAN DR

CRYSTAL SHORES PL
ST 32
ST

CRYSTAL GREEN PT WY
CRYSTAL GREEN CT
CRYSTAL GREEN CL
CRYSTAL GREEN MS
CRYSTAL GREEN WY
CRYSTAL GREEN DR
CRYSTAL GREEN RS
CRYSTAL GREEN
CRYSTAL GREEN BY
CRYSTAL GREEN PL
CRYSTAL GREEN

CRYSTAL GREEN MR
CRYSTAL GREEN DR
CRYSTAL GREEN GV

RANCH RD
WY
WINTERS WY
BILLY HAYNES TR
LANG PL
ROWLAND LN
RD
RANCH

Okotoks Flight Centre

N

Dr. Morris Gibson Sch

00 PL
00 PL
200 PL
200 PL
100 PL
200 PL
600 PL
800 PL
WELCH CR
DOWNEY GN
DOWNEY PL
CRYSTALRIDGE CR
CRYSTALRIDGE PL
CRYSTALRIDGE LK
CRYSTALRIDGE CR
CRYSTALRIDGE DR
CRYSTALRIDGE RS
CRYSTALRIDGE CL
CRYSTALRIDGE BY
CRYSTALRIDGE GT
CRYSTALRIDGE RS
CRYSTALRIDGE TER
CRYSTALRIDGE WY
CRYSTALRIDGE VW
CRYSTAL RIDGE PT
CRYSTALRIDGE DR
RIDGE WY
DR

CTL
DOWNEY BY
DOWNEY

5

6

ELM AV
OAK AV
OAK PL
STANLEY AV
HERITAGE CR
HERITAGE DR
HERITAGE GT
CRYSTALRIDGE
SAIT
FISHER CR
FISHER AV
STOCKTON PT
STOCKTON ST

Town of Okotoks
MD of Foothills

7

ST N 32 RAILWAY
ST N
ST E 370
42 ST E
AV E

Sheep River

Okotoks Wilderness Campground

River Bend Campground

Camp Okotoks

48 ST E

Sheep River

8

CIMARRON DR
CIMARRON CL
CIMARRON DR
CIMARRON
CIMARRON BLVD
CIMARRON BLVD
BLVD
ST 32
48

ary's ool

MD of Foothills
Town of Okotoks

KILOMETERS
0   0.5   1

9

7

ST E

Town of Okotoks
MD of Foothills

E · F · G · H

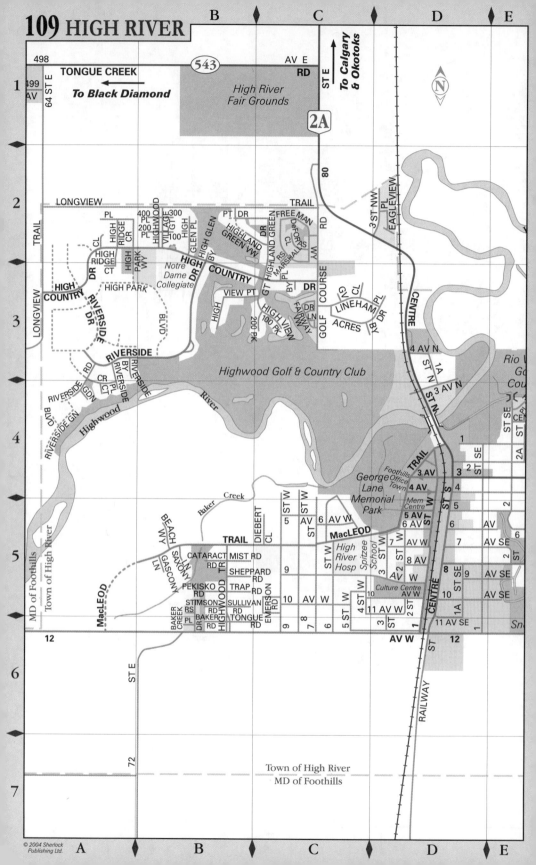

109 HIGH RIVER

A

498
499 AV
64 ST E
TONGUE CREEK
→ **To Black Diamond**

LONGVIEW
TRAIL
LONGVIEW
HIGH COUNTRY DR
RIVERSIDE DR
HIGH COUNTRY DR
RIVERSIDE RD
RIVERSIDE BLVD
RIVERSIDE GDN
RIVERSIDE GN
Highwood

MD of Foothills
Town of High River
72 ST E

B

543
AV E
RD

LONGVIEW
TRAIL
PL
HIGH RIDGE CL
HIGH RIDGE CT
WOOD
VILLAGE GT
400 PL
300 PL
200 PL
100 PL
HIGH RIDGE CR
HIGH PARK WY
HIGH PARK
BLVD
Notre Dame Collegiate
HIGH COUNTRY DR
HIGH GLEN BY
GLEN PL
HIGHLAND GREEN VW
HIGHLAND GREEN
HIGH VIEW PT
HIGH VIEW
100 PK
200 PK
HIGH FAIRWAY
DR
LN
FREEMAN
DeFORAS
MARSHALL RS
CL
RS

River
Baker Creek
Creek

BEACH WY
SAXONY LN
GASCONY LN
CATARACT RD
MIST RD
SHEPPARD RD
PEKISKO RD
TRAP RD
STIMSON RS
SULLIVAN RD
BAKER CREEK PL
HIGHWOOD TR
TONGUE RD
DIEBERT CL
EMERSON RD
TRAIL
MacLEOD
MacLEOD
BAKER CREEK RD

12
ST E

C

2A
80
ST E
To Calgary & Okotoks

High River Fair Grounds

TRAIL
DR
PT DR
VIEW PT
GT
LINEHAM ACRES
GV
CL
BY
PL
DR
DR
GOLF COURSE RD
MAN WY
DR

Highwood Golf & Country Club

5
6 AV W
ST W
ST W
AV
ST W
9
AV W
10
AV W
9
6 ST W
7
8
5 ST W
6
MacLEOD
High River Hosp
Spitzee School
Culture Centre
George Lane Memorial Park
Foothills Office Town
3 AV
4 AV
5 AV
6 AV
7 W
8 AV
W
10
11 AV W
ST W
2 ST
4 ST W
3 ST W
2 ST

D

AV E
RD
ST E
3 ST NW
EAGLEVIEW PL
CENTRE
4 AV N
1A
3 AV N
ST N
ST N
3 AV
TRAIL
ST S
ST S
CENTRE
1
3 ST
2 ST
1A ST
11 AV SE
1
12
AV W
ST
RAILWAY

Mem Centre
1
3
4
5
6
7
8
9
10
11 AV SE

E

N

Rio G Cou
ST SE
ST SE
2A
AV
AV SE
2 ST
AV
AV SE
AV SE
6
5
Sn

Town of High River
MD of Foothills

© 2004 Sherlock Publishing Ltd.

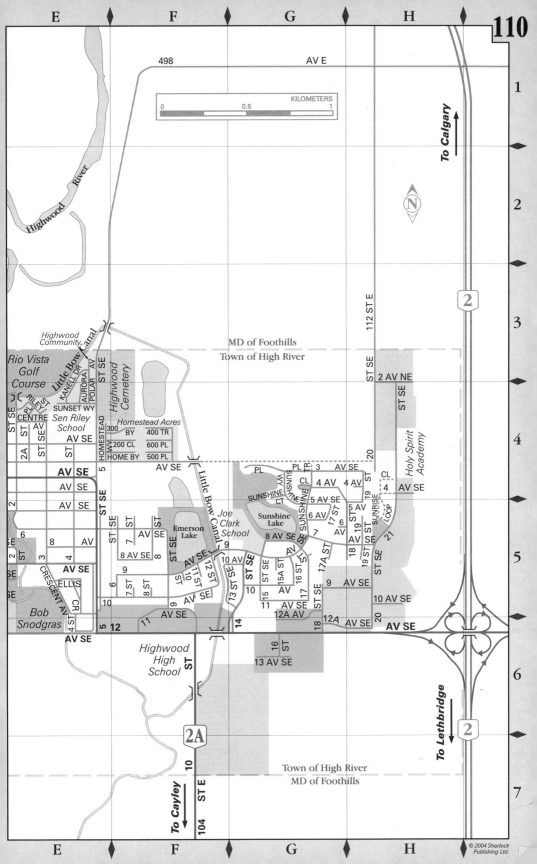

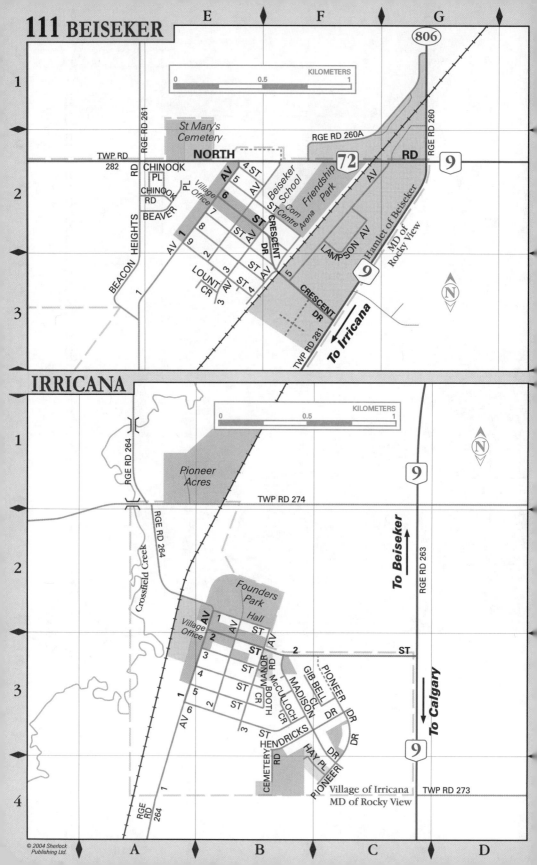

111 BEISEKER

806

KILOMETERS
0   0.5   1

1

RGE RD 261

St Mary's Cemetery

RGE RD 260A

NORTH

72 **RD**

9

RGE RD 260

TWP RD 282

CHINOOK PL

CHINOOK RD

BEAVER

AV

4 ST

5 AV

6

Village Office

7

PL

8

1

9

AV

2

LOUNT CR

3

3 AV

ST AV

ST AV

4 ST

5

ST AV

DR

CRESCENT

ST

Beiseker School

Com Centre

Arena

Friendship Park

LAMPSON AV

AV

Hamlet of Beiseker

MD of Rocky View

9

2

BEACON HEIGHTS

1

3

CRESCENT DR

TWP RD 281

To Irricana

N

IRRICANA

KILOMETERS
0   0.5   1

N

1

RGE RD 264

Pioneer Acres

TWP RD 274

9

Crossfield Creek

RGE RD 264

To Beiseker

RGE RD 263

2

Founders Park Hall

Village Office

AV

1 AV

ST

2

ST

2 **ST**

3

ST

AV

MANOR RD

McCULLOCH CR

BOOTH CR

MADISON

GIB BELL

PIONEER DR

CL

DR

PIONEER DR

DR

To Calgary

9

4

5

1

6

AV

2

3 ST

HENDRICKS RD

CEMETERY RD

HAY PL

PIONEER

Village of Irricana
MD of Rocky View

TWP RD 273

9

3

4

© 2004 Sherlock Publishing Ltd.

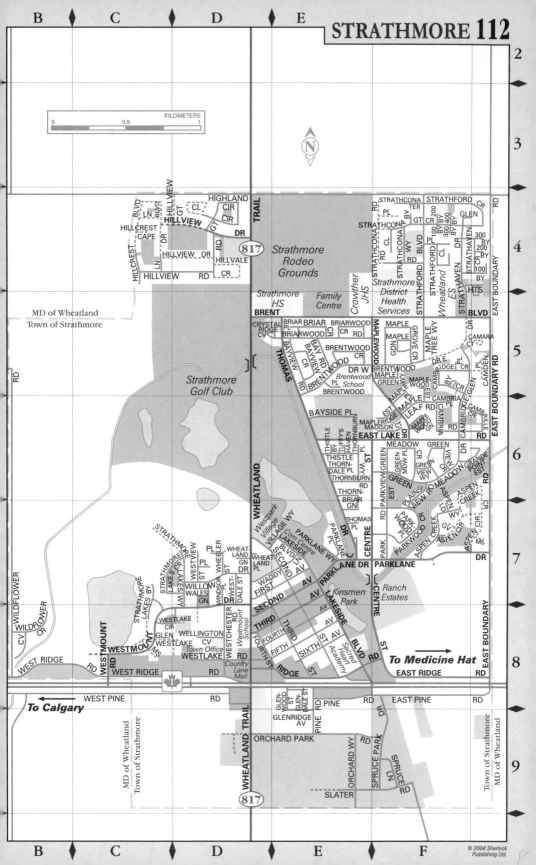

KILOMETERS
0   0.5   1

N

MD of Wheatland
Town of Strathmore

HILLCREST
CAPE

HILLCREST

HILLVIEW BLVD
HILLVIEW GT
HILLVIEW LN
HILLVIEW DR

HILLVIEW
HILLVIEW DR
HILLVIEW RD

HILLCREST LN
HILLCREST DR

CL

HIGHLAND
CIR
CIR
DR

HILLVALE
RD
CR

817

*Strathmore
Rodeo
Grounds*

TRAIL

BRENT

*Strathmore
HS*

*Family
Centre*

Crowther JHS

*Strathmore
District
Health
Services*

STRATHCONA RD
STRATHCONA PL
STRATHCONA CL
STRATHCONA GT
STRATHCONA WY
STRATHCONA RD
STRATHCONA CL

STRATHFORD
TER
CR 200
BY 200
BY 400
BY 300
BY 100

GLEN

STRATHFORD
CL

STRATHFORD
BLVD
STRATHLAND

STRATHAVEN
DR

STRATHAVEN
ES
Wheatland

CAMARA
CT

300
BY 200
BY 100
BY

HTS

BLVD

EAST BOUNDARY

*Strathmore
Golf Club*

THOMAS

BAYVIEW

CRYSTAL
RIDGE
CV

BRIAR
PL

BRIAR

BRIARWOOD
CR

BRIARWOOD
CR RD

BAY RD
BAYVIEW

BRENTWOOD
DR W
BRENTWOOD

BRENTWOOD
CR

BRENTWOOD
PL
*Brentwood
School*
BRENTWOOD

MAPLEWOOD

MAPLE
GDN

GROVE CR

MAPLE

MAPLE
GREEN

MAPLE WY

MAPLE
TREE WY

MAPLE
DR E

MAPLE
WOOD

MAPLE
PL
MAPLE

LEAF RD

MAPLE
WOOD

RIDGE

CAMBRIA
GLEN CR
CR

CAMBRIDGE
CR

CAMDEN
PL
CAMILLE

CAMBRIA
PL

CAMBRIA
RD

EAST BOUNDARY RD

BAYSIDE PL

MAPLERIDGE
MADISON CT

EAST LAKE

THISTLE
THORN-
DALE PL
THORNBURN

THISTLE
THORNBURN

TUFFYS
HAVEN

THORN-
BRIAR
GN

THORN-
BRIAR
GN

ST

MEADOW
GREEN
PL
GREEN
MDW PL

GREEN

GREEN
CR

GREEN
VIEW WY

VIEW
CR

RD

DR

RD

GRANDE
POINT
EST

RD

WHEATLAND

*Westpark
Village*

VILLAGE WY

Com Centre

PARKLANE
LAKESIDE
BLVD
LN

PARKLANE

PARKLANE
PL

DR

THOMAS
PL

GREEN

PARKVIEW GREEN

RD
RD

PLAINS
VIEW

MEADOW
GN

PARK
WOOD
PL

PARKWOOD
CR

MEADOW

ASPEN
GN

ASPEN

ASPEN
CREEK

ASPEN
WY

ASPEN
PL

GRANDE
POINT
EST

RD

ASPEN
CREEK
CR

ASPEN CIR
MS

STRATHMORE LAKES BY
STRATHMORE LAKES BY
STRATHMORE
LAKES BY

PL
WESTVIEW
ST
PL

WILLOW
WALES
GN

WINDSOR
DR

WHEELER
WEST-
DALE ST
GN

WHEAT-
LAND
GN DR

WHEAT-
LAND
PL

VILLAGE
BLVD

SECOND
AV

PARK

PARK

CENTRE

DR

PARKLANE WY

*Ranch
Estates*

PARKLANE

DR

WESTMOUNT
RD

WILDFLOWER
CV
WILDFLOWER
CR

WEST RIDGE
RD

WESTMOUNT

WESTMOUNT
RD

WEST RIDGE

WESTLAKE
CIR
MS

WESTLAKE
GLEN

WELLINGTON
CV

WESTLAKE

Town Office

WESTCHESTER
RD

WEST-
DALE ST

*Westmount
School*

*Country
Lane Mall*

WHEAT-
LAND
PL

WADDY
WY

FIRST

SECOND

THIRD

FOURTH ST

FIFTH

SECOND
AV

FIRST

THIRD
ST

FOURTH

RIDGE

LAKESIDE
AV
AV
AV
AV

SIXTH
ST

*Kinsmen
Park*

*Sacred
Heart
Academy*

CENTRE

ST

LAKESIDE
BLVD
RD

To Medicine Hat

EAST RIDGE

EAST BOUNDARY

RD

DR

MD of Wheatland
Town of Strathmore

WEST PINE

To Calgary

WHEATLAND TRAIL

RD

GLEN-
WOOD
ST
GLEN-
WOOD
DALE ST

PINE

GLENRIDGE
AV

PINE

PINE

RD
RD

EAST PINE

RD

DR

ORCHARD PARK

ORCHARD WY

SPRUCE PARK

SPRUCE
LN

SPRUCE
RD

SLATER

Town of Strathmore
MD of Wheatland

817

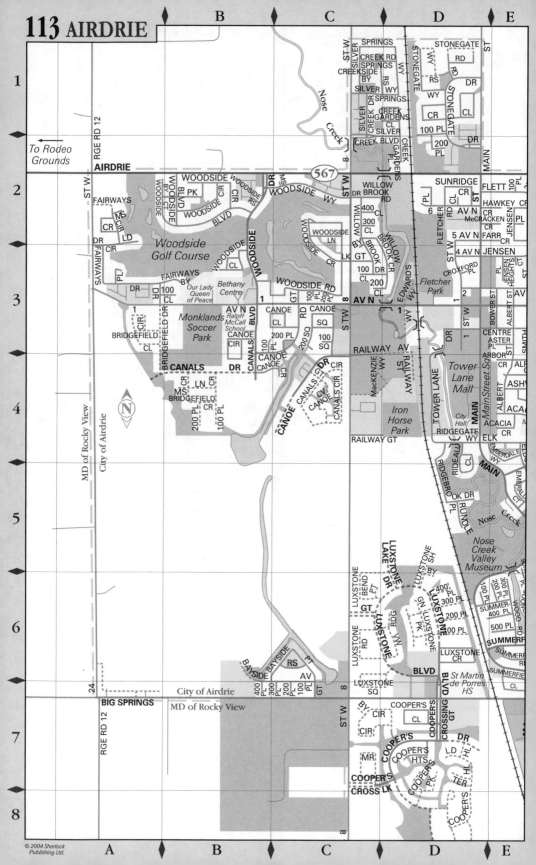

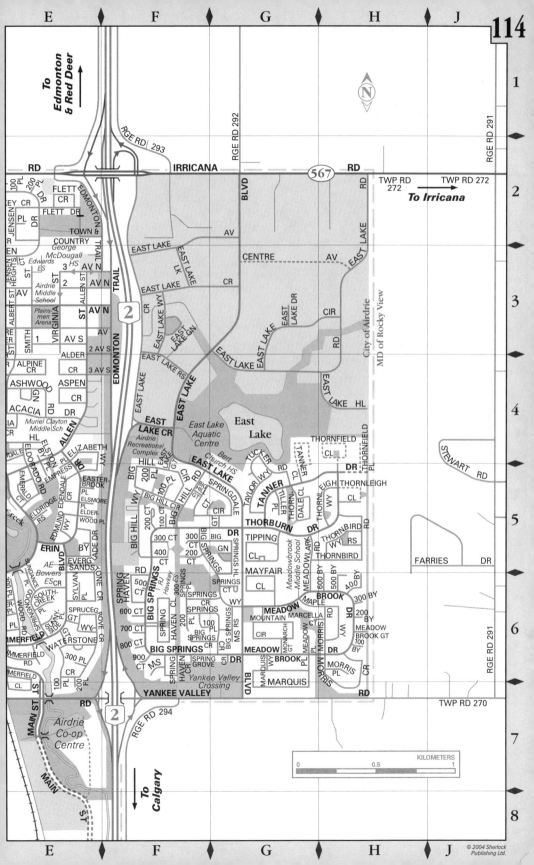

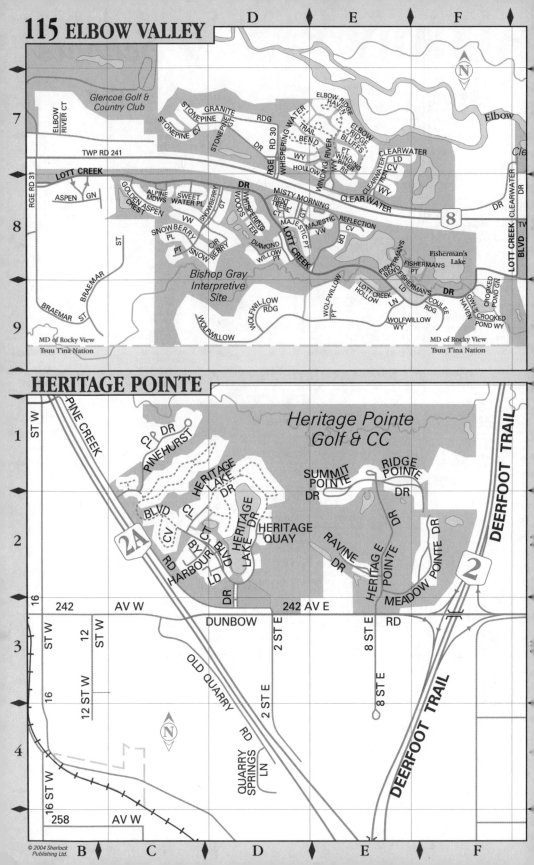

115 ELBOW VALLEY

D   E   F

N

Elbow
Cle

7

Glencoe Golf &
Country Club

ELBOW
RIVER CT

STONEPINE CV

STONEPINE

GRANITE
RDG

STONEPINE
DR

RGE RD 30

STONEPINE CV

RGE

ELBOW RIDGE
HAVEN

WHISPERING WATER

TRAIL
BEND

ELBOW
RIDGE
BLUFFS

WINDING RIVER PT

CLEARWATER
LD

CLEARWATER
CV

CLEARWATER
WY

Elbow

TWP RD 241

WY
HOLLOW

WINDING
RIVER RS

CLEARWATER

Cle

LOTT CREEK

RGE RD 31

ASPEN

GN

GOLDEN ASPEN
CREST

ALPINE
MDWS

VW

SWEET
WATER PL

SNOWBERRY

DR

WHISPERING WATER

GT

SCOOM

MISTY MORNING

BENT
TREE
CT

LD

MAJESTIC PT

MAJESTIC
VW

REFLECTION
CV

8

DR

CLEARWATER
DR

LOTT CREEK
BLVD

CLEARWATER
DR

TV

8

SNOWBERRY
PL

SNOW
BERRY
PT

VW

CIR

BERRY

DIAMOND

WILLOW
PT

LOTT CREEK

DR

FISHERMAN'S
BEND

FISHERMAN'S
PT

FISHERMAN'S
Lake

FISHERMAN'S
DR

FISHERMAN'S
LD

DR

CROOKED
POND GN

OWL'S
HAVEN

CROOKED
POND WY

9

BRAEMAR
ST

ST

BRAEMAR
ST

Bishop Gray
Interpretive
Site

WOLFWILLOW
RDG

WOLFWILLOW

WOLFWILLOW

WOLFWILLOW
PT

WOLFWILLOW

LOTT CREEK
HOLLOW

LN

COULEE
RDG

WOLFWILLOW
WY

MD of Rocky View
Tsuu T'ina Nation

MD of Rocky View
Tsuu T'ina Nation

© 2004 Sherlock
Publishing Ltd.

HERITAGE POINTE

ST W

PINE CREEK

CL

DR

PINEHURST

Heritage Pointe
Golf & CC

1

HERITAGE
LAKE
DR

HERITAGE
LAKE
DR

SUMMIT
POINTE
DR

RIDGE
POINTE

DR

DEERFOOT TRAIL

2A

BLVD

CL

CV

BY

CT

HARBOUR

BLVD

LD

HERITAGE
LAKE
DR

HERITAGE
QUAY

RAVINE
DR

HERITAGE
POINTE

DR

MEADOW POINTE DR

2

2

RD

DR

16

242

AV W

242 AV E

3

ST W

12 ST W

12 ST W

DUNBOW

OLD QUARRY

2 ST E

2 ST E

8 ST E

8 ST E

RD

N

4

16 ST W

QUARRY
SPRINGS

LN

RD

DEERFOOT TRAIL

16

258

AV W

B   C   D   E   F

CALGARY *Sports & Schools*

Arenas

ACADIA RECREATION COMPLEX
240 90 Av SE **75 AF52**
AIRDRIE RECREATIONAL COMPLEX
200 East Lake Cr *(AIR)* **113 G5**
BANFF RECREATION CENTRE
Mt Norquay Rd *(BNF)* **21 B3**
BEISEKER ARENA
410 5 St *(BSKR)* **111 F8**
BOB SNODGRASS RECREATION COMPLEX
228 12 Av SE *(H RV)* **109 E5**
BOWNESS SPORTSPLEX
7904 43 Av NW **35 L23**
BRENTWOOD SPORTSPLEX
5107 33 St NW **38 U22**
BURNS STADIUM
2431 Crowchild Tr NW **38 X27**
CALGARY CENTENNIAL ARENAS
2390 47 Av SW **58 X42**
CALGARY RUGBY UNION
9025 Shepard Rd SE **77 AQ52**
CALGARY SOCCER CENTRE
7000 48 St SE **70 AV47**
CALGARY WINTER CLUB
4611 14 St NW **39 AB23**
CANADIAN HOCKEY CENTRE
2424 University Dr NW **38 W27**
CANMORE RECREATION CENTRE
1900 8 Av *(CAN)* **101 C3**
CROWCHILD TWIN ARENAS
185 Scenic Acres Dr NW **23 J18**
CROWFOOT ARENA
8080 John Laurie Blvd NW **12 M14**
DON HARTMAN SPORTSPLEX
5206 68 St NE **32 AZ20**
EAST CALGARY TWIN ARENAS
299 Erin Woods Dr SE. **62 AV39**
ED WHALEN ARENA
2000 Southland Dr SW **74 Z54**
ERNIE STARR ARENA
4808 14 Av SE **62 AV35**
FAIRVIEW ARENA
8038 Fairmount Dr SE. **67 AG49**
FAMILY LEISURE CENTRE
11150 Bonaventure Dr SE **75 AG57**
FATHER DAVID BAUER ARENA
2424 University Dr NW **38 W27**
FORBES INNIS ARENA
5600 Centre St N **28 AG21**
FRANK McCOOL ARENA
1900 Lake Bonavista Dr SE **83 AH60**
GEORGE BLUNDUN ARENA
5020 26 Av SW **57 R37**
GLENMORE VELODROME
5300 19 St SW **58 Z43**
HENRY VINEY ARENA
814 13 Av NE **51 AI29**
HUNTINGTON HILLS COMMUNITY ASSOCIATION
520 78 Av NW **15 AE15**
JACK SETTERS ARENA
2020 69 Av SE **69 AO47**
JIMMIE CONDON ARENA
502 Heritage Dr SW. **67 AE50**
JOE KRYCZKA ARENA
2000 Southland Dr SW **74 Z54**
LAKE BONAVISTA COMMUNITY ASSOCIATION
1401 Acadia Dr SE. **83 AI61**
MAX BELL ARENA
1001 Barlow Tr SE **52 AP35**
McMAHON STADIUM
1817 Crowchild Tr NW **38 X28**
MOUNT PLEASANT SPORTSPLEX
610 23 Av NW **40 AE27**
MURRAY COPOT ARENA
6715 Centre St N **28 AF18**
NICKEL ARENA
9504 Oakfield Dr SW **73 V53**
NORMA BUSH ARENA
2424 University Dr NW **38 W27**
NORTH EAST SPORTSPLEX
5206 68 St NE **32 AZ20**
OAKRIDGE COMMUNITY ASSOCIATION
9504 Oakfield Dr SW **73 V53**
OILFIELDS REGIONAL ARENA
611 3 St SW *(B DMD)* **106 G3**
OKOTOKS RECREATION CENTRE
99 Okotoks St *(OKS)* **107 E2**
OPTIMIST ARENA
5020 26 Av SW **57 R37**
PETE KNIGHT MEMORIAL CENTRE
920 Mountain Av *(CRS)* **8 G2**

PLAINSMEN ARENA
320 Centre Av *(AIR)* **113 F3**
RENFREW ARENAS
814 13 Av NE **51 AI29**
ROSE KOHN ARENA
502 Heritage Dr SW **67 AE50**
SHOULDICE ARENA
1515 Home Rd NW **37 Q28**
SOUTH FISH CREEK ARENAS
333 Shawville Blvd SE **91 AG70**
SOUTHLAND LEISURE CENTRE
2000 Southland Dr SW **74 Z54**
SPRING LAKES SAWMILLS FAMILY SPORTS CENTRE
Griffin Rd *(COCR)* **103 G7**
SPRINGBANK PARK FOR ALL SEASONS
32224a Springbank Rd *(SPNG)* **99 C2**
STEW HENDRY ARENA
814 13 Av NE **51 AI29**
STRATHMORE FAMILY CENTRE
160 Brent Blvd *(STMR)* **112 E2**
STU PEPPARD ARENA
5300 19 St SW **58 Z43**
THORNCLIFFE GREENVIEW
5600 Centre St N **28 AG21**
TRIWOOD COMMUNITY ASSOCIATION
2244 Chicoutimi Dr NW. **39 Y25**
VILLAGE SQUARE ARENAS
2623 56 St NE **43 AW27**
VOLLEYDOME
2825 24 Av NW **38 W27**
WEST HILLHURST COMMUNITY ASSOCIATION
1940 6 Av NW **48 Z31**
WESTSIDE ARENA
2000 69 St SW **46 N36**

Athletic Parks & Leisure Centres

ACADIA PARK ATHLETIC FIELD
315 90 Av SE **75 AG52**
CARDEL PLACE
250 Country Village Wy NE **5 AF7**
CHESTERMERE RECREATION CENTRE
201 West Chestermere Dr *(CHST)* **80 C4**
DON HARTMAN SPORTSPLEX
5206 68 St NE **32 AZ20**
FAMILY LEISURE CENTRE
11150 Bonaventure Dr SE **75 AG57**
FOOTHILLS ATHLETIC PARK
2431 Crowchild Tr NW **38 W27**
FOREST LAWN ATHLETIC PARK
1425 52 St NE **62 AV35**
FRANK McCOOL ATHLETIC PARK
1900 Lake Bonavista Dr SE **83 AH60**
GLENMORE ATHLETIC PARK
5300 19 St SW **58 Z43**
JAYCEE SLOWPITCH PARK
1899 39 Av NE **41 AN24**
NORTH MOUNT PLEASANT ARTS CENTRE
523 27 Av NW **40 AE27**
OPTIMIST ATHLETIC PARK
5020 26 Av SW **57 R37**
POP DAVIES ATHLETIC PARK
6415 Ogden Rd SE **69 AO46**
RENFREW ATHLETIC PARK
814 13 Av NE **51 AI29**
ROTARY CHALLENGER PARK
8925 Barlow Tr NE **31 AS21**
ROTARY PARK RECREATION CENTRE
617 1 St NE **50 AG31**
SHOULDICE ATHLETIC PARK
1515 Home Rd NW **37 Q28**
SOUTH FISH CREEK RECREATION CENTRE
333 Shawville Blvd SE **91 AG70**
SOUTHLAND LEISURE CENTRE
2000 Southland Dr SW **74 Z54**
TOM BROOK ATHLETIC PARK
2000 Southland Dr SW **74 Z54**
UPLANDS RECREATION CENTRE
20 Hawkside Rd NW **12 N14**
VILLAGE SQUARE LEISURE CENTRE
2623 56 St NE **43 AW27**
WESTSIDE RECREATION CENTRE
2000 69 St SW **46 N36**
WILDFLOWER ARTS CENTRE
3363 Spruce Dr SW. **47 V34**
WOODBINE ATHLETIC PARK
24 St SW **81 X60**

Golf

ALLSHOTS DRIVING RANGE
Old Banff Coach Rd *(SPNG)* **99 J3**
BANFF SPRINGS GOLF COURSE
Bow Falls Dr *(BNF)* **21 F8**
BEDDINGTON GOLF PARK
9284 Harvest Hills Blvd NE **16 AF12**
CALGARY ELKS GOLF & COUNTRY CLUB
2502 6 St NE. **40 AI27**
CANMORE GOLF & COUNTRY CLUB
2000 8 Av *(CAN)* **101 B2**
CANYON MEADOWS GOLF AND COUNTRY CLUB
12501 14 St SW **82 AB59**
COCHRANE GOLF CLUB
240 Riverview Dr *(COCR)* **103 E6**
COLLICUT SIDING GOLF COURSE
Western Dr *(CRS)* **8 E5**
CONFEDERATION PARK GOLF COURSE
3204 Collingwood Dr NW **39 Z26**
COUNTRY CLUB OF THE HAMPTONS
69 Hamptons Dr NW **13 S9**
COUNTRY HILLS GOLF CLUB
1334 Country Hills Blvd NW. **15 AC10**
D'ARCY RANCH GOLF CLUB
Milligan Dr *(OKS)* **107 B2**
EAGLE QUEST GOLF CENTER
Douglas Range Rd SE **76 AN57**
EAGLE QUEST GOLF COURSE
7 Douglas Woods Dr SE **85 AP59**
EAGLE QUEST GOLF DOME
999 32 Av NE **41 AK27**
EARL GREY GOLF CLUB
6540 20 St SW **66 Z46**
ELBOW SPRINGS GOLF CLUB
Hwy 8 West *(SPNG)* **99 H7**
FAMILY GOLF CENTRE
9550 Bearspaw Dam Rd NW **23 H20**
FOX HOLLOW GOLF CLUB
999 32 Av NE **41 AK27**
GLENCOE GOLF & COUNTRY CLUB
Elbow Dr SW **67 AB44**
GLENCOE GOLF & COUNTRY CLUB
Hwy 8 West *(SPNG)* **99 E6**
GLENEAGLES GOLF COURSE
100 Gleneagles Dr *(COCR)* **103 A5**
GOLF CENTRE HARVEST HILLS
Country Hills Blvd NW **6 AJ8**
HARVEST HILLS GOLF COURSE
1450 Harvest Hills Dr NE **16 AJ9**
HERITAGE POINTE GOLF & COUNTRY CLUB
1 Heritage Pointe Dr *(H PT)* **115 D6**
HIGHLAND GOLF AND COUNTRY CLUB
4304 3 St NW **40 AF23**
HIGHWOOD GOLF & COUNTRY CLUB
Golf Course Rd *(H RV)* **109 B3**
INGLEWOOD GOLF & CURLING CLUB
19 Gosling Wy SE **61 AP38**
LAKESIDE GREENS GOLF & COUNTRY CLUB
555 Lakeside Greens Dr *(CHST)* **80 C5**
LAKEVIEW GOLF CLUB
5840 19 St SW **66 Z45**
LYNX RIDGE GOLF CLUB
Twelve Mile Coulee Rd NW. **22 B18**
MAPLE RIDGE GOLF CLUB
1240 Mapleglade Dr SE **75 AK57**
McCALL LAKE GOLF CLUB
1600 32 Av NE **41 AM25**
McCOWANS GOLF DOME
50 50 Av SW **59 AF43**
McKENZIE MEADOWS GOLF CLUB
17215 McKenzie Meadows Dr SE **95 AP70**
PINEBROOK GOLF & COUNTRY CLUB
Pinebrook Wy *(SPNG)* **99 H5**
RCGA GOLF LEARNING CENTRE
7100 15 St SE **68 AL47**
REDWOOD MEADOWS GOLF & COUNTRY CLUB
Redwood Meadows Dr *(RED)* **33 B4**
RICHMOND GREEN GOLF CLUB
2539 33 Av SW **58 W39**
RIO VISTA GOLF COURSE
2 St SE *(H RV)* **109 E3**
RIVERSIDE GOLF PARK
Deerfoot Tr SE **76 AL55**
SHAGANAPPI POINT GOLF CLUB
1200 26 St SW **48 W34**
SHAW-NEE SLOPES GOLF CLUB
820 James McKevitt Rd SW **82 AD64**
SILVER SPRINGS GOLF AND COUNTRY CLUB
1600 Varsity Estates Dr NW **25 P21**
SILVERTIP GOLF & COUNTRY CLUB
Silvertip Tr *(CAN)* **101 E3**

STEWART CREEK GOLF COURSE
Three Sisters Parkway *(CAN)* **101 G9**
STRATHMORE GOLF CLUB
80 Wheatland Tr *(STMR)* **112 D2**
SWINGSHOTS
1755 18 Av NE **51 AM29**
TARGET GREENS GOLF CENTRE
1851 84 St NE. **44 BD28**
TEE IT UP GOLF CENTRE
8220 McKnight Blvd NE. **44 BC22**
TRAIL WEST PARKS
34 Commercial Ct *(SPNG)* **99 D1**
TURNER VALLEY GOLF COURSE
Imperial Dr *(T VAL)* **105 E4**
VALLEY RIDGE GOLF & COUNTRY CLUB
11618 Valley Ridge Pk NW **34 C21**
WILLOW PARK GOLF AND COUNTRY CLUB
639 Willow Park Dr SE. **75 AI55**
WOODSIDE GOLF COURSE
525 Woodside Dr *(AIR)*. **113 A3**

Points of Interest

BOW VALLEY RANCH
Bow Bottom Tr SE **92 AN67**
BUTTERFIELD ACRES
11829 Rocky Ridge Blvd NW **1 F7**
CALAWAY PARK
Trans Canada Hwy *(SPNG)*. **99 B1**
CALGARY ZOO BOTANICAL GARDENS &
PREHISTORIC PARK
1300 Zoo Rd NE **51 AK34**
CANADA OLYMPIC PARK
Canada Olympic Dr SW **35 I26**
HERITAGE PARK HISTORICAL VILLAGE
1900 Heritage Dr SW **66 Z49**
INGLEWOOD BIRD SANCTUARY
2425 9 Av SE **61 AO39**
MOUNT ROYAL COLLEGE
4825 Richard Rd SW **57 V42**
NAVAL MUSEUM OF ALBERTA
1820 24 St SW **48 X36**
OLYMPIC HALL OF FAME
88 Canada Olympic Rd SW **35 I25**
PUMPHOUSE THEATRES
2140 Pumphouse Av SW **48 Y34**
RACE CITY SPEEDWAY
68 St SE **79 BA57**
SAM LIVINGSTON FISH HATCHERY
1440 17a St SE **52 AN35**
TOURIST INFORMATION CENTRE
8925 Barlow Tr NE **17 AO14**

Schools

Colleges & Universities

ALBERTA BIBLE COLLEGE
635 Northmount Dr NW. **39 AC24**
HEALTH SCIENCES CENTRE
3350 Hospital Dr NW **38 V29**
MOUNT ROYAL COLLEGE
4825 Richard Rd SW **57 V42**
KELLAR HALL
2550 Dieppe Av SW **58 X41**
ROCKY MOUNTAIN COLLEGE
4039 Brentwood Rd NW **38 V24**
ST MARY'S COLLEGE
14500 Bannister Rd SE **91 AF64**
SOUTHERN ALBERTA INSTITUTE OF TECHNOLOGY
1301 16 Av NW. **49 AC29**
FOOTHILLS REGIONAL CAMPUS
145 Fisher St *(OKS)* **107 F4**
MAYLAND HEIGHTS CAMPUS
2015 Centre Av E. **52 AO33**
THE BANFF CENTRE
100 St Julien Rd *(BNF)*. **21 D5**
UNIVERSITY OF CALGARY
2500 University Dr NW **38 W26**
VICTORY BIBLE COLLEGE
101 St NW **34 F24**

Public, Private & Catholic

ABBEYDALE ELEMENTARY
320 Abergale Dr NE **54 BA31**
ABC CHARTER SCHOOL
2519 Richmond Rd SW **58 X38**
ACADIA ELEMENTARY
9603 5 St SE **75 AH53**
AE BOWERS ES
1721 Summerfield Blvd *(AIR)* **113 F6**
AE CROSS JUNIOR HIGH
3445 37 St SW **57 T40**
AKIVA ACADEMY
140 Haddon Rd SW **74 AD52**

ALBERT PARK ELEMENTARY
1317 27 St SE. **52 AQ35**
ALBERTA HIGH SCHOOL OF FINE ARTS
229 Woodhaven Dr *(OKS)* **107 D5**
ALEX FERGUSON ELEMENTARY
1704 26 St SW **48 W36**
ALEX MUNRO ELEMENTARY
427 78 Av NE **28 AG16**
ALICE JAMIESON GIRLS' ACADEMY
950 6 St NE **51 AI31**
ALTADORE ELEMENTARY
4506 16 St SW **58 AA42**
ALTERNATIVE HIGH SCHOOL
5003 20 St SW **58 Y43**
ANDREW SIBBALD ELEMENTARY
1711 Lake Bonavista Dr SE **83 AJ61**
ANNIE FOOTE ELEMENTARY
6320 Temple Dr NE **44 AY24**
ANNIE GALE JUNIOR HIGH
577 Whiteridge Wy NE **43 AU24**
ASCENSION OF OUR LORD ES & JHS
509 Harvest Hills Dr NE **16 AG10**
BALMORAL JUNIOR HIGH
220 16 Av NW **40 AF29**
BANFF COMMUNITY HIGH SCHOOL
330 Banff Av *(BNF)* **21 C4**
BANFF ELEMENTARY SCHOOL
325 Squirrel St *(BNF)*. **21 C3**
BANFF TRAIL ELEMENTARY
3232 Cochrane Rd NW **38 X26**
BANTING & BEST ELEMENTARY
1819 66 Av SE **69 AN47**
BATTALION PARK SCHOOL
369 Sienna Park Dr SW. **56 N39**
BEDDINGTON HEIGHTS ELEMENTARY
95 Bermuda Rd NW. **15 AD13**
BEISEKER COMMUNITY SCHOOL
415 2 Av *(BSKR)* **111 F8**
BELFAST ELEMENTARY
1229 17a St NE **52 AN30**
BELVEDERE-PARKWAY ELEMENTARY
4631 85 St NW **35 J23**
BERT CHURCH HIGH SCHOOL
1010 East Lake Blvd *(AIR)* **113 G5**
BIG ROCK SCHOOL
33 Hunters Gt *(OKS)* **107 C5**
BISHOP CARROLL SENIOR HIGH SCHOOL
4624 Richard Rd SW **58 X42**
BISHOP GRANDIN SENIOR HIGH SCHOOL
111 Haddon Rd SW **74 AD51**
BISHOP KIDD JUNIOR HIGH SCHOOL
1420 28 St SE. **52 AQ36**
BISHOP McNALLY HS
5700 Falconridge Blvd NE. **31 AX20**
BISHOP PAUL O'BYRNE HIGH SCHOOL
333 Shawville Blvd SE. **90 AF70**
BISHOP PINKHAM JUNIOR HIGH
3304 63 Av SW **65 V46**
BLESSED DAMIEN ELEMENTARY SCHOOL
3619 28 St SE. **61 AQ40**
BLESSED KATERI TEKAKWITHA SCHOOL
1005 Abbotsford Dr NE **54 BA30**
BOB EDWARDS JUNIOR HIGH
4424 Marlborough Dr NE **53 AU31**
BOW VALLEY HIGH SCHOOL
2000 River Heights Dr *(COCR)* **103 G9**
BOWCROFT ELEMENTARY
3940 73 St NW **36 M24**
BOWNESS HIGH SCHOOL
4627 77 St NW **35 L23**
BRAESIDE ELEMENTARY
1747 107 Av SW **74 AA56**
BRANTON JUNIOR HIGH
2103 20 St NW **38 Z28**
BRENTWOOD ELEMENTARY
1231 Northmount Dr NW **38 W24**
BRENTWOOD ELEMENTARY SCHOOL
95 Brentwood Dr W *(STMR)* **112 E2**
BRIAR HILL ELEMENTARY
1233 21 St NW. **48 Y30**
BUCHANAN ELEMENTARY
3717 Centre St N **40 AG24**
C IAN McLAREN SCHOOL
402 3 St SW *(B DMD)* **106 G3**
CALGARY ACADEMY
9400 17 Av SW. **45 H36**
CALGARY CHRISTIAN SCHOOL
5029 26 Av SW. **57 R38**
CALGARY CHRISTIAN SCHOOL
2839 49 St SW. **57 R38**
CALGARY FRENCH SCHOOL
700 77 St SW. **35 L29**
CALGARY FRENCH SCHOOL
6304 Larkspur Wy SW **66 Y46**
CALGARY ISLAMIC SCHOOL
225 28 St SE. **52 AQ33**
CALGARY JEWISH ACADEMY
6700 Kootenay St SW. **67 AB47**
CALGARY MONTESSORI SCHOOL
2828 19 St NW **38 Z27**

CALGARY MONTESSORI SCHOOL
8710 Ancourt Rd SE. . . . . **75 AH**
CALGARY PREPARATORY SCHOOL
140 Haddon Rd SW . . . . **74 AD**
CALGARY WALDORF SCHOOL
515 Cougar Ridge Dr SW . . . . **35 I**
CAMBRIAN HEIGHTS ELEMENTARY
640 Northmount Dr NW . . . . **39 AC**
CANADIAN BAPTIST SCHOOL
100 Convention Wy *(COCR)* . . . . . . **103 I**
CANMORE COLLEGIATE
1800 8 Av *(CAN)* . . . . **101 G**
CANYON MEADOWS ELEMENTARY
395 Canterbury Dr SW . . . . **82 AD**
CAPITOL HILL ELEMENTARY
2210 18 St NW. . . . . **39 AA**
CAPPY SMART ELEMENTARY
5808 Madigan Dr NE . . . . **54 AY**
CAPTAIN JOHN PALLISER ELEMENTARY
1484 Northmount Dr NW . . . . **38 U.**
CARDINAL NEWMAN ES & JHS
16201 McKenzie Lake Blvd SE . . . . . . **95 AR**
CATHERINE NICHOLS GUNN ELEMENTARY
6625 4 St NE . . . . **28 AG**
CECIL SWANSON ELEMENTARY
4820 Rundlewood Dr NE . . . . **43 AU**
CEDARBRAE ELEMENTARY
10631 Oakfield Dr SW . . . . **73 V**
CENTRAL MEMORIAL HIGH SCHOOL
5111 21 St SW . . . . **58 Y**
CHESTERMERE HIGH SCHOOL
Highway *(CHST)* **80**
CHESTERMERE LAKE MIDDLE SCHOOL
128 West Lakeview Dr *(CHST)*. **80**
CHIEF JUSTICE MILVAIN ELEMENTARY
3428 42 St NE. . . . . **43 AU**
CHINOOK COLLEGE
2519 Richmond Rd SW. . . . . **58 X**
CHINOOK PARK ELEMENTARY
1312 75 Av SW . . . . **67 AC**
CHINOOK WINDS ADVENTIST ACADEMY
10101 2 Av SW . . . . **35 G**
CHRIS AKKERMAN ELEMENTARY
5004 Marbank Dr NE . . . . **53 AV**
CHRISTINE MEIKLE SCHOOL
64 12 St NE . . . . **51 AK**
CHRISTOPHER ROBIN SCHOOL
1011 Beverley Blvd SW . . . . **67 AC**
CLARENCE SANSOM COMMUNITY SCHOOL
5840 24 Av NE . . . . **43 AX**
CLEAR WATER ACADEMY
2521 Dieppe Av SW . . . . **58 X**
COCHRANE HIGH SCHOOL
529 4 Av N *(COCR)* **103**
COLLINGWOOD ELEMENTARY
3826 Collingwood Dr NW . . . . **39 Z**
COLONEL IRVINE JUNIOR HIGH
412 Northmount Dr NW . . . . **40 AD.**
COLONEL J FRED SCOTT ELEMENTARY
171 Whitehorn Rd NE. . . . . **43 AU**
COLONEL MACLEOD ELEMENTARY & JUNIOR HIGH
1610 6 St NE. . . . . **51 AI.**
COLONEL SANDERS ELEMENTARY SCHOOL
226 Northmount Dr NW . . . . **27 AE.**
COLONEL WALKER COMMUNITY SCHOOL
1921 9 Av SE. . . . . **61 AM**
CORPUS CHRISTI ELEMENTARY SCHOOL
5607 Thornton Rd NW. . . . . **28 AF.**
COVENTRY HILLS SCHOOL
10 Covepark Dr NE . . . . **6 A**
CRESCENT HEIGHTS HIGH SCHOOL
1019 1 St NW. . . . . **50 AF**
CROSSFIELD ELEMENTARY SCHOOL
1120 Mountain Av *(CRS)* **8**
CROSSING PARK ELEMENTARY SCHOOL
500 Martindale Blvd NE . . . . **31 AV**
CROWTHER MEMORIAL JUNIOR HIGH SCHOOL
220 Brent Blvd *(STMR)* **112**
DALHOUSIE ELEMENTARY
4440 Dallyn St NW . . . . **25 S**
DAVID D OUGHTON ELEMENTARY
1511 34 St SE. . . . . **52 AS.**
DAVID THOMPSON MIDDLE SCHOOL
9320 Arbour Cr SE . . . . **75 AH**
DEER RUN ELEMENTARY
2127 146 Av SE . . . . **84 AO**
DELTA WEST ACADEMY
414 11a St NE. . . . . **51 AK**
DEVRY INSTITUTE OF TECHNOLOGY
2700 3 Av SE . . . . **52 AP**
DON BOSCO ELEMENTARY JUNIOR HIGH SCHOOL
13615 Deer Ridge Dr SE . . . . **84 AM**
DOUGLAS HARKNESS COMMUNITY SCHOOL
6203 24 Av SE . . . . **44 AY**
DOUGLASDALE ELEMENTARY
400 Douglas Park Blvd SE. . . . . . . **86 AS**
DR EP SCARLETT HIGH SCHOOL
220 Canterbury Dr SW . . . . **74 AC**
DR EW COFFIN ELEMENTARY
5615 Barrett Dr NW . . . . **26 V**

DR GLADYS McKELVIE EGBERT SCHOOL
6033 Madigan Dr NE **54** AY31
DR GORDON HIGGINS JUNIOR HIGH
155 Rundlehill Dr NE **43** AU27
DR GORDON TOWNSEND
1820 Richmond Rd SW **48** Z36
DR JK MULLOY ELEMENTARY
7440 10 St NW **27** AD16
DR OAKLEY SCHOOL
3904 20 St SW **58** Z41
DR. MORRIS GIBSON SCHOOL
147 Crystalridge Dr (OKS) **107** F3
ECOLE AIRDRIE MIDDLE SCHOOL
332 1 Av NW (AIR) **113** F3
ECOLE DE LA SOURCE
360 94 Av SE **75** AG53
ECOLE EDWARDS ELEMENTARY SCHOOL
324 3 Av NE (AIR) **113** F3
ECOLE ELEMENTAIRE PERCY PEGLER
69 Okotoks Dr (OKS) **107** E3
ECOLE ELIZABETH BARRETT SCHOOL
605 4 Av N (COCR) **103** E3
ECOLE JOE CLARK SCHOOL
1208 9 Av SE (H RV) **109** F5
ECOLE NOTRE-DAME DES VALLEES
Hwy 1A (COCR) **103** D3
EDGEMONT SCHOOL
55 Edgevalley Cir NW **13** T14
ELBOW PARK ELEMENTARY
721 38 Av SW **59** AD40
ELBOW VALLEY ELEMENTARY SCHOOL
244209 Rge Rd 33 (SPNG) **99** C1
ELBOYA ELEMENTARY & JUNIOR HIGH
4804 6 St SW **59** AD43
ELIZABETH RUMMEL SCHOOL
1033 Cougar Creek Dr (CAN) **101** F5
EMILY FOLLENSBEE CENTRE
5139 14 St SW **59** AB43
ERIN WOODS ELEMENTARY
25 Erin Park Dr SE **62** AV40
ERNEST MANNING HIGH SCHOOL
3600 16 Av SW **47** U36
ERNEST MORROW JUNIOR HIGH
1212 47 St SE **62** AV35
ETHEL M JOHNSON ELEMENTARY
255 Sackville Dr SW **74** AC56
EUGENE COSTE ELEMENTARY
10 Hillgrove Cr SW **74** AC53
FAIRVIEW JUNIOR HIGH
7840 Fairmount Dr SE **67** AG49
FALCONRIDGE ELEMENTARY
1331 Falconridge Dr NE **32** AY21
FATHER DOUCET ELEMENTARY SCHOOL
65 Shannon Dr SW **90** AC67
FATHER JAMES WHELIHAN SCHOOL
70 Sunmills Dr SE **91** AI68
FATHER LACOMBE SENIOR HIGH SCHOOL
3615 Radcliffe Dr SE **52** AS34
FATHER SCOLLEN SCHOOL
6839 Temple Dr NE **44** AY23
FE OSBORNE JUNIOR HIGH
5315 Varsity Dr NW **37** Q23
FISH CREEK ELEMENTARY SCHOOL
1039 Suncastle Dr SE **91** AK69
FOOTHILLS ACADEMY
745 37 St NW **47** U30
FOOTHILLS COMPOSITE HIGH SCHOOL
229 Woodhaven Dr (OKS) **107** D5
FOREST LAWN HIGH SCHOOL
1304 44 St SE **62** AU35
FOUNDATIONS FOR THE FUTURE
ALICE M CURTIS
9711 Academy Dr SE **75** AI53
NORMAN BETHUNE
315 86 Av SE **75** AF51
NORTH CALGARY
719 44 Av NW **40** AD23
RENFREW
1210 Russet Rd NE **51** AJ30
FRED SEYMOUR ELEMENTARY
809 Willingdon Blvd SE **75** AJ57
FROEBEL GARDEN OF CHILDREN
119 Pinetown Pl NE **43** AW27
GEORGE McDOUGALL HIGH SCHOOL
412 3 Av NE (AIR) **113** F3
GEORGES P VANIER JUNIOR HIGH
509 32 Av NE **40** AH26
GLAMORGAN ELEMENTARY
50 Grafton Dr SW **57** T41
GLENBOW ELEMENTARY SCHOOL
55 Glenpatrick Rd (COCR) **103** D4
GLENBROOK ELEMENTARY
4725 33 Av SW **57** S40
GLENDALE ELEMENTARY
2415 Kelwood Dr SW **57** T37
GLENMORE CHRISTIAN ACADEMY
16520 24 St SW **89** Y68
GOOD SHEPHERD SCHOOL
52 Robinson Dr (OKS) **107** E2
GRANT MacEWAN ELEMENTARY
180 Falshire Dr NE **32** AY19

GREENVIEW ELEMENTARY
211 McKnight Blvd NE **28** AG22
GUY WEADICK ELEMENTARY
5612 Templehill Rd NE **43** AX24
GW SKENE ELEMENTARY SCHOOL
6226 Penbrooke Dr SE **54** AY34
HAROLD PANABAKER JUNIOR HIGH
23 Sackville Dr SW **74** AC55
HAROLD W RILEY ELEMENTARY
3743 Dover Ridge Dr SE **62** AS40
HAULTAIN MEMORIAL ELEMENTARY
605 Queensland Dr SE **84** AM60
HAWKWOOD SCHOOL
650 Hawkwood Blvd NW **12** O13
HAYSBORO ELEMENTARY
1123 87 Av SW **74** AC51
HD CARTWRIGHT JUNIOR HIGH
5500 Dalhart Rd NW **25** R18
HENRY WISE WOOD SENIOR HIGH SCHOOL
910 75 Av SW **67** AC48
HERITAGE CHRISTIAN ACADEMY
2003 McKnight Blvd NE **42** AO23
HIDDEN VALLEY ELEMENTARY SCHOOL
10951 Hidden Valley Dr NW **14** X9
HIGHWOOD ELEMENTARY SCHOOL
11 Holmwood Av NW **40** AD23
HIGHWOOD HIGH SCHOOL
12 Av SE (H RV) **109** F6
HILLHURST COMMUNITY SCHOOL
1418 7 Av NW **49** AB31
HOLY ANGELS ELEMENTARY SCHOOL
275 Riverglen Dr SE **76** AO51
HOLY CROSS ELEMENTARY JUNIOR HIGH SCHOOL
3719 26 Av SE **62** AS38
HOLY FAMILY ELEMENTARY SCHOOL
904 32 St SE **52** AR34
HOLY NAME FRENCH IMMERSION SCHOOL
3011 35 St SW **57** U39
HOLY REDEEMER FRENCH IMMERSION SCHOOL
708 47 St SE **53** AV34
HOLY SPIRIT ACADEMY
708 21 St SE (H RV) **109** H4
HOLY SPIRIT ELEMENTARY JUNIOR HIGH
129 Powell St (COCR) **103** F4
HOLY TRINITY ACADEMY
53 Cimarron Dr (OKS) **107** E6
HOLY TRINITY ELEMENTARY SCHOOL
1717 41 St SE **62** AT36
HUNTINGTON HILLS ELEMENTARY
820 64 Av NW **27** AD18
IAN BAZALGETTE JUNIOR HIGH
3909 26 Av SE **62** AT38
INSTITUTE OF RELIGION
3120 32 Av NW **38** W25
INTERNATIONAL SCHOOL OF EXCELLENCE
3915 34 St NE **42** AR24
ISLAMIC CENTRE OF CALGARY
5615 14 Av SW **46** Q36
JACK JAMES HIGH SCHOOL
5105 8 Av SE **53** AV34
JAMES FOWLER HIGH SCHOOL
4004 4 St NW **40** AF24
JAMES SHORT MEMORIAL ES
6333 5 Av SE **54** AY34
JANET JOHNSTONE ELEMENTARY
224 Shawnessy Dr SW **90** AD67
JENNIE ELLIOTT ELEMENTARY
3031 Lindsay Dr SW **66** W46
JERRY POTTS ELEMENTARY
3720 42 St NW **37** S25
JOHN G DIEFENBAKER HIGH SCHOOL
6620 4 St NW **28** AF18
JOHN PAUL II ELEMENTARY SCHOOL
119 Castleridge Dr NE **31** AW19
JOHN W COSTELLO ES
300 Strathcona Dr SW **46** O33
JOHN WARE JUNIOR HIGH
10020 19 St SW **74** Z54
JOHN XXIII ELEMENTARY JUNIOR HIGH SCHOOL
1420 Falconridge Dr NE **32** AZ20
JUNO BEACH ACADEMY OF CANADIAN STUDIES
2215 Uxbridge Dr NW **38** V28
KEELER ELEMENTARY
4807 Forego Av SE **53** AV33
KILLARNEY ELEMENTARY
3008 33 St SW **57** V38
KING GEORGE ELEMENTARY
2108 10 St SW **39** AC28
KINGSLAND ELEMENTARY
7430 5 St SW **67** AE48
LAKE BONAVISTA ELEMENTARY
1015 120 Av SE **83** AJ59
LAWRENCE GRASSI MIDDLE SCHOOL
730 4 St (CAN) **101** C5
LEROI DANIELS
47 Fyffe Rd SE **68** AH49
LESTER B PEARSON HIGH SCHOOL
3020 52 St NE **43** AW27
LORD BEAVERBROOK HIGH SCHOOL
9019 Fairmount Dr SE **75** AG52

LORD SHAUGHNESSY HIGH SCHOOL
2336 53 Av SW **66** Y44
LOUIS RIEL ELEMENTARY & JUNIOR HIGH
9632 Oakfield Dr SW **73** V53
LOUISE DEAN CENTRE
120 23 St NW **48** Y32
LYCEE LOUIS PASTEUR
4099 Garrison Blvd SW **58** Y41
MADELEINE D'HOUET FRENCH IMMERSION SCHOOL
108 22 St NW **48** Y32
MANACHABAN MIDDLE SCHOOL
724 Chiniki Dr (COCR) **103** E3
MAPLE RIDGE ELEMENTARY
10203 Maplemont Rd SE **75** AJ54
MARION CARSON ELEMENTARY
5225 Varsity Dr NW **37** R23
MARLBOROUGH ELEMENTARY
4711 Maryvale Dr NE **53** AV32
MASTERS ACADEMY
4414 Crowchild Tr SW **58** X42
MAYLAND HEIGHTS ELEMENTARY
2324 Maunsell Dr NE **52** AO31
McKENZIE LAKE ES
16210 McKenzie Lake Wy SE **95** AS68
MEADOWBROOK MIDDLE SCHOOL
1796 Meadow Brook Dr (AIR) **113** H6
MENNO SIMONS CHRISTIAN SCHOOL
7000 Menno Simons Gt SW **56** N39
MIDNAPORE ELEMENTARY
55 Midpark Rs SE **91** AH66
MIDSUN SCHOOL
660 Sunmills Dr SE **92** AL69
MILTON WILLIAMS JUNIOR HIGH SCHOOL
92 Malibou Rd SW **67** AD46
MITFORD MIDDLE SCHOOL
110 Quigley Dr (COCR) **103** B3
MONSIGNOR AJ HETHERINGTON ES
4 Coral Springs Blvd NE **32** AZ21
MONSIGNOR EL DOYLE ELEMENTARY SCHOOL
8887 Scurfield Dr NW **23** I16
MONSIGNOR JJ O'BRIEN SCHOOL
99 Bridlewood Rd SW **90** AA69
MONSIGNOR JS SMITH ES & JHS
2919 Douglasdale Blvd SE **85** AR59
MONSIGNOR NEVILLE ANDERSON ELEMENTARY
327 Sandarac Dr NW **15** Z12
MONTEREY PARK ELEMENTARY
2823 Catalina Blvd NE **44** BA26
MONTESSORI SCHOOL OF CALGARY
5915 Lewis Dr SW **65** V45
MONTGOMERY JUNIOR HIGH
2116 MacKay Rd NW **37** S28
MOTHER MARY GREENE ELEMENTARY SCHOOL
115 Edenwold Dr NW **26** U15
MOTHER TERESA ELEMENTARY SCHOOL
121 Midlake Blvd SE **91** AH66
MOUNT VIEW ELEMENTARY
2004 4 St NE **40** AH28
MOUNTAIN VIEW ACADEMY
7659 26 Av SW **55** L38
MOUNTAIN VIEW ELEMENTARY
2031 Sable Dr SE **62** AR37
MURIEL CLAYTON MIDDLE SCHOOL
305 Acacia Dr (AIR) **113** F5
NATIONAL SPORT SCHOOL
3009 Morley Tr NW **38** Y26
NATIONAL SPORTS SCHOOL
3600 16 Av SW **47** U36
NELLIE McCLUNG ELEMENTARY
2315 Palliser Dr SW **73** Y53
NICKLE JUNIOR HIGH
2500 Lake Bonavista Dr SE **83** AG60
NORTH HAVEN ELEMENTARY
4922 North Haven Dr NW **39** AC22
NOTRE DAME COLLEGIATE
1500 High Country Dr (H RV) **109** B3
OGDEN ELEMENTARY
1919 76 Av SE **69** AO49
OILFIELDS HIGH SCHOOL
511 3 St SW (B DMD) **106** G3
OKOTOKS JUNIOR HIGH SCHOOL
1 Pacific Av (OKS) **107** E3
OLYMPIC HEIGHTS SCHOOL
875 Strathcona Dr SW **46** O34
OS GEIGER ELEMENTARY
100 Castlebrook Dr NE **31** AV20
OUR LADY OF PEACE ES & JHS
14826 Millrise Hi SW **90** AC65
OUR LADY OF THE ASSUMPTION ES & JHS
7311 34 Av NW **36** M25
OUR LADY QUEEN OF PEACE
1820 1 Av NW (AIR) **113** B3
PARKDALE ELEMENTARY
728 32 St NW **47** V31
PATRICK AIRLIE ELEMENTARY
1520 39 St SE **62** AT36
PEARBOROUGH MEADOWS ES
5645 Pensacola Cr SE **53** AX35
PIITOAYIS FAMILY SCHOOL
4105 26 Av SE **62** AT38

PINERIDGE COMMUNITY SCHOOL
1927 61 St NE. **43 AX28**
PRAIRIE GRADUATE SCHOOL
2540 5 Av NW **48 X31**
PRAIRIE WATERS ELEMENTARY SCHOOL
201 Invermere Dr *(CHST)* **80 A4**
PRINCE OF WALES ELEMENTARY
253 Parkland Wy SE. **91 AK63**
QUEEN ELIZABETH ELEMENTARY
402 18 St NW. **49 AA32**
QUEEN ELIZABETH JUNIOR & SENIOR HIGH
512 18 St NW. **49 AA31**
QUEENSLAND DOWNS ELEMENTARY
199 Queen Charlotte Wy SE **84 AM61**
RALPH McCALL SCHOOL
1505 1 Av NW *(AIR)* **113 B3**
RAMSAY ELEMENTARY
2223 Spiller Rd SE **51 AI37**
RANCHLANDS COMMUNITY
610 Ranchlands Blvd NW. **24 O16**
RB BENNETT ELEMENTARY
6305 33 Av NW **36 O25**
RENFREW EDUCATION MAIN SCHOOL
2050 21 St NE. **42 AO28**
RENFREW EDUCATION SUNDANCE
75 Sunpark Dr SE **91 AH69**
RICHMOND ELEMENTARY
2701 22 St SW **58 Y38**
RIDEAU PARK ELEMENTARY & JUNIOR HIGH
829 Rideau Rd SW **59 AE39**
RIVERBEND SCHOOL
65 Rivervalley Dr SE **76 AM52**
RJ HAWKEY ELEMENTARY SCHOOL
233 Big Springs Dr *(AIR)* **113 G6**
ROBERT WARREN JUNIOR HIGH
12424 Elbow Dr SW. **82 AC59**
ROLAND MICHENER ELEMENTARY
5958 4 Av NE **53 AX31**
ROSEDALE ELEMENTARY & JUNIOR HIGH
905 13 Av NW **49 AD30**
ROSEMONT ELEMENTARY
19 Rosevale Dr NW **39 AB26**
ROSSCARROCK ELEMENTARY
1406 40 St SW **47 T35**
RT ALDERMAN JUNIOR HIGH
725 Mapleton Dr SE **75 AI55**
RUNDLE ACADEMY
4330 16 St SW **58 AA42**
RUNDLE COLLEGE ELEMENTARY SCHOOL
2634 12 Av NW **48 W30**
RUNDLE COLLEGE HS
2612 37 Av NE **42 AP24**
RUNDLE ELEMENTARY
4120 Rundlehorn Dr NE **43 AT28**
SACRED HEART ACADEMY
709 Second St *(STMR)* **112 E5**
ST ALPHONSUS ELEMENTARY SCHOOL
928 Radnor Av NE **51 AJ29**
ST AMBROSE ELEMENTARY JUNIOR HIGH
1500 Arbour Lake Rd NW. **11 K13**
ST ANDREW ELEMENTARY SCHOOL
4331 41 Av SW **57 T41**
ST ANNE SENIOR HIGH SCHOOL
1010 21 Av SE. **51 AJ37**
ST ANTHONY SCHOOL
4811 6 St SW **59 AD43**
ST AUGUSTINE ELEMENTARY JUNIOR HIGH SCHOOL
7112 7 St SW. **67 AD47**
ST BEDE ELEMENTARY SCHOOL
333 Bermuda Dr NW **15 AD13**
ST BENEDICT ELEMENTARY SCHOOL
10340 19 St SW **74 Z54**
ST BERNADETTE ELEMENTARY SCHOOL
55 Lynndale Cr SE **69 AO47**
ST BONAVENTURE JUNIOR HIGH SCHOOL
1710 Acadia Dr SE **83 AI62**
ST BONIFACE ELEMENTARY SCHOOL
927 Lake Sylvan Dr SE **83 AJ59**
ST BRIGID SCHOOL
730 Citadel Wy NW **12 N10**
ST CATHERINE ELEMENTARY SCHOOL
11 Canata Cl SW **82 AC59**
ST CECILIA FRENCH IMMERSION SCHOOL
610 Agate Cr SE **75 AI54**
ST CHARLES CONGREGATED SCHOOL
2445 23 Av SW. **58 X37**
ST CLARE ES
12455 Coventry Hills Wy NE **6 AI5**
ST CLEMENT ELEMENTARY SCHOOL
1140 Mayland Dr NE **52 AO30**
ST CYRIL ELEMENTARY JUNIOR HIGH SCHOOL
2990 Cedarbrae Dr SW **73 V56**
ST DOMINIC ELEMENTARY SCHOOL
4820 Dalhart Rd NW **25 S19**
ST ELIZABETH STETON SCHOOL
10845 Hidden Valley Dr NW **14 Y9**
ST FRANCIS SENIOR HIGH SCHOOL
877 Northmount Dr NW. **39 AA25**
ST GABRIEL THE ARCHANGEL
197 Invermere Dr *(CHST)* **80 A4**

ST GERARD FRENCH IMMERSION SCHOOL
1204 96 Av SW **74 AC53**
ST GREGORY ELEMENTARY JUNIOR HIGH SCHOOL
5340 26 Av SW **56 Q38**
ST HELENA JUNIOR HIGH SCHOOL
320 64 Av NW **28 AF18**
ST HENRY ELEMENTARY SCHOOL
7423 10 St NW **27 AD17**
ST HUBERT ELEMENTARY SCHOOL
320 72 Av NE **28 AG17**
ST JAMES ELEMENTARY & JUNIOR HIGH SCHOOL
2227 58 Av SW **66 Y45**
ST JEAN BREBEUF JUNIOR HIGH SCHOOL
5030 Northland Dr NW **26 U21**
ST JOHN BOSCO
712 Fortalice Cr SE **53 AW34**
ST JOSEPH ELEMENTARY JUNIOR HIGH SCHOOL
2512 5 St NW. **40 AE27**
ST JUDE ELEMENTARY SCHOOL
730 Woodbine Blvd SW **81 V59**
ST LEO CENTRE
6220 Lakeview Dr SW **65 V46**
ST LUKE FRENCH IMMERSION SCHOOL
1232 Northmount Dr NW **38 X23**
ST MARGARET SCHOOL
3320 Carol Dr NW **39 AB25**
ST MARIA GORETTI ELEMENTARY SCHOOL
375 Hawkstone Dr NW **12 O13**
ST MARK ELEMENTARY SCHOOL
4589 Marbank Dr NE **53 AU30**
ST MARTHA ELEMENTARY JUNIOR HIGH SCHOOL
6020 4 Av NE **54 AY31**
ST MARTIN DE PORRES SCHOOL
410 Big Springs Rd *(AIR)* **113 E7**
ST MARY'S SCHOOL
42 Cimarron Tr *(OKS)* **107 E6**
ST MATTHEW SCHOOL
416 83 Av SW **67 AG50**
ST MICHAEL ELEMENTARY JUNIOR HIGH SCHOOL
4511 8 Av SW **47 S34**
ST PATRICK ELEMENTARY SCHOOL
6006 Rundlehorn Dr NE **43 AX28**
ST PAUL CENTRE
124 24 Av NE **40 AG27**
ST PETER ELEMENTARY SCHOOL
720 58 St SE **53 AX34**
ST PHILIP ELEMENTARY SCHOOL
13825 Parkside Dr SE **91 AJ63**
ST PIUS FRENCH IMMERSION SCHOOL
2312 18 St NW **39 AA28**
ST RITA ELEMENTARY SCHOOL
7811 Ranchview Dr NW **24 O16**
ST ROSE OF LIMA SCHOOL
2419 50 St SE. **43 AV27**
ST RUPERT ELEMENTARY SCHOOL
111 Rundlehill Dr NE **43 AU27**
ST STEPHEN ELEMENTARY JUNIOR HIGH SCHOOL
10910 Elbow Dr SW. **74 AC56**
ST SYLVESTER ELEMENTARY SCHOOL
7318 Silver Springs Blvd NW **24 M19**
ST THOMAS AQUINAS ELEMENTARY SCHOOL
4540 26 Av SW. **57 S37**
ST THOMAS MORE ELEMENTARY SCHOOL
6110 Temple Dr NE **44 AY24**
ST VINCENT DE PAUL SCHOOL
4525 49 St NW **37 R23**
ST WILFRID ELEMENTARY SCHOOL
4225 44 Av NE **43 AU23**
ST WILLIAM ELEMENTARY SCHOOL
11020 Fairmount Dr SE **75 AG56**
STE MARGUERITE BOURGEOYS ES
4700 Richard Rd SW **58 X42**
SALVATION ARMY CHILDREN'S VILLAGE
1731 29 St SW **47 V36**
SAM LIVINGSTON ELEMENTARY
12011 Bonaventure Dr SE. **83 AG58**
SCENIC ACRES SCHOOL
50 Scurfield Wy NW. **23 I16**
SCIENCE ALBERTA SCHOOL
5915 Lewis Dr SW **65 V45**
SENATOR PATRICK BURNS JUNIOR HIGH
2155 Chilcotin Rd NW **39 Y24**
SENATOR RILEY SCHOOL
338 1 Av SE *(H RV)* **109 E4**
SHERWOOD COMMUNITY
2011 66 Av SE **69 AO47**
SILVER SPRINGS ELEMENTARY
7235 Silver Mead Rd NW **24 M20**
SIMON FRASER JUNIOR HIGH
5215 33 St NW. **26 U21**
SIMONS VALLEY ELEMENTARY
375 Sandarac Dr NW **15 Z11**
SIR JAMES LOUGHEED ELEMENTARY
3519 36 Av SW. **57 U40**
SIR JOHN A MACDONALD JUNIOR HIGH
6600 4 St NW **28 AF18**
SIR JOHN FRANKLIN JUNIOR HIGH SCHOOL
2215 8 Av NE **52 AO31**
SIR WILFRID LAURIER JUNIOR HIGH SCHOOL
819 32 St SE **52 AR34**

SIR WILLIAM VAN HORNE HIGH
2215 Uxbridge Dr NW . . . . **38 V**
SIR WINSTON CHURCHILL HIGH
5220 Northland Dr NW . . . . **26 U**
SOMERSET SCHOOL
150 Somerset Mr SW. . . . . **90 AC**
SOUTH CALGARY HIGH SCHOOL
55 Sun Valley Blvd SE . . . . **91 AH**
SOUTHWOOD ELEMENTARY
898 Sylvester Cr SW . . . . **74 AD**
SPITZEE ELEMENTARY SCHOOL
409 MacLeod Tr *(H RV)* **109**
SPRINGBANK COMMUNITY HIGH SCHOOL
32226 Springbank Rd *(SPNG)* **99**
SPRINGBANK MIDDLE SCHOOL
244235 Rge Rd 33 *(SPNG)* **99**
SPRUCE CLIFF ELEMENTARY
3405 Spruce Dr SW . . . . **47 U**
STANLEY JONES ELEMENTARY
950 6 St NE . . . . **51 AI**
STRATHMORE HIGH SCHOOL
100 Brent Blvd *(STMR)* **112**
SUNALTA ELEMENTARY
536 Sonora Av SW . . . . **48 Y**
SUNDANCE ELEMENTARY
200 Sunmills Dr SE. . . . . **91 AI**
SUNNYSIDE COMMUNITY SCHOOL
211 7 St NW . . . . **49 AD**
TERRACE ROAD ELEMENTARY
2103 46 St NE . . . . **37 R**
TERRY FOX JHS
139 Falshire Dr NE. . . . . **32 AY**
THE HAMPTONS SCHOOL
10330 Hamptons Blvd NW . . . . **13 S**
THOMAS B RILEY JUNIOR HIGH
3915 69 St NW . . . . **36 M**
THORNCLIFFE ELEMENTARY
5646 Thornton Rd NW. . . . . **28 AF**
TOM BAINES JHS
250 Edgepark Blvd NW . . . . **13 R**
TRADITIONAL LEARNING CENTRE
226 Northmount Dr NW . . . . **27 AE**
TURNER VALLEY SCHOOL
114 Royal Av *(T VAL)* **105**
TUXEDO PARK ELEMENTARY
202 28 Av NE . . . . **40 AG**
UNIVERSITY ELEMENTARY
3035 Utah Dr NW . . . . **38 V**
VALLEY CREEK MIDDLE SCHOOL
10959 Hidden Valley Dr NW **14**
VALLEY VIEW ELEMENTARY
4105 26 Av SE. . . . . **62 AT**
VARSITY ACRES ELEMENTARY
4255 40 St NW . . . . **37 T**
VINCENT MASSEY JUNIOR HIGH
939 45 St SW . . . . **47 S**
VISTA HEIGHTS ELEMENTARY
2411 Vermillion St NE. . . . . **41 AN**
WEBBER ACADEMY
1515 93 St SW . . . . **45 H**
WEST DALHOUSIE ELEMENTARY
6502 58 St NW . . . . **25 P**
WEST DOVER ELEMENTARY
3113 30 Av SE . . . . **62 AP**
WEST ISLAND COLLEGE
7410 Blackfoot Tr SE . . . . **68 AI**
WESTGATE ELEMENTARY
150 Westminster Dr SW . . . . **47 R**
WESTMOUNT SCHOOL
220 Wheatland Tr *(STMR)* **112**
WG MURDOCH SCHOOL
1020 Mountain Av *(CRS)* **8**
WHEATLAND ELEMENTARY SCHOOL
220 Brent Blvd *(STMR)* **112**
WILDWOOD ELEMENTARY
120 45 St SW. . . . . **47 S**
WILLIAM ABERHART HIGH SCHOOL
3009 Morley Tr NW. . . . . **38 V**
WILLIAM REID SCHOOL
1216 36 Av SW . . . . **59 AC**
WILLIAM ROPER HULL SCHOOL
2266 Woodpark Av SW . . . . **81 V**
WILLOW PARK ELEMENTARY
343 Willow Park Dr SE . . . . **75 AG**
WILMA HANSEN JUNIOR HIGH
963 Queensland Dr SE . . . . **84 AM**
WINDSOR PARK ELEMENTARY
5505 4a St SW . . . . **67 AE**
WO MITCHELL ELEMENTARY
511 Silvergrove Dr NW. . . . . **24 M**
WOODBINE ELEMENTARY
27 Woodfield Wy SW. . . . . **81 V**
WOODLANDS ELEMENTARY
88 Woodgreen Dr SW. . . . . **81 Z**
WOODMAN JUNIOR HIGH
8706 Elbow Dr SW . . . . **74 AD**
YOUTH WITH A MISSION
1205 Okalta Rd *(T VAL)* **105**

CALGARY *Street Index*

NOTES

Numbered streets within Calgary are included in the index.

Named streets outside the City of Calgary include an abbreviation (listed below) indicating the town or rural area in which they are located.

(AIR) . . . . Airdrie
(B CK) . . . . Bragg Creek
(B DMD) . . . . . . Black Diamond
(BNF) . . . . Banff
(BSKR) . . . . Beiseker
(CAN) . . . . Canmore
(CHST) . . . . Chestermere
(COCR) . . . . Cochrane
(CRS) . . . . Crossfield
(FOOT) . . . . MD Foothills
(H RV) . . . . High River
(IRR) . . . . Irricana
(LNG) . . . . Langdon
(OKS) . . . . Okotoks
(RED) . . . . . Redwood Meadows
(RCKY) . . . . . . MD Rocky View
(SHP) . . . . Shepard
(STMR) . . . . Strathmore
(T VAL) . . . . Turner Valley

1

Street	Page Grid
1 AV NE (300-700)	51 AI32
AV NW (600-1000)	47 U31
AV NW (600-1000)	49 AD32
AV NW (1700-2800)	48 W32
AV SE	53 AX32
AV SW (700-800)	49 AD33
AV SW (9800-10100)	34 E25
ST NE (300-3200)	50 AG32
ST NE (3300-3900)	40 AG26
ST NE (4800)	28 AG22
ST NW (700-3200)	50 AF31
ST NW (3300-4200)	40 AF25
ST NW (4800-5000)	28 AG22
ST SE (200-2200)	59 AG37
ST SE (4000-5000)	59 AG43
ST SE (5500-5700)	67 AG45
ST SE (14800-15300)	91 AF64
ST SW (100-1500)	50 AF36
ST SW (2200-2400)	59 AF38
ST SW (3000-3200)	59 AG37
ST SW (3600-3800)	59 AF40
ST SW (4700-5700)	67 AF45
1A ST NW (1400)	40 AF29
ST NW (4300)	40 AF23
ST SE	67 AG44
ST SW (3600-4200)	59 AF41
ST SW (5200-6400)	67 AF46
2 AV (200-1200)	50 AG32
AV NW (600-1000)	49 AC32
AV NW (1500-2600)	48 X32
AV SE (100)	50 AG33
AV SE (2000-3000)	52 AO33
AV SE (6200)	54 AY33
AV SW (100)	50 AF33
AV SW (400-800)	49 AD33
AV SW (3500-3700)	47 U33
AV SW (9700-10100)	34 E25
ST NE (200-1200)	50 AH32
ST NE (2700-4000)	40 AH27
ST NE (9600)	16 AF11
ST NW (800-3200)	50 AF30
ST NW (3300-4300)	40 AF25
ST NW (5000)	28 AF22
ST SE (5100-5700)	67 AG45
ST SE (6100-6500)	67 AG46
ST SE (9500-9800)	75 AF54
ST SE (10000-10400)	75 AG55
ST SW (100-1800)	50 AF36
ST SW (1900-2400)	59 AF38
ST SW (3000-3800)	59 AF40
ST SW (5300-5800)	67 AF45
2A AV NE	40 AF29
ST SE	59 AG38
3 AV NE (200-600)	50 AG32
AV NW (2200-3000)	52 AO32
AV NW (600-1000)	49 AC32
AV NW (1900-2700)	48 W32
AV NW (3300-3500)	47 U31
AV SE	52 AN33, 53 AX33
AV SE (100)	50 AG33

Street	Page Grid
AV SE (2500-2600)	52 AP34
AV SE (4300)	53 AU33
AV SE (6700)	54 AZ33
AV SW (100-900)	40 AD33
AV SW (3400-4000)	47 T33
ST NE (200-500)	50 AH32
ST NE (3600)	40 AH25
ST NE (4400-4800)	28 AH22
ST NE (7200)	28 AH17
ST NE (9600)	16 AG12
ST NW (1300-1800)	50 AF30
ST NW (3300-4000)	40 AF25
ST SE (300-1300)	50 AH36
ST SE (2400)	60 AH38
ST SE (5100-6400)	68 AH46
ST SE (9500-9800)	75 AG53
ST SW (200-700)	59 AF34
ST SW (3000-3200)	59 AF39
ST SW (3600)	59 AF40
ST SW (5700-6100)	67 AF46
3A AV NE	52 AP32
ST NE	40 AH24
4 AV NE	52 AP32
AV NE (200-1100)	50 AG32
AV NE (5400-6900)	53 AW32
AV NW (800-1000)	49 AC31
AV NW (2000-2900)	48 W32
AV NW	AN30
AV SE (100-500)	50 AG33
AV SE (4300-4600)	53 AU33
AV SE (6600-6800)	54 AY33
AV SW (100-1100)	49 AD33
AV SW (3800-4000)	47 T33
ST NE (1-300)	50 AH33
ST NE (700-2700)	50 AH32
ST NE (5900-6400)	28 AH19
ST NE (6500-8000)	28 AH18
ST NW (700-3200)	40 AE29
ST NW (3300-6400)	40 AE25
ST NW (6500-7200)	27 AE18
ST SE (600-700)	50 AH34
ST SE (4000)	60 AH41
ST SE (5300-6100)	68 AH46
ST SW (100-2500)	59 AE38
ST SW (3900-4000)	59 AE41
ST SW (4600-5600)	67 AE44
ST SW (30100-3600)	59 AE40
4A AV SE	53 AU33
ST NE (500-800)	51 AI31
ST NE (6400)	28 AH19
ST NE (8000)	28 AH15
ST NW (700-1600)	50 AE30
ST NW (3100-3200)	40 AE26
ST SE (3900)	59 AE41
ST SW (4200-5500)	59 AE44
ST SW (6700-7300)	67 AE48
5 AV NE (200-1000)	50 AG31
AV NE (2700-3400)	52 AQ32
AV NW (800-1300)	49 AB31
AV NW (1900-3700)	47 V31
AV SE (100-600)	50 AG34
AV SE (4300)	53 AU33
AV SE (5200-6300)	53 AW33
AV SW (100-1100)	49 AC33
AV SW (3700)	47 U34
AV SW (4000-4800)	47 R33
ST NE (500-2300)	51 AI31
ST NE (3400)	40 AI25
ST NE (4300-4600)	41 AI22
ST NW (700-3200)	50 AE30
ST NW (6900-7300)	27 AE16
ST NW (7800)	27 AE16
ST SE (600-1500)	50 AI34
ST SE (5100-6000)	68 AI45
ST SE (7000)	68 AI48
ST SE (9200-9800)	75 AH54
ST SE (99000-10200)	75 AH55
ST SW (300-2500)	59 AE38
ST SW (3000)	59 AE39
ST SW (3600-4000)	59 AE41
ST SW (4600-6500)	67 AE46
ST SW (6800-8200)	67 AD50
ST SW (10800-11000)	74 AD56
ST SW (14700-15200)	82 AE64
ST SW (16200)	90 AE68
5A AV SE	53 AU34
ST NW (700-900)	50 AE31
ST NW (3100)	40 AE26
ST NW (1700-1900)	58 AE37
ST SW (3000)	59 AE39
ST SW (4200)	59 AE41
6 AV NE	50 AG31
AV NW (100)	50 AF31
AV NW (1500-2900)	48 W31
AV SE (100-600)	50 AG34
AV SE (4300)	53 AU34
AV SW (100-1100)	49 AC34
ST NE (1-3200)	51 AI33

Street	Page Grid
ST NE (3300-3800)	40 AI25
ST NE (4000-5900)	40 AI24
ST NE (14000-14400)	6 AI2
ST NW (200-300)	49 AD31
ST NW (1300-2400)	50 AE30
ST SE (800-1300)	50 AI35
ST SE (1900-2400)	60 AI38
ST SE (4200-4400)	60 AI42
ST SE (5200-5800)	68 AI45
ST SE (6100)	68 AH46
ST SE (6700-7500)	68 AI48
ST SE (8500-9100)	75 AI52
ST SE (15800)	91 AI66
ST SW (300-1500)	50 AE33
ST SW (3000-3800)	59 AD40
ST SW (4700-5500)	67 AD44
ST SW (6800-6900)	67 AD47
ST SW (11200)	74 AD57
ST SW (13000-13100)	82 AE61
ST SW (14300-14600)	82 AD64
ST SW (16200)	90 AE68
ST SW (17000-17800)	90 AE69
6A AV SE	53 AU34
ST NE (1-500)	51 AI33
ST NE (4500-4800)	41 AI23
ST NW	49 AD30
ST SE (6200-6400)	68 AI46
ST SW	59 AD41
7 AV NW (100-1500)	50 AG31
AV NE (2500-2800)	52 AP31
AV NW (100)	50 AF31
AV NW (400-500)	50 AE31
AV NW (1700)	49 AA31
AV NW (2000-3700)	47 U30
AV SE (100-600)	50 AG34
AV SE (1900-2000)	52 AM36
AV SE (4300-4500)	53 AU34
AV SE (100-1100)	49 AC34
ST NE (1-500)	51 AI33
ST NE (2100-2400)	41 AI28
ST NE (5700)	29 AJ20
ST NW (100-400)	49 AD31
ST NW (1300-2700)	49 AD30
ST NW (3100-3200)	40 AD26
ST NW (7300-7800)	27 AD16
ST SE	68 AI43
ST SE (2000)	51 AJ37
ST SE (3400-4200)	60 AI41
ST SE (9800)	75 AI53
ST SW (100-2300)	59 AD37
ST SW (3000-3800)	59 AD40
ST SW (4100)	59 AD41
ST SW (6800-8600)	67 AD50
ST SW (10100-10300)	74 AD54
ST SW (10800-11000)	74 AD56
7A AV SE	53 AU34
ST NE	51 AJ33
ST NW	49 AD30
ST SW	59 AD40
8 AV NE (100-1200)	50 AG31
AV NE (1700-3500)	51 AM31
AV NE (6700-6800)	54 AZ31
AV NW (100-200)	50 AF31
AV NW (1300-2000)	48 Z31
AV NW (2900-3700)	38 U29
AV SE (100-200)	50 AG34
AV SE (400-600)	50 AH34
AV SW (900-1500)	51 AJ35
AV SE (1900-2200)	52 AN36
AV SE (4100-6000)	52 AS34
AV SW (100-1100)	49 AC34
AV SW (3300)	47 V34
AV SW (3500-5200)	47 R34
ST NE	41 AJ28, 51 AJ33
ST NE (100-500)	51 AJ32
ST NE (2100-2200)	41 AJ28
ST NE (5200-5700)	28 AJ21
ST NE (6600-7800)	29 AJ18
ST NW (100)	49 AD31
ST NW (1400-2400)	40 AD29
ST NW (6900-7200)	27 AE17
ST SE (600-1800)	51 AJ35
ST SE (2100-2400)	51 AJ37
ST SE (3400-4100)	60 AJ41
ST SE (3500-3800)	59 AC40
ST SW (3600-3800)	59 AC40
ST SW (4100)	59 AD43
ST SW (10200-10400)	74 AC54
ST SW (11400)	74 AC57
8A AV NE	51 AM31
ST NE (100-500)	51 AM31
ST SE (4500)	41 AJ23
ST SW	59 AC38
9 AV NE	51 AM30
AV NE (100-600)	50 AG30

Street	Page Grid
AV NW (100-200)	50 AF30
AV NW (500-600)	50 AE30
AV NW (1900)	48 Z31
AV NW (2100-2400)	48 X31
AV SE (100-700)	50 AG34
AV SE (800-2400)	51 AJ35
AV SE (2500-2800)	52 AP34
AV SE (7900-8300)	54 BC34
AV SW (100-1600)	49 AA34
AV SW (7400-7700)	45 L31
AV SW (8700-9400)	45 I31
ST NE	29 AJ20
ST NE (100-500)	51 AJ32
ST NE (6500-6800)	29 AJ18
ST NW	40 AD24
ST NW (100-300)	49 AD32
ST NW (1100-2400)	49 AD30
ST NW (3000-3200)	40 AD26
ST NW (7900)	27 AD16
ST SE (800-1700)	51 AJ35
ST SE (2200-2700)	51 AJ37
ST SE (3000-4100)	60 AJ42
ST SE (5800)	68 AJ45
ST SW	59 AC41, 67 AC47
ST SW (500-2000)	59 AC39
ST SW (3400-3900)	59 AC39
9A AV NE	52 AN30
ST NE	51 AJ32
ST NW	49 AC32
ST SW	49 AC36

10

Street	Page Grid
10 AV NE (100-600)	50 AG30
AV NE (1700-1900)	51 AM30
AV NE (2500-2900)	52 AP30
AV NW (100-400)	50 AF30
AV NW (1500-1600)	49 AB30
AV NW (1900)	48 Z30
AV NW (2100)	48 Y30
AV SE	53 AX35
AV SE (100-400)	50 AG35
AV SW (100-1500)	51 AK35
AV SE (1820-1840)	61 AM37
AV SE (2500-2800)	52 AP35
AV SE (3700-4300)	52 AS35
AV SW (5400)	53 AW35
AV SW (100-2200)	49 Z34
AV SW (3800-4900)	47 R35
AV SW (7000-7800)	46 M31
ST NE (100-800)	51 AJ32
ST NE (4100-4500)	41 AJ23
ST NE (5700)	29 AK20
ST NE (7000-7800)	29 AJ17
ST NW (100-2300)	49 AC32
ST NW (2400-3900)	39 AC26
ST NW (7400-7800)	27 AD16
ST SE (1000)	51 AJ35
ST SE (1100)	51 AJ36
ST SE (3100-3400)	60 AJ39
ST SE (6300)	68 AJ46
ST SE (12000)	83 AJ58
ST SW	59 AC41
ST SW (3000-3500)	59 AC39
ST SW (8000-8200)	67 AC50
ST SW (16200)	90 AC68
10A ST NW	49 AC32
ST SW (1700-1900)	59 AC37
11 AV NE	50 AG30
AV NW (100-400)	50 AF30
AV NW (900)	49 AC30
AV NW (1500-1600)	49 AB30
AV NW (1800)	48 Z30
AV NW (2500-2900)	48 W30
AV SE	53 AW35, 62 AU35
AV SE (100-600)	50 AG35
AV SE (800-1400)	51 AJ36
AV SE (2500-2800)	52 AP35
AV SW (100-2100)	49 AA35
AV SW (700-7800)	46 M32
ST NE (1-400)	51 AK33
ST NE (2800-3100)	41 AL26
ST NE (5000-7200)	29 AK21
ST NW	39 AC29
ST NW (200-400)	49 AC32
ST NW (5200-5800)	27 AC20
ST SW (500-1900)	51 AK36
ST SE (2000-2300)	60 AK38
ST SE (2900-4300)	60 AK41
ST SE (5000-6400)	68 AJ46
ST SE (6500-7300)	68 AJ48
ST SW (500-1900)	59 AC37
ST SW (3400-3800)	59 AC40

ST SW (7200-7300)....67 AC48
ST SW (8300-8700)....74 AC51
ST SW (11200-11300)..74 AC57
11A ST NE (10-400)....51 AK33
ST NE (3500-3800)....41 AK24
ST NW............49 AC32
ST SE............60 AK41
12 AV NE............54 AZ30
AV NE (100-600)....50 AG30
AV NE (1700)....51 AM30
AV NE (3200-3600)....52 AS30
AV NW (100-400)....50 AE30
AV NW (1700-2400)....48 Y30
AV NW (2500-2900)....48 W30
AV SE (100-700)....50 AX35
AV SE (2600-4000)....52 AP35
AV SE (6000-6100)....53 AX35
AV SW (100-2000)....48 Z35
AV SW (2600-3300)....47 V35
AV SW (3900)....47 T35
AV SW (8800)....45 I33
ST NE (40-200)....51 AK33
ST NE (2500-3200)....41 AL26
ST NE (3400-4800)....41 AK22
ST NW (100-900)....49 AB33
ST NW (2100)....39 AC29
ST SE (600-1100)....51 AK36
ST SE (4300-4600)....60 AK42
ST SE (5900-6400)....68 AK46
ST SE (7100-7300)....68 AK47
ST SW (1100-2300)....59 AB37
ST SW (3400-3800)....59 AB40
ST SW (9000-9600)....74 AB52
12A ST NE (100-200)....51 AK32
ST NE (700)....51 AK31
ST SE............60 AK43
13 AV NE (100-800)....50 AG30
AV NE (4000-4100)....53 AT30
AV NW (100-900)....49 AD30
AV NW (1700-1900)....48 Z30
AV NW (2400-2900)....47 V30
AV NW (4900-5200)....37 P27
AV SE (100-600)....50 AG35
AV SE (2600)....52 AP35
AV SE (2800)....52 AQ35
AV SW (100-1700)....49 AA35
AV SW (3000-3100)....47 V35
AV SW (3800-4500)....47 S35
AV SW (8100-8500)....45 J34
ST NE (100-700)....51 AL32
ST NE (4600-4700)....41 AL23
ST NW (1-400)....49 AB32
ST NW (1800-2200)....39 AB29
ST NW (8100)....15 AB15
ST SE (700-1200)....51 AK36
ST SE (4900-5000)....60 AK43
ST SE (6800-7000)....68 AK47
ST SW (1000-2200)....59 AB37
ST SW (3400-3800)....59 AB40
13A ST NE............51 AL31
ST SE............61 AL41
ST SW............59 AB40
14 AV NE (200-600)....40 AG29
AV NE (1700-1900)....51 AM29
AV NE (3800-3900)....52 AS29
AV NW (100)....40 AF29
AV NW (500)....40 AD29
AV NW (1400-2400)....48 Y29
AV NW (2600-2900)....48 W29
AV SE............51 AM36
AV SE (100)....50 AG36
AV SE (300-600)....50 AH36
AV SE (2500-2800)....52 AP35
AV SE (3500-5400)....52 AS35
AV SE (6600)....54 AZ35
AV SW (100-1700)....49 AA35
AV SW (2500-3300)....47 V36
AV SW (5600-5800)....46 P36
AV SW (7000-7700)....45 L34
AV SW (8600-9200)....45 I34
ST NE (4300-4700)....41 AL23
ST NE (11500)....6 AL8
ST NW (1-2400)....49 AB33
ST NW (2500-6400)....39 AB27
ST NW (6500-9500)....15 Z11
ST NW (12000-14100)..5 AB6
ST SE (700-1000)....51 AL36
ST SE (3800-4000)....61 AL41
ST SW (800-3400)....59 AB39
ST SW (3500-3800)....59 AB40
ST SW (6700-8900)....74 AB54
ST SW (11000-12500)..82 AB59
14A ST SE (700)....51 AL36
ST SE (3600-4100)....61 AL41
ST SE (1800)....49 AB36
ST SW (2100-2400)....59 AB38
ST SW (3500-5000)....59 AB43

15

15 AV NE (200-1100)....40 AG29
AV NW............48 W29
AV NW (100-200)....40 AF29
AV NW (4600)....37 Q28

AV SE............51 AM36
AV SE (100-400)....50 AG36
AV SE (2500-2800)....52 AP36
AV SE (6900-7000)....54 AZ36
AV SW............45 L35
AV SW (100-1600)....58 AA36
AV SW (2400)....48 X36
AV SW (3000-3100)....47 V36
AV SW (3900-4500)....47 S36
ST NE (2900-3000)....41 AM26
ST NE (8400-14100)...17 AM10
ST NW (100-1300)....49 AB32
ST NW (1700-2000)....39 AB29
ST NW (3200)....39 AB26
ST SE (1000-1800)....51 AL36
ST SE (3400-4600)....60 AL43
ST SW (1100-3300)....59 AB39
ST SW (3400-5000)....58 AA43
15A ST NE............41 AM26
ST SE (2200-3200)....61 AM37
ST SE (3600-4100)....61 AM41
ST SW (2500-2600)....58 AA38
ST SW (3500-4200)....58 AA41
16 AV NE (100-2200)....40 AG29
AV NE (1500-3500)....51 AM29
AV NE (3600-6200)....43 AX29
AV NW (100-1900)....39 AC29
AV NW (2000-3300)....37 T29
AV NW (3400-4900)....37 Q28
AV NW (6800-8200)....35 H24
AV SE............54 AZ36
AV SE (2500-5200)....52 AP36
AV SW............45 L36, 47 U36
AV SW (800-1600)....49 AB36
AV SW (2700)....48 W36
ST NE............7 AM6
ST NE (900-1600)....51 AM31
ST NE (2600-3000)....41 AM27
ST NW (1-1300)....49 AA32
ST NW (1700-2500)....48 AA29
ST SE (200)....52 AN33
ST SE (1400-1600)....51 AM36
ST SE (2000-2900)....61 AM38
ST SE (3600-4200)....61 AM41
ST SE (7600)....69 AM49
ST SW (1000-1800)....58 AA39
ST SW (3500-4800)....58 AA43
16A AV SE............54 AZ36
ST NE............51 AM31
ST NW (200-600)....49 AA32
ST NW (1100-1300)....48 AA30
ST NW (2500-2800)....39 AA27
ST SE (1400-1600)....51 AM36
ST SE (2300-2700)....61 AM38
ST SE (3800-4200)....61 AM41
ST SW (1800-2500)....58 AA37
ST SW (3800-4400)....58 AA42
16B ST SW............58 AA37
17 AV NE (100-800)....40 AG29
AV NW (100-2000)....48 Z29
AV NW (4200-5200)....36 P26
AV SE............51 AI36
AV SE (100-200)....50 AG36
AV SE (800-1500)....51 AI36
AV SE (1700-7600)....52 AC36
AV SW............45 G36
AV SW (100-1400)....49 AB36
AV SW (1500-3400)....47 V36
AV SW (3500-5300)....46 Q36
AV SW (5400-6800)....46 N36
ST NE (900-1600)....51 AM31
ST NW (10-20)....49 AA33
ST NW (1000)....49 AA31
ST NW (1700-2700)....39 AA27
ST SE (100-300)....52 AN33
ST SE (1400-1700)....51 AM36
ST SE (2300-2900)....61 AM38
ST SE (4100-4200)....61 AM41
ST SW (1200)....49 AA35
ST SW (1800-3400)....58 AA39
ST SW (3500-5000)....58 AA43
ST SW (12300-12700)..82 AA60
17A ST NE............52 AN31
ST NW (1000-1400)....48 AA30
ST NW (2500-2700)....39 AA27
ST SE (1400-1600)....52 AN36
ST SE (4100-4200)....61 AM41
ST SE (6000-6400)....69 AM46
ST SW (1800-2600)....58 AA38
17B ST SW............58 AA37
18 AV NE (100-500)....40 AG28
AV NE (1600-2300)....42 AO28
AV NE (5700-6100)....43 AX28
AV NW (100-2000)....38 Z28
AV NW (5100-5200)....37 Q27
AV SE (100-200)....50 AG36
AV SE (900-1000)....51 AJ36
AV SW (100-500)....50 AE36
AV SW (800-900)....49 AC36
AV SW (2000)....48 Z36
ST NE (900-1400)....52 AN31
ST NE (1600)....52 AN29
ST NE (2600-2900)....41 AN27
ST NE (4100-4200)....41 AN24
ST NE (11600-11800)...7 AN7
ST NW (100-500)....49 AA33
ST NW (1200)....48 AA30
ST NW (2000-2800)....48 Z29
ST SE............76 AO55
ST SE (200-600)....52 AO34

ST SE (6000)....69 AN45
ST SE (6200-9200)....76 AN52
ST SW (1300)....48 Z35
ST SW (1800-2300)....58 Z37
ST SW (2600-4200)....58 Z41
18A ST NE............52 AN31
ST NW (100-500)....48 Z32
ST NW (100-1300)....49 AA31
ST SE (6000-6600)....69 AN46
ST SW (1800-2100)....58 Z37
19 AV NE............40 AG28
AV NW (100-2000)....38 Z28
AV NW (4200-5200)....37 Q26
AV SE (900-1000)....51 AJ36
AV SE (2700-4700)....52 AQ36
AV SW............47 U36
AV SW (200-500)....50 AE36
AV SW (800-900)....49 AC36
AV SW (1400-2100)....58 Z37
AV SW (2600-2900)....48 W36
AV SW (3100-4500)....57 S37
ST NE (400-2400)....52 AN30
ST NE (2800-4200)....42 AO27
ST NE (9500-10000)...17 AN12
ST NW (100-2800)....48 Z33
ST NW (2900-4300)....38 Z27
ST SE (200-400)....52 AO33
ST SE (700-800)....61 AM37
ST SE (6200-6600)....69 AM46
ST SW............48 Z35
ST SW (1800-3400)....58 Z39
ST SW (3500-5700)....58 Z43
ST SW (9600-10700)...74 Z55
19A ST SW (1800)....48 Z36
ST SW (2500)....58 Z37

20

20 AV NE (100-600)....40 AG28
AV NE (2200-2300)....42 AO28
AV NE (3300-3600)....42 AR28
AV NW (200-2200)....38 Z28
AV NW (4300-5200)....37 Q26
AV SE............61 AM37
AV SE (900-1000)....51 AJ37
AV SE (5000-5100)....62 AV37
AV SE (300-500)....59 AE37
AV SW (2200-2400)....58 Y37
ST NE............52 AO29
ST NW (100-800)....42 Z30
ST NW (1000-2400)....48 Z33
ST SE (800-900)....52 AM37
ST SE (6400-6600)....69 AO46
ST SE (7000-7600)....69 AO49
ST SW (2200-3400)....58 Z39
ST SW (3500-6500)....66 Z46
20A AV NE............41 AJ28
ST NW (1300-1600)....48 Z30
ST SE (6600-8000)....69 AO49
ST SW............58 Y43
21 AV NE............40 AG28
AV NW (200-2200)....38 Z28
AV NW (4400-5200)....37 Q26
AV SE (800-1000)....51 AJ37
AV SE (3600-4400)....62 AS37
AV SW (200-500)....59 AE37
AV SW (1400-3600)....57 U37
ST NE (1400)....52 AO30
ST NE (2000)....52 AO29
ST NE (2500-3000)....42 AO27
ST NE (3600-3800)....42 AO25
ST NE (4200)....42 AO23
ST NE (7900-8000)....30 AO16
ST NW (600)....48 Y33
ST NW (2400)....38 Y27
ST SE (7200-7800)....69 AO50
ST SW (9000-9600)....76 AO53
ST SW (2500-3500)....58 Y40
ST SW (4900-5800)....66 Y45
21A AV SE............63 AW37
ST NW............48 Y30
ST SE............69 AO50
ST SW............58 Y43
22 AV NE (100-800)....40 AG28
AV NE (5800-5900)....43 AX28
AV NE (6500-6800)....44 AY28
AV NW (200-1100)....40 AD28
AV NW (1400-2000)....38 Z28
AV NW (4500-5300)....37 Q26
AV SE............61 AM37, 61 AQ37
AV SE (800)....51 AJ37
AV SW (90)....59 AG37
AV SW (300-600)....59 AE37
AV SW (1400-1600)....58 AA37
AV SW (1800-2400)....58 Y37
ST NE (2100-2400)....42 AO28
ST NE (2600-2700)....42 AO27
ST NE (7900-8000)....17 AP14
ST NE (10000)....17 AO11
ST NW (100-1000)....48 Y33
ST NW (2300-2800)....38 Y27
ST SE............52 AN37
ST SE (4700-5100)....69 AO44
ST SE (7200-7800)....69 AO50

ST SW............81 Y61
ST SW (1400-1700)....48 Y35
ST SW (2200-2500)....58 Y37
ST SW (2700-3000)....58 Y39
ST SW (4900-5000)....58 Y43
ST SW (9400)....73 Y53
22A ST NW (2300)....38 Y27
ST SE............69 AP49
ST SW............58 Y37
23 AV NE (100-600)....40 AG28
AV NE (2400)....42 AP27
AV NE (2500-2900)....42 AQ28
AV NE (3000-3200)....42 AR28
AV NE (5500)....43 AW27
AV NE (6500-6800)....44 AZ27
AV NE (8400)....44 BC27
AV NW (100-1100)....39 AC27
AV NW (1400-2000)....38 Z27
AV NW (2100-2400)....38 Y28
AV NW (4500-5300)....37 S26
AV SE (700-900)....51 AJ37
AV SE (1200)....60 AK37
AV SE (3700-5000)....62 AS37
AV SE (5500-6000)....63 AW37
AV SW (100)....59 AF37
AV SW (300-600)....59 AE37
AV SW (1400-3900)....57 T37
ST NE (100-200)....52 AP32
ST NE (1900-4200)....42 AP28
ST NW (100-700)....48 Y33
ST NW (1300-1600)....48 Y30
ST NW (2300-2700)....38 Y27
ST SW (3400)....39 Y25
ST SE............52 AP33, 61 AP43
ST SE (7400-7600)....69 AP49
ST SW (1400-1700)....48 X36
ST SW (2000-2200)....58 Y37
23A ST NW............38 Y27
ST SW............58 X37
23B ST NE............42 AP24
24 AV NE............42 AS27
AV NE (100-700)....40 AG27
AV NE (1600-2500)....41 AM27
AV NE (2500-2700)....42 AQ27
AV NE (5700-6800)....43 AX27
AV NW (100-1000)....40 AD27
AV NW (1500-3400)....38 V27
AV NW (3500-3800)....38 U27
AV SE (700-800)....51 AI37
AV SE (1600-1800)....54 AA37
AV SE (2700)....61 AQ37
AV SW (100-600)....59 AE37
AV SW (1500-1700)....58 AA37
AV SW (3200)....58 X37
ST NE (2400-2600)....42 AP27
ST NE (12900-14400)...7 AP4
ST NE (1100-1200)....48 X31
ST SE (5300-5500)....69 AP44
ST SE (7000-10500)...76 AP55
ST SW (10600-11800)..76 AP57
ST SW (1400-2000)....48 X36
ST SW (2300-2600)....58 X38
ST SW (9400-9900)....73 X54
ST SW (10700-13400)..81 X61
ST SW (15000-18100)..89 X72
24A ST NW............48 X31
ST SE............69 AP49
ST SW (1700-1900)....48 X36
ST SW (2000-2800)....58 X38
ST SW (3200)....58 X39
25 AV NE............42 AS27
AV NE (100-600)....40 AG27
AV NE (1300-2100)....41 AN27
AV NE (6600-6700)....44 AY27
AV NW (100-900)....40 AD27
AV SE (300-600)....60 AH38
AV SW (10-600)....58 AE38
AV SW (1500-2000)....58 Z38
AV SW (3400-4500)....57 S37
ST NE............42 AP25
ST NW............48 X32
ST SE............61 AO38
ST SE (300)....52 AP34
ST SE (1200-1300)....52 AP35
ST SE (4400-5000)....61 AP42
ST SE (7200-8000)....69 AP49
ST SW (1700-3200)....58 X39
25A ST SE............61 AQ41
26 AV NE (100-600)....40 AG27
AV NE (3300-3500)....42 AR26
AV NE (6100-6800)....44 AY27
AV NW (100-800)....40 AD27
AV NW (2000-2400)....38 X27
AV SE............38 U29, 63 AW38
AV SE (800-1400)....60 AJ38
AV SE (1700-1800)....61 AA38
AV SE (2700-4500)....61 AQ38
AV SW............55 L38
AV SW (100-300)....59 AE38
AV SW (1500-3300)....57 V38
AV SW (3400-5300)....56 Q38
ST NE (800-1000)....52 AQ31
ST NE (2500-3600)....42 AQ25
ST NW (100-400)....48 W32
ST NW (3100-4600)....38 X25
ST SE (1000-1600)...52 AQ35

ST SE (2000-4300) ... 61 AP41
ST SE (5800)....... 69 AQ44
ST SE (8200-8500) .. 76 AP51
ST SW (1200-3200) .. 58 W39
ST SW (9300)....... 73 W53
ST SW (9800-9900) .. 73 W54
ST SW (10800-11200) .. 73 X56
26A ST SE (3600-3900) .. 61 AQ40
ST SE (7400-7800) .. 69 AQ49
ST SW (1400-3200) .. 58 W39
27 AV NE (100-600).... 40 AG27
AV NE (1500-2300).. 41 AL27
AV NW (100-700) .. 40 AD27
AV NW (2000) 38 Y26
AV NW (2300-2400).. 38 X27
AV SE 62 AS38
AV SW (1-60) 59 AG38
AV SW (1500-2200).. 58 Y38
ST NE (2700-4000).. 42 AQ26
ST NW (700)........ 48 W32
ST SE 61 AQ41
ST SE (900-1700) ... 52 AQ36
ST SE (2000-2400) .. 61 AQ37
ST SE (5300-5400) .. 69 AQ44
ST SE (7600-7800) .. 69 AQ49
ST SE (8400-8500) .. 77 AQ51
ST SE (10800)....... 85 AQ56
ST SW (1400-3200) .. 58 W39
ST SW (11200)....... 73 W57
27A AV SE.............. 62 AS38
28 AV NE 41 AL27
AV NE (100-600).... 40 AG26
AV NE (5800-6400) .. 43 AX27
AV NW (100-700) .. 40 AE26
AV NW (2000) 38 Y26
AV SE (1800)....... 61 AM38
AV SE (2700)....... 61 AQ38
AV SE (3600)....... 62 AQ38
AV SW (10-50) 59 AG38
AV SW (1500-2400).. 58 X38
AV SW (2500-4300).. 57 T38
AV SW (4900)....... 57 R38
ST NE (200-1400).... 52 AQ32
ST NW 48 W32
ST SE 77 AQ51
ST SE (100-200) 52 AQ33
ST SE (1000-1600) .. 52 AQ36
ST SE (2000)....... 61 AQ37
ST SE (2400-3900) .. 62 AR41
ST SE (4800-5000) .. 62 AR43
ST SW 73 W52
ST SW (1400-3200) .. 58 W39
28A AV SE.............. 62 AS38
AV SE 62 AR39
29 AV NE 43 AW26
AV NE (100-500).... 40 AG26
AV NE (1100)....... 41 AL26
AV NE (6600-6800) .. 44 AZ26
AV NW (100-600) .. 40 AE26
AV NW (4600)....... 37 S26
AV NW (6400)....... 36 O26
AV NW (6900)....... 36 N26
AV SE 62 AT38
AV SW (10-60) 59 AG38
AV SW (600-700) 59 AD38
AV SW (1500-2400).. 58 X38
AV SW (4600-4800).. 57 S38
ST NE (2000-4000).. 42 AR28
ST NW.............. 47 V32
ST SE (6200)....... 70 AR46
ST SE (10800-11800).. 85 AQ54
ST SW (1400-3500) .. 57 V39
ST SW (9200)....... 73 V52
29A AV SE (3600)....... 62 AS38
AV SE (3900)....... 62 AR39
ST SE 62 AR39

30

30 AV NE 41 AL26
AV NE 43 AV26
AV NE (100-600).... 40 AG26
AV NE (1700-2300).. 41 AN26
AV NW (100-1000) .. 39 AC26
AV NW (6300-6400) .. 36 O26
AV SE.............. 60 AI39
AV SE (1700-1900) .. 61 AM39
AV SE (2700-4100) .. 62 AR39
AV SW (20-60) 59 AG39
AV SW (100-700) 59 AD39
AV SW (1500-2500).. 58 W39
AV SW (3000-5300).. 57 R39
ST NE 52 AR32
ST NW.............. 47 V32
ST SE 62 AR37
ST SE (1900)....... 52 AR36
ST SE (5400)....... 70 AR44
ST SE (5900-8200) .. 70 AR50
ST SW 66 W46
ST SW (1900-3200) .. 57 V39
ST SW (11200-11400) .. 73 V57
30A AV SE.............. 62 AR39
ST SE 62 AR39
31 AV NE 43 AX26
AV NE (100-300).... 40 AG26

AV NE (1200)........ 41 AL26
AV NE (4600-4700).. 43 AU26
AV NW 39 AA26
AV NW (100-400) .. 40 AF26
AV NW (900-1000) .. 39 AC26
AV NW (6200-6400) .. 36 N26
AV SW 59 AE39
AV SW (10-60) 59 AG39
AV SW (1700-2400).. 58 X39
AV SW (2900)....... 58 W39
ST NW (100)........ 47 V32
ST NW (3500)....... 38 M25
ST SE (1900)....... 52 AR36
ST SE (8200)....... 70 AR50
ST SW (1400-2800) .. 57 V38
ST SW (3400-3900) .. 57 V40
ST SW (4500)....... 57 U42
31A AV SE.............. 62 AR39
ST SE 62 AR39
32 AV NE (100-700) .. 40 AG26
AV NE (900-2600).. 41 AJ26
AV NE (2700-5600).. 42 AU26
AV NE (6900-7800).. 43 AX26
AV NW (100-400) .. 40 AE26
AV NW (900-1000) .. 39 AC26
AV NW (1600)....... 39 AA26
AV NW (3100-4900).. 37 S25
AV NW (6100-6500).. 36 O26
AV NW (6900)....... 36 N25
AV SW (700-1000) .. 59 AC39
AV SW (1500-2400).. 58 Y39
AV SW (2500-2900).. 58 W39
AV SW (3800-5300).. 57 R39
ST NE (2000-3900).. 42 AR28
ST NE (8300-8700).. 30 AR15
ST NW.............. 47 V31
ST SE (800-1200) ... 52 AR35
ST SE (1800)....... 52 AR36
ST SW (4500-5000) .. 62 AR43
ST SW (1400-2800) .. 57 V38
ST SW (3400)....... 57 V39
32 CONNECTOR AV NE .. 40 AI24
32A AV SE.............. 62 AR39
33 AV NE 42 AR25
AV NE 43 AW25
AV NE (100-600).... 40 AG25
AV NW (400)....... 40 AE25
AV NW (6000-6900) .. 36 N25
AV NW (7800-9000) .. 35 I22
AV NW (200-400).. 59 AF39
AV SW (900)....... 59 AE39
AV SW (1500-2400).. 58 W39
AV SW (3800-5100).. 57 R39
ST NE 52 AR33
ST NW (500-900) 47 V31
ST NW (3300-4000).. 38 V25
ST NW (5100-5200).. 26 V21
ST SE (1800-2000) .. 62 AR37
ST SE (3100-3500) .. 62 AS40
ST SW 47 U36
ST SW (1400-3300) .. 57 V39
ST SW (3400-3600) .. 57 V40
33A AV SE.............. 62 AR39
ST NW.............. 47 V31
ST SE 62 AS39
34 AV NE (100-600).... 40 AG25
AV NE (1200)....... 41 AK25
AV NE (3000-3400).. 42 AR25
AV NE (4800)....... 43 AV25
AV NE (6700)....... 44 AZ25
AV NW 37 R25
AV NW (200-400).. 40 AE25
AV NW (2300-2600).. 38 X25
AV NW (3100)....... 38 W25
AV NW (6300-6500).. 36 N25
AV NW (7000-9000).. 35 L25
AV SE 63 AW39
AV SE (300-600).... 60 AH40
AV SE (800-1600) ... 60 AI40
AV SE (2600-3200) .. 61 AQ40
AV SE 56 N40
AV SW (20-60)....... 59 AG40
AV SW (500-1100) .. 59 AC40
AV SW (1300-2400).. 58 Y40
AV SW (3000-3500).. 57 U40
AV SW (8000-9200).. 55 I40
ST NE (2000)....... 42 AR28
ST NE (3400-3900).. 42 AS25
ST NW.............. 38 U22, 38 U27
ST NW (100-900).... 47 U31
ST SE 62 AS39
ST SE (1000-1800) .. 52 AS36
ST SE (4700)....... 62 AS42
ST SE (1900-3000) .. 57 U39
ST SW (5900-6600) .. 65 U45
34A ST NW (100-500) .. 47 U31
ST NW (900)....... 47 V30
ST SE 62 AS42
35 AV NE 44 AY25
AV NE (200-600).... 40 AG25
AV NE (2200-2300).. 42 AO25
AV NE (2600)....... 42 AP25
AV NW (400)....... 40 AE25
AV NW (6300-6400).. 36 O25
AV NW (6500-7600).. 35 L25
AV SE 62 AS41
AV SW (1700-2100).. 58 Y40
AV SW (3100-3700).. 57 U40
AV SW (4100-5300).. 57 R40

ST NE (3500-3700) ... 42 AS25
ST NW (900-1800) ... 47 U31
ST SE (900-1800) ... 52 AS36
ST SE (5700-5900) .. 70 AS45
ST SE (6300-6400) .. 70 AS46
ST SE (7500-7800) .. 70 AS50
ST SE (11500-11800) .. 86 AS58
ST SW (1700-3100) .. 57 U38
35A ST NW 47 U30
ST SE 62 AS43
ST SE 47 U33
35B ST SE 62 AT43
36 AV NE (200-600).... 40 AG25
AV NE (1200-1300).. 41 AK25
AV NW (6500)....... 40 AE25
AV NW (7000-8900).. 35 I22
AV SE 61 AM40
AV SW (300-500).... 59 AG40
AV SW (300)....... 59 AF40
AV SW (600-1200) .. 59 AC40
AV SW (1300-2100).. 58 Y40
AV SW (3100-3700).. 57 U40
ST NE (500-1300).. 52 AS32
ST NE (2000-4800).. 42 AS27
ST NE (5000-8000).. 42 AS22
ST NW (700-900) 47 U30
ST NW (3600-3700).. 38 U25
ST SE (100-1700) ... 52 AS36
ST SE (1800-4900) .. 62 AS43
ST SE (5200-6900) .. 70 AS46
ST SE (8000)....... 70 AS50
ST SE (11100-11200) .. 77 AS56
ST SW (400-700) 47 U34
ST SW (1900-3100) .. 57 U38
36A ST NW 47 U30
36B ST NW 47 U30
37 AV NE (200-700).... 40 AG24
AV NE (2400-3500).. 42 AP24
AV NE (6700-6800).. 44 AZ24
AV NW (400)....... 40 AF24
AV NW (7100-7700).. 35 L24
AV SW 59 AF40
AV SW (200-300).... 59 AE40
AV SW (1600-2400).. 58 Z40
AV SW (3400-4500).. 57 S40
ST NW (100-700).... 47 U31
ST NW (3300-4500).. 38 U25
ST SE (900-2600) ... 62 AS38
ST SW (1-3500) 57 U40
ST SW (3600-6600) .. 65 U46
ST SW (12000-13900) .. 81 U63
38 AV NE (200-600).... 40 AG24
AV NE (1200)....... 41 AK24
AV NW 40 AF24
AV SE 61 AL40
AV SW (200-1200) .. 59 AC40
AV NW (1300-2000).. 58 AA40
ST NE (900-1100) ... 53 AT31
ST NE (1800)....... 43 AT28
ST NE (2400-2600) .. 43 AT27
ST NE (3300-3400) .. 43 AT25
ST NE (4200-4400) .. 43 AT24
ST NE (9200)....... 18 AT13
ST SE (900-2600) ... 62 AT38
ST SW (300-1600) .. 47 U36
ST SW (300-3300) .. 57 U39
38A AV SE 59 AG40
AV SW 59 AF40
39 AV NE............. 42 AO24
AV NE (200)....... 40 AG24
AV NE (3500)....... 42 AR24
AV NW (900-1000) .. 39 AC24
AV NW (7400-7700).. 35 L24
AV SE 59 AG41
AV SW 57 V41, 59 AG41
AV SW (200-300).... 59 AE41
AV SW (1000-1200).. 59 AB41
AV SW (1800)....... 58 Z41
AV SW (4800-5000).. 57 R40
ST NE 43 AT22
ST NE (2400-2500) .. 43 AT28
ST NE (3600-3700) .. 43 AT24
ST NW.............. 37 T25
ST NW (4400-4500).. 37 T23
ST SE (100)....... 53 AT33
ST SW (900-1600) .. 62 AT38
ST SW (2800-3300) .. 57 T39

40

40 AV NE (200-600).... 40 AG24
AV NE (1100-1400).. 41 AK24
AV NW (100-1200) .. 39 AC23
AV NW (3500-6100).. 37 P23
AV NW (8100)....... 35 K24
AV NW (9600-9700).. 35 G24
AV NW (100)....... 59 AF41
AV SW (200-400) 59 AE41
AV SW (1700-2000).. 58 Z41
AV SW (3100-3500).. 57 U40
AV SW (4700-5000).. 57 R41
ST NE 43 AT28

ST NE (400-600)..... 53 AT32
ST NE (5100)....... 31 AT21
ST NW.............. 31 AT18
ST NW (6800-8000).. 31 AT18
ST NW.............. 37 T24
ST SE (600-700) 53 AT34
ST SE (800-2600) ... 62 AT38
ST SE (5500-8000) .. 70 AT50
ST SE (10700-11200).. 70 AT46
ST SE (12700)....... 86 AU61
ST SW (15000-12300).. 77 AT57
ST SW (300-1600) .. 47 T36
ST SW (2700-3700) .. 57 T40
41 AV NE (200-900).... 40 AG23
AV NE (2000-2300).. 42 AO23
AV NE (6700)....... 44 AZ23
AV NW (100-200) .. 40 AF24
AV NW (7500-7700).. 35 L23
AV SE 60 AH41
AV SE (1500-1700) .. 61 AL41
AV SW 59 AF41
AV SW (2000)....... 58 Z41
AV SW (3800-4500).. 57 R41
ST NE 43 AT29
ST NW (1800)....... 37 S29
ST NW (4500-4800).. 37 T23
ST SW (900-3300) .. 62 AT39
ST SW (900-1600) .. 47 T36
ST SW (2700-3700) .. 57 T40
41A AV SE 61 AQ41
42 AV NE (100-600).... 40 AG23
AV NE (2400)....... 42 AP23
AV NW (100-200) .. 40 AF23
AV NW (500)....... 40 AE23
AV SE (100-1300) .. 59 AG41
AV SW (100-400) .. 59 AE42
AV SW (1600-2000).. 58 Z41
ST NE 18 AT13, 53 AU32
ST NE (1300-1400) .. 53 AU30
ST NE (1700)....... 43 AU29
ST NE (3300-3500) .. 43 AT25
ST NE (7400-7600) .. 31 AT17
ST NW (1900)....... 37 S29
ST NW (3400-4000).. 37 S24
ST SE (400-900) 53 AU34
ST SE (1500-2600) .. 62 AT38
ST SE (6400)....... 70 AT46
ST SE (7900-8000) .. 70 AT50
ST SE (10300-11400).. 77 AT57
ST SE (11500-11600).. 77 AT57
ST SW (300-600) 47 T33
ST SW (900-1600) .. 47 T36
ST SW (2700-3700) .. 57 T40
42A AV NW 40 AF23
AV SE 53 AU34
43 AV NE (100)....... 40 AG23
AV NE (900)....... 41 AJ23
AV NE (6700-6800).. 44 AZ23
AV NW (100-200) .. 40 AF23
AV NW (7900-8300).. 35 K23
AV SE 60 AK42
AV SW (200)....... 59 AF42
AV SW (1900-2000).. 58 Z42
ST NW.............. 37 R28
ST SE (900-1700) .. 53 AU33
ST SE (1800-2600) .. 62 AU38
ST SE (4600-5000) .. 62 AU43
ST SW (900-1600) .. 47 S36
ST SW (2700-3800) .. 57 S40
ST SW (4700)....... 57 T43
43A ST SE 53 AU33
44 AV NE (100)....... 40 AG23
AV NE (1300-1400).. 41 AK23
AV NE (3700-5200).. 42 AS23
AV NW (100-300) .. 40 AF23
AV NW (500-700) .. 40 AD23
AV NW (5200)....... 37 R23
AV NW (7300-8500).. 35 J23
AV NW (9600-10000).. 35 G23
AV SE (1100)....... 60 AJ42
AV SE (3200-3500) .. 62 AR42
AV SW 57 U41
AV SW (1700-2000).. 58 Z42
ST NE.......... 31 AU21, 53 AU31
ST NE (200)....... 53 AU32
ST NE (6800-8600).. 31 AU16
ST NW.............. 37 R28
ST SE (100-1700) .. 62 AU36
ST SE (1800-2600) .. 62 AU38
ST SE (5400-8000) .. 70 AU50
ST SE (8100-9400) .. 77 AU54
ST SE (11500-12000).. 77 AU57
ST SW (1400-1600) .. 47 S36
ST SW (3100-3800).. 57 S40
45 AV NE 41 AI23
AV NE (1100-1400).. 41 AJ23
AV SE 61 AQ42
AV SW (300)....... 59 AF42
AV SW (1600-2000).. 58 Z42
AV SW (3700)....... 57 U42
ST NW.............. 37 R28
ST SE (1500-1700) .. 62 AU36
ST SE (1800-2600) .. 62 AU38
ST SW (1-3800) 57 S40
ST SW (3900-5000) .. 57 S43
46 AV NE 41 AI22
AV NW.............. 37 T23
AV NW (4800) 25 R22
AV NW (7700-8800).. 35 J22

123 **46 AV NW - 85 ST SW**

AV NW (10000) **35** G22
AV SE (700-1100) **60** AI42
AV SE (3200-5200) **62** AR42
AV SW (100-600) **59** AD42
AV SW (1500-2000) **58** Z42
AV SW (3800-5000) **57** R42
ST NE **43** AU26
ST NE (4200) **43** AV24
ST NW (1500-2100) **37** R28
ST NW (3000) **37** R26
ST SE (100) **53** AU33
ST SE (1500-1700) **62** AU36
ST SE (1800-2800) **62** AU38
ST SE (5500-7900) **70** AU49
ST SE (10300-11100) **77** AU56
ST SE (12900-13000) **97** AU62
ST SW **47** S33
ST SW (3100-3300) **57** S39
ST SW (4000) **57** S41
47 AV NE **41** AL22
AV NW (7700-8900) **35** I22
AV SE (2200) **61** AO42
AV SE (2500) **61** AP42
AV SE (2900-3000) **62** AR42
AV SW (300-800) **59** AD43
AV SW (1700-2300) **58** Y43
ST NE **43** AV22
ST NW **37** Q27
ST SE (100-800) **62** AV35
ST SE (1500-2600) **62** AV38
ST SE (4600-5000) **62** AV43
ST SW (1100-1700) **47** R36
ST SW (3100) **57** S39
ST SW (3700-3900) **57** S40
ST SW (4300-4500) **57** S42
48 AV NE (300) **28** AH22
AV NE (1200) **41** AK22
AV NE (2500-2800) **30** AP22
AV NW (900-1200) **39** AC21
AV NW (2700) **26** W22
AV NW (7700-9400) **35** I22
AV SE (800-6000) **68** AI43
AV SE (2200) **61** AO43
AV SE (2500-2600) **61** AP43
AV SE (3300-3600) **62** AR43
AV SE (4800-5200) **62** AV43
AV SW (400-900) **59** AC43
AV SW (1600-2000) **58** Z43
ST NE (800-1000) **53** AV30
ST NE (1800-2300) **43** AV28
ST NE (2700-3500) **43** AV27
ST NW (2300-2500) **37** Q27
ST NW (4600-5100) **25** R22
ST SE (1500-2600) **62** AV38
ST SE (5500-8000) **70** AV50
ST SE (8100-9800) **78** AV53
ST SE (10500-11400) **78** AV57
ST SE (12500-13000) **97** AV62
ST SW **57** R41
ST SW (3100) **57** R39
49 AV NE **41** AK22
AV NW **25** R22
AV SE (2200-2300) **61** AO43
AV SE (2500) **61** AP43
AV SE (2900-3200) **62** AR43
AV SW **59** AF43
AV SW (400-900) **59** AC43
AV SW (1600-2200) **58** Y43
AV SW (4500) **57** S43
ST NE **43** AV24
ST NW **37** Q27
ST NW (3400-4000) **37** R25
ST SE **62** AV36
ST SW **47** R34
ST SW (2700-3500) **57** R40

50

50 AV NE **28** AI21
AV NE (4800) **43** AV22
AV SE **63** AZ43
AV SE (100-300) **59** AG43
AV SE (2000-5800) **61** AO43
AV SW (300-900) **59** AD43
AV SW (1500-2100) **58** W43
ST NE **43** AV25
ST NE (500-700) **53** AV31
ST NE (2200-2500) **43** AV28
ST NW (2300) **37** R26
ST NW (3300-3700) **37** R25
ST SE (1500-2400) **62** AV37
ST SE (5300) **70** AV44
ST SE (10300-11000) **78** AV56
ST SW (3100-3200) **57** R39
ST SW (4500-4900) **57** R42
51 AV SE (400-600) **60** AH43
AV SE (2200-2400) **61** AO43
AV SE (5300-6800) **63** AX43
AV SW (400-700) **59** AD43
AV SW (2000-2100) **58** Y43
ST NE (2300-2400) **43** AW28
ST NW **37** P27
ST SE (1500-1700) **53** AW36
ST SE (4600-5200) **62** AV43
ST SE (5700-6100) **70** AV45
ST SE (7400-8000) **70** AV50
ST SW **57** R40
52 AV NE **31** AT21
AV NW (3200-3600) **26** U21
AV SE **67** AG44
AV SE (2200-2400) **69** AO44
AV SE (5300-5500) **71** AW44
AV SW (300-700) **67** AD44
AV SW (2000-2400) **66** Y44
ST NE (200-1600) **53** AW30
ST NE (1700-4800) **43** AW27
ST NE (8200-10000) **19** AW15
ST NW (1700-2100) **36** P26
ST NW (4100-4400) **37** R24
ST SE **97** AW62
ST SE (200-1700) **53** AW36
ST SE (1800-5000) **63** AW41
ST SE (5100-8000) **71** AW50
ST SE (8100-11400) **78** AW57
52A ST SE **53** AW35
53 AV NE **29** AJ21
AV NW (400) **27** AE21
AV NW (5200-5400) **25** Q20
AV SE (200-600) **67** AG44
AV SE (5400-5500) **71** AW44
AV SW (300-700) **67** AD44
AV SW (2000-2400) **66** X44
ST NE **43** AW23
ST NW (4100-5500) **37** Q23
ST NW (6500-6900) **25** R18
ST SE (1100-1200) **53** AW35
ST SE (5400-5700) **71** AW45
53A ST SE **53** AW35
53B ST SE **53** AW35
53C ST SE **53** AW35
54 AV NE (100-140) **28** AG21
AV NE (3800-4700) **31** AT20
AV NW (100-500) **27** AE21
AV NW (6600-7100) **24** N21
AV SE (2600-3900) **69** AQ44
AV SE (4200-5400) **70** AT44
AV SE (5500) **71** AX44
AV SW (400-700) **67** AD44
AV SW (2000-2400) **66** Y44
AV SW (3400-3700) **65** U44
ST NE (5300-5500) **31** AW21
ST NE (6300-6400) **31** AW19
ST SE **78** AW57
ST SE (1100-1200) **53** AW35
ST SE (1700-1800) **53** AW36
ST SE (5200-5300) **71** AW44
ST SE (6900) **71** AW47
ST SE (7500-8000) **71** AW50
55 AV NE **29** AJ20
AV NW **28** AG21
AV SE **67** AG44
AV SW **66** X44
AV SW (300-700) **67** AD44
AV SW (2000) **66** Z44
ST NE (400) **53** AX31
ST NE (3600-4400) **43** AW24
ST SE (600-700) **53** AX34
ST SE (5300-5600) **71** AX45
ST SE (6900) **71** AX47
56 AV NE **28** AG20
AV NW (1300) **27** AC20
AV SE (3500-3900) **70** AS45
AV SE (5000-5200) **70** AV45
AV SE (5400-5500) **71** AX45
AV SW (400-700) **67** AD44
AV SW (2000) **66** Z44
ST NE (1800-3500) **43** AX28
ST SE **78** AX57
ST SE (7700-8000) **71** AX50
57 AV NE **28** AI20
AV NW **27** AC20
AV SE **69** AQ44
AV SW (200-700) **67** AD45
AV SW (2000) **66** Z45
ST SE (5500-6700) **71** AX46
58 AV NE **71** AX45
AV NW **23** J20
AV SE (100-1200) **67** AG45
AV SE (2500-3300) **69** AP44
AV SE (4100-4400) **70** AT45
AV SW (100-700) **67** AD45
AV SW (2000-2400) **66** Y45
AV SW (3400-3700) **65** U45
ST NE **43** AX26
ST NE (300) **53** AX32
ST NE (1700-1800) **43** AX29
ST NE (4100-4400) **43** AX23
ST NW (6300-6500) **25** P19
ST SE (600-700) **53** AX34
ST SE (8800-9000) **78** AX52
ST SW **46** P35
59 AV NW **28** AF20
AV SE (800) **68** AI45
AV SW **67** AF45
ST NE **43** AX28, **53** AX32
ST NW **36** P25
ST SE **68** AK45
59A AV SE **69** AN45
60 AV NE (100-500) **28** AG20
AV NW **23** J19
AV SE **67** AG46, **69** AN45
AV SE (100-500) **68** AH45
AV SE (1100) **68** AJ46
AV SE (3600) **70** AS45
AV SW **67** AF46, **67** AF45
ST NE (2500-3500) **43** AX27
ST NE (4700-4800) **43** AX23
ST NE (8000-9600) **19** AX15
ST NW **36** P25
ST SE (200-500) **53** AX33
ST SE (900-1200) **53** AX35
ST SE (2000) **63** AX37
ST SE (8500-9400) **78** AX53
61 AV NW (7000) **24** N19
AV NW (7300) **24** M19
AV NW (8400) **23** J19
AV SE **69** AQ46
AV SE (100-200) **67** AG46
AV SE (2600-5200) **69** AP45
AV SW (100-300) **67** AF46
AV SW (600) **67** AD46
AV SW (3600-3700) **65** U46
ST NE **44** AY28
ST NW **36** O25
ST SE **54** AY36
62 AV NW (6600) **24** N19
AV NW (8400) **23** J19
AV SE (100-400) **67** AG46
AV SE (1600-1900) **69** AN46
AV SE (3500) **70** AS46
AV SW (3400) **65** U46
ST NE (1700-1900) **44** AY29
ST NE (2500) **44** AY27
ST NW **36** O25
63 AV NW **27** AE19
AV SW **65** V46
ST NW **36** O25
64 AV NE (100-600) **28** AG18
AV NE (900-1100) **29** AJ18
AV NE (5200) **31** AU18
AV NE (6400) **31** AX18
AV NW **23** J18, **28** AF19
AV NW (100-1200) **27** AD19
AV SE **69** AN46
AV SE (700-800) **68** AI46
AV SE (1000-1200) **68** AJ46
AV SE (3500-4400) **70** AS46
AV SE (4900-5200) **70** AV46
ST NE (3300-3600) **44** AY25
ST NE (4500-4600) **44** AY23
ST NW **36** N25
ST SE **78** AY52
65 AV NE **29** AJ18
AV NW **24** M18
AV SE **67** AG46
ST NE (1700-2200) **44** AZ29
ST NE (2400) **44** AZ27
ST NW **36** N24
ST SE **54** AZ36
66 AV NW **24** M18
AV NW (5800) **25** P18
AV SE (1700-2100) **69** AM47
AV SE (3500) **70** AS47
AV SE (8200-8300) **72** BC47
AV SW (2500-3600) **65** U46
ST NE **44** AZ27
ST NW (3700-3900) **36** N24
ST NW (5200-5300) **24** N21
67 AV NE **31** AS18
AV NW **23** L18
AV SW **67** AD47
ST NE **44** AZ27
ST NE (3700) **44** AZ24
ST NW **24** N21
ST NW (3600) **36** N25
ST NW (4100) **36** N24
68 AV NE (200) **28** AG18
AV NE (900-1100) **29** AJ17
AV NW (400-800) **27** AE18
AV NW (7600-7700) **23** L18
AV SE (2400) **69** AP47
AV SE (4300-4800) **70** AU47
AV SW **67** AC47
ST NE (200-2200) **54** AZ32
ST NE (2300-6400) **44** AZ27
ST NE (6500-10000) **20** AZ15
ST NW (3100) **36** N25
ST NW (5200) **24** N21
ST SE (200-1700) **54** AZ36
ST SE (1800-8000) **71** AZ50
ST SE (8100-10100) **78** AZ54
ST SE (10200-13500) **87** AZ62
ST SE (13600-14600) **98** AZ64
69 AV SE **67** AE47
AV SE (1900-2100) **69** AN47
AV SE (2200-2400) **69** AP47
AV SE (5800) **71** AW47
AV SW **67** AD47
ST NW (3000) **36** N27
ST NW (3400-4100) **36** N24
ST NW (4200-4900) **35** L22
ST NW (5100) **24** N21
ST SW (100-1700) **46** N36
ST SW (1800-4400) **56** N41

70

70 AV SE (1200) **68** AJ47
AV SE (3800-4000) **70** AS47
AV SW (500) **67** AE47
AV SW (900-1400) **67** AB47
ST NW (4200-4800) **35** L22
ST NW (6400) **24** N19
ST SE (1600-1700) **54** BA36
ST SE (11300) **79** BA57
71 AV NW (600-800) **27** AE17
AV NW (7900) **23** K17
AV SE (100) **67** AF48
AV SE (400-600) **68** AH48
AV SE (2100) **69** AO48
AV SW (100-500) **67** AE48
AV SW (700) **67** AD48
ST NW **36** M25
ST NW (6600-6700) **24** M18
72 AV NE (100-400) **28** AF17
AV NE (900) **29** AJ17
AV NE (4100-4400) **31** AT17
AV NW **27** AD17
AV SE (2100-2500) **69** AO48
AV SE (3500-6800) **70** AS48
ST NW (4200-4600) **35** L23
ST NW (6200) **24** M19
ST SE (9700-10200) **79** BA54
73 AV SE (500) **67** AF48
AV SE (1200-1300) **68** AJ48
AV SE (3500) **70** AS48
AV SW (500) **67** AE48
AV SW (900-1300) **67** AB48
ST NW **35** L23
ST SW (600-1100) **46** M31
ST SW (1200-1700) **46** M36
74 AV SE (2300-2700) **69** AO48
AV SE (4000) **70** AS48
AV SE (4900-5100) **70** AV48
AV SE (7400-8000) **71** AZ48
ST NW **36** M24
ST SE **79** BB56
75 AV NW **27** AE16
AV SE (4200-4400) **70** AT48
AV SW (500-1400) **67** AB48
ST NW **23** L18
ST NW (4300-4600) **35** L23
ST SW **45** L36
76 AV NE **31** AT16
AV SE (1600-2700) **69** AN49
AV SE (3700-6000) **70** AS49
ST NW **35** L24
ST SE **54** BB36
77 AV SE **69** AP49
AV SE (500-600) **68** AI49
AV SE (4900-5100) **70** AV49
AV SW **67** AD49
ST NW **35** L25
ST SW (500-1000) **45** L32
ST SW (2000) **45** L36
ST SW (2200-4200) **55** L39
78 AV NE **30** AQ16
AV NE (100-400) **28** AF16
AV NE (1900-2300) **30** AP16
AV NW **15** AC15
AV SE **71** AX49
AV SE (100-200) **67** AG49
AV SE (2100-2700) **69** AO49
AV SE (3700-4800) **70** AS49
AV SE (5500-5600) **71** AW49
AV SW **67** AB49
AV SW (400-500) **67** AE49
AV SW (900-1000) **67** AC49
ST NW **35** L25
ST NW (6800-7200) **23** L18
ST SE **79** BB53
79 AV SE **68** AI49
ST NW **35** K24
80 AV NE (2900-5100) **30** AQ15
AV NE (7800-8000) **20** AY15
AV SE (2100-2200) **69** AO50
AV SE (2600-2700) **69** AP50
AV SE (3100-3500) **70** AR50
AV SE (4200-5000) **70** AT50
AV SE (5600) **71** AW50
AV SE (5700) **71** AX50
AV SW **67** AC50
ST NW **35** K24
ST NW (4600) **35** K23
81 ST NW **35** K23
ST SW (700-1000) **45** K31
ST SW (2000) **45** K36
ST SW (2000-2900) **55** K37
82 ST NW **35** K23
83 AV SE (400) **67** AG50
AV SE (2500) **69** AP50
AV SE (2700-3300) **69** AQ50
ST NW **35** J24
84 AV NE **17** AP14
AV NE (4500-5100) **18** AU14
AV SE (200-300) **75** AF51
AV SE (2500) **76** AP51
AV SE (2700-3100) **77** AQ51
AV SE (6100-6800) **78** AY51
AV SW **74** AD51
ST NE (1700-3200) **44** BD29
ST NW (4400-4600) **35** J23
ST NW (5900-6200) **23** J20
ST SE (1800-8000) **72** BD45
ST SE (9000) **79** BD54
85 AV SE (2500-2700) **76** AP51
ST NW (4600) **35** J23
ST NW (11000-14400) **10** J9
ST SW (300-500) **35** J27
ST SW (500-1700) **45** J36

ST SW (1800-4200) 55 J40
36 AV SE 78 AW51
AV SE (200-300) ... 74 AE51
AV SE (2600-2800) ... 77 AQ51
AV SE (6200-7200) ... 78 AX51
AV SW 74 AC51
ST NW 35 J22
37 AV NW (900-1300) ... 74 AB51
AV SW 23 I20, 35 I23
38 AV NE (2900-5600) ... 18 AS13
AV NE (5700-6000) ... 19 AX13
AV SE 75 AG52
ST SW 35 I22
39 AV NE 20 AY13
AV SW (800-1400) ... 74 AB51
ST NW 35 I22
ST SW (2100-2200) ... 45 I31
ST SW (2100-2200) ... 55 I37
40 AV SE (200-300) ... 75 AF52
AV SE (3800-6700) ... 77 AS52
AV SW (1300-1400) ... 74 AB52
AV SW (1600-3500) ... 73 V51
42 AV NE 18 AT12
AV SE 75 AJ52
AV SE (200) ... 75 AG52
AV SW 73 X52
AV SW (1500-1800) ... 74 AA52
43 AV SW 73 U52
ST SW 45 H36
44 AV SE (100-400) ... 75 AF53
AV SE (600-800) ... 75 AH53
AV SE (5500-6000) ... 78 AW53
AV SW 74 AC52
46 AV SE (100-700) ... 16 AF11
AV NW 10 G11
AV SE (300-500) ... 75 AF53
AV SE (4000) ... 77 AT53
AV SE (6900-7800) ... 78 AZ53
AV SW (1000-1200) ... 74 AA53
AV SW (1300-1800) ... 74 AB53
47 AV SE 75 AH53
AV SW 74 AB53
ST SW 35 G25
48 AV SE (4000-5600) ... 78 AW54
AV SE (6900-7700) ... 79 BA53
AV SW 73 X54
49 AV SE (200-500) ... 74 AE55

100

00 AV NE 17 AN10
01 AV SW 74 AD54
ST NW 35 G21
ST SW (100-300) ... 35 G25
ST SW (700-1700) ... 45 G36
ST SW (1800-3600) ... 55 G40
02 AV SE (4300-5000) ... 77 AU54
AV SW (6900-7800) ... 78 AZ54
04 AV SE (4300-4800) ... 77 AU55
AV SW (600-900) ... 74 AC55
AV SW (1300-1400) ... 74 AB55
AV SW (1800) ... 74 AA55
ST NW 9 F12
05 AV SW (1100-1400) ... 74 AB55
06 AV SE (2400) ... 76 AO55
AV SE (3700-5200) ... 77 AS55
AV SE (6900-8000) ... 78 AZ54
AV SW (1300-1400) ... 74 AB55
AV SW (2500-2600) ... 73 X55
AV SW (3100) ... 73 V55
07 AV SE (2500-3000) ... 76 AP56
AV SE (6900) ... 78 AZ55
AV SE (1300-1400) ... 74 AB55
AV SW (1700) ... 74 AA55
AV SW (3100) ... 73 V55
ST NW 22 E12
08 AV SE 78 AZ55
AV SW (1300-1400) ... 74 AB56
AV SW (3200-3300) ... 73 V56
09 AV SE 78 AZ55
AV SW 74 AE56
AV SW (1300-1400) ... 74 AB56
AV SW (3100) ... 73 V56
10 AV SE 78 AZ56
AV SE (3700-5200) ... 77 AS56
AV SW (600) ... 74 AD56
AV SW (1500-1700) ... 74 AA56
AV SW 74 AA56
12 AV NW (5900) ... 2 O8
AV NW (7500) ... 1 J8
AV NW (10300-10800) ... 9 E8
AV SE 78 AZ57
AV SE (3700-4800) ... 77 AS57
14 AV SE (2500-8400) ... 85 AQ57
15 AV NE 7 AM7
16 AV SE 86 AT58
AV SW (1300) ... 82 AB58
17 AV SW 81 Z58
ST NW 22 C13
18 AV NE 7 AM6
AV SE 85 AQ58, 86 AT58
AV SW 82 AE58
20 AV NE 7 AM6
AV SE (700-1100) ... 83 AI58
AV SE (4100-4400) ... 86 AT59

AV SW 82 AE58
122 AV SE 86 AU60
124 AV SW 82 AD59
126 AV SW 86 AU61
AV SW 81 W60
128 AV NE 7 AM4
AV SE 86 AU61
129 AV SE 83 AG61
130 AV SE 97 AX63
AV SE (4000-5200) ... 95 AR62
AV SW (700) ... 82 AE61
AV SW (3700) ... 81 U61
135 AV SE 83 AG62
136 AV SE 84 AN62
137 AV SE (1100) ... 84 AL63
AV SE (1500-1600) ... 84 AM62
138 AV SE 84 AM63
145 AV SE 82 AE64
146 AV SE (100-500) ... 82 AE64
AV SE (2000-2600) ... 92 AM65
AV SE (5300-5700) ... 97 AW64
AV SW (1400-3500) ... 81 V64
148 AV SE 90 AE65
149 AV SE 91 AF65
151 AV SE 91 AF65
153 AV SE 92 AN66
AV SE (200) ... 91 AF66
154 AV SW 90 AB66
157 AV SW 90 AD66
159 AV SW 90 AD67
162 AV SE 91 AF68
AV SW (900-10900) ... 90 AC69
AV SW (14900) ... 89 Y68
170 AV SW 89 X70
178 AV SE (4100-5500) ... 96 AU71
194 AV SE 93 AJ75
196 AV SE 96 AT74

A

ABADAN CR NE 44 BA29
PL NE 100, 200 .... 54 BA30
300, 400, 500 ... 54 BA30
ABALONE CR NE 54 BA32
PL NE 100, 200 .... 54 BA32
300, 400 ... 54 BB32
500 ... 54 BA32
WY NE 54 BB32
ABBERCOVE DR SE 54 AZ33
LN SE 54 AZ33
RD SE 54 AZ33
WY SE 54 AZ33
ABBERFIELD CR NE 54 AZ32
CT NE 54 BA32
PL NE 54 AZ32
WY NE 54 BA32
ABBEYDALE DR NE 54 BA32
DR SE 54 BA31
VL NE 54 BA31
ABBOT AV NE 51 AK32
ABBOTSFORD DR NE ... 54 AZ30
PL NE 54 BA30
ABBOTT PL SE 75 AI53
ABERDARE CR NE 54 BB31
PL NE 54 BA31
RD NE, WY NE ... 54 BB32
ABERDEEN RD SE 75 AH51
ABERFOYLE CL NE 54 BB30
PL NE 54 BB31
ABERGALE CL NE 54 BA31
DR NE, PL NE, WY NE . 54 BA31
ABINGDON CR NE 44 BA29
CT NE 54 BB30
PL NE 100, 200 ... 54 BB30
WY NE 44 BA29
ABINGER CR NE 54 BA31
RD NE 54 BA31
ABOYNE CR NE 54 AZ30
PL NE 100, 200, 300... 54 BA30
WY NE 54 BA30
ACACIA WY NE 113 E4
DR (AIR) 113 E4
ACADEMY DR SE 75 AI53
ACADIA DR SE (200-500) 75 AH52
DR SE (600-1700) ... 75 AI54
ACTON AV SW 58 AA42
ADAMS CR SE 75 AF53
ADDISON DR SE 68 AH50
PL SE 75 AI51
ADELAIDE ST SE 51 AJ35
ADRIAN PL SE 75 AJ54
AERIAL PL NE 30 AO16
AERO DR NE 29 AK16
GT NE 29 AK16
RD NE 29 AK19
AGATE CR SE 75 AI54
AIR SERVICES PL NE ... 17 AP14
AIRDRIE RD (AIR) ... 113 A2
AIRPORT RD NE 17 AO13
TR NE (2000) ... 17 AK11
ALANDALE LK (SPNG) ... 99 E3
PL 100, 200 (SPNG) ... 99 E3
ALANWOOD ST SE 75 AH51
ALBANY PL SE 75 AH53

ALBERNI RD SE 75 AH54
ALBERT ST (AIR) 113 E4
ALBERTA AV SE 51 AJ36
AV (OKS) ... 107 D6
ST (CRS) ... 8 G2
ALCOCK CL (OKS) ... 107 C5
ST (OKS) ... 107 C5
ALCOTT CR SE 75 AG54
RD SE 75 AG53
ALDER CR (AIR) 113 E4
WY NW 35 I23
ALDERWOOD CL SE ... 75 AI51
PL SE 75 AI51
ALEXANDER CR NW ... 49 AD30
ST SE 51 AI37
ALFEGE ST SW 59 AB39
ALLAN CR SE 75 AF53
ALLANDALE CL SE ... 75 AI52
RD SE 75 AI53
ALLDEN PL SE 75 AI53
ALLEN ST (AIR) 113 E4
ALLISON DR SE 75 AG53
ALLSTON AV SE 75 AH51
ALMOND CR SE 75 AI52
ALPINE CR (AIR) 113 E4
MDWS (EV) ... 115 C8
ALTADORE AV SW ... 58 AA42
ALYTH CT SE 60 AL37
PL SE 60 AL37
RD SE 61 AM37
AMBER AV SE 68 AI50
AMHERST ST SW ... 59 AD37
AMIENS CR SW 58 Y42
RD SW 58 Y41
ANAHEIM BY NE ... 44 BB24
CIR NE, CR NE ... 44 BB24
CT NE ... 44 BB25
GDN NE ... 44 BA24
GN NE, PL NE ... 44 BA25
ANATAPI LN SW 45 H36
ANCOURT RD SE 75 AH51
ANDERSON AV (LNG) ... 88 D6
CR (T VAL) ... 105 C4
GV SW ... 73 W57
RD SE ... 75 AF57
RD SW (500-900) ... 73 U57
ANDREW HEIGHTS
PL (SPNG) ... 99 E3
ANNE AV SW 59 AD42
ANTELOPE LN (BNF) ... 21 F4
ST (BNF) ... 21 E4
APPLE WY NE 35 H23
APPLEBROOK CIR SE .. 54 BB35
APPLEBURN CL SE ... 54 BB34
APPLECREST CR SE ... 54 BA34
CT SE, PL SE ... 54 BA34
APPLECROFT RD SE ... 54 BA36
APPLEFIELD CR NE ... 54 BA35
APPLEGLEN PK SE ... 54 BB33
PL SE 100 ... 54 BB33
200, 300 ... 54 BB33
APPLEGROVE CR SE ... 54 BA33
PL SE ... 54 BB34
APPLEMEAD CL SE ... 54 BB34
APPLEMONT CL SE ... 54 BA34
PL SE ... 54 BA34
APPLERIDGE GN SE ... 54 BA34
APPLESIDE CL SE ... 54 BB33
APPLESTONE PK SE ... 54 BB36
PL SE 100, 200 ... 54 BB36
APPLETREE CL SE ... 54 AZ35
CR SE, RD SE, WY SE . 54 BA35
APPLEVILLAGE CT SE .. 54 AZ36
APPLEWOOD CT SE ... 54 BA34
DR SE ... 54 BA34
LN SE ... 54 BA34
PL SE 100 ... 54 AZ34
200, 300, 400 ... 54 BA34
APRIL RD (B CK) ... 33 E6
ARBOR CR (AIR) ... 113 E4
ARBOUR CR SE ... 75 AG53
ARBOUR BUTTE CR NW 11 L11
PL NW, RD NW, WY NW 11 L11
ARBOUR CLIFF CL NW ... 12 M12
CT NW ... 12 M13
ARBOUR CREST CIR NW .. 11 K12
CL NW ... 11 K13
CL NW 100 ... 11 K13
200 ... 11 K13
CT NW ... 11 K12
DR NW ... 11 J12
HTS NW 100 ... 11 J12
MS NW 100 ... 11 J12
MT NW ... 11 K12
RD NW ... 11 K12
RS NW ... 11 J12
TER NW ... 11 K11
WY NW ... 11 K11
ARBOUR ESTATES GN NW 11 L13
LD NW, VW NW, WY NW 11 L13
ARBOUR GLEN CL NW ... 12 M12
GN NW ... 12 M12
ARBOUR GROVE CL NW .. 11 J14
ARBOUR LAKE DR NW... 11 K13
GN NW, PL NW ... 12 M12
RD NW ... 11 I13
WY NW ... 11 L12

ARBOUR MEADOWS
CL NW ... 11 I13
ARBOUR RIDGE CIR NW.. 12 M11
CL NW, CT NW ... 12 M11
GN NW, HE NW ... 12 N11
HTS NW ... 12 M11
PK NW ... 12 N11
PL NW, WY NW ... 12 M11
ARBOUR STONE CL NW .. 11 I12
CR NW ... 11 I12
PL NW 100, 200 ... 11 H13
RS NW ... 11 J12
WY NW ... 11 H13
ARBOUR SUMMIT CL NW. 12 N12
PL NW 100, 200, 300 .. 12 N12
ARBOUR VISTA CL NW .. 11 L12
GT NW ... 12 M12
HL NW, HTS NW, PT NW 11 L12
RD NW ... 11 L13
TER NW ... 11 L12
WY NW ... 11 L13
ARBOUR WOOD CL NW .. 11 K13
CR NW ... 11 K13
MS NW ... 11 J14
PL NW ... 11 K13
ARCHIBALD WY (T VAL) .. 105 B4
ARCHWOOD RD SE ... 75 AJ53
ARDIEL DR (OKS) ... 107 C5
ARLINGTON BY SE ... 75 AI51
DR SE ... 75 AH51
PL SE ... 75 AI51
ARMSTRONG CR SE ... 75 AG52
DR SW ... 58 Y42
ARRAS DR SW ... 58 Y42
ARTISTS VIEW DR (SPNG) . 99 G1
GT, PT (SPNG) ... 99 G2
WY (SPNG) ... 99 G1
ASH CR SE ... 52 AQ36
CR SE ... 75 AG51
ASHLEY CL (CAN) ... 101 B5
CR SE ... 75 AG51
ASHWOOD GN (AIR) ... 113 E4
RD (AIR) ... 113 E4
ASHWORTH RD SE ... 68 AH50
ASPEN CIR (STMR) ... 112 F7
CR SE ... 62 AR37
CR (AIR) ... 113 E4
DR NW ... 35 I23
GLEN (CAN) ... 101 D2
GN (EV) ... 115 B8
GV (STMR) ... 112 F7
LD (STMR) ... 112 F7
MS (STMR) ... 112 G7
WY NW ... 35 I23
ASPEN CREEK CR (STMR) 112 G7
WY (STMR) ... 112 F7
ASPEN DALE CT SW ... 45 K35
GT SW ... 45 K35
WY SW ... 45 L35
ASPEN GLEN CL SW ... 45 K36
PL SW 100 ... 45 K36
200, 300, 400 ... 45 L36
ASPEN GROVE PL (CHST) . 80 A6
ASPEN MEADOWS CT SW 46 M35
CT SW 100, 200 ... 46 M35
GN SW, PL SW ... 46 M35
PL SW 100, 200 ... 46 M35
WY SW ... 46 M35
ASPEN RIDGE CR SW ... 46 M35
CT SW ... 45 L34
LK SW ... 46 M35
LN SW ... 46 M34
MS SW ... 46 M35
PL SW, WY SW ... 45 L34
ASPEN STONE BLVD SW . 45 I36
RD SW ... 45 I35
ASPEN SUMMIT BLVD SW 45 J35
CL SW ... 45 J35
DR SW ... 45 K34
GT SW, HTS SW ... 45 J35
MS SW ... 45 J34
PL SW 100 ... 45 J35
200, 300 ... 45 K35
ASPEN VISTA PL SW 100 . 45 K34
200 ... 45 K34
RD SW ... 45 K35
WY SW ... 45 L35
ASSINIBOINE RD SE ... 75 AI53
ASTER PL (AIR) ... 113 E3
ASTORIA CR SE ... 75 AH54
ATHABASCA AV (CRS) ... 8 F1
ST SE ... 75 AH51
ST (CRS) ... 8 F2
ATHENS RD SE ... 75 AI54
ATHLONE RD SE ... 75 AH52
ATLANTA CR SE ... 75 AG53
ATLAS DR SE ... 75 AH51
ATTICA DR SE ... 68 AH50
AUBURN RD SE ... 75 AJ53
AURORA DR (H RV) ... 109 E4
PL SE ... 75 AI52
AUSTIN RD SE ... 75 AH54
AVALON RD SE ... 75 AG54
AVERY PL SE ... 75 AI53
AVIATION BLVD NE ... 41 AK22
PK NE ... 29 AK21
PL NE ... 41 AL21
RD NE ... 41 AL22
WY NE ... 29 AL21
AVONBURN RD SE ... 75 AF51
AVONLEA PL SE ... 75 AI52

B

BAGOT AV SW 59 AB37
BAILEY RIDGE CL *(T VAL)* 105 C7
PL *(T VAL)* 105 C7
BAINES RD NW 26 V21
BAIRD AV *(COCR)* 103 G5
BAKER CR NW 38 W23
RD *(H RV)* 109 B6
BAKER CREEK DR *(H RV)* 109 B6
PL *(H RV)* 109 B6
RS *(H RV)* 109 B5
BALDWIN CR SW 67 AC45
BALSAM AV *(B CK)* 33 G7
DR SW 47 U34
BANDED PEAK PL *(SPNG)* 99 E3
BANFF AV *(BNF)* 21 D6
TR NW 38 X28
BANISTER DR *(OKS)* 107 D4
GT *(OKS)* 107 C4
BANNERMAN DR NW 26 V20
BANNISTER MR SE 91 AF65
RD SE 91 AF63
BANTRY ST NE 51 AK31
BARBERRY WK SW 47 U35
BARCLAY PR SW 50 AF33
ST SW 50 AF34
BARLOW TR NE 30 AQ20
TR NE *(100-1600)* 52 AP32
TR NE *(1600-4800)* 42 AP28
TR NE *(11100-14000)* 17 AP12
TR SE *(700-1000)* 52 AP34
TR SE *(4400-5900)* 61 AP42
TR SE *(6000-8000)* 70 AS46
TR SE *(8100-11800)* 86 AS58
BAROC RD NW 25 P19
BARR RD NW 38 V23
BARRETT DR NW 26 V21
PL NW 26 V20
BARRON CR NW 26 V21
DR NW 26 V21
BATCHELOR CR NW 38 V22
BATTLEFORD AV SW 58 W41
BAY RD *(STMR)* 112 E5
BAY CROFT RD SW 74 Z52
BAY FIELD PL SW 74 Z52
BAY RIDGE DR SW 73 Y51
BAY SHORE RD SW 74 Z52
BAY VIEW DR SW 73 X52
PL SW 73 X52
BAY WOOD PL SW 73 Y52
BAYCREST CT SW 73 Y51
PL SW 73 Y51
BAYLOR CR SW 73 Y52
BAYSIDE AV *(AIR)* 113 B6
GT *(AIR)* 113 C7
PL 100, 200, 300 *(AIR)* 113 C7
400 *(AIR)* 113 B7
PL *(STMR)* 112 E6
PT *(AIR)* 113 C6
RS *(AIR)* 113 C6
BAYVIEW CR *(STMR)* 112 E5
RD *(STMR)* 112 E5
BEACH WY *(H RV)* 109 B5
BEACHAM CL NW 15 AB14
RD NW, RS NW 15 AB14
WY NW 15 AB14
BEACON HEIGHTS
RD *(BSKR)* 111 D3
BEACONSFIELD CL NW 15 AA13
CR NW 15 AA14
GT NW 15 AA13
PL NW, RD NW 15 AA14
RS NW 15 AA14
WY NW 15 Z14
BEAR ST *(BNF)* 21 C6
BEARBERRY BY NW 15 AB13
CL NW, CR NW, PL NW 15 AB13
BEARSPAW DR NW 26 V21
BEARSPAW DAM
RD NW *(8600-9600)* 23 H20
RD NW *(9700-11400)* 34 D20
BEAUPRE CR NW 35 L24
BEAVER PL *(BSKR)* 111 E2
RD NW 26 U20
ST *(BNF)* 21 D5
BEAVER DAM PL NE 28 AG19
RD NE 28 AI21
WY NE 28 AG19
BEDDINGTON BLVD NE 28 AF15
BLVD NW 15 AD14
CIR NE, CR NE, DR NE 16 AF14
GDN NE 16 AF14
GN NE, PL NE 16 AG14
RD NE, RS NE 16 AF14
TR NE 16 AF13
TR NW 15 AC11, 4 AA8
WY NE 16 AF14
BEDFIELD CL NE 28 AH15
CT NE 100 28 AI15
200 28 AH15
GT NE 28 AH15
BEDFORD CIR NE 16 AG14
DR NE 16 AG14
MR NE 16 AH14
PL NE 100, 200 16 AG14
300 16 AH14
RD NE 16 AH14
ST SW 67 AC45
BEDRIDGE PL NE 28 AF15
RD NE, WY NE 28 AF15
BEDWOOD BY NE 28 AG15
CR NE 16 AG14
HL NE 28 AG15
PL NE 16 AG14
RD NE, RS NE 28 AG15
BEIL AV NW 38 W23
BEIRUT DR SW 66 W45
BEL-AIRE DR SW 67 AC45
PL SW 67 AB45
BELAVISTA CR SW 67 AC45
BELL ST NW 38 W24
ST SW 57 S43
BELLEVUE AV SE 51 AJ36
BELVEDERE RD SW 67 AB46
BENCHLANDS DR *(COCR)* 103 G5
PL *(COCR)* 103 G5
TER 100 *(CAN)* 101 F4
200 *(CAN)* 101 E4
TR *(CAN)* 101 E4
BENCROFT PL *(COCR)* 103 G5
BENNETT CR NW 38 W23
BENSON RD NW 38 V22
BENT TREE CT *(EV)* 115 D8
CT *(EV)* 115 D8
BENTLEY PL *(COCR)* 103 G5
BENTON DR NW 26 U20
BERGEN CR NW 15 AE14
PL NW, RD NW 15 AE14
BERKLEY CL NW 15 AD14
CR NW 15 AD15
CT NW 15 AD14
DR NW 15 AA13
GT NW 15 AA15
PL NW 15 AE15
RD NW 15 AD14
RS NW 15 AD15
WY NW 15 AC14
BERKSHIRE BLVD NW 15 Z13
CL NW, CT NW 15 AC13
MS NW 15 AC13
PL NW 100, 200 15 AD13
300 15 AD12
RD NW 15 AC12
BERMONDSEY CR NW 15 AB15
CT NW 15 AB15
PL NW 26 V15
RD NW 15 AC14
RS NW 15 AC15
WY NW 15 AB15
BERMUDA CL NW 15 AD14
CT NW 15 AD14
DR NW 15 AC13
GT NW 15 AE14
LN NW 15 AE13
PL NW 15 AD13
RD NW 15 AD14
WY NW 15 AE14
BERNARD CL NW 15 AE13
CT NW, DR NW 15 AD13
MS NW 100, 200 15 AE12
300, 400, 500 15 AD12
PL NW 15 AD13
RD NW, WY NW 15 AD12
BERWICK CL NW 15 AC14
CR NW 15 AC13
CT NW 15 AC14
DR NW 15 AB14
HL NW, PL NW 15 AC14
RD NW 15 AC14
RS NW, WY NW 15 AC14
BEVERLEY BLVD SW 67 AC46
PL SW 67 AB46
BIG HILL CIR *(AIR)* 113 F5
GT *(AIR)* 113 F5
PL 100, 200 *(AIR)* 113 F5
RD *(AIR)* 113 F5
RD *(COCR)* 103 G3
WY *(AIR)* 113 F5
BIG HORN ST *(BNF)* 21 C5
BIG ROCK GT *(OKS)* 107 B7
LN, RD *(OKS)* 107 B7
TR *(OKS)* 107 A7
BIG SPRINGS CR *(AIR)* 113 F6
CT 200, 300 *(AIR)* 113 F5
DR *(AIR)* 113 F6
GN, HL *(AIR)* 113 G5
MS *(AIR)* 113 G6
RD *(AIR)* 113 A7
RS *(AIR)* 113 G6
WY *(AIR)* 113 F5
BILLY HAYNES TR *(OKS)* 107 G4
BIRCH AV *(BNF)* 21 C7
CR SE 61 AQ37
DR *(BNF)* 21 C7
BIRCHWOOD PL *(CAN)* 101 C3
BISON PH SE 51 AJ36
BLACK ROCK CR *(CAN)* 101 E4
BLACKBURN RD SE 60 AH40
BLACKFOOT TR SE 51 AJ36
TR SE *(2200-6200)* 68 AI44
TR SE *(6500-9800)* 68 AH48
BLACKLOCK WY *(T VAL)* 105 A5
BLACKTHORN BY NE 28 AH19
CR NE, GN NE 28 AH19
PL NE 28 AH20
RD NE 28 AG19
RD NW 28 AF19
BLAKISTON DR NW 38 V24
BLOW ST NW 38 V23
BLUE GROUSE RDG *(CAN)* 101 E3
BONAVENTURE
DR SE *(8300-9800)* 75 AF53
DR SE *(9900-13600)* 75 AF55
BONITA CR NW 36 M25
BONNYBROOK PL SE 61 AL38
RD SE 61 AL38
BOOTH CR *(IRR)* 111 B3
BOTSFORD ST *(LNG)* 88 C8
BOULDER CR *(CAN)* 101 F6
BOULTON RD NW 38 U22
BOW AV *(BNF)* 21 C6
CL *(COCR)* 103 C5
CR NW 36 M22
CT *(COCR)* 103 C5
LD NW 36 P26
PL *(COCR)* 103 C5
PT *(COCR)* 103 C5
ST *(COCR)* 103 F5
TR SW *(1700-3700)* 47 U35
TR SW *(3800-5600)* 46 O33
WY *(COCR)* 103 C5
BOW ANNE RD NW 36 N24
BOW BOTTOM TR SE 83 AK60
TR SE *(13000-15900)* 84 AL62
BOW FALLS DR *(BNF)* 21 D8
BOW GREEN CR NW 35 L22
BOW MEADOWS
CR *(CAN)* 101 G6
DR *(COCR)* 103 C5
BOW RIDGE CL *(COCR)* 103 A5
CR *(COCR)* 103 A5
CT 100, 200 *(COCR)* 103 B5
DR, LK, LN *(COCR)* 103 A5
RD *(COCR)* 103 A5
BOW VALLEY DR NE 51 AJ33
LN NE 51 AK33
TR *(CAN)* 101 D3
BOW VILLAGE CR NW 35 L22
BOWBANK CR NW 37 Q25
BOWCLIFFE CR NW 35 K25
BOWCROFT PL *(COCR)* 103 G5
BOWDALE CR NW 36 N27
BOWER ST *(AIR)* 113 E3
BOWFORT RD NW 35 J25
RD SW 35 J25
BOWGLEN CR NW 35 K23
RD NW 35 K23
BOWLAKE PL NW 35 K24
BOWLEN ST NW 38 W23
BOWMANTEN PL NW 35 L25
BOWMONT CR NW 36 O26
BOWNESS CTR NW 35 L23
RD NW *(1600-2400)* 48 Y33
RD NW *(3700-6700)* 36 N24
RD NW *(6800-8500)* 35 J23
BOWRIDGE CR NW 35 K25
DR NW 35 J24
BOWVIEW RD NW 36 O26
BOWWATER CR NW 36 P25
BOWWOOD DR NW 36 N24
BOYCE CR NW 49 AB30
BRABOURNE MS SW 73 Y56
RD SW, RS SW 73 Y56
BRACEBRIDGE CR SW 74 AA55
BRACEWOOD CR SW 74 Z57
DR SW, PL SW, RD SW 73 Y57
RS SW, WY SW 73 Y57
BRACKEN PT *(B CK)* 33 F7
RD *(B CK)* 33 E8
BRACKENRIDGE RD SW 74 AA55
BRADBURY DR SW 74 AA55
BRADEN CR NW 38 V23
BRADFORD ST SW 74 AA56
BRADLEY AV SW 74 AA55
BRAE PL SW 74 Z56
RD SW 74 Z56
BRAE GLEN CL SW 74 Z55
CR SW, CT SW, LN SW 74 Z55
RD SW 74 Z55
BRAEMAR PL SW 74 AA55
ST *(SPNG)* 99 E7
BRAEMAR GLEN
RD *(SPNG)* 99 E7
BRAESIDE DR SW 73 X56
PL SW 74 AA55
BRALORNE CR SW 74 AA55
BRAMPTON CR SW 74 AA55
BRANDER AV *(LNG)* 88 B6
BRANDON ST SE 60 AH41
BRANIFF CR SW 74 AA57
GN SW 74 AA57
PL SW 100 74 AA57
200, 300 74 AA56
RD SW 74 AA56
BRANTFORD CR NW 38 X23
DR NW 38 W24
BRATON PL SW 74 AA56
BRAXTON PL SW 100 74 Z56
200 74 AA57
300 74 Z57
RD SW 74 Z56
BRAZEAU CR SW 74 AA56
BRECKEN RD NW 38 W24
BREEN CR NW 38 V22
RD NW 38 V22
BRENNER CR NW 26 U20
DR NW, PL NW 26 U20
BRENT BLVD *(STMR)* 112 D5
BRENTWOOD BLVD NW 38 V23
CR *(STMR)* 112 E5
DR E *(STMR)* 112 F5
DR W *(STMR)* 112 E5
GN NW 38 U23
PL *(STMR)* 112 E5
RD NW 38 V24
BRESKENS DR SW 58 X41
BRETON BY NW 26 V20
CL NW, PL NW 26 V20
BRIAR CR NW 48 Y30
CR *(STMR)* 112 E5
PL *(STMR)* 112 E5
BRIARWOOD CR *(STMR)* 112 E5
RD *(STMR)* 112 E5
BRIDGE CR NE 51 AI31
BRIDGEFIELD CIR *(AIR)* 113 A3
CL *(AIR)* 113 A3
CR, CR *(AIR)* 113 B4
DR *(AIR)* 113 A4
LN *(AIR)* 113 B4
PL 100, 200 *(AIR)* 113 B4
BRIDLECREEK
GN SW 100 90 AB70
200, 300 90 AB70
400 90 AA71
500 90 AA70
GT SW 90 AA70
HE SW 90 AA69
PK SW 90 AB70
TER SW 90 AA70
BRIDLECREST BLVD NE 89 X69
CR NE 89 X68
CT NE 89 X69
DR NE, GDN NE 89 X68
LK NE, MR NE, PL NE 89 X69
RD NE, ST NE, WY NE 89 X69
BRIDLEGLEN LK SW 89 Z69
MR SW, PK SW, RD SW 89 Z68
BRIDLEMEADOWS CM SW 89 Y70
CM SW 100, 200, 300 89 Y70
400 89 Y70
MR SW 89 Y70
1000, 2000 89 Y70
BRIDLEPOST GN SW 89 Z69
BRIDLERIDGE CIR SW 89 Z71
CR SW 89 Z70
CT SW, GDN SW 89 Y70
HTS SW 89 Y69
LK SW 89 Z70
RD SW 89 Y70
VW SW 89 Y69
WY SW 89 Z70
BRIDLEWOOD AV SW 89 Y70
BLVD SW 89 Z68
CIR SW 90 AA68
CL SW 89 Z68
CM SW 89 Z70
CR SW 89 Z69
CT SW 89 Z70
CT SW 100 90 AA69
200 90 AA70
300 89 Z70
400 89 Z71
DR SW 90 AA70
GDN SW 89 Z69
GN SW 90 AA68
GV SW, LK SW 90 AA69
LN SW 100, 200 90 AA70
300 90 AA71
MR SW 89 Z69
PK SW 89 Z70
PL SW 100, 200, 300 90 AA68
400 90 AA69
RD SW 90 AA68
ST SW 89 Z69
VW SW 90 AA70
WY SW 90 AA69
BRIGHTON DR NW 38 X24
BRIGHTONCREST CM SE 97 AX64
CM SE 100 97 AX63
200 97 AY63
CV SE 98 AZ64
GN SE 100, 200 97 AY63
MR SE, PL SE 97 AX63
PT SE 98 AZ63
RS SE, TER SE 97 AY64
BRIGHTONDALE BY SE 97 AX65
CL SE, CR SE, GN SE 97 AX65
PK SE, PR SE 97 AX65
BRIGHTONSTONE BY SE 97 AX64
CM SE 97 AX64
GDN SE, GN SE 97 AW64
GV SE, LD SE, LK SE 97 AX64
PS SE 97 AX64
BRIGHTONWOODS
BY SE 97 AY65
CR SE, GDN SE 97 AY65
GN SE 98 AZ64
GV SE 98 AZ65
BRISEBOIS DR NW 38 V23
BRITANNIA DR SW 59 AC42
LN SW 59 AD41
BROADVIEW RD NW 48 Y33
BROCKINGTON RD NW 26 W22
BROOKGREEN DR SW 73 X55
BROOKLYN CR NW 38 X24

BROOKMERE BY SW 100...74 Z55
200...........74 Z56
CR SW, GDN SW 73 Y55
PL SW, RD SW 74 Z55
BROOKPARK BLVD SW ..73 Y55
BY SW...........73 Y56
CR SW...........73 X55
DR SW, MS SW, PL SW. 73 Y55
RS SW 73 Y55
BROWN CR NW 38 V22
BROWNSEA DR NW 48 Z33
BRUNSWICK AV SW ...59 AE42
BUCKBOARD RD NW ...25 P19
BUCKTHORN CR NW ...28 AF19
RD NW 28 AF21
BUFFALO ST (BNF) 21 B7
BUILDERS RD SE 59 AG42
BULYEA CR NW 38 U22
RD NW 38 V22
BURBANK CR SE 68 AI44
RD SE.........68 AI46
BURGESS DR NW 38 W24
BURLEIGH CR SE 68 AJ44
BURNEY RD (B CK) 33 G8
BURNS AV SE 51 AI36
BURNSIDE DR (B CK) ..33 G7
BURNSLAND RD SE 59 AG41
BURNTALL DR (B CK) ..33 G8
BURROUGHS CIR NE ..44 BB26
MR NE 44 BA26
PL NE 44 BB26
BUTLER CR NW 38 W23
BUTTE PL NW 38 X23
BUTTON RD NW........38 U22

C

CABOT ST SW 59 AB39
CADOGAN RD NW......39 AB25
CAEN AV SW 58 W41
CAFFARO CT (CAN)....101 G9
CALAIS AV SW 58 W41
CALANDAR RD NW 39 AAA24
CALIFORNIA BLVD NE ..44 BA28
PL NE 100, 200......44 BA27
300, 400 ....44 BA27
CALKINS PL (T VAL) ...105 C6
CALLA DONNA PL SW . 67 AC49
CAMARA CT (STMR)...112 G5
CAMBRAI AV SW 58 Y41
CAMBRIA PL (STMR) ...112 F6
RD (STMR) 112 F6
CAMBRIAN DR NW 39 AB25
CAMBRIDGE BY (STMR). 112 F5
CR (STMR) 112 F5
PL NW 40 AD26
PL (STMR) 112 F5
RD NW 39 AC26
CAMBRIDGE GLEN
DR (STMR) 112 F6
CAMBRILLE CR (STMR) . 112 G5
CAMDEN PL (STMR)....112 G5
CAMERON AV SW 49 AB36
CAMPUS DR NW 38 W26
GT NW 38 W27
PL NW 100........38 W27
400, 500, 600 .. 38 W26
700 ....38 W26
800..........38 V26
CANADA OLYMPIC DR SW 35 H24
GN SW, LN SW, RD SW 35 H25
VW SW 35 J27
CANALS BLVD (AIR) 113 B4
CIR (AIR) 113 C4
DR (AIR) 113 B4
CANATA CL SW 82 AC59
CANAVERAL CR SW ...82 AD59
RD SW 82 AD58
CANBERRA PL NW 39 Z25
RD NW........39 Z25
CANDIAC RD SW 82 AE58
CANDLE CR SW 82 AC60
CT SW 82 AC61
PL SW 100 ....82 AC60
200 ....82 AC61
300, 400 .....82 AC60
TER SW 82 AC60
CANFIELD CR SW 82 AD58
GN SW 82 AE58
PL SW 82 AE59
RD SW 74 AE57
WY SW 82 AD58
CANFORD CR SW 82 AD58
PL SW........82 AD58
CANMORE RD NW 38 Y26
CANNA BY SW........82 AD59
CR SW 82 AD59
CANNELL PL SW 82 AC60
200 ....82 AD60
RD SW 82 AD60
CANNES RD SW 82 AD59
CANNIFF PL SW 100 ...82 AE61
200, 300 ....82 AE61
CANNINGTON
CL SW 400 ....82 AD61

PL SW 100, 200, 300 .. 82 AD60
WY SW 82 AD60
CANNOCK PL SW 82 AD59
RD SW........82 AC59
CANNON RD NW 26 X22
CANOE CIR (AIR) 113 B3
CL (AIR) 113 C3
CR (AIR) 113 B4
CV, DR, GT (AIR) ... 113 C4
PL 100 (AIR) 113 B3
200 (AIR) 113 C3
RD, SQ (AIR) 113 C3
SQ 100, 200 (AIR) .. 113 C3
CANOVA CL SW.......82 AB58
200, 300 ......82 AB59
PL SW 100, 200 .....82 AB59
RD SW 82 AB59
CANSO BY SW 82 AB60
CT SW 82 AC60
GN SW, PL SW......82 AC60
CANTABRIAN DR SW .. 82 AC58
CANTER PL SW 100 ...82 AB58
200, 300 ......82 AB58
CANTERBURY CT SW .. 82 AC60
CT SW 100 ......82 AC59
200 ....82 AC60
DR SW 82 AC58
GDN SW 82 AD61
PL SW 100, 200, 300 .. 82 AC58
400 ......82 AC58
500 ......82 AC59
CANTERVILLE BY SW .. 82 AB59
DR SW, RD SW .. 82 AB59
CANTREE BY SW 100 . 82 AE60
200 ....82 AE60
PL SW, RD SW 82 AE60
CANTRELL BY SW 82 AE61
DR SW 82 AE59
PL SW 100, 200, 300 .. 82 AE59
400 ......82 AE60
500, 600, 700 . 82 AE61
800 ....82 AE61
CANYON CL (CAN) 101 G5
DR NW........39 Z24
PL (CAN) 101 G5
RD (CAN) 101 G5
CANYON MEADOWS
DR SE 83 AF62
DR SW 82 AB60
CAPILANO CR NW 39 Y23
CAPITOL HILL
CR NW (2200-2400) ... 38 Y28
CR NW (2600-3300) .. 38 X26
CAPRI AV NW 26 W22
CR NW 26 X22
CARDELL ST NE 51 AK32
CARDIFF DR NW 39 AC25
PL NW........39 AC25
CARDSTON CR NW 39 Z25
CARIBOU DR NW 39 Y25
ST (BNF) 21 C6
CARLETON ST SW 59 AC38
CARLSON TR (COCR) .. 103 E2
CARLYLE RD SW 67 AB49
CARMANGAY CR NW .. 39 Z24
CARMEL CL NE.......44 AZ24
PL NE 44 BA24
CARNARVON WY NW .. 39 AB24
CARNEY RD NW 26 W21
CAROL DR NW 39 AA26
CAROLINA CR (COCR) .. 103 G5
DR (COCR) 103 G5
PL 100, 200 (OKS) 107 D4
CARRAGANA CR NW... 38 X23
CARRIAGE LN (SPNG).. 99 E2
CARTIER ST SW 59 AC38
CASALE PL (CAN) 101 G9
ST SW 65 S45
CASCADE CT (BNF)....21 D8
PL (COCR) 103 D5
RD NW 38 X26
CASSON GN NW 37 T26
CASTLE PL (COCR) 103 D5
RD NW 38 X26
CASTLEBROOK CT NE . 31 AV20
DR NE 31 AV19
MS NE 31 AU20
PL NE 31 AU20
RD NE, RS NE 31 AU20
WY NE 31 AV19
CASTLEBURY CT NE ... 31 AV20
RD NE, WY NE 31 AV20
CASTLEDALE CR NE ... 31 AV19
GT NE, PL NE, WY NE 31 AV19
CASTLEFALL CR NE 31 AW20
GV NE 31 AW21
RD NE, WY NE 31 AV21
CASTLEGLEN CR NE ... 31 AW20
CT NE, PL NE, RD NE . 31 AW20
WY NE 31 AW19
CASTLEGREEN CL NE .. 31 AW19
CASTLEGROVE PL NE .. 31 AW19
RD NE, WY NE 31 AW19
CASTLEPARK RD NE .. 31 AW19
WY NE 31 AX19
CASTLERIDGE BLVD NE . 31 AU20
CL NE........31 AW19
CR NE 31 AX19

DR NE 31 AV19
RD NE, WY NE 31 AX19
CATALINA BLVD NE ... 44 BA27
CIR NE........44 AZ23
PL NE 100, 200......44 BA27
CATARACT RD (H RV) .. 109 B5
CATHEDRAL RD NW .. 38 X26
CAVANAUGH PL NW .. 39 AB24
CAVE AV (BNF) 21 B7
CAVENDISH BEACH
BY (CHST) 80 B7
CAWDER DR NW 39 AA25
CAYUGA CR NW 39 Z23
DR NW 39 Z23
CEDAR CR SW 47 V33
WY NW 35 H23
CEDAR RIDGE CR SW .. 73 W55
DR SW 73 V55
PL SW 73 W55
CEDAR SPRINGS GDN SW 73 X56
CEDARBRAE CR SW ... 73 W55
DR SW 73 V56
CEDARBROOK BY SW 100 73 X56
200 ....73 W56
CL SW 73 W55
PL SW 73 W56
WY SW........73 W56
CEDARDALE BY SW 100 . 73 U56
200 ....73 V57
CR SW 73 V57
HL SW 73 U57
MS SW 73 U57
PL SW 100 ......73 U55
200, 300 ... 73 U55
RD SW 73 V57
RS SW 73 V57
CEDARGROVE CT SW 100 73 W57
200 ....73 W57
LN SW........73 X57
PL SW, RD SW, WY SW 73 V57
CEDARILLE CR SW 73 U55
DR SW 73 U55
GN SW........73 U55
PL SW 73 V55
WY SW 73 U54
CEDARPARK DR SW ... 73 V55
GN SW........73 X55
GT SW 73 W55
CEDARVIEW MS SW ... 73 X55
CEDARWOOD DR SW... 73 V56
HL SW, MS SW 73 V56
PK SW 100, 200 .....73 V56
PL SW 73 V56
RS SW 73 V56
CEDUNA LN SW 73 X56
PK SW 73 W56
CELTIC RD NW........39 AC25
CEMETERY RD SE 60 AH39
RD (IRR) 111 B4
CENTRE AV E 52 AN33
AV NE 51 AJ33
AV (AIR) 113 E3
AV (B DMD) 106 G2
AV (B CK) 33 E7
AV (COCR) 103 F4
AV (H RV) 109 E4
AV (OKS) 107 C5
CR NW 28 AG21
CT (OKS)........107 C5
ST N (600-3200) 50 AG31
ST N (3300-6300) .. 40 AG25
ST N (6400-8400) ... 15 AE15
ST N (14400) 5 AE6
ST S (200-1500) 50 AG34
ST S (5900-6600) ... 67 AG46
ST SW 59 AF43
ST N (H RV) 109 D3
ST S (H RV) 109 D5
ST (LNG) 88 C8
ST (STMR) 112 E7
CENTRE A
ST NE (1400-1600) .. 40 AG29
ST NE (3300-4400) .. 40 AG25
ST NW 50 AG31
CENTRE B
ST NW (1400-1500) .. 40 AG29
ST NW (3300-4000) .. 40 AG25
CENTURY GT SE 52 AP34
CHALICE RD NW 26 W21
CHAMPLAIN ST SW ... 59 AC39
CHANCELLOR WY NW . 39 AC24
CHANDLER RD NW 26 W21
CHAPALA BY SE......93 AL73
CL SE 93 AK74
CR SE, CT SE, DR SE . 93 AL73
GT SE, GV SE 93 AK74
HE SE, LE SE 93 AL73
RD SE, SQ SE, TER SE 93 AK74
WY SE 93 AL74
CHAPALINA CL SE 93 AI73
CR SE 93 AI73
GN SE, HE SE, HTS SE 93 AJ74
LK SE........93 AJ74
MR SE 93 AI72
PL SE 100, 200 .....93 AJ74
RS SE, TER SE 93 AJ74
WY SE 93 AI72
CHAPALINA PARK CR SE . 93 AI73
CHAPARRAL BLVD SE .. 93 AL72

BY SE, CIR SE........93 AJ72
CL SE.........93 AJ73
CM SE 93 AJ72
CR SE 93 AK72
CT SE 100, 200.......93 AK72
CV SE 93 AJ73
DR SE 93 AJ72
GN SE 93 AL72
GV SE, HE SE 93 AJ73
LK SE.........93 AJ73
MR SE 93 AJ73
MS SE 93 AJ73
PK SE 93 AJ72
PL SE 100, 200, 300 .. 93 AK72
PT SE 93 AK72
RD SE 93 AL73
ST SE 93 AL73
TER SE 93 AJ72
VL SE.........93 AJ73
WY SE.........93 AL73
CHAPARRAL RIDGE
BY SE 100 ......94 AM72
CIR SE, DR SE, LK SE . 94 AM72
PT SE 100 ......94 AM72
200, 300 ... 94 AM73
TER SE 94 AM73
WY SE 94 AM72
CHAPEL RD NW 26 Y22
CHAPMAN CIR SE 93 AL74
CL SE, CT SE, HE SE . 93 AL74
LK SE, MS SE, PL SE . 93 AL74
RD SE, TER SE 93 AL73
WY SE 93 AL74
CHARDIE PL SW 67 AB49
RD SW 67 AB49
CHARLEBOIS DR NW .. 38 X25
CHARLES AV SW 59 AC42
CHARLESWOOD CR NW . 38 W25
DR NW 38 W25
CHARLESWORTH
AV (COCR) 103 F5
CHATEAU PL NW 38 X25
CHATHAM DR NW 39 Y24
PL NW........39 Y23
CHELSEA ST NW 39 AB26
CHELTENHAM RD NW . 39 AA25
CHEROKEE DR NW.... 38 X25
PL NW 39 Y24
CHEROVAN DR SW ... 67 AC49
CHERRY WY NW 35 H23
CHERRY TREE WK SW . 47 U35
CHESTER PL NW 39 AA26
CHESTERMERE STATION
WY (CHST) 80 B5
CHESTNUT WK SW ... 47 U35
CHEYENNE CR NW.... 39 Y24
CHICOUTIMI DR NW .. 38 X24
CHILCOTIN RD NW 39 Y24
CHILD AV NE 51 AK31
CHILDRENS GT NW ... 37 T27
CHINA CL (CAN)......101 B5
CHINIKI DR (COCR) ... 103 E3
CHINOOK DR SW..... 67 AC50
DR (COCR) 103 E3
PL (BSKR) 111 E2
RD (BSKR) 111 E2
CHINOOK ARCH LN (SPNG) 99 D4
CHIPPENDALE DR NW .. 39 Y25
CHIPPEWA RD NW 39 Y23
CHISHOLM AV (CRS) ...8 G2
CR NW 39 Y24
CHRISTIE GDN SW 46 P35
PT SW 46 O36
RD NW 39 O36
CHRISTIE BRIAR GN SW . 46 N36
HE SW, LN SW, MR SW 46 N36
ROW SW.......46 N36
CHRISTIE CAIRN HE SW . 46 O36
GV SW 46 O36
CHRISTIE ESTATE
BLVD SW 46 N35
GDN SW 46 O35
GV SW, HE SW 46 O36
MR SW 46 O35
TER SW 46 O35
CHRISTIE KNOLL GN SW . 46 N35
HTS SW¹ 46 N35
PT SW 100, 200, 300 .. 46 N35
400 ......46 N35
CHRISTIE PARK
GN SW 100 ......46 P36
200 ....46 O36
GT SW, HL SW.......46 O36
MR SW 46 P36
MS SW 100 ......46 P36
200, 300 ... 46 P35
TER SW 46 P35
VW SW........46 O36
CHURCHILL DR SW ... 67 AB50
CIMARRON BLVD (OKS) . 107 D8
BY, CIR, CL (OKS) ... 107 D8
CM (OKS)........107 C9
CR (OKS) 107 D8
CT (OKS) 107 D7
DR (OKS) 107 D7
HL (OKS) 107 D7
PT (OKS) 107 D8
RS (OKS) 107 D9
TR (OKS) 107 D7
WY (OKS) 107 D7

CIMARRON GROVE
CR *(OKS)* **107** D9
CIMARRON MEADOWS
BY *(OKS)* **107** C8
CL, CR *(OKS)* **107** C8
LK *(OKS)* **107** D8
RD *(OKS)* **107** D8
WY *(OKS)* **107** D8
CIMARRON PARK
BY *(OKS)* **107** D9
CL *(OKS)* **107** D8
PL *(OKS)* **107** D9
CITADEL BLVD NW. ... **12** P10
BY NW **12** O10
CIR NW **12** P10
CL NW, CT NW **12** P11
DR NW **12** O9
GDN NW **12** P11
GN NW **13** Q10
GT NW **12** O11
GV NW **13** Q11
HTS NW **12** P11
LK NW **12** N11
LN NW **12** O10
MR NW **12** O11
PK NW **12** O11
PT NW **12** M9
TER NW **12** O11
WY NW **12** M10
CITADEL ACRES CL NW . **11** L10
PL NW **11** L10
CITADEL BLUFF CL NW . **12** M10
CITADEL CREST CIR NW . **12** O10
GN NW, HE NW, LK NW **12** O10
PK NW **12** O9
PL NW **12** O10
CITADEL ESTATES
HTS NW **12** M10
LK NW, MR NW, PL NW **12** M10
TER NW **12** M10
CITADEL FOREST CL NW . **11** L10
LK NW, PL NW **11** L10
CITADEL HILLS CIR NW . **12** P11
GN NW **12** P11
PL NW 100 .... **12** P12
200 .... **12** Q12
300 .... **12** P11
CITADEL MEADOW
BY NW 100, 200 ..... **12** P9
300, 400, 500 .... **12** O9
CL NW. **12** N9
CR NW **12** O9
CT NW **12** P9
GDN NW **12** N9
GV NW **12** P9
PT NW **12** N9
CITADEL MESA CL NW .. **12** M9
CITADEL PASS CR NW .. **12** O11
CT NW 100, 200 ..... **12** O11
CITADEL PEAK CIR NW .. **12** P10
MS NW **12** P10
CITADEL RIDGE CL NW .. **12** N10
GN NW, PK NW, PL NW **12** N10
CITADEL VISTA CL NW .. **11** L10
GN NW **11** L10
CITY WORKS RD SW **56** P42
CLARENDON RD NW .. **39** AA24
CLARET ST NW. **26** X22
CLARK AV *(OKS)* **107** C6
CLARKE RD SW **67** AC50
CLATTER ST NW. **39** AB25
CLEAR MOUNTAIN
RS *(SPNG)* **99** G4
CLEARWATER CV *(EV)* . **115** E7
DR *(EV)* **115** E8
LD *(EV)* **115** E7
RUN, WY *(EV)* **115** E8
CLEVELAND CR SE **60** AH41
CLIFF ST SW. **59** AE37
CLIFFE AV SW **59** AE41
COACH CR NW **46** N31
COACH BLUFF CR SW ... **46** N31
COACH GATE CT SW **46** P32
PL SW, WY SW. **46** P32
COACH GROVE PL SW 100 **46** O32
200, 300 .... **46** O32
RD SW **46** O32
COACH HILL RD SW ... **46** N31
COACH LIGHT BY SW 100 **46** O32
200, 300, 400 .... **46** O32
500 .... **46** O32
COACH MANOR RS SW... **46** P32
TER SW **46** P32
COACH RIDGE CR NW .. **46** N32
CL SW, PL SW, RD SW . **46** N32
RS SW. **46** N32
COACH SIDE CR SW **46** O31
PL SW **46** O31
RD SW, TER SW. **46** O31
COACHWAY GDN SW ... **46** N31
GN SW **46** N31
LN SW 100, 200, 300 .. **46** N31
RD SW **46** N31
COACHWOOD CR SW ... **46** O32
PL SW **46** O32
COCHRANE CR *(COCR)* . **103** E4
RD NW **38** Y26
COLBORNE CR SW **59** AB37
COLEMAN RD NW. **26** W21
COLERIDGE CR NW... **39** AB24

RD NW **39** AB24
COLGROVE AV NE **51** AK31
COLLEEN AV SW **67** AB50
CR SW **67** AC50
COLLEGE LN SW **49** AD36
COLLEGIATE BLVD NW .. **38** U26
CT NW, CV NW **38** U26
PL NW **38** V26
PL NW 100, 300 ..... **38** V26
RD NW **38** U27
COLLICUTT ST SW **67** AB49
COLLINGWOOD DR NW .. **39** Z26
PL NW **39** AA24
COLLINS CR *(CRS)*. **8** F2
COLONEL BAKER PL NE . **51** LK33
COLUMBIA PL NW **39** Z24
COLWELL ST *(LNG)* **88** D8
COMANCHE RD NW ... **39** AA24
COMMERCE ST NW ... **39** AB25
COMMERCIAL CT *(SPNG)* . **99** C1
DR *(SPNG)* **99** C1
COMMUNITY WY *(OKS)* . **107** C6
COMPOUND RD *(BNF)* .. **21** F2
CONFEDERATION VL NW **39** AA25
CONGO CR SW **66** W45
RD NW **66** W45
CONNAUGHT DR NW .. **39** AB24
CONRAD CR NW **26** W21
DR NW **26** W21
PL *(SPNG)* **99** F4
CONSTABLE PL NW .. **39** AA26
RD NW **39** AA26
CONSTANCE AV SE **51** AI37
CONVENTION WY *(COCR)* **103** D1
COOPER'S BY *(AIR)* **113** C7
CIR *(AIR)* **113** C7
CL, DR, HL *(AIR)* ... **113** D7
HTS, LD *(AIR)* **113** D7
MR *(AIR)* **113** C7
PK, TER *(AIR)* **113** D7
COOPER'S CROSSING
GT *(AIR)* **113** D7
LK *(AIR)* **113** D7
COPELAND AV *(LNG)* .. **88** B7
COPITHORNE RD NW .. **39** AA25
COPPERFIELD BLVD SE. . **97** AY67
CL SE **97** AY67
CM SE **97** AZ67
CR SE, GDN SE **97** AY67
GDN SE 100, 200, 300. **97** AX67
GN SE 100, 200 ..... **97** AY66
GT SE **97** AX67
GV SE **98** AZ67
GV SE 100 .... **98** AZ68
200, 300 .... **98** AZ67
HTS SE **97** AX66
LK SE **97** AY66
LN SE **97** AY68
MR SE **98** AZ67
MR SE 100 .... **97** AY66
200 .... **98** AZ67
MS SE 100 .... **97** AY67
200 .... **97** AY68
RS SE **97** AY66
TER SE **97** AY67
COPPERSTONE GT SE. . **98** AZ66
GV SE **98** BA67
GV SE 100, 200, 300 .. **98** BA67
MS SE, PL SE, ST SE . **98** AZ66
CORAL CV NE. **32** BA21
CORAL KEYS CT NE. ... **32** BA19
CT NE 100, 200 ..... **32** AZ19
DR NE **32** BA19
NE 100, 200 .... **32** BA19
PL NE 200, 300, 400. . **32** BA20
VL NE **32** AZ20
VL NE 100, 200 ..... **32** BA20
300 .... **32** AZ20
400 .... **32** BA20
500 .... **32** AZ20
CORAL REEF BY NE **32** BB19
CL NE, CR NE, LK NE . **32** BB19
MR NE 200, 300 .... **32** BB19
CORAL SANDS CT NE .. **32** BB21
PL NE **32** BA21
PL NE 100 .... **44** AZ22
200 .... **44** BA22
TER NE **32** BA21
TER NE 100 .... **44** BA22
200 .... **32** BA21
300 .... **32** BB21
CORAL SHORES
BY NE 100 .... **32** BA21
200 .... **32** BB20
CAPE NE **32** BB20
CAPE NE 100 .... **32** BA20
200 .... **32** BB20
CT NE 100, 200 ..... **32** BA20
CV NE, DR NE **32** BA21
LD NE **32** BA20
LD NE 100, 200 ..... **32** BA20
CORAL SPRINGS
BLVD NE. **32** BA21
BY NE, CIR NE **32** AZ19
CL NE, CT NE **32** BA19
GDN NE **32** BB20
GN NE **32** BA19
GV NE **32** BB20
LD NE **32** BB21

LD NE 100 .... **32** BA21
200 .... **32** BB21
MS NE 100, 200 ..... **32** BA19
PK NE **32** BB20
PL NE 100, 200, 300 .. **32** BB21
400 .... **32** BB20
CORNELL PL NW **39** AB25
RD NW **39** AB25
CORNWALLIS DR NW .. **39** AB24
CORONADO PL NE **44** BA27
CORONATION DR SW.. **59** AC42
CORTINA BY SW 100.. ... **55** I37
200 .... **55** H37
CT SW **55** H37
DR SW **45** H36
WY SW **55** H37
COSGROVE ST NW **26** Y22
COSTA MESA CL NE ... **44** AZ24
PL NE **44** AZ24
COSTELLO BLVD SW ... **46** P36
COTTAGE ST NW. **39** AC23
COTTONWOOD CR SE . **62** AR37
ST NW. **35** H23
COUGAR CT *(CAN)* ... **101** F5
PL *(BNF)* **21** D4
ST *(BNF)* **21** D4
COUGAR CREEK DR *(CAN)* **101** F5
COUGAR PLATEAU
CIR SW **35** K28
GT SW **35** J28
MS SW 100. .... **35** K28
200 .... **35** K29
PL SW **35** K28
PT SW **35** K27
WY SW **35** K28
COUGAR POINT RD *(CAN)* **101** E4
COUGAR RIDGE BY SW . **35** L28
CIR SW **35** K29
CR SW **35** K28
CT SW **35** L29
DR SW **35** I28
GT SW **35** J28
HTS SW **35** L28
LK SW **35** K29
MS SW **35** L29
VW SW **35** K28
COUGARSTONE BY SW. . **35** J28
CIR SW **35** J28
CL SW **35** H29
CM SW **35** H28
CR SW **35** H28
CT SW **35** H28
CV SW **35** I28
GDN SW 100 .... **35** J29
200 .... **35** J28
GT SW, GV SW **35** I28
LK SW **35** J28
MR SW **35** H27
MS SW **35** I27
PK SW **35** I28
PL SW, SQ SW. **35** I29
TER SW **35** I27
VL SW **35** J28
WY SW **35** I28
COULEE LN SW **36** M28
PK SW **36** M29
RDG *(EV)* **115** F9
VW SW **36** M29
COUNCIL WY SW **59** AB39
COUNTRY HILLS BLVD NE . **5** AF8
BLVD NW **10** I8
BLVD NW *(100-2900)* . **15** AC10
BLVD NW *(3000-8000)* . **11** L10
BY NW **15** AC10
CIR NW 1000, 2000 .. **16** AF10
CL NW **15** AC11
CR NW **16** AF10
CT NW 100, 200. .... **15** AD11
300, 400, 500 .... **15** AC11
600, 700, 800 .... **15** AC11
CV NW **15** AE10
DR NW **15** AE10
GDN NW, GN NW ... **15** AD10
GT NW **15** AE10
GV NW **16** AF9
HTS NW **15** AE11
LD NW **16** AF9
LK NW **15** AC10
MR NW **15** AF9
MS NW **16** AF9
PK NW **15** AC10
PL NW 100 .... **16** AF10
200, 300, 400 .... **16** AF9
RD NW **16** AF9
RS NW **16** AF9
SQ NW **5** AE9
TER NW, VL NW. **16** AF9
VW NW. **15** AD10
WY NW **16** AF9
COUNTRY VILLAGE BY NE. **6** AH7
CAPE NE 100, 200, 300. . **6** AH7
400 .... **6** AH7
CIR NE **6** AH7
CV NE **5** AG8
LD NE **6** AH7
LK NE **5** AF7
RD NE **5** AF6
WY NE. **5** AF7
COVE BY *(CHST)* **80** C5
CR *(CHST)* **80** C4

CT 100, 200 *(CHST)* **80** C4
DR *(CHST)* **80** C5
LD *(CHST)* **80** B5
LK *(CHST)* **80** C4
PL *(CHST)* **80** C5
PT 100, 200 *(CHST)* .. **80** C5
RD *(CHST)* **80** C5
COVEBROOK CL NE **5** AG4
GN NE, GT NE, PL NE . **6** AH4
COVECREEK CL NE **6** AH4
GN NE **6** AI4
GT NE. **6** AI3
PL NE **6** AI3
COVEHAVEN CR NE. ... **5** AF6
CT NE. **5** AG6
GDN NE **5** AG5
LK NE **5** AG6
MS NE. **5** AF6
RD NE, RS NE **5** AG6
TER NE **5** AF5
VW NE **5** AG6
COVEMEADOW CL NE .. **5** AG4
CR NE **5** AF4
RD NE. **5** AG4
COVENTRY BLVD NE **6** AJ7
CIR NE **6** AH7
CL NE **6** AI8
CR NE **6** AI7
CT NE 100 .... **6** AI6
200 .... **6** AH6
DR NE. **6** AI7
GDN NE **6** AI6
GN NE **6** AI7
GT NE **6** AJ8
LK NE. **6** AI6
LN NE **6** AJ8
MS NE 100, 200. .... **6** AI8
PL NE 100, 200 ..... **6** AI8
RD NE. **6** AI6
VW NE, WY NE. **6** AH6
COVENTRY HILLS BLVD NE **6** AH6
DR NE **5** AF5
WY NE **5** AH5
COVEPARK CIR NE **6** AI4
CL NE **6** AH5
CR NE **6** AI5
CT NE **6** AI4
DR NE, GN NE, MS NE . **6** AH5
PL NE **6** AH4
RD NE **6** AH4
SQ NE **5** AG5
TER NE **6** AH5
WY NE **6** AH5
COVERDALE CT NE 100 .. **6** AI6
200, 300 .... **6** AI6
PL NE **6** AI7
RD NE **6** AJ7
WY NE **6** AJ7
COVERTON CIR NE **6** AJ5
CL NE, CT NE **6** AJ6
GN NE **6** AJ6
GT NE **6** AJ6
HTS NE **6** AJ4
MS NE. **6** AJ5
COVETTE BY NE. **6** AJ5
GN NE **6** AJ6
COVEWOOD CIR NE **6** AJ5
CL NE **6** AJ5
GN NE **6** AJ4
GT NE **6** AI4
LK NE **6** AI5
MR NE **6** AI5
PK NE, PL NE. **6** AI5
COVILLE BY NE. **6** AI3
CIR NE **6** AJ3
CL NE **6** AI3
CR NE **6** AK4
GDN NE **6** AJ3
GT NE **6** AJ4
SQ NE **6** AJ3
COVINGTON BY NE 100 .. **6** AJ7
200, 300 .... **6** AJ7
CL NE, CT NE **6** AJ6
MS NE. **6** AJ7
PL NE 200 .... **6** AJ7
RD NE, RS NE. **6** AJ7
COWAN ST *(LNG)* **88** B8
COYOTE DR *(BNF)* **21** G4
WY *(CAN)* **101** F5
CRABAPPLE WK SW ... **47** U34
CRAIG RD SW. **67** AB49
CRAMOND CIR SE **96** AT71
CL SE, CR SE, DR SE . **96** AS71
PL SE 100, 200 ..... **96** AS71
CRANBERRY CL SE ... **96** AU73
CR SE, GN SE, WY SE . **96** AT72
CRANFIELD CIR SE **96** AT72
CR SE, GDN SE **96** AS71
GDN SE 100, 200, 300. **96** AS71
400 .... **96** AS72
GN SE **96** AS72
LK SE **96** AT73
MR SE **96** AT73
PK SE **96** AS72
PL SE. **96** AT72
CRANLEIGH BY SE 100 .. **96** AR71
200 .... **96** AR71
CL SE **96** AR71
CM SE **96** AQ72
CT SE **96** AR72

DR SE 96 AQ71
GDN SE 96 AR72
GN SE 96 AQ71
GT SE 96 AR72
HTS SE, MR SE 96 AQ72
MS SE 96 AQ72
PK SE 96 AQ71
PL SE 100 . . . . 96 AR72
    200 . . . . 96 AR73
VW SE 100, 200 . . . . . 96 AQ73
WY SE 96 AQ71
CRANSTON BLVD SE . . 96 AR71
DR SE, PL SE 96 AR72
RD SE 96 AS73
WY SE 96 AR73
CRANWELL CL SE . . . 96 AS72
CR SE 96 AR73
GN SE 100 . . . . 96 AR73
    200 . . . . 96 AS73
LK SE, MR SE 96 AS73
PL SE 96 AR72
CRAWFORD RD NW . . . 26 W21
CREEK GARDENS CL (AIR)113 D1
PL (AIR) 113 D2
CREEK SPRINGS RD (AIR) 113 C1
RS (AIR) 113 C1
CREEKSIDE BY (AIR) . . 113 C1
CRESCENT AV (H RV) . . 109 E5
BLVD SW 59 AD42
DR (BSKR) 111 F3
RD NW 39 AC29
RD E (OKS) 107 D6
RD W (OKS) 107 B5
CRESTBROOK CR SW . 34 A25
PL SW, TER SW 34 A25
CRESTHAVEN BY SW . . 34 B25
PL SW 100, 200, 300 . . 34 B24
    400 . . . . 34 B24
    500 . . . . 34 A24
RS SW, VW SW, WY SW 34 B25
CRESTMONT
BLVD SW, DR SW 34 B25
WY SW 34 B25
CRESTON CR NW 38 X27
CRESTRIDGE GT SW . . 34 B25
HTS SW 34 B25
MS SW 100 . . . . 34 B25
    200 . . . . 34 C25
PL SW 100 . . . . 34 C24
    200 . . . . 34 C25
WY SW 34 C25
CRESTVIEW RD SW . . . 59 AB41
CRESTWOOD RD SE . . 69 AO46
CRILLY CL (LNG) 88 E8
CROCUS CR (COCR) . . 103 E4
RD NW 39 Y23
CROMWELL AV NW . . . 39 AA24
CROOKED POND GN (EV) . 115 F9
WY (EV) 115 F9
CROSS CR SW 67 AC50
CROWCHILD
TR NW (100-3200) . . . 38 X28
TR NW (3300-6900) . . . 25 O19
TR NW (7000-8000) . . . 23 L16
TR NW (8000-11300) . . 22 C11
TR SW (1400-2000) . . . 58 X38
TR SW (6300-6600) . . . 66 X47
CROWFOOT CIR NW . . . 11 K15
CR NW 11 K14
GT NW 100, 200 . . . . . 11 L14
RD NW 11 L15
RS NW 11 J15
TER NW 11 K14
WY NW 11 K15
CROWN AV SW 59 AC42
CROXFORD PL (AIR) . . . 113 D3
CROYDON RD NW 39 AC25
CRYSTAL BEACH
BY (CHST) 80 B8
CRYSTAL GREEN BY (OKS)107 F5
CL, DR (OKS) 107 F3
GV (OKS) 107 G4
MR (OKS) 107 G3
MS (OKS) 107 F3
PL (OKS) 107 F4
PT, PT, RS (OKS) 107 F3
WY (OKS) 107 F3
CRYSTAL RIDGE
CV (STMR) 112 D5
CRYSTAL SHORES
BY (OKS) 107 E3
CR (OKS) 107 E3
CT (OKS) 107 E4
CV (OKS) 107 D3
DR, GN, HL (OKS) 107 E3
HTS, LD (OKS) 107 D3
LN (OKS) 107 D3
MR (OKS) 107 D3
MS (OKS) 107 D3
PL, PT, RD (OKS) 107 E3
VW (OKS) 107 E3
WY (OKS) 107 E3
CRYSTALRIDGE BY (OKS). 107 E4
CL, CR, CT (OKS) 107 E6
DR (OKS) 107 E6
GT, LK, PL (OKS) 107 E5
PT, RS, TER (OKS) . . . 107 E6
VW (OKS) 107 E5
WY (OKS) 107 E5
CULLEN CREEK EST (SPNG)99 F3

CULVER RD NW 39 AA25
CUMBERLAND DR NW . . 39 AC25
CUMMER PL (B CK) . . . 33 F7
CUTHBERT PL NW 39 Z24
CYMRIE ST NW 39 AC24
CYPRUS AV SW 66 W45
CR SW 66 X45
GN SW, VL SW 66 X44

D

DAGGETT ST (OKS) 107 C6
DALARNA BY NW 25 T19
DALBEATTIE GN NW . . . 25 T19
HL NW 25 T19
DALBROOK BY NW 25 Q19
DALCASTLE CL NW . . . 25 Q17
CR NW 25 Q17
CT NW, DR NW, HL NW . 25 P18
LK NW 24 P17
MS NW 100, 200, 300 . . 24 P17
    400, 500 . . . . 25 P18
PL NW 25 Q17
RS NW, WY NW 25 P18
DALCROFT CR NW 25 S18
HL NW 25 R19
DALFORD HL NW 25 R19
RD NW 25 R19
DALGETTY BY NW 100 . . 25 S20
    200 . . . . 25 S20
DR NW, HL NW, PL NW . 25 S20
DALGLEISH BY NW 100 . 25 S19
    200, 300 . . . . 25 S19
RD NW 25 S19
DALHAM CR NW 25 R19
RD NW 25 R18
DALHART HL NW 25 R18
RD NW 25 R19
DALHOUSIE CR NW . . . 25 Q19
DR NW 25 Q19
RD NW 25 Q19
DALHURST CR NW 25 R18
GT NW, PL NW, WY NW 25 S18
DALKEITH HL NW 25 T20
DALLYN ST NW 25 S19
DALMARNOCK CR NW . . 25 T19
GN NW 25 T19
DALMEAD CR NW 25 T19
DALMENY BY NW 100 . . 25 R17
    200, 300 . . . . 25 R17
GT NW, HL NW 25 R17
DALRIDGE HL NW 25 R19
DALROY CR NW 25 T20
DALRYMPLE CR NW . . . 25 R18
GN NW 25 Q18
HL NW 25 Q19
WY NW 25 Q18
DALSBY GT NW 25 S18
RD NW 25 S19
DALTON BY NW 25 T20
DR NW 25 T20
DALWOOD WY NW 25 Q18
DALZELL PL NW 25 T18
DANLOE ST NE 51 AK31
DAQING AV SW 50 AF33
DARTMOUTH RD SE . . . 60 AI39
DAWES RD (FOOT) 93 AL75
DEADHORSE RD (LNG) . . 88 D9
DEER BY SE 84 AO62
PL SE 84 AO62
PL (CAN) 101 B5
ST (BNF) 21 E5
DEER LANE SE 84 AO64
CL SE, PL SE, RD SE . . 84 AO64
DEER PARK PL SE 100 . . 92 AO65
    200 . . . . 92 AO65
    300 . . . . 92 AO64
RD SE 92 AO65
WY SE 92 AO65
DEER RIDGE CL SE . . . 84 AL62
CT SE 84 AN63
DR SE 84 AL62
LN SE 84 AL63
MS SE 84 AM63
WY SE 84 AM64
DEER RIVER CIR SE . . . 84 AO61
GN SE 84 AO60
GT SE 84 AO61
PL SE 100, 200 . . . . . . 84 AO61
DEER RUN BLVD SE . . . 84 AO62
BY SE, CL SE, CR SE . . 92 AO65
DR SE, PL SE 92 AO65
DEER SIDE DR SE 92 AO65
PL SE 100, 200 . . . . . . 92 AO65
    300, 400, 500 . . . . . 92 AP65
    600 . . . . 92 AP65
RD SE 92 AP65
DEERBOW CIR SE 92 AN65
CT SE, GT SE, PL SE . . 92 AN65
DEERBROOK BY SE . . . 92 AP64
CR SE 92 AO64
CT SE 92 AO64
MS SE 92 AO65
PL SE, RD SE 92 AQ64
DEERCLIFF RD SE 84 AN62

DEERCREST CL SE 84 AN62
PL SE, WY SE 84 AN63
DEERCROFT PL SE 100 . 92 AP65
    200, 300 . . . . 92 AP65
WY SE 92 AP65
DEERCROSS PL SE . . . 84 AO63
RD SE, WY SE 84 AO63
DEERFIELD BY SE 84 AM64
CIR SE, CT SE, DR SE . 84 AM64
GDN SE, GN SE 84 AN64
GV SE 84 AN64
MR SE, PL SE 84 AM63
TER SE 84 AN64
VL SE 84 AN64
DEERFOOT TR NE 17 AK10
TR NE 28 AI19, 41 AJ23
TR NE 51 AL29
TR NE 68 AK46, 76 AN57
TR SE 96 AT70
TR SE (100-5000) 52 AO35
TR SE (5900-10300) . . 68 AJ51
TR SE (10000) 75 AK54
TR SE (13000-16700) . . 95 AT69
DEERMEADE BY SE . . . 92 AP64
PL SE, RD SE 92 AP64
DEERMONT CT SE 100 . 84 AN63
    200, 300, 400 . . . . . 84 AN64
    500 . . . . 84 AN64
PL SE, RD SE 84 AM62
DEERMOSS BY SE 84 AO62
CR SE, PL SE 84 AO62
DEERPATH CT SE 100 . . 84 AL63
    500, 600 . . . . 84 AM64
RD SE 84 AM64
DEERPOINT GDN SE . . . 84 AO63
LN SE, RD SE 84 AL63
DEERSAXON CIR SE . . . 84 AN64
GT SE, RD SE 84 AN64
DEERVIEW CT SE 100 . . 84 AO62
    200 . . . . 84 AM63
DR SE, HTS SE 84 AN63
PL SE 84 AN63
TER SE, WY SE 84 AM63
DEERWOOD BY SE 84 AO63
RD SE 84 AO63
DEFORAS CL (H RV) . . . 109 C2
DEKALTA DR (T VAL) . . . 105 C5
DEL MONICA BY NE . . . 44 BA26
PL NE 44 BA26
VL NE 44 BD26
DEL RAY CL NE 44 BB27
CR NE, CT NE 44 BB28
GT NE, PL NE, RD NE . 44 BB27
DEL RIO PL NE 44 AZ27
DENISE RD (B CK) 33 E6
DIAMOND BY SE 100 . . . 84 AL59
    200, 300, 400 . . . . . 84 AL59
    500 . . . . 84 AL59
    600 . . . . 84 AL58
CR SE (B DMD) 106 J3
CT SE 100 . . . . 84 AM58
    200 . . . . 84 AM58
    300, 400 . . . . 84 AM59
    500, 600, 700 . . . . . 84 AN59
    800 . . . . 84 AN59
DR SE 84 AL59
PT SE 100, 200 . . . . . . 84 AM58
TER SE 84 AL58
VW SE 84 AM58
DIAMOND WILLOW
PT (EV) 115 D8
DIEBERT CL (H RV) 109 C5
DIEPPE AV SW 58 W40
DINGMAN CL (T VAL) . . . 105 D5
DISCOVERY DR SW . . . 55 L43
HTS SW 55 L42
PL SW 100, 200 . . . . . 55 L42
    300 . . . . 56 M42
RS SW 55 L43
DISCOVERY RIDGE
BLVD SW 55 K42
BY SW 100, 200 . . . . . 55 H41
    300, 400 . . . . 55 G41
CIR SW 55 H41
CR SW 55 K42
CT SW 55 J42
CV SW 55 J42
GDN SW 55 I41
GN SW 55 I42
GT SW 55 L42
HE SW 55 J42
HL SW 55 I41
HTS SW 55 H41
LD SW 55 J41
LK SW 55 K42
LN SW, MR SW 55 I42
MS SW, MT SW 55 J41
PK SW 55 H40
PL SW 55 H40
PT SW, RD SW, RS SW . 55 K42
TER SW 100, 200 . . . . . 55 H41
VW SW 55 K42
WY SW 55 H40
DISCOVERY VALLEY
CV SW 55 K43
DISCOVERY WOODS
VW SW 55 K41
DOGWOOD CR SE 61 AQ40
WY NW 35 H23

DORCHESTER AV SW . . 59 AC38
DOUGLAS AV (LNG) 88 E7
DOUGLAS GLEN
BLVD SE 76 AO56
BY SE 100, 200 . . . . . . 76 AO57
CIR SE 76 AN55
CL SE 100 . . . . 76 AO57
    200 . . . . 76 AO56
    300, 400 . . . . 76 AN56
CM SE 76 AP57
CR SE 76 AP56
CT SE 76 AP57
CT SE 100, 200 . . . . . . 76 AO57
GDN SE 100 . . . . 76 AO56
    200, 300 . . . . 76 AN56
GN SE 76 AO57
GT SE 76 AN56
GV SE 76 AN56
HE SE 100, 200, 300 . . 76 AN56
HTS SE 76 AN56
MR SE 100, 200 . . . . . 76 AO57
MS SE 76 AO57
PK SE 76 AN56
PL SE 76 AN57
PT SE 100 . . . . 76 AN57
    200 . . . . 76 AN56
    300 . . . . 76 AN57
    400, 500, 600 . . . . . 76 AN56
VW SE 76 AO56
DOUGLAS PARK
BLVD SE 85 AQ60
CL SE, MR SE, PL SE . . 85 AQ60
VW SE 100, 200, 300 . . 85 AR61
    400 . . . . 85 AR60
DOUGLAS RANGE RD SE 85 AQ60
DOUGLAS RIDGE
BLVD SE 86 AS59
CIR SE 86 AS61
CL SE 86 AS59
GN SE 86 AS60
GV SE 86 AT61
LK SE 86 AS61
MS SE 100 . . . . 86 AT60
    200 . . . . 86 AT60
    300, 400 . . . . 86 AS60
PL SE 100 . . . . 86 AS60
    200 . . . . 86 AT60
    300 . . . . 86 AT61
VW SE, WY SE 86 AS61
DOUGLAS SHORE CL SE 85 AP60
DOUGLAS WOODS
BY SE 85 AQ60
CL SE 85 AQ60
CL SE 100 . . . . 85 AQ60
    200 . . . . 85 AP59
    300 . . . . 85 AP59
CT SE 100 . . . . 85 AP59
DR SE 85 AP59
GDN SE 85 AQ59
GV SE 85 AP59
HL SE, HTS SE 85 AP58
LK SE 85 AQ59
MR SE 85 AQ58
MS SE 100, 200 . . . . . 85 AP58
    300, 400 . . . . 85 AS60
    500 . . . . 86 AS60
PK SE 85 AR59
PL SE 100, 200 . . . . . . 85 AP58
    300, 400 . . . . 85 AP58
    500, 600, 700 . . . . . 85 AR59
    800 . . . . 85 AR59
PT SE 100, 200 . . . . . . 85 AQ59
RD SE 86 AS60
RS SE 85 AQ58
TER SE 85 AP58
VW SE 85 AQ59
WY SE 85 AP59
DOUGLASBANK
BY SE 100 . . . . 85 AO58
    200, 300 . . . . 85 AO58
CR SE 84 AO59
CT SE 100, 200 . . . . . . 85 AN58
    300, 400 . . . . 85 AN58
DR SE 85 AO58
GDN SE 85 AP59
GN SE 100, 200 . . . . . 85 AO58
    300 . . . . 76 AO57
MS SE 100, 200 . . . . . 84 AO59
PL SE 100, 200 . . . . . . 84 AO59
    300 . . . . 85 AO58
PT SE 76 AN57
RS SE 85 AO58
WY SE 76 AN57
DOUGLASDALE BLVD SE 85 AP58
CR SE 85 AR61
CT SE 100 . . . . 86 AS61
    200, 300, 400 . . . . . 85 AR61
PT SE 85 AR61
DOUGLASPARK
HE SE 100 . . . . 85 AP60
DOUGLASVIEW BLVD SE 85 AR60
BY SE, CIR SE 85 AR60
CT SE 100 . . . . 86 AS60
    200 . . . . 86 AS61
PK SE 85 AR60
RD SE 85 AR61
RS SE 85 AR60
DOVELY CR SE 61 AQ40
CT SE, PK SE, PL SE . . 61 AQ40

WY SE 61 AQ40
DOVER CR SE 62 AT38
 PT SE 61 AQ41
 RD SE 62 AT39
DOVER MEADOW CL SE. 62 AS40
DOVER RIDGE BY SE... 62 AR40
 CL SE 62 AS40
 CT SE 62 AT40
 DR SE 61 AQ41
 PL SE 62 AR40
DOVERBROOK RD SE .. 61 AQ41
DOVERCLIFFE CL SE ... 62 AS39
 RD SE 62 AT39
 WY SE 62 AS39
DOVERCREST DR SE ... 62 AR41
 PL SE 100, 200 .... 62 AR41
 RD SE 62 AR41
 WY SE 61 AQ41
DOVERCROFT PL SE ... 62 AR41
 RD SE 62 AR41
DOVERDALE CR SE 62 AT38
 MS SE 62 AT38
DOVERGLEN CR SE 61 AP41
 PL SE 100, 200 .... 61 AP40
DOVERTHORN BY SE ... 62 AR40
 CL SE 61 AQ40
 PL SE, RD SE, WY SE. 62 AR40
DOVERTREE PL SE 62 AU38
DOVERVIEW CR SE 62 AS41
 DR SE 62 AS41
 PL SE 62 AS40
 RD SE 62 AR40
DOVERVILLE CR SE 62 AT38
 WY SE 62 AU38
DOVERWOOD PL SE ... 62 AT38
DOWNEY BY (OKS) 107 E6
 GN (OKS) 107 D6
 PL 100, 200, 300 (OKS) 107 D5
 500 (OKS) 107 D5
 600, 800 (OKS) ... 107 E5
 RD (OKS) 107 D5
DR CARPENTER CIR NW. 39 AC29
DRAGOON ST SW 65 T45
DRURY AV NE 51 AJ31
DUFFERIN BLVD SE ... 78 AW56
 PL SE 78 AW55
DUNHAM LN (T VAL) .. 105 B3
 LOOP, ST (T VAL) .. 105 B4
DURHAM AV SW 59 AC37
DYRGAS GT (CAN) 101 G9

E

EAGLE CR (BNF) 21 E3
 HTS (CAN) 101 F4
 LD (CAN) 101 G4
EAGLE CREST PL SW .. 66 AA49
EAGLE RIDGE DR SW .. 66 AA49
 PL SW 66 AA49
EAGLE TERRACE RD (CAN)101 F4
EAGLEVIEW GT (COCR) . 103 J4
 HTS (COCR) 103 J4
 PL (COCR) 103 J4
 PL (H RV) 109 D2
 WY (COCR) 103 J4
EAMON RD NW. 9 E11
EARL GREY CR SW 59 AD38
EAST BOUNDARY
 RD (STMR) 112 G8
EAST CHESTERMERE
 DR (CHST) 80 C8
EAST FREEWAY NE ... 32 BB18
 NE 44 BC27
 SE. 54 BD36
EAST LAKE AV (AIR) ... 113 F3
 BLVD (AIR) 113 F4
 CIR (AIR) 113 G3
 CR (AIR) 113 F3
 DR (AIR) 113 G3
 GN (AIR) 113 F3
 GT (AIR) 113 F4
 HL (AIR) 113 H4
 LK (AIR) 113 C3
 RD (AIR) 113 G4
 RD (STMR) 112 F6
 RS (AIR) 113 F4
 WY (AIR) 113 F3
EAST LAKEVIEW RD (CHST)80 C8
EAST PINE RD (STMR) .. 112 F8
EAST RIDGE RD (STMR) . 112 F8
EASTERBROOK PL (AIR). 113 E5
EASTRIDGE BLVD (CHST). 80 F8
 BY, DR (CHST) 80 E8
 GT (CHST) 80 F8
EAU CLAIRE AV SW. ... 50 AE32
ECHLIN CT (B CK) 33 F7
 DR (B CK) 33 F7
EDCATH BY NW 26 U16
 CT NW, MS NW 26 U16
 PL NW 100 ...... 26 U16
 200 .... 26 U16
 RD NW. 25 T15
 RS NW 26 U16
EDELWEISS CR NW 26 U16
 CT NW, DR NW ... 26 U16

PL NW 100 .... 26 U16
 200, 300 .... 26 U17
 PT NW. 26 U17
 RD NW 26 U16
EDENDALE CR NW 25 T15
 CR (AIR) 113 E5
 PL NW 25 T15
 WY NW 25 T15
EDENSTONE PL NW 25 T16
 RD NW. 25 T16
 VW NW 25 S16
 WY NW 25 T16
EDENWOLD CR NW 26 V15
 DR NW. 25 T15
 GN NW, HTS NW ... 26 V15
 PL NW 26 V15
EDFORTH CR NW 25 T15
 PL NW 100, 200, 300 .. 26 U15
 RD NW, WY NW ... 26 U15
EDGAR AV (T VAL) 105 B4
EDGEBANK CIR NW 13 U14
 PL NW 100, 200, 300 . 13 U14
 400 .... 13 U14
 500, 600 .... 13 U14
 700 .... 13 U14
EDGEBROOK BLVD NW .. 13 V11
 CIR NW, CL NW ... 13 U13
 CT NW 100 ..... 14 W13
 200 .... 13 V13
 CV NW 13 V12
 DR NW 13 U14
 GDN NW 100, 200, 300 . 13 V13
 GN NW 13 V14
 GV NW 100, 200 ... 14 W12
 300 .... 14 X12
 400 .... 13 V12
 HTS NW 13 V13
 LD NW. 13 V14
 MS NW 13 V14
 PK NW 14 W12
 PL NW 13 V14
 PT NW 14 W13
 RD NW 13 V14
 RS NW. 13 V13
 TER NW. 13 V12
 VW NW 14 W12
EDGEBURN CR NW 13 R12
 GDN NW 13 R13
 LN NW. 13 R12
 PL NW 13 R12
EDGEBYNE CR NW 13 S14
 DR NW 25 R16
 GDN NW 100, 200, 300 . 13 S15
 PL NW, RD NW, WY NW 25 R17
EDGEFORD PL NW 25 R16
EDGEHILL BY NW 25 R16
 CL NW 13 S15
 CR NW, CT NW 25 R16
 DR NW 25 Q16
 MS NW 13 R15
 PL NW 100, 200 ... 25 Q16
 RS NW 25 Q16
EDGELAND BY NW 13 R15
 CL NW. 13 R14
 CR NW. 13 R14
 CT NW. 13 R15
 GT NW 13 R13
 MS NW 13 R15
 RD NW 13 R14
 RS NW. 13 R14
EDGEMONT BLVD NW .. 25 S16
 BY NW 100, 200, 300 ... 25 T18
 400 .... 26 U18
 500, 600 .... 25 T18
 CT NW. 26 U18
 DR NW 25 S17
 HL NW 25 T16
 PL NW 100, 200, 300 ... 25 T17
 RD NW 25 S17
 RS NW 25 T18
EDGEMONT ESTATES
 DR NW 25 S17
 RD NW 25 S17
EDGEPARK BLVD NW... 13 R12
 CR NW. 13 R14
 CT NW. 13 R13
 DR NW 13 S13
 MS NW 13 S13
 RS NW, RD NW 13 R13
 VL NW 13 R13
EDGERIDGE BY NW 13 T12
 CIR NW 13 T12
 CL NW 13 T12
 CT NW 100 ..... 13 S12
 200 .... 13 S12
 GDN NW 100, 200, 300. 14 W11
 GN NW 13 U12
 GT NW. 13 T12
 MS NW 13 V12
 PK NW. 13 S12
 PL NW 13 S12
 200 .... 13 S12
 TER NW. 13 V11
 VW NW 14 W11
 WY NW 13 S13
EDGEVALLEY CIR NW .. 13 T14

CL NW. 13 U13
 DR NW, GDN NW 13 T13
 GN NW 100, 200. ... 13 T14
 LD NW. 13 T13
 MR NW 13 U13
 MS NW 100 ...... 13 U13
 200 .... 13 V13
 300 .... 13 U13
 PL NW. 13 U13
 VW NW, WY NW 13 T13
EDGEVIEW DR NW 13 S14
 HTS NW 13 S14
 PL NW 100 ..... 13 T14
 200 .... 13 S14
 300. .... 13 S13
 400 .... 13 T13
 RD NW. 13 T14
EDGEWOOD DR NW ... 13 R15
 PL NW, RS NW 13 S15
EDINBURGH RD SW ... 59 AC42
EDISON CR SW 59 AF41
EDMONTON TR NE ... 40 AH28
 TR (AIR) 113 F4
EDMUND WY (AIR) 113 E5
EDWARD AV (T VAL) ... 105 B4
 CL (T VAL) 105 B4
 ST NE 51 AL32
 ST (T VAL) 105 B4
EDWARD'S WY (AIR) ... 113 D3
EDWORTHY PK SW 47 R32
 ST SW. 46 Q32
ELBOW
 DR SW (500-6500) ... 67 AD46
 DR SW (6700-9900) .. 74 AC54
 DR SW (10000-13100). 82 AC60
 RS (B CK) 33 G5
ELBOW PARK LN SW ... 59 AE40
ELBOW RIDGE
 BLUFFS (EV) 115 E7
 HAVEN (EV) 115 E7
ELBOW RIVER CIR (SPNG) 99 E6
 CT (SPNG) 99 E6
 DR, PT, RD (SPNG) .. 99 D6
ELDERWOOD PL (AIR) .. 113 E5
ELDORADO CL NE 44 BA28
 PL NE 100, 200, 300... 44 BA28
 400 .... 44 BA28
 RD (AIR) 113 E4
ELDRIDGE RS (AIR) 113 E5
ELGIN AV SE 97 AU68
 BY SE 97 AU68
 CT SE 97 AU69
 DR SE 97 AU68
 GN SE 95 AT67
 GT SE 97 AU67
 HE SE 95 AT68
 MR SE 97 AU68
 MS SE 95 AT68
 PL SE 97 AV68
 PT SE 97 AU69
 RS SE, ST SE, VW SE . 97 AV68
 WY SE 97 AU67
ELGIN PARK CM SE 97 AU67
 GV SE, HL SE 97 AV67
 RD SE 97 AU67
ELIZABETH RD SW 59 AC42
 ST SE 51 AJ36
 ST (OKS) 107 A6
 WY (AIR) 113 E4
ELK AV (OKS) 107 C6
 HL (AIR) 113 E4
 ST (BNF) 21 C5
ELK RUN BLVD (CAN) .. 101 G5
ELKTON DR SW....... 55 L39
 PL SW, WY SW 56 M39
ELLIS CR (H RV) 109 E5
ELM AV (OKS) 107 D6
 PL (OKS) 107 D6
ELMA ST (OKS) 107 B6
ELMONT BY SW 100 ... 56 M38
 200 .... 56 M39
 CT SW 56 M38
 DR SW 56 M38
 MR SW 56 M38
 MS SW 56 N38
 PL SW 100 ..... 56 M39
 RS SW 56 M39
ELMWOOD DR SE 62 AR38
ELSMORE PL (AIR) 113 E5
ELSTON PL (AIR) 113 E4
 PL (AIR) 113 E5
ELTON CT (B CK) 33 F8
ELVEDEN DR SW 55 L38
EMBERDALE WY (AIR) .. 113 E4
EMERALD CT (AIR) 113 E5
 WY SE (B DMD)..... 106 H3
EMERSON RD (H RV) .. 109 C5
EMPRESS PL (AIR) 113 E5
ERIN CIR SE 62 AV41
 CR SE 62 AU41
 DR (AIR) 113 E5
 GV SE 62 AV41
 LK SE, PL SE 62 AV41
 RD SE 62 AU41
ERIN CROFT CR SE 62 AU39
 GN SE, PL SE 62 AU39
ERIN DALE CR SE 62 AT40
 PL SE 100, 200 ... 62 AU40
ERIN GREEN MS SE ... 62 AU41
 PL SE, WY SE 62 AU41

ERIN GROVE BY SE 62 AV39
 CL SE 62 AU40
 CT SE, PL SE 62 AV39
ERIN MEADOW BY SE.. 62 AV40
 CL SE 62 AU40
 CR SE 62 AU40
 CT SE 62 AV39
 GN SE, MR SE, WY SE 62 AV40
ERIN MOUNT CR SE ... 62 AT40
 PL SE 100 ...... 62 AU40
 200 .... 62 AU40
ERIN PARK BY SE 62 AU40
 CL SE 62 AU40
 DR SE 62 AV40
 PL SE 100, 200 ... 62 AV40
ERIN RIDGE CT SE 62 AT41
 PL SE, RD SE 62 AT41
ERIN WOODS BLVD SE . 62 AT41
 CIR SE 62 AS41
 DR SE 62 AU41
 GN SE 100, 300 ... 62 AS41
 LN SE 62 AU39
 PL SE. 62 AT41
 TER SE 62 AU40
ERLTON CT SE 59 AG40
 PL SW 59 AG37
 RD SW, ST SW 59 AG38
 TR SW. 59 AF40
ESCARPMENT DR (SPNG). 99 F4
 PK (SPNG) 99 G4
 PL (SPNG) 99 G2
EVANSBROOKE HTS NW . 4 X5
 LD NW. 4 X6
 LK NW. 4 X5
 MR NW. 4 W5
 PK NW, PL NW. 4 X6
 PT NW, TER NW, WY NW 4 W5
EVANSCOVE CIR NW.... 4 Y5
 HTS NW, PL NW. ... 4 Y5
EVANSCREEK CT NW ... 4 X5
 CT NW 100, 200 ... 4 W5
EVANSFORD GV NW ... 4 Z5
 RD NW. 4 Z5
EVANSMEADE CIR NW .. 4 Y6
 CL NW, CM NW 4 Y5
 CR NW, MR NW 4 Y6
 PT NW 100, 200 ... 4 Y6
 PL NW 4 Y6
EVANSTON RS NW 4 X6
 VW NW 4 X5
EVERBROOK DR SW ... 89 Y65
EVERCREEK BLUFFS
 CR SW. 81 X64
 GT SW 81 W63
 MS SW 81 W63
 PL SW, PT SW, RD SW. 81 W64
 VW SW, WY SW. ... 81 X64
EVERGLADE BY (AIR) ... 113 E5
 CIR SW 81 V64
 DR (AIR) 113 E5
 GT SW 81 V64
 LK SW 81 V64
 PL SW, WY SW ... 81 W64
EVERGLEN MR SW 89 W66
 RD SW. 89 W67
 RS SW, WY SW. ... 89 W66
EVERGREEN AV SW 89 Z65
 BLVD SW. 89 Z65
 BY SW 82 AA63
 CIR SW 89 Z65
 CIR (CAN) 101 A5
 CL SW 82 AA63
 CM SW 90 AA65
 CR SW 82 AA63
 CT SW, CV SW 82 AA63
 DR SW 82 AA62
 GDN SW 82 AA62
 GT SW 89 Z65
 GV SW 82 AA63
 HE SW 100. ...... 82 AA62
 200 .... 82 AA63
 HL SW 82 AA62
 HTS SW 82 AB64
 LD SW 82 AA64
 LK SW, LN SW. 82 AA64
 MR SW 82 AA63
 MS SW 100, 200 .... 81 Z64
 PL SW 100 ...... 82 AA63
 200 .... 82 AB64
 PLAZA SW 100, 200 .. 82 AA64
 PT SW. 82 AB64
 RS SW 82 AA63
 SQ SW. 89 Z65
 ST SW. 82 AA64
 TER SW 82 AA62
 VW SW, WY SW. ... 82 AB63
EVERHOLLOW AV SW .. 89 X65
 CR SW. 89 X65
 GN SW 89 X66
 HE SW. 89 X65
 PK SW. 81 X64
 PL SW. 89 X65
 RS SW 89 W65
 ST SW, WY SW. ... 89 X65
EVERMEADOW DR SW .. 89 X66
 GT SW 89 X67
 MR SW. 89 X66
EVEROAK CL SW 89 Y66
 CR SW. 89 X65
 DR SW. 81 Y64

GDN SW 89 Y66
GN SW 89 X66
PK SW, PL SW 89 Y65
EVERRIDGE CIR SW . . 89 W66
CL SW 89 W66
DR SW, GN SW, GT SW 89 W65
LK SW 89 W66
MR SW 89 X67
PK SW 89 W65
RD SW, WY SW 89 Y67
EVERSTONE AV SW . . 90 AA67
BLVD SW, CT SW . . 90 AA67
DR SW 89 Z68
GT SW 90 AA67
LK SW, PL SW 89 Z67
RD SW 90 AA67
RS SW 90 AA68
WY SW 90 AA67
EVERSYDE AV SW . . 89 Y67
BLVD SW 89 Y67
BY SW, CIR SW 89 Z66
CT SW 89 Y68
GN SW, HE SW 89 Z67
MR SW 89 Z66
RD SW 89 Z65
ST SW, WY SW 89 Z66
EVERWILLOW BLVD SW 89 Z66
CIR SW 89 Z66
CL SW, GN SW . . 90 AA66
PL SW 90 AA66
EVERWOODS CL SW . . 89 W65
CT SW 100, 200 . . . . 81 W64
RD SW 81 W64
EXSHAW RD NW 38 X26

F

FAIRHOLM DR (CAN) 101 C3
PL (BNF) 21 B8
FAIRMOUNT
DR SE (6700-9900) . . . 67 AG47
DR SE (10000-11000) . . 75 AG56
FAIRVIEW CR SE 67 AG48
DR SE 67 AG49
FAIRWAY DR (H RV) . . 109 C3
LN, VW (H RV) 109 C3
FAIRWAYS BY NW (AIR) . . 113 B3
CIR (AIR) 113 A2
CL NW 100 (AIR) 113 B3
CR (AIR) 113 A2
DR NW (AIR) 113 A3
LD, MS (AIR) 113 A3
PL NW (AIR) 113 A3
FALAISE AV SW 58 W42
FALBURY BY NE 32 AZ21
CR NE 32 AZ21
FALCHURCH CR NE . . 31 AX20
PL NE 32 AY21
RD NE 31 AX20
FALCON ST (BNF) 21 E3
FALCONER TER NE 32 AZ20
FALCONRIDGE BLVD NE 31 AW21
CL NE 43 AX22
CR NE 31 AX21
DR NE 31 AW21
GDN NE 32 AZ20
PL NE 43 AX22
FALDALE CL NE 32 AZ19
CT NE, PL NE 31 AX20
FALLINGWORTH BY NE . 31 AX21
CT NE, PL NE 31 AX20
FALLSWATER CR NE . . 32 AY21
GT NE 44 AY22
RD NE 32 AY21
FALMEAD BY NE 31 AX20
CL NE, PL NE, RD NE . . 31 AX20
FALMERE CT NE 32 AY19
RD NE, WY NE 32 AY19
FALSBRIDGE DR NE . . 31 AW21
GT NE 31 AW21
FALSBY CT NE 31 AW21
PL NE 31 AX21
RD NE, WY NE 31 AW21
FALSHIRE CL NE 32 AY19
DR NE 31 AX19
PL NE 31 AX19
TER NE 31 AX19
WY NE 32 AZ19
FALTON CL NE 32 AZ20
CT NE, DR NE 32 AZ20
MS NE 32 AZ20
RD NE 32 AY21
RS NE, WY NE 32 AY20
FALWOOD CR NE 32 AY21
PL NE 44 AY22
WY NE 32 AY21
FALWORTH BY NE . . 31 AX21
CT NE 31 AX20
PL NE 31 AX21
RD NE 31 AW20
WY NE 31 AX20
FARNHAM DR SE 68 AH24
FARR CR (AIR) 113 D2
FARRELL RD SE 67 AG47
FARRIES DR (AIR) 113 J5
FAWN CR SE 67 AG48

FAY RD SE 67 AF49
FENTON RD SE 67 AG49
FERNCLIFF CR SE 67 AG48
FERNIE PL SE 67 AF49
FESTUBERT AV SW 65 S45
FIELDING DR SE 67 AF49
FIR DR SE 62 AR38
FIRST ST (COCR) 103 F5
FISHER AV (COCR) 103 F5
CR (OKS) 107 E6
RD SE 67 AF48
ST SE 67 AF48
ST (OKS) 107 E6
FISHERMAN'S BEND (EV) . 115 E8
LD (EV) 115 E8
PT (EV) 115 F8
FITZGERALD RS (CAN) . . 101 G9
FLANDERS AV SW 58 X41
FLARE AV (T VAL) 105 C5
FLAVELLE RD SE 67 AG50
FLEETWOOD DR SE . . 68 AH49
FLETCHER RD (AIR) . . 113 D2
FLETT CR (AIR) 113 E2
DR (AIR) 113 E2
PL 100, 200 (AIR) 113 E2
FLINT PL SE 67 AF48
RD SE 67 AF49
FLOWER DEW AV SW . . 57 S43
FOLEY RD SE 67 AG49
FONDA CL SE 53 AT33
CR SE 52 AS33
CT SE 100 . . . . 53 AT34
400, 600, 700 . . 53 AT33
1000 . . . . 53 AT33
1100, 1200 . . . . 53 AT34
DR SE 53 AT33
GN SE 52 AS34
HL SE 53 AT33
MS SE 52 AS34
PL SE, RS SE 53 AT34
WY SE 53 AT33
FORD ST SW (B DMD) . . 106 G2
FORDHAM CR SE 53 AU33
FOREGO AV SE 53 AV33
FOREST CR SE 53 AW33
GN SE 53 AW33
PL SE 53 AW34
RD SE, WY SE 53 AW33
FOREST GROVE PL SE . 53 AV34
FORGE RD SE 67 AG47
FORITANA RD SE 53 AV33
FORLEE DR SE 53 AV34
FORMAN CR SE 53 AU33
FORTALICE CR SE 53 AV34
FORTRESS DR SW 55 J40
MR SW 100, 200 . . . . 55 K40
RS SW 55 K40
FORTUNE RD SW 53 AU33
FOSTER RD SE 67 AG48
FOUNTAIN RD SE 68 AH48
FOURIER DR SE 53 AV33
FOWLER DR NW 39 AD29
FOX ST (BNF) 21 E4
FOXWELL RD SE 67 AF49
FRANKLIN DR SE 67 AG48
FRASER RD SE 68 AH50
FREDSON DR SE 67 AG49
FREEMAN WY (H RV) . . 109 C2
FREEPORT BLVD NE . . 17 AP9
DR NE, LD NE 7 AO8
PL NE 7 AP8
WY NE 17 AO9
FRESNO PL NE 100 . . 44 BA24
200 . . . . 44 BA24
FROBISHER BLVD SE . . 67 AF50
FRONTAGE RD (CAN) . . 101 D3
FRONTENAC AV SW . . 59 AB38
AV (T VAL) 105 B4
FULHAM ST SE 68 AH49
FULLERTON RD SE 68 AH50
FYFFE RD SE 68 AH49

G

GAINSBOROUGH DR SW . 57 S41
GT SW 57 S41
GALBRAITH DR SW 57 T43
GALWAY CR SW 57 T42
GARDEN CR SW 59 AE38
GARLAND ST SW 57 S38
GARNET CL SE (B DMD) . 106 H3
GARRICK DR SW 57 S43
GARRISON BLVD SW . . 58 Y41
GT SW, SQ SW 58 Y40
GARRY CR SE 28 AH22
GASCONY LN (H RV) . . 109 B5
GATEFIELD AV SW 57 T37
GATEWAY DR SW 57 R37
PL SW 57 R37
GAZA CR SW 66 X44
GENERAL AV NE 51 AJ32
GEORGE ST (T VAL) . . 105 B4
GEORGE CRAIG
BLVD NE 29 AN22
GEORGE FOX TR (COCR) . 103 A5

GEORGIA ST SW 57 S37
GEORGIAN VL NE 54 AY30
200, 300, 400 . . 54 AY30
GIB BELL CL (IRR) 111 C3
GILMER PL SW 57 S43
GISSING DR SW 57 U41
GLACIER DR SW 57 T43
DR (BNF) 21 B8
DR (CAN) 101 F6
PL SW 57 T43
GLADEVIEW CR SW 57 T42
GLADSTONE GDN SW . . 57 R42
RD NW 49 AB32
GLADYS RIDGE RD SW . . 57 R37
DR SW, GDN SW . . 56 Q42
GN SW 57 R42
TER SW 57 R43
GLAMORGAN CR SW . . 57 R42
DR SW 57 S42
PL SW 200 . . . . 57 S42
300 . . . . 57 S41
400 . . . . 57 S42
WY SW 57 R41
GLASGOW DR SW 46 Q36
GLEN AV (BNF) 21 D7
CR (BNF) 21 D8
GLENBOW DR (COCR) . . 103 D4
GLENBROOK BY (COCR) . 103 E4
CR (COCR) 103 D4
DR SW 57 S40
MS (COCR) 103 D4
PL SW 56 Q40
PL (COCR) 103 D4
RD (COCR) 103 E4
GLENCASTLE ST SW . . 57 T38
GLENCOE RD SW 59 AD39
GLENDALE CR (COCR) . . 103 D4
PL (COCR) 103 D4
ST (STMR) 112 E8
WY (COCR) 103 D3
GLENDEER CIR SE 68 AK48
GLENEAGLE PL SW 57 R39
GLENEAGLES
BLVD (COCR) 103 K5
CL (COCR) 103 K5
DR (COCR) 103 H4
GN (COCR) 103 K5
GT (COCR) 103 H4
LD (COCR) 103 B5
PT 100 (COCR) 103 B5
TER (COCR) 103 K5
VW (COCR) 103 B5
GLENFIELD RD SW 57 R38
GLENGROVE CL SW . . 56 Q39
GLENHILL CR (COCR) . . 103 D5
CT, DR, PL (COCR) . . 103 D5
GLENMERE RD SW 57 S37
GLENMORE GN SW . . 67 AB47
TR (300-1200) 67 AF47
TR SE (1300-2800) . . 68 AL47
TR SE (2900-5200) . . 70 AR50
TR SE (5300-8400) . . 71 AX50
TR SW (600-1100) . . 67 AC47
TR SW (2100-3100) . . 57 R43
TR SW (4900) 56 O43
TR SW (9000) 55 G40
GLENMORE BRIDGE
RD SW 67 AB46
GLENMORE HILL RD SW 66 AA45
GLENMOUNT CR SW . . 47 S36
DR SW 47 S36
GLENPARK CR SW 57 T38
GLENPATRICK CR (COCR) 103 E5
CT (COCR) 103 D4
DR SW 57 R40
DR (COCR) 103 D5
PL, RD (COCR) 103 D4
GLENPORT RD (COCR) . . 103 D5
GLENRIDGE AV (STMR) . 112 E9
GLENSIDE DR SW 46 Q36
GLENVIEW CR SW 57 R37
DR SW 47 S36
GLENVISTA KEY (COCR) . 103 K3
PL (COCR) 103 K3
GLENWAY DR SW 57 T41
GLENWOOD AV SW 57 T37
BY (COCR) 103 D4
CR SW 57 T37
CT (COCR) 103 D4
DR SW 47 S36
PL (COCR) 103 D4
ST (STMR) 112 E8
GLOUCESTER CR SW . . 57 T41
DR SW 57 T41
GODDARD AV NE 28 AH22
GOLAN AV SW 66 W44
ST SW 66 X44
GOLDEN ASPEN
CREST (EV) 115 C8
GOLF COURSE RD (H RV) 109 C3
GOLF COURSE LOOP
RD (BNF) 21 F9
GOODING LN (T VAL) . . 105 C4
GOPHER ST (BNF) 21 C5
GORDON DR SW 57 S43
GOSLING WY SE 61 AP39
GOVERNMENT
RD N (B DMD) 106 H2
RD S (B DMD) 106 H4

GOVERNOR DR SW 57 S42
GRACEWOOD EST (SPNG) . 99 B3
GV, VW (SPNG) 99 B3
GRAFTON DR SW 57 T41
DR SW 57 T41
GRAHAM DR SW 57 R38
GRAND DR SW 57 R37
GRAND BEACH BY (CHST) . 80 B7
GRAND OAKS DR SW . . 47 T36
GRANDE POINT
EST (STMR) 112 G6
GRANITE RDG (EV) 115 D7
GRANLEA PL SW 47 R36
GRANT CR SW 57 S38
GRANVILLE CR SW 57 S38
ST SW 57 T38
GRASSI PL 100 (CAN) . . 101 B5
200, 300 (CAN) . . 101 B5
GRASSMERE CL (CHST) . 80 A5
GT, MS, PL (CHST) . . 80 A5
RD, VW, WY (CHST) . . 80 A5
GREEN MEADOW
CR (STMR) 112 F6
DR, PL (STMR) 112 F6
GREEN VALLEY
EST (COCR) 103 J2
GREEN VIEW CR (STMR) . 112 F6
WY (STMR) 112 F6
GREENFIELD PL NE 40 AG23
RD NE 28 AH23
GREENHILL CR NE 28 AH22
GREENRIDGE RD SW . . 47 T36
GREENVIEW DR NE 28 AG22
PL NE 28 AH23
GREENWOOD CR SW . . 57 T42
GREY AV (CRS) 8 F3
GREYHOUND WY SW . . 49 AA34
GRIER AV NE 28 AH21
PL NE, TER NE 28 AH21
GRIFFIN RD (COCR) 103 D5
GRIFFIN INDUSTRIAL
PT (COCR) 103 G5
GRIZZLY CR (CAN) 101 F5
ST (BNF) 21 D6
GROSVENOR PL SW . . 47 T36
GROTTO CL (COCR) . . 101 F6
PL, RD (CAN) 101 F5
TER (CAN) 101 G5
WY (CAN) 101 F6
GROVE HILL DR SW 57 S37
PL SW 57 S37
RD SW 47 R36

H

HADDOCK RD SW 74 AC53
HADER RD SW 74 AD53
HAGER PL SW 74 AC54
HALIFAX CR NW 38 Y28
HALLBROOK DR SW 74 AB52
BY SW 74 AB52
HALLMARK PL SW 74 AB53
HAMILTON ST NW 48 X30
HAMLET RD SW 67 AC50
HAMMOND AV (CRS) 8 F2
HAMPSHIRE CIR NW 13 R11
CL NW 13 S11
CT NW 100, 200, 300 . . 13 S11
400 . . . . 12 Q12
500 . . . . 13 R11
GV NW 13 Q11
PL NW 100, 200, 300 . . 13 Q11
HAMPSTEAD CIR NW . . 13 T11
CL NW 13 S11
GDN NW 14 W10
GDN NW 100 . . . . . . 14 W10
200 . . . . 13 S11
GN NW 13 U11
GV NW 13 U11
HE NW 100, 200 . . . . 13 U11
HL NW 13 U10
MR NW 13 U10
PL NW 100, 200 . . . . 13 S11
PT NW, RD NW 13 U11
RS NW, TER NW 13 V10
VW NW, WY NW 13 U11
HAMPTON CR SW 57 V39
HAMPTONS BLVD NW . . 13 R11
BY NW 13 T9
CIR NW 13 S10
CL NW, CV NW 13 S9
DR NW 13 S10
GDN NW 100, 200, 300 . 13 T10
GN NW 13 Q10
GV NW 13 R10
HE NW 13 U10
HTS NW 13 U10
LD NW 100 . . . . 13 S10
200 . . . . 13 S10
LK NW 13 U11
MR NW 13 R9
MS NW 100 . . . . 13 S10
200 . . . . 13 S11
300, 400, 500 . . 13 R11
PK NW 13 R10

PL NW 13 S9
RS NW 13 T10
SQ NW 13 R10
SQ NW 100, 200 . . . 13 R10
TER NW 13 T10
WY NW 13 R9
HANOVER RD SW 74 AC52
HARCOURT RD SW 67 AC50
HARDISTY PL SW 74 AD53
HARLEY RD SW 74 AB53
HARLOW AV NW 40 AD23
HARMON PL SW 74 AE51
HARPER ST NW 40 AE22
HARRIS PL NW 38 U26
HARRISON CT 100 (CRS) . . . 8 F1
    200, 300, 400 (CRS) . 8 F1
    PL, ST (CRS) 8 F2
HARROW CR SW 74 AD52
    PL SW 74 AD52
HARTFORD PL NW 40 AE22
    RD NW 40 AE23
HARVARD ST NW 40 AD24
HARVEST CREEK CL NE . 16 AI10
    CT NE 100, 200 . . . . . 16 AI10
    LK NE 16 AI10
HARVEST GLEN CT NE . . 16 AH11
    HTS NE 16 AH11
    LK NE 16 AH10
    MS NE 16 AH10
    PL NE 100 . . . . 16 AH10
        200 . . . . 16 AH11
    RS NE 16 AH10
    WY NE 16 AI10
HARVEST GOLD CIR NE . 16 AG10
    HTS NE 16 AG10
    MR NE 16 AF11
    PL NE 16 AG11
HARVEST GROVE CL NE . 16 AI9
    GN NE 16 AJ9
    PL NE 100 . . . . 16 AI10
        200 . . . . 16 AI10
        300, 400 . . . . 16 AI9
HARVEST HILLS
    BLVD NE 15 AE12
    BLVD NE (9700-11200) . . 5 AF8
    BY NE 16 AG11
    DR NE 16 AG10
    GT NE 16 AI9
    LK NE 16 AH11
HARVEST LAKE CR NE . . 16 AI9
    DR NE 16 AH10
    GN NE 100, 200, 300 . . 16 AI9
    VL NE 16 AH10
    WY NE 16 AI9
HARVEST OAK CIR NE . . 5 AG8
    CR NE 5 AG8
    DR NE 16 AG9
    GN NE 6 AH8
    GT NE 16 AG10
    PL NE 5 AG8
    RS NE 16 AG9
    RS NE 100, 200 . . . . . 16 AG9
    VW NE 16 AG9
    WY NE 5 AG8
HARVEST PARK CIR NE . 16 AH10
    CT NE 16 AH9
    GT NE, MS NE 16 AH10
    PL NE 16 AH9
    RD NE 16 AG9
    TER NE 16 AG10
    WY NE 16 AH9
HARVEST ROSE CIR NE . 16 AG11
    GDN NE 16 AG10
    PK NE, PL NE 16 AG11
HARVEST WOOD GT NE . . 6 AI8
    LK NE, PL NE, RD NE . . 6 AH8
    WY NE 6 AH8
HARVEY PL SW 74 AE51
HARWOOD ST (B CK) . . 33 G7
HASKAYNE PL NW 38 W27
HASTINGS CR SE 60 AK42
HAULTAIN PL SW 74 AD51
HAVENHURST CR SW . . 74 AD53
HAVERHILL RD SW 67 AC50
HAWK AV (BNF) 21 E3
HAWKBURY CL NW 12 O13
    PL NW 12 O13
HAWKCLIFF CT NW 12 Q14
    GT NW 12 Q14
    MS NW, PL NW 12 Q15
    WY NW 12 Q14
HAWKDALE BY NW 100 . 12 N14
        200 . . . . 12 N14
        300 . . . . 12 N13
    CIR NW 12 N14
    CL NW 12 O13
    GT NW, PL NW 12 N14
HAWKEY CR (AIR) 113 C2
HAWKFIELD CR NW . . . 12 M14
    PL NW, RS NW, WY NW 12 N14
HAWKFORD CR NW 12 P13
    CT NW, GT NW 12 P13
    PL NW 12 P14
    WY NW 12 P13
HAWKHILL CT NW 100 . . 12 Q14
    200 . . . . 12 Q14
MS NW 13 R14
PL NW 100, 200 . . . . . 13 R14
    300, 400, 500 . . 12 Q13
    600 . . . . 12 Q13

RD NW 12 Q13
WY NW 12 Q14
HAWKLAND CIR NW . . . 12 O11
    CR NW 12 O11
    PL NW 100, 200, 300 . . 12 O12
        400 . . . . 12 N12
HAWKLEY VALLEY PL NW 12 O15
    RD NW 12 O15
HAWKMOUNT CL NW . . . 12 O12
    GN NW 12 O12
    HTS NW 12 O13
HAWKRIDGE CT NW . . . 12 P14
    PL NW 12 P15
HAWKS CT NW 12 P15
HAWKSBROW DR NW . . 12 O14
    MS NW 100, 200, 300. . 12 O15
    PL NW 12 O14
    PT NW 12 O14
    RD NW 12 O14
HAWKSIDE CL NW 12 O14
    MS NW 100 . . . . 12 O14
        200 . . . . 12 N15
        300 . . . . 12 N15
        400, 500, 600 . . . . 12 N15
        700 . . . . 12 N15
    PK NW 12 O14
    RD NW 12 O15
HAWKSLEY BY NW 12 O15
    CR NW 12 O15
HAWKSLOW BY NW . . . 12 P15
    CT NW, PL NW 12 P15
HAWKSTONE CL NW . . . 12 P13
    CT NW 100, 200 . . . . . 12 P13
    DR NW 12 N12
    GT NW, MR NW 12 P12
    MR NW 100, 200, 300. . 12 P12
        400, 500, 600. . . . . 12 P12
    PL NW 100 . . . . 12 Q13
HAWKTREE BY NW 100 . 12 Q13
        200 . . . . 12 Q12
    CIR NW 12 Q12
    CL NW 12 P12
    GN NW 12 Q12
HAWKVIEW MANOR
    BY NW 12 Q15
    CIR NW 12 P14
    CT NW 100 . . . . 12 P14
    LK NW 12 P14
    PL NW 100, 200 . . . . . 12 P14
    RD NW 12 P14
HAWKVILLE CL NW 12 N13
    MS NW 12 N13
    PL NW 12 N14
HAWKWOOD BLVD NW . 12 O14
    CR NW 12 M14
    DR NW 12 N15
    HL NW 12 O15
    PL NW, RD NW, WY NW 12 M14
HAWTHORN DR NW . . . 28 AF20
HAWTHORNE CR NW. . . 48 Y30
HAY PL (IRR) 111 C4
HAYS DR SW 74 AC52
HAYSBORO CR SW . . . 74 AB51
HAZELWOOD CR SW . . 74 AD54
HEADLAND CL (COCR) . 103 G4
HEALY DR SW 67 AD50
HEATHER PL SW 74 AB54
HEATHERSTONE PL SE . 75 AF51
HEMLOCK CR SW 47 V34
HENDERSON BY (LNG) . 88 E6
    CL (LNG) 88 E6
    RD (LNG) 88 D6
HENDON DR NW 40 AD22
    PL NW 40 AE23
HENDRICKS DR (IRR) . . 111 B3
HENEFER RD SW 74 AD53
HEPBURN RD SW 74 AC51
HERITAGE BY (H PT) . . 115 C2
    CR (OKS) 107 E6
    CT (H PT) 115 C2
    CV (H PT) 115 C2
    DR SE 67 AF50
    DR SW 67 AB50
    DR (OKS) 107 E6
    GT SE 68 AJ48
    GT (OKS) 107 E6
    HARBOUR (H PT) . . 115 D2
    QUAY (H PT) 115 D2
HERITAGE LAKE
    BLVD (H PT) 115 C2
    CL (H PT) 115 C2
    DR (H PT) 115 D1
HERITAGE MEADOWS
    RD SE 68 AK49
    WY SE 68 AJ49
HERITAGE POINTE
    DR (H PT) 115 C2
HERITAGE WOODS
    DR (SPNG) 99 H3
    PL 100 (SPNG) 99 J4
        200, 300 (SPNG) . 99 H4
HESTON ST NW 39 AC24
HIDDEN CIR NW 14 Y10
    CL NW 14 W10
    CR NW, CT NW 14 X10
    CV NW 100, 200, 300. . 14 Y10
    GN NW 14 W10
    MS NW 14 W10
    PK NW 14 Y10

PT NW 14 X10
WY NW 14 W10
HIDDEN CREEK BLVD NW . 4 AA6
    BY NW 5 AB6
    CIR NW 5 AB6
    CR NW 4 AA7
    CV NW. 4 Z7
    DR NW 4 Z8
    GDN NW 4 AA7
    GN NW 4 AA8
    HTS NW 4 AA7
    MR NW 4 Z6
    MS NW 4 AA7
    PK NW 4 AA8
    PL NW 4 Z8
    PT NW. 5 AB7
    RD NW, RS NW 4 AA6
    TER NW 5 AB7
    VW NW, WY NW 4 AA7
HIDDEN HILLS PL NW 100 . 13 V9
    200, 300 . . . . 13 V9
    RD NW 13 V9
    TER NW 200 . . . . 14 Y9
    WY NW 13 V10
HIDDEN RANCH BLVD NW 14 X9
    CIR NW 14 X9
    CL NW 14 W9
    CR NW, CT NW 14 X9
    HL NW 14 W10
    MS NW 14 W9
    PL NW 100 . . . . 14 X9
        200 . . . . 14 X10
        300 . . . . 14 X9
    RD NW, TER NW 14 W9
    WY NW 14 W9
HIDDEN RIDGE BY NW . 14 Y9
    CL NW, CT NW, PL NW . 14 Y9
    VW NW 14 Y9
HIDDEN SPRING CIR NW . . 4 Z8
    CL NW, CT NW 14 Z9
    GN NW 14 Y8
    MS NW 100, 200 . . . . 14 Y8
    PL NW 14 Y9
HIDDEN VALE CL NW . . 14 Z10
    CR NW, CT NW 14 AA10
    PL NW 100, 200, 300 . 14 AA10
        400 . . . . 15 AA11
        500, 600 . . . . 14 AA10
HIDDEN VALLEY CR NW. 14 AA10
    DR NW 13 V9
    GDN NW 14 Z9
    GN NW 14 AA10
    GT NW, GV NW 14 AA9
    GV NW 100 . . . . 14 AA9
        200 . . . . 14 AA9
        300 . . . . 14 Z9
        400 . . . . 14 AA10
    HTS NW 14 Z10
    LD NW 100 . . . . 14 Z10
        200, 300. . . . . 14 Y10
    LK NW 14 Z9
    MR NW 14 AA9
    MR NW 100 . . . . 14 AA9
        200 . . . . 14 Z9
        300 . . . . 14 AA9
    PK NW 14 AA9
    PL NW 100 . . . . 14 AB10
        200 . . . . 14 AA10
        300 . . . . 14 AB10
    VL NW 14 Z9
HIGH ST SE. 97 AV66
HIGH COUNTRY BY (H RV) 109 C3
    DR (H RV) 109 B3
    PL (H RV) 109 C3
HIGH GLEN BY (H RV) . 109 B2
    DR (H RV) 109 B2
HIGH PARK BLVD (H RV). 109 A3
    WY (H RV) 109 A3
HIGH POINT
    EST 100 (CHST) 80 E8
        200 (CHST) 80 E7
HIGH RIDGE CL (H RV) . 109 A2
    CR (H RV) 109 A2
    CT (H RV) 109 A2
    PL (H RV) 109 A2
HIGH VIEW GT (H RV) . 109 C3
    PK 100, 200 (H RV) . 109 C3
    PT (H RV) 109 B3
HIGHFIELD AV SE 60 AI42
    BLVD SE 60 AK41
    CIR SE 60 AI42
    CR SE 60 AK43
    PL SE 60 AJ42
    RD SE 60 AI39
HIGHLAND CIR (STMR) . 112 D4
    CL, GT (STMR) 112 D4
    PL NW 40 AE22
HIGHLAND GREEN
    DR (H RV) 109 B2
    PT, VW (H RV) 109 B2
HIGHWOOD PL NW . . . 40 AD23
    TR (H RV) 109 B5
HIGHWOOD VILLAGE
    GT (H RV) 109 B2
    PL 100, 200, 300 (H RV). 109 B2
        400 (H RV) 109 B2
HILL RD NE 51 AL32
HILLARY CR SW. 74 AC52
HILLCREST AV SW 59 AC38
    BLVD (STMR) 112 C4

CAPE (STMR) 112 C4
EST (SPNG) 99 B3
LN (STMR) 112 C4
HILLGREEN PL SW 74 AB53
HILLGROVE CR SW . . . 74 AC53
    DR SW (50-110) 74 AB53
HILLVALE CR (STMR) . . 112 D4
HILLVIEW DR (STMR) . . 112 D4
    GT (STMR) 112 D4
    LN, RD (STMR) 112 C4
HILTON AV NW 40 AD22
HOBART RD SW 74 AB53
HOCHWALD AV SW . . . 58 W40
    CT SW 58 W40
HODSON CR (OKS) . . . 107 D4
    PL, WY (OKS) 107 D5
HOGARTH CR SW 74 AD52
HOLDEN PL SW 74 AB51
    RD SW 74 AB51
HOLLAND ST NW 39 AC23
HOLLY DR SE 62 AR37
    ST NW 39 AC23
HOLLYBURN RD SW . . . 74 AC52
HOLMWOOD AV NW . . . 40 AD22
HOLY CROSS LN SW . . 59 AF37
HOME BY (H RV) 109 F4
    RD NW 37 Q27
HOMESTEAD
    BY 300 (H RV) 109 F4
    CL 200 (H RV) 109 F4
    PL 500, 600 (H RV) . 109 F4
    TR 400 (H RV) 109 F4
    WY (H RV) 109 E4
HOODOO CR (CAN) . . . 101 F5
HOOKE RD SW 74 AB53
HOOVER PL SW 74 AC51
HOPE ST SW 59 AD38
HOPEWELL PL NE 42 AQ23
    WY NE 30 AQ22
HORIZON VIEW CT (SPNG) 99 F2
    LN, PL (SPNG) 99 F3
    RD (SPNG) 99 F5
HORSE CREEK RD (COCR) 103 A1
HORTON RD SW 74 AE52
HOSPITAL DR NW 38 V29
    PL (CAN) 101 D4
HOUNSLOW DR NW . . . 39 AC23
HUB AV SW 74 AC52
HUBALTA RD SE 63 AW37
HUBERT ST (T VAL) . . 105 C4
HUDSON RD NW 40 AD24
HUGGARD RD (SPNG) . 99 B2
HULL AV SW 74 AE51
HUNTBOURNE GN NE . 28 AG17
    GT NE, HL NE 28 AG17
    PL NE 28 AH17
    RD NE 28 AG18
    WY NE 28 AG18
HUNTCHESTER CR NE . 28 AG18
HUNTCROFT PL NE . . . 28 AF16
    RD NE, WY NE 28 AF16
HUNTER ST NW 39 AC24
HUNTERBOW CR NW . . 27 AD18
HUNTERBROOK
    PL NW 100, 200 . . . . 15 AC15
        300 . . . . 15 AB15
    RD NW 15 AC15
HUNTERBURN CR NE . . 27 AC16
    HL NW, PL NW. 27 AC16
HUNTERCOVE PL NW . . 27 AD17
HUNTERCREST RD NW . 27 AD17
HUNTERDALE PL NW . . 27 AD18
    RD NW 27 AD17
HUNTERFIELD PL NW . . 27 AE16
    RD NW 27 AE16
HUNTERHAVEN PL NW . 27 AD17
    RD NW 27 AD17
HUNTERHORN CR NE . . 28 AI17
    DR NE, GDN NE 28 AH18
    GT NE 28 AH18
    LN NE, MR NE 28 AH18
    PL NE 28 AH17
    RD NE. 28 AH17
    TER NE 28 AI18
HUNTERPLAIN HL NW . . 27 AE16
HUNTERQUAY HL NW . . 27 AC16
    PL NW 15 AC15
    RD NW 15 AC15
    WY NW 27 AC16
HUNTERS CR (OKS) . . . 107 B6
    GT, MS (OKS). 107 B7
    PL 100, 200 (OKS) . . 107 B6
HUNTERSLEA CR NW . . 27 AD16
HUNTERSTON BY NW . . 15 AC15
    CR NW, HL NW 15 AD15
    PL NW 15 AD15
    RD NW 15 AD15
HUNTERTOWN CR NW . 27 AE16
HUNTERVALLEY RD NW . 27 AE16
HUNTERVIEW DR NW . . 15 AC15
HUNTERVILLE RD NW . . 27 AE17
HUNTERWOOD RD NW . 27 AE17
HUNTFORD CL NE. 28 AG18
    GN NE, HL NE, RD NE . 28 AF17
    WY NE. 28 AF17
HUNTHAM GT NE 28 AF15
    PL NE 100, 200, 300. . 28 AF15
    RD NE 28 AF15
HUNTINGTON CL NE . . . 28 AH15

GN NE	28 AH16
RD NE	28 AG16
ST NE, WY NE	28 AH15
HUNTINGTON PARK	
BY NW	27 AD16
GN NW, PL NW	27 AD16
HUNTLEY CL NE	28 AG16
RD NE, WY NE	28 AH16
HUNTMEADOW RD NE	28 AH17
HUNTRIDGE CR NE	28 AF16
GT NE	28 AF17
HL NE	28 AG17
PL NE	28 AG16
RD NE, WY NE	28 AF16
HUNTS CR NW	27 AE18
PL NW	27 AE18
HUNTSBAY RD NW	27 AD18
HUNTSTROM BY NE 100	28 AI15
200	28 AI15
DR NE	28 AH15
PL NE	28 AH15
RD NE	28 AH15
HUNTSVILLE CR NW	28 AF18
HUNTWELL CT NE 100	28 AH16
200	28 AH16
PL NE 100, 200	28 AI16
RD NE	28 AI17
WY NE	28 AH16
HUNTWICK CR NE	28 AG16
HL NE, WY NE	28 AG16
HURON AV NW	39 AC23
HURST RD SE	51 AJ37
HUSKY OIL GDN NW	35 H26
HUSSAR ST SW	65 T44
HUTTON CR SW.	74 AD53
PL SW.	74 AD53
HUXLEY PL SW	74 AB51
HYLER PL SW	74 AB51
HYSLOP DR SW	74 AD51

I

IJSSELMEER ST SW.	65 S44
IMPERIAL DR SW *(B DMD)*	106 E5
DR *(T VAL)*	105 D6
WY SW.	59 AD42
INDUSTRIAL PL *(CAN)*	101 C3
INGLEWOOD CV SE	51 AM35
GV SE, LD SE, PT SE	51 AM35
INVERLAKE RD *(CHST)*	80 B3
INVERMERE CL *(CHST)*	80 A6
DR *(CHST)*	80 A5
INVERNESS BLVD SE	97 AU66
CL SE	97 AU66
CT SE	97 AU65
CV SE	97 AV66
DR SE	95 AT67
GDN SE, GN SE.	97 AV66
GT SE	97 AV66
GV SE	95 AT66
LN SE	97 AU66
PK SE	95 AT66
PL SE.	95 AT67
RS SE, SQ SE.	97 AU66
VW SE	97 AV66
WY SE.	95 AT66
IRRICANA RD *(AIR)*	113 F2

J

JACKSON PL NW.	38 U26
JAMES McKEVITT	
RD SW	90 AA69
JAMIESON AV NE	51 AK31
JASPER WY *(BNF)*	21 B8
JAY ST *(BNF)*	21 E3
JENSEN CR *(AIR)*	113 E2
DR *(AIR)*	113 E3
PL *(AIR)*	113 E2
JENSEN HEIGHTS	
CT *(AIR)*	113 E3
PL *(AIR)*	113 E3
JERUSALEM RD SW	74 AA52
WY SW.	74 AA52
JOHN ST *(T VAL)*	105 B5
JOHN LAURIE BLVD NW	11 L14
BLVD NW	25 Q16
26 U19, 39 AC23	25 Q16
JOLIET AV SW	59 AB39
JOYCE CR NW	49 AB30
JUNIPER DR NW.	35 H23
RD NW	48 Y30
RDG *(CAN)*	101 E2

# K	
KAMENKA GN *(CAN)*	101 B7
KANANASKIS DR SW	67 AB48
WY *(CAN)*	101 E5
KANELL DR *(H RV)*	109 E4
KEEWATIN ST SW	67 AC48
KELOWNA CR SW	67 AB47
KELSEY PL SW	67 AC48
KELVIN PL SW	67 AD50
KELWOOD CR SW	57 T38
DR SW	47 T36
PL SW	57 T37
KENDALL PL SW	67 AD48
KENMARE CR SW	57 V39
KENNEDY DR SW	67 AB47
KENOSEE PL SW	67 AC47
KENSINGTON CL NW	49 AB33
CR NW	49 AC33
RD NW	48 Y33
KENT PL SW	67 AB47
KENTISH DR SW	67 AE49
KERFOOT CR SW	67 AC48
KERRY PARK RD SW	57 U39
KERRYDALE RD SW	57 U40
KERWOOD CR SW	67 AB48
KETCHEN AV SW	65 S44
KEW ST SW	67 AB48
KILDARE CR SW	57 U39
KILDONAN CR SW	67 AC48
PL SW 1000, 1100	67 AC47
KILKENNY RD SW	57 U39
KILLARNEY GLEN	
CT SW 100, 200, 300	57 V39
400, 500, 600	57 V39
KILLEARN AV SW	67 AB48
KINCORA BLVD NW	4 W6
BY NW 100, 200	4 W8
300, 400.	3 V8
500, 600, 700	3 U7
CV NW 100, 200	4 W7
DR NW	4 W7
GDN NW, GV NW.	3 U6
HL NW.	3 U6
HTS NW	4 V7
LD NW	4 W7
MR NW	3 U7
PK NW	4 W7
PL NW 100	3 V8
200	4 W7
PT NW.	3 U7
RS NW.	3 V6
TER NW.	4 W6
VW NW	3 V7
KINCORA GLEN BY NW.	3 V5
CR NW, GN NW, LN NW	3 V6
MS NW, RD NW.	3 U5
RS NW	3 V6
KINGFISHER LN *(CHST)*	80 C9
KINGSLAND CT SW.	67 AE48
PL SW.	67 AD49
VL SW.	67 AE48
KINGSMERE CR SW	67 AE48
KINGSTON ST NW	48 W30
KINSALE RD SW.	57 U39
KIRBY PL SW.	67 AD49
KLAMATH PL SW.	67 AD48
KLONDIKE AV SW.	67 AB47
KLUANE DR *(BNF)*	21 C8
KNIGHT PL *(CRS)*	8 F2
ST *(OKS)*	107 C5
KNOWLES AV *(OKS)*	107 C5
PL *(OKS)*	107 C5
KODIAK RD *(CAN)*	101 F5
KOOTENAY AV *(BNF)*	21 D8
ST SW.	67 AB47
KOREA AV SW	65 T45
PL SW 100.	65 T45
KRIZAN BY *(CAN)*	101 G9

# L	
LA CAILLE PL SW	49 AD33
LA SALLE CR SW	65 U44
LA VALENCIA GDN NE	44 AZ26
GN NE	44 BA26
LACHINE CR SW.	66 X47
LACOMBE WY SW	66 X45
LADBROOKE DR SW	57 V44
PL SW	57 V44
LADY MacDONALD	
CR *(CAN)*	101 F5
DR *(CAN)*	101 G5
LAGUNA CIR NE	44 AZ25
CL NE	44 BA25
WY NE	44 BA23
LAIRD CT SW	66 W47
LAKE CT SW	65 V47
PL	80 C7
LAKE ACADIA GN SE	83 AI61
PL SE, RD SE	83 AI61

LAKE ADAMS CR SE	83 AG59
GN SE	83 AG59
PL SE.	83 AF59
LAKE ARROW GN SE	83 AJ61
RD SE	83 AI61
WY SE	83 AI61
LAKE ASPEN RD SE	83 AF58
LAKE BONAVENTURE	
DR SE	83 AG58
LAKE BONAVISTA DR SE	83 AG58
GN SE	83 AI59
LAKE CHRISTINA CL SE	83 AK59
PL SE.	83 AJ59
RD SE	83 AJ60
WY SE.	83 AJ59
LAKE CRIMSON CL SE	83 AK62
DR SE	83 AJ62
LAKE EMERALD CR SE	83 AI58
PL SE, RD SE.	83 AI58
LAKE ERIE EST *(CHST)*	80 C8
GN SE	83 AH59
RD SE	83 AH60
WY SE	83 AH59
LAKE FRASER CM SE	83 AF58
CT SE	83 AF59
DR SE, GN SE	83 AF58
GT SE	83 AF59
PL SE 100	83 AF59
200	83 AF59
WY SE.	83 AF59
LAKE GENEVA PL SE	83 AJ60
RD SE	83 AJ60
LAKE HURON BY SE	83 AK58
CR SE, PL SE	83 AK58
LAKE LINNET CL SE	83 AI58
CR SE	83 AI58
GN SE.	83 AH58
LAKE LOUISE WY SE	83 AI58
LAKE LUCERNE CL SE	83 AJ61
CR SE	83 AJ62
DR SE, RD SE	83 AJ61
WY SE.	83 AJ62
LAKE MEAD CR SE	83 AG60
DR SE	83 AG60
GN SE	83 AG60
PL SE	83 AH60
RD SE.	83 AG60
LAKE MICHIGAN CR SE.	84 AL59
DR SE	84 AL59
RD SE.	83 AK60
LAKE MORAINE GN SE.	83 AH60
PL SE 100, 200.	83 AG59
RD SE	83 AG59
RS SE.	83 AG60
WY SE.	83 AH60
LAKE NEWELL CR SE.	83 AF58
GN SE.	83 AF58
LAKE ONTARIO DR SE.	83 AJ62
PL SE 100	83 AK60
200, 300, 400	83 AK60
RD SE.	83 AK60
LAKE PATRICIA PL SE	83 AJ60
LAKE PLACID BY SE.	83 AI62
CL SE	83 AI62
DR SE.	83 AI61
GN SE 100, 200	83 AG61
300, 400	83 AH62
HL SE	83 AI62
PL SE.	83 AI61
RD SE	83 AI61
RS SE.	83 AH62
LAKE ROSEN CR SE	83 AG58
PL SE	83 AG58
LAKE SIMCOE CL SE.	83 AG62
CR SE	83 AG61
CT SE	83 AG62
GN SE.	83 AG61
RS SE.	83 AG62
LAKE SUNDANCE CR SE.	83 AJ60
PL SE.	83 AK60
LAKE SYLVAN CR SE	83 AK59
DR SE	83 AJ59
PL SE	83 AK59
LAKE TAHOE GN SE.	83 AH61
PL SE.	83 AH60
LAKE TOPAZ CR SE.	83 AG60
CR SE.	83 AG60
DR SE	83 AJ60
PL SE, RD SE, WY SE	83 AJ61
LAKE TWINTREE BY SE.	83 AJ60
GN SE.	83 AI60
DR SE	83 AJ60
PL SE, RD SE, WY SE	83 AJ60
LAKE WAPTA PL SE.	83 AK58
RD SE, RS SE, WY SE	83 AJ58
LAKE WASA GN SE.	83 AF58
PL SE.	83 AF58
LAKE WATERTON CR SE	83 AF59
WY SE.	83 AF59
LAKE WILLOW RD SE.	83 AF60
LAKE WOOD PL SE 100.	83 AF60
200	83 AF60
LAKESIDE BLVD *(STMR)*	112 E7
CR SW	65 V46
LAKESIDE GREENS	
CL *(CHST)*	80 B6
CR *(CHST)*	80 B6
CT *(CHST)*	80 A7
CT 100, 200, 300 *(CHST)*	80 A6
DR *(CHST)*	80 B6
GT *(CHST)*	80 A7
PL 100, 200, 300 *(CHST)*	80 B6

400 *(CHST)*	80 B6
500 *(CHST)*	80 B7
LAKEVIEW BY *(CHST)*	80 B7
CV *(CHST)*	80 B7
DR SW	65 U44
GT *(CHST)*	80 B7
INLET *(CHST)*	80 B7
RS *(CHST)*	80 C8
LAKEVIEW SHORES	
CT *(CHST)*	80 B7
LAMBERT AV NE	51 AL32
LAMONT CT SW	65 X47
LAMPSON AV *(BSKR)*	111 F2
LANCASTER WY SW	65 V45
LANCING AV SW	66 Y46
LANE CR SW	65 V45
LANEHAM PL SW	66 Y44
LANG PL *(OKS)*	107 G3
LANGRIVILLE DR SW	66 Y45
LANGTON DR SW	66 Y44
LANSDOWNE AV SW	59 AC41
EST 100 *(CHST)*	80 E8
200 *(CHST)*	80 E8
300 *(CHST)*	80 D8
LARCH AV *(CAN)*	101 B2
CL, CR *(CAN)*	101 B2
CT SW	66 X47
PL 100 *(CAN)*	101 C3
200, 300, 400 *(CAN)*	101 B3
500 *(CAN)*	101 B3
600, 700, 800 *(CAN)*	101 B2
900 *(CAN)*	101 A2
1000 *(CAN)*	101 B3
1100 *(CAN)*	101 B3
WY NW	35 H23
LARKSPUR WY SW	66 Y46
LAS AMERICAS VL NE	44 BA25
LASSITER CT SW	65 V47
LATHOM CR SW	66 W45
LAUDEN AV *(OKS)*	107 B6
LAUREL CR SW	66 W46
LAURENTIAN WY SW	66 Y46
LAURIER CT SW	66 X47
LAUT AV *(CRS)*	8 G3
CR *(CRS)*	8 F4
LAVAL AV SW	59 AC38
LAW DR SW	65 U46
LAWRENCE CT SW	66 X47
LAWRENCE GRASSI	
RDG *(CAN)*	101 B7
LAWSON PL SW	65 U45
LAXTON PL SW.	25 Z45
LAYCOCK DR NE	28 AG22
DR NW	28 AF22
LAYZELL RD SW	66 X45
LEASIDE DR SW	65 V47
LEDUC CR SW	65 V45
LEESON CT SW	66 X47
LEFROY CT SW	66 W47
LEGARE DR SW	66 W45
LEGSBY RD SW	66 Y45
LENTON PL SW.	66 Y44
LEPINE CT SW	66 W47
LETHBRIDGE CR SW	65 U46
LEVIS AV SW	59 AC39
LEWIS DR SW.	65 U46
LIDDEL CT SW	65 V47
LILAC WY NW	35 I24
LIMIT AV *(CRS)*.	8 E2
LINCOLN DR SW	66 Y45
GN SW	57 U42
MR SW	57 U43
PK *(CAN)*	101 E5
PL SW	57 U43
WY SW	57 U43
LINDEN DR SW	65 V46
LINDSAY DR SW	66 W46
LINDSTROM DR SW	66 W47
LINEHAM AV *(OKS)*	107 D6
LINEHAM ACRES	
BY 400 *(H RV)*	109 C3
CL 200 *(H RV)*	109 C3
DR *(H RV)*	109 C3
GV 100 *(H RV)*	109 C3
PL 300 *(H RV)*	109 D3
LINK ST *(CRS)*	8 F2
LIONEL CR SW	66 W46
LIRI AV SW	65 U46
MS SW.	65 U46
LISMER GN NW	37 T26
LISSINGTON DR SW	66 Y44
LITTLE RAVINE RD *(CAN)*	101 E2
LIVINGSTONE DR SW.	65 V47
LLOYD DR SW	66 W45
CR *(LNG)*	88 E7
LOCK CR *(OKS)*	107 C5
PL *(OKS)*	107 C5
LOCKE CT SW	65 V47
LOCKINVAR RD SW	65 U45
LODGE CR SW	65 U45
LOGAN CR SW	65 U45
LOMBARDY CR SW	66 X46
LONDON ST NW	48 W30
LONDONDERRY CR SW.	65 V45
LONG BEACH LD *(CHST)*	80 B8
LONGEWAY PL *(SPNG)*	99 D1
LONGMOOR WY SW	66 Y46
LONGRIDGE DR SW	66 Y46
LONGVIEW TR *(H RV)*	109 A2
LONGWOOD CT SW	66 X47

LORNE PL SW 66 Y46
LOS ALAMOS CR NE 44 BA23
PL NE 100, 200, 300 . . . 44 BB23
LOTT CREEK BLVD (EV) . . . 115 F8
DR (EV) 115 D8
HOLLOW (EV) 115 E9
LOUGHEED CIR (BNF) 21 D8
DR SW 66 X45
LOUISE RD SW 66 W46
LOUNT CR (BSKR) 111 E3
LOWELL CT SW 65 V47
LOWER SPRINGBANK
RD (SPNG) 99 H5
LOWES CT SW 66 W47
LUXSTONE BEND (AIR) . . . 113 C6
BLVD, BY, CR (AIR) 113 D6
GN (AIR) 113 C6
GT (AIR) 113 D6
PK (AIR) 113 D6
PL 100, 200, 300 (AIR) . 113 D6
400 (AIR) 113 D6
PT, RD (AIR) 113 C6
RDG (AIR) 113 D6
SH (AIR) 113 C7
SQ (AIR) 113 C7
VW (AIR) 113 D6
LUXSTONE LAKE
DR (AIR) 113 D5
LYLE AV SW 66 Y46
LYNCH CR SW 66 X46
LYNN RD SE 69 AP47
LYNNBROOK BY SE 69 AM47
CL SE 69 AM47
GT SE, PL SE, RD SE . . 69 AM47
RD SE 69 AO47
LYNNDALE CR SE 69 AO47
RD SE 69 AN48
LYNNOVER CR SE 69 AN48
PL SE 100, 200, 300 . . 69 AN48
RD SE 69 AN48
WY SE 69 AM47
LYNNRIDGE BY SE 69 AM45
CT SE 69 AM45
MS SE, PL SE, VL SE . . 69 AM45
LYNNVIEW CR SE 69 AM46
CT SE, PL SE 69 AM45
RD SE 69 AM46
RS SE 69 AM46
TER SE 69 AM46
WY SE 69 AM46
LYNNWOOD DR SE 69 AO47
LYNX ST (BNF) 21 C6
LYSANDER CR SE 69 AN48
DR SE 69 AN47
PL SE 100, 200, 300 . . 69 AN48
LYTTON CR SE 69 AN48

M

MacDONALD AV SE 51 AJ35
PL (CAN) 101 B4
MacEWAN DR NW 14 Y11
TER NW 14 Y11
MacEWAN GLEN CL NW . 15 Z13
DR NW 14 Y13
PL NW 100, 200 . . . . . . 14 Y13
RD NW, WY NW 14 Y13
MacEWAN MEADOW
CR NW 14 Y12
GT NW 15 Z11
LK NW 15 Z12
RS NW 14 Y11
WY NW 14 Y12
MacEWAN PARK CIR NW . 14 X12
CL NW 14 X13
GN NW 14 Y13
GT NW 15 Z13
HTS NW, LK NW 14 Y12
MR NW 14 X13
MS NW 14 Y13
PL NW, RD NW 14 Y12
RS NW 14 X12
VW NW 14 X13
WY NW 14 Y12
MacEWAN RIDGE CIR NW . 14 X11
CL NW, GT NW 14 X11
PL NW 14 Y11
VL NW 100, 200 . . . . . . 14 X11
VW NW 14 X11
MacEWAN VALLEY GT NW 14 Y11
MS NW 100, 200, 300 . . 14 Y11
RD NW 14 Y11
MacKAY DR SW 67 AD46
RD NW 37 S29
MACKENZIE AV (AIR) . . . 113 C4
MacCKID CR NE 52 AO30
RD NE 52 AO30
MacLEAY RD NE 52 AO31
MacLEOD
TR S (2300-4200) 59 AG41
TR S (2500-14600) . . . 91 AF63
TR S (6500-9800) 74 AE54
TR S (9900-13000) . . . 74 AE57
TR SE (300-1800) 50 AG36
TR SE (15100-18100) . . 91 AF65

TR SE (18200-19000) . . 91 AG69
TR SW 67 AE46
TR (H RV) 109 C5
MADDOCK CR NE 53 AX32
DR NE 53 AX32
LN NE 100 . . . . 53 AX32
WY NE 53 AX32
MADEIRA CL NE 53 AX30
CR NE, DR NE 53 AX30
GT NE 53 AX31
PL NE 100, 200 . . . . . . 53 AW30
RD NE 53 AX30
WY NE 53 AW30
MADIGAN CT NE 54 AZ31
DR NE 53 AW30
MADISON AV SW 59 AD42
CT (STMR) 112 F6
DR (IRR) 111 B3
ST (T VAL) 105 D5
MAGGIE ST SE 51 AJ36
MAIDSTONE BY NE 53 AW31
CR NE 53 AX31
DR NE 53 AW31
GN NE 100, 200 . . . . . . 53 AW31
PL NE, RD NE, WY NE . 53 AW31
MAIN ST (AIR) 113 D4
ST (CAN) 101 C4
ST (T VAL) 105 C4
MAITLAND CR NE 44 AY29
DR NE 44 AY29
GN NE, GT NE 44 AZ29
HL NE 54 AZ30
PL NE 100, 200 . . . . . . 54 AZ30
RD NE 54 AY30
RS NE 44 AY30
WY NE 54 AZ30
MAJESTIC GT (EV) 115 D8
PT (EV) 115 D8
VW (EV) 115 E8
MALIBOU RD SW 67 AD46
MALLARD AL (CAN) 101 C4
MALVERN CL NE 54 AZ32
CR NE 54 AZ31
CT NE 54 AZ32
DR NE 54 AY32
GN NE 54 AZ32
GT NE 54 AY31
PL NE 54 AZ31
RD NE 54 AZ32
WY NE 54 AZ32
MANCHESTER RD SE . . . 59 AG41
MANHATTAN RD SE 60 AH42
MANILLA RD SE 60 AH42
MANITOBA RD SE 60 AH42
MANITOU RD SE 60 AH42
MANNING CL NE 52 AN32
RD NE 51 AM31
MANOR RD SW 67 AD46
RD (IRR) 111 B3
MANORA CR NE 43 AX29
DR NE 43 AX29
HL NE 53 AX30
PL NE 53 AW30
RD NE, RS NE, WY NE . 53 AX30
MANY HORSES BY (RED) . 33 F1
CIR (RED) 33 F2
CL (RED) 33 F1
CR, CT (RED) 33 E2
DR (RED) 33 F2
GDN (RED) 33 F1
GN (RED) 33 F2
GT, PK (RED) 33 E2
PL, RS (RED) 33 F1
MAPLE AV (CRS) 8 F1
GDN (STMR) 112 F5
PL SW 67 AD45
PL (CRS) 8 G1
PL (STMR) 112 F6
ST (OKS) 107 D6
WK (CRS) 8 F1
WY NW 35 I23
WY (AIR) 113 G6
MAPLE BROOK PL SE . . . 75 AI54
MAPLE COURT CR SE . . . 75 AJ54
MAPLE GREEN WY (STMR) 112 F5
MAPLE GROVE CR (STMR) 112 F5
PL SE 75 AI54
MAPLE LEAF RD (STMR) . 112 F6
MAPLE RIDGE CR SE . . . 75 AK55
MAPLE TREE WY (STMR) . 112 F5
MAPLEBEND DR SE 75 AJ55
MAPLEBURN DR SE 75 AJ56
MAPLECREEK DR SE . . . 75 AJ54
MAPLECREST RD SE . . . 75 AK56
MAPLECROFT RD SE . . . 75 AJ55
MAPLEDALE PL SE 75 AJ55
MAPLEFORD RD SE 75 AJ56
MAPLEGLADE CL SE . . . 75 AJ57
CR SE 75 AK57
DR SE 75 AK57
PL SE 75 AK57
MAPLEGLEN CR SE 75 AJ55
MAPLEMONT RD SE 75 AJ55
MAPLERIDGE EST (STMR) 112 F6
MAPLESHIRE RD SE 75 AK55
MAPLETON DR SE 75 AI54
MAPLEWOOD CR SE . . . 75 AJ54
DR SE (B DMD) 106 H3
DR (STMR) 112 F5
EST (STMR) 112 F5

GN (STMR) 112 F6
PL SE (B DMD) 106 H3
WY SE (B DMD) 106 H3
MARANDA CL NE 53 AT30
MARBANK DR NE 53 AT30
PL NE 53 AV30
WY NE 52 AS30
MARBROOKE CIR NE . . . 53 AV32
MARBURY PL NE 53 AV32
MARCELLA CT (AIR) . . . 113 G6
MARCHAND CR SE 53 AV32
MARCOMBE CR NE 53 AV30
DR NE 53 AV30
PL NE 53 AV30
RD NE 53 AV30
WY NE 53 AV30
MARDA LK SW 58 Y40
MARDALE CR NE 43 AU29
DR NE 43 AU29
RD NE, WY NE 43 AV29
MARGARET AV SE 51 AI37
MARGATE CL NE 53 AT30
PL NE 53 AT31
MARIAN CR NE 53 AV31
RD NE, WY NE 53 AV31
MARIPOSA DR NE 52 AN32
PL NE 52 AN31
MARKERVILLE RD NE . . 52 AN32
PL NE 53 AW31
WY NE 53 AT32
MARLOWE PL NE 51 AI29
MARLYN CT NE 43 AT29
PL NE 100, 200 . . . . . . 43 AT29
WY NE 43 AT29
MARMOT CR (BNF) 21 E4
PL (BNF) 21 F3
ST (BNF) 21 F4
MARPOLE BY NE 53 AT30
PL NE 53 AT31
RD NE 53 AT30
MARQUETTE ST SW . . . 59 AC38
MARQUIS PL (AIR) 113 G7
WY (AIR) 113 G6
MARQUIS OF LORNE
TR SE 89 W71
TR SE 91 AJ71, 96 AR70
MARSDEN RD NE 41 AI28
MARSH RD NE 50 AH32
MARSHALL RD NE 53 AV31
RS (H RV) 109 C2
MARSHAM RD NE 53 AV32
MARTELL RD NE 53 AW32
MARTHAS CL NE 31 AV16
GN NE 31 AV16
MR NE 100, 200, 300 . 31 AW16
PL NE 31 AV16
WY NE 19 AV15
MARTHAS HAVEN
GDN NE 31 AU17
GN NE, GT NE 31 AV16
HE NE 31 AV15
MR NE 31 AV16
PK NE 31 AV16
PL NE 31 AV16
PR NE 31 AU17
WY NE 19 AV15
MARTHAS MEADOW
BY NE 19 AV15
CL NE, DR NE, GN NE . 19 AV15
GT NE, LK NE, PL NE . . 19 AV15
MARTIN AV (OKS) 107 B5
MARTIN CROSSING
BY NE 31 AW16
CL NE 31 AV17
CR NE 31 AW17
CT NE 31 AU17
CV NE, DR NE 31 AV17
GN NE, GV NE 31 AW17
LK NE 31 AV16
MR NE 31 AV17
PK NE, RS NE 31 AV17
WY NE 31 AW16
MARTINBROOK GT NE . 31 AW16
LK NE 31 AV17
PL NE 100, 200, 300 . . 31 AW17
RD NE 31 AV17
MARTINDALE BLVD NE . 31 AU17
CL NE, CR NE 31 AV18
CT NE 31 AX18
DR NE 31 AW18
GT NE 31 AV18
MS NE 31 AX18
MARTINGLEN CL NE . . . 31 AU18
LK NE, MS NE, PL NE . 31 AU18
WY NE 31 AU18
MARTINGROVE CT NE . . 31 AX18
DR NE, MS NE, PL NE . 31 AX18
RD NE, WY NE 31 AX18
MARTINPARK MS NE . . . 31 AU18
WY NE 31 AU17
MARTINRIDGE CL NE . . . 31 AV18
GV NE 31 AW18
PL NE 31 AW18
RD NE 31 AV17
WY NE 31 AW18
MARTINVALLEY CR NE . 19 AW15
CT NE 19 AW15
MS NE 100, 200 . . . . . . 19 AX15

PL NE 31 AW16
RD NE 19 AX15
WY NE 31 AW16
MARTINVIEW CL NE . . . 31 AV18
CR NE, RD NE 31 AV18
MARTINWOOD CT NE . . 31 AX17
MS NE 31 AX17
PL NE 100, 200, 300 . . 31 AX17
RD NE, WY NE 31 AX17
MARWOOD CIR NE 53 AU32
PL NE 53 AU32
RD NE 53 AT32
WY NE 53 AU32
MARYLAND PL SW 67 AC46
MARYVALE CR NE 53 AU31
DR NE 53 AU32
PL NE 53 AT31
RD NE, WY NE 53 AU31
MASSEY PL SW 67 AB46
MATADOR CR NE 52 AO31
MATHESON DR NE 52 AN32
MAUNSELL CL NE 52 AP31
DR NE 52 AO31
MAYDAY WK SW 47 U35
MAYFAIR CL (AIR) 113 G6
RD SW 67 AD45
MAYLAND DR NE 52 AO30
MAYNARD RD SE 52 AO34
McCALL LD NE 30 AP21
WY NE 30 AO22
McCANN ST (LNG) 88 D8
McCASKILL DR (CRS) . . . 8 G1
McCOOL CR (CRS) 8 F5
ST (CRS) 8 G5
McCRACKEN CR (AIR) . . 113 D2
McCULLOCH CR (IRR) . . 111 B3
McDONNELL AV SW . . . 57 S43
McDOUGALL CT NE . . . 51 AI33
PL (LNG) 88 C6
RD NE 51 AI33
ST (LNG) 88 C6
McGONIGAL DR NE 52 AN31
McHUGH CT NE 52 AO29
PL NE, RD NE 52 AP30
McINTOSH RD NE 52 AP31
McKENNA CR SE 95 AR69
LN SE 95 AR69
MR SE 95 AR69
MS SE 96 AR70
PL SE, RD SE, WY SE . 95 AR69
McKENZIE DR SE 95 AS68
PL SE 95 AS68
McKENZIE LAKE
BLVD SE 95 AQ69
BY SE 100, 200, 300 . . 95 AS66
400, 500 . . . . 95 AS66
600, 700, 800 . 95 AT66
900, 1000 . . . 95 AT66
CR SE 95 AT67
CV SE 100 . . . . 95 AT67
200, 300 . . . . 95 AS68
GDN SE 95 AR66
GN SE 95 AT67
GT SE, ISLAND SE 95 AS66
LD SE 95 AS67
MR SE 95 AS67
PL SE 95 AS66
PT SE 95 AS66
VW SE, WY SE 95 AS66
McKENZIE MEADOWS
DR SE 95 AQ70
McKENZIE TOWNE
AV SE 97 AV65
BLVD SE 97 AU65
DR SE 97 AU67
GT SE, LK SE . . . 97 AW66
McKERNAN CT SE 95 AS69
PL SE, RD SE 95 AS69
McKERRELL CL SE 95 AS69
CR SE 95 AS68
CT SE 95 AS68
GDN SE 100, 200 . . . . 95 AT68
PL SE 100, 200 . . . . . . 95 AS68
300, 400, 500 . 95 AT68
WY SE 95 AS68
McKINLEY BY SE 95 AR69
CT SE 95 AR68
PL SE, RD SE 95 AR68
RS SE, WY SE 95 AR68
McKINNON CR NE 52 AP31
DR NE 52 AO29
PL NE 100 . . . . 52 AP32
200 . . . . 52 AP32
RD NE, TER NE 52 AO29
McKIVOR BLVD SE 97 AX66
McKNIGHT
BLVD NE (200-700) . . . 41 AI22
BLVD NE (1200-2400) . 41 AK22
BLVD NE (7000-8400) . 44 AR22
BLVD NW 40 AE22
McNEILL RD NE 52 AN31
McPHERSON RD NE 51 AJ33
McRAE ST (OKS) 107 D6
McTAVISH CT NE 29 AN22
PL NE, RD NE 29 AN22
MEADOW CL (COCR) . . . 103 C5
CT (COCR) 103 C5
PL (AIR) 113 G6
PL (COCR) 103 C5
WY (COCR) 103 C5

MEADOW BROOK
BY 100 (AIR) 113 H6
200, 300, 400 (AIR) 113 H6
500, 600 (AIR) 113 H6
DR (AIR) 113 G6
GT (AIR) 113 H6
MEADOW LARK LN (SPNG) 99 C3
MEADOW POINTE
DR (H PT) 115 E2
MEADOWLARK CR SW 67 AD46
RD (AIR) 113 G6
MEADOWVIEW PL SW 67 AD46
RD SW 67 AD45
MEDFORD PL SW 67 AC46
MELVILLE PL SW 67 AC46
MEMORIAL DR E 53 AX32
DR NE 50 AG32
DR NW 48 Y33
DR SE 50 AG32
MENNO SIMONS GT SW 56 N40
MEOTA RD NE 52 AN31
MEREDITH RD NE 50 AH33
MERGANSER DR E (CHST) 80 D7
DR W (CHST) 80 A7
MERIDIAN RD NE 52 AP32
RD SE 52 AP33
MERRILL DR NE 40 AI26
MIDBEND CR SE 91 AG67
PL SE 100, 200 91 AG67
300 91 AH67
MIDCREST CR SE 91 AG65
RS SE 91 AG65
MIDDLE SPRINGS DR (BNF) 21 B8
MIDDLETON DR NE 52 AO30
MIDGLEN DR SE 91 AI65
GDN SE, LN SE 91 AI65
PL SE 100, 200, 300 91 AI65
RD SE 91 AI66
TER SE 100 91 AH65
200, 300 91 AI65
WY SE 91 AH65
MIDLAKE BLVD SE 91 AF66
GN SE 91 AH66
PL SE 91 AI66
MIDLAND CR SE 91 AI67
PL SE 91 AI68
PL SE 100, 200 91 AI67
MIDLAWN CL SE 91 AF65
GN SE 91 AG64
PL SE 91 AG65
MIDNAPORE PL SE 91 AF65
MIDPARK BLVD SE 91 AG66
CL SE 91 AH67
CR SE, DR SE, GDN SE 91 AG66
GT SE 91 AG67
HL SE 91 AG66
PL SE, RS SE 91 AH66
WY SE 91 AG68
MIDRIDGE BY SE 91 AH64
CL SE 91 AH65
CR SE, DR SE, GDN SE 91 AG65
GN SE 91 AH65
PL SE 100 91 AG64
200 91 AH64
RD SE, RS SE 91 AH65
MIDVALLEY CR SE 91 AJ67
DR SE 91 AI66
PL SE 100 91 AI66
200 91 AJ66
300 91 AJ67
RD SE 91 AJ66
RS SE, WY SE 91 AI66
MILLAR RD NE 52 AO31
MILLBANK BY SW 90 AE66
CL SW 90 AD65
CR SW 90 AD66
CT SW 90 AD65
DR SW 90 AC65
HL SW 90 AD66
RD SW 90 AE66
MILLCREST CT SW 90 AC66
GN SW 90 AC66
PL SW 90 AB65
RD SW 90 AC66
RS SW, WY SW 90 AB65
MILLICAN RD SE 69 AO45
MILLIGAN DR (OKS) 107 D5
MILLPARK PL SW 82 AC64
RD SW, RS SW 90 AC65
WY SW 90 AC65
MILLRISE BLVD SW 90 AE65
CL SW 90 AC65
CR SW 90 AC66
DR SW 90 AB65
GN SW 90 AB66
HL SW 90 AC65
LN SW 90 AE65
MR SW 90 AB66
MS SW 90 AE65
PT SW 82 AE64
SQ SW 90 AB66
SQ SW 100, 200 90 AB66
300, 400 90 AA66
WY SW 90 AD65
MILLROSE PL SW 90 AE65
MILLSIDE CR SW 82 AD64
CT SW, DR SW 90 AD65
PL SW 90 AE65
RD SW, WY SW 90 AD65
MILLVIEW BY SW 100 90 AA65
200 90 AA65
300 82 AA64
400, 500 82 AB64
CM SW 90 AB65
CT SW 100, 200 90 AB65
DR SW 82 AB64
GDN SW 100, 200 90 AB65
GN SW, GT SW 90 AA65
MR SW 90 AB65
PK SW 90 AA65
PL SW 100, 200, 300 82 AB64
RD SW, RS SW 90 AB65
SQ SW 90 AB65
WY SW 90 AB66
MILLWARD PL NE 52 AP30
RD NE 52 AO30
MILNE DR NE 52 AO31
MISANO AV SW 65 T46
CT SW 100, 200, 300 65 U46
400 65 U46
500, 600 65 T46
MISKOW CL (CAN) 101 F9
MISSION RD SW 59 AF39
MIST RD (H RV) 109 B5
MISTY MORNING DR (EV) 115 D8
MOE AV (LNG) 88 C5
MONARCH GT (AIR) 113 G6
MONCTON RD NE 41 AJ28
MONS AV SW 58 Y42
MONSERRAT DR NW 37 P27
MONTALBAN AV NW 37 R26
CR NW 37 S27
DR NW 37 R26
MONTANA CR NW 37 R26
DR NW 37 S26
MONTANE RD (CAN) 101 E5
MONTCALM CR SW 59 AB38
MONTEREY AV NW 37 Q28
MONTGOMERY AV NW 37 Q28
BLVD NW 37 Q29
RD NW 37 R29
VW NW 37 S29
MONTREAL AV SW 59 AB38
MONTROSE CR NE 41 AI28
MONUMENT PL SE 52 AQ33
MOODIE RD NE 52 AO30
MOOR ST SW 67 AD45
MOORCROFT RD SW 67 AB46
MOORGATE PL SW 67 AC46
MOOSE ST (BNF) 21 D5
MORAINE RD NE 52 AP32
RD (CAN) 101 F5
MOREUIL CT SW 58 Y42
MORLEY CR NW 38 X25
TR NW (2500-3500) 38 X25
TR NW (5700-5800) 25 P19
MORO DR SW 58 X40
MORRIS CR (AIR) 113 H6
PL, RD (AIR) 113 H6
MORRISON AV (T VAL) 105 C4
ST SW 59 AC38
MOSSIP AV (CRS) 8 F1
MOTHERWELL RD NE 52 AO30
MT ABERDEEN CIR SE 95 AT63
CL SE 95 AT62
GV SE 95 AS62
LK SE 95 AT62
MR SE 95 AS62
MT ALBERTA BY SE 95 AR64
CT SE 95 AR65
GN SE, MR SE 95 AR66
PL SE 100, 200 95 AR65
VW SE 95 AR65
MT ALLAN CIR SE 95 AT64
MT APEX CR SE 95 AT63
GN SE 95 AT63
MT ASSINIBOINE CIR SE 95 AQ68
PL SE 100, 200 95 AQ68
MT BELCHER PL SE 95 AQ67
MT BREWSTER CIR SE 95 AS64
PL SE 95 AS65
MT CASCADE CL SE 95 AQ67
PL SE 100, 200, 300 95 AQ67
400 95 AP68
MT COPPER GN SE 95 AQ68
PK SE 95 AQ67
PK SE 100, 200 95 AQ67
MT CORNWALL CIR SE 95 AS65
MS SE 100, 200 95 AT65
MT DOUGLAS CIR SE 95 AS63
CL SE 95 AS64
CT SE 100 95 AR62
200 95 AS62
300 95 AR62
400 95 AS62
GN SE 100, 200 95 AS64
300 95 AS63
400 95 AS64
MR SE 100, 200, 300 95 AS64
PL SE 100, 200 95 AS63
300, 400 95 AR63
PT SE 95 AR62
VL SE 95 AS63
MT GIBRALTER HTS SE 95 AQ70
PL SE 95 AQ69
MT KIDD GDN SE 95 AQ69
PT SE, RD SE 95 AQ69
MT LORETTE CL SE 95 AS64
PL SE 100 95 AT64
200 95 AT65
300, 400 95 AT64
MT McKENZIE BY SE 95 AS62
DR SE 95 AS62
GDN SE 100 95 AR65
200, 300 95 AR66
VL SE 95 AR66
WY SE 95 AR65
MT NORQUAY GT SE 95 AQ68
PK SE 100 95 AP68
200 95 AQ68
RD (BNF) 21 B4
MT PEECHEE PL (CAN) 101 C4
MT RELIANT PL SE 100 95 AQ67
MT ROBSON CIR SE 95 AR67
CL SE, GT SE 95 AR67
MT ROYAL CT SW 58 W42
MT RUNDLE PL (CAN) 101 C4
MT SELKIRK CL SE 95 AS65
PL SE 95 AS65
MT SPARROWHAWK
LD SE 95 AR68
PL SE 100, 200 95 AR68
300 95 AQ68
400 95 AR67
MT VICTORIA PL SE 100 95 AR66
200, 300 95 AQ66
MT YAMNUSKA CT SE 95 AQ69
PL SE 95 AQ69
MOUNTAIN AV (BNF) 21 C8
AV (CAN) 101 C2
AV (CRS) 8 G2
CIR (AIR) 113 G6
LN (BNF) 21 D8
PL (OKS) 107 C5
ST (CAN) 101 D4
ST (COCR) 103 F4
ST (OKS) 107 B5
MOUNTAIN GOAT
LN (BNF) 21 C5
MOUNTAIN PARK CIR SE 95 AR66
DR SE 95 AQ67
MOUNTAIN RIVER
EST (SPNG) 99 C4
MOUNTAIN VISTA
EST (SPNG) 99 B3
MOUNTVIEW CR NE 41 AI28
MUNRO DR NE 52 AO31
MUNSON ST (CRS) 8 F3
MURDOCH CL (CRS) 8 F3
ST (CRS) 8 F2
MURPHY PL NE 52 AO32
RD NE 52 AO32
MURRAY PL NE 52 AO32
PL (SPNG) 99 D4
MUSKOKA DR NE 52 AN32
MUSKRAT ST (BNF) 21 D6

N

NAHANNI DR (BNF) 21 C8
NAMAKA CR NW 39 AB23
NANTON AV (CRS) 8 F2
RD NW 39 AC22
NELSON RD NW 39 AB22
NEMISKAM RD NW 39 AC21
NESBITT AV (LNG) 88 D6
CL (LNG) 88 E5
RD NW 39 AC21
NEW PL SE 51 AL35
ST SE 51 AL35
NEW BOW LN SE 51 AL35
NEW BRIGHTON BY SE 98 AZ65
CIR SE, CL SE 97 AW64
CM SE 97 AY66
CT SE 98 AZ65
CV SE, DR SE 97 AW63
GDN SE 100, 200 97 AX66
GN SE 97 AX66
GT SE 97 AW65
GV SE 100, 200 98 AZ65
300, 400 98 AZ64
LD SE 97 AW63
LK SE, MR SE 97 AW65
MS SE 100, 200 97 AW65
PK SE 1000, 2000 98 AZ65
PL SE 100, 200, 300 97 AW64
400 97 AW64
WY SE 97 AY66
NEWCOMBE PL NW 39 AC21
NEWTON ST (LNG) 88 C8
NICKLE RD NW 39 AB22
NICOLA PL NW 39 AC22
NINA GDN NE 51 AK33
NINGA RD NW 39 AC21
NIPAWIN CR NW 39 AC22
NIVEN PL NW 39 AB21
RD NW 39 AB22
NOBLE RD NW 39 AB22
NOKOMIS PL NW 39 AC21
NOLAN RD NW 39 AC21
NORDEGG CR NW 39 AC22
NORFOLK DR NW 27 AC20
RD NW, WY NW 27 AD20
NORMANDY DR SW 58 X41
NORQUAY CT NW 39 AB22
DR NW 39 AB23
HTS NW 39 AB22
NORRIS RD NW 39 AB21
NORSEMAN PL NW 27 AC20
RD NW 27 AC20
NORTH RD (BSKR) 111 E2
NORTH HAVEN DR NW 39 AB23
NORTH ROYALITE
WY (T VAL) 105 D5
NORTHCOTE RD NW 39 AB23
NORTHLAND DR NW 38 U22
NORTHMOUNT CR NW 27 AD21
DR NW (100-1100) 39 AB25
DR NW (1200-1600) 38 U22
PL NW 27 AE20
NORTHRIDGE DR (OKS) 107 C4
NOSE HILL DR NW 22 E18
DR NW (5300-7000) 23 H20
DR NW (8500-8900) 12 M14
NOTTINGHAM GT NW 27 AC20
RD NW 27 AC20
NUTANA PL NW 39 AB23

O

OAK AV (OKS) 107 D6
OAKBRIAR CL SW 73 Y54
OAKBURY PL SW 73 W54
OAKCHURCH BY SW 73 V53
CR SW 73 V53
PL SW 73 W53
OAKCLIFFE DR SW 73 U53
PL SW 100 73 U53
OAKDALE PL SW 100 73 X53
OAKFERN CR SW 73 V52
RD SW 73 V52
WY SW 73 V51
OAKFIELD DR SW 73 V54
PL SW 100 73 V53
OAKHAMPTON
PL SW 100 73 W53
200 73 W53
OAKHILL DR SW 73 W53
PL SW 100, 200, 300 73 X53
400 73 X53
500 73 W53
600, 700 73 W54
OAKLAND GT SW 73 V53
PL SW 100 73 U52
200 73 U53
RD SW 73 V53
WY SW 73 U53
OAKLAWN PL SW 73 W54
OAKMERE CL (CHST) 80 A6
GN (CHST) 80 A5
PL 100, 200 (CHST) 80 A6
PT (CHST) 80 A6
WY (CHST) 80 A5
OAKMOOR CR SW 73 V54
DR SW 73 V54
PL SW 100 73 W54
200 73 V54
WY SW 73 W54
OAKMOUNT CT SW 73 U51
DR SW 73 U53
PL SW 73 U52
RD SW 73 V51
WY SW 73 U52
OAKRIDGE GT SW 73 V54
PL SW 100, 200 73 V54
300 73 U54
RD SW 73 V54
WY SW 73 U54
OAKSIDE BY SW 100 73 W52
200 73 W52
CIR SW, CL SW 73 V52
GT SW 73 W52
PL SW 100 73 W52
RD SW 73 W52
OAKTREE CL SW 73 X54
LN SW 73 X54
OAKVALE PL SW 73 W54
OAKVIEW PL SW 73 W54
OAKWOOD DR SW 73 U53
PL SW 100 73 W53
200 73 W54
300, 400 73 V54
500, 600 73 U54
OGDEN CR SE 69 AN48
DR SE 69 AM49
RD SE (2800-4200) 61 AL41
RD SE (4300-8000) 69 AO45
RS SE, WY SE 69 AM49
OGDEN DALE PL SE 69 AQ48
RD SE 69 AP47
OGMOOR CR SE 69 AN49
PL SE 69 AN49
OKALTA RD (T VAL) 105 B6
OKOTOKS DR (OKS) 107 C5
OLD BANFF COACH
RD SW 35 H29
RD SW (6400) 46 O32
RD (SPNG) 99 F1
OLD CANMORE RD (CAN) 101 E4
OLD HAULAGE RD (CAN) 101 C7

OLYMPIA BY SE........**69** AP49
  CR SE, DR SE.......**69** AO50
  PL SE................**69** AP49
OLYMPIC DR *(CAN)*....**101** B5
  WY SE.............**50** AH36
ORCHARD WY *(STMR)* ...**112** E9
ORCHARD PARK
  RD *(STMR)*..........**112** D9
OSBORNE CR SW.......**58** Y37
OSLER AV *(CRS)*........**8** F2
OTTER LN *(BNF)*.......**21** F4
  ST *(BNF)*...........**21** D5
OWL'S HAVEN *(EV)* ...**115** F9
  ST *(BNF)*...........**21** E3

P

PACIFIC AV *(OKS)* **107** D5
  RD NE.............**41** AI22
PALERMO WY SW **74** Z52
PALIS WY SW **73** Y53
PALISADE DR SW.......**73** X53
PALISAN PL SW **73** Y54
PALISBRIAR PK SW 100 ..**73** Y54
  200...............**73** Y54
PALISCLIFFE RD SW **73** Y54
PALISDALE RD SW.......**74** Z54
PALISFIELD RD SW......**74** Z54
PALISHALL RD SW.......**73** Y54
PALISMOUNT PL SW **73** Y52
PALISPRIOR RD SW......**73** Y53
PALISTONE RD SW **73** X53
PALISVIEW PL SW **73** Y52
PALISWOOD BY SW **73** Y53
  GT SW **73** Y52
  PK SW 100 ....**74** Z52
  200...............**74** Z53
  PL SW, RD SW **73** Y52
  WY SW **73** Y53
PALLISER DR SW **73** V51
  PL SW **73** X53
  TR *(CAN)* **101** C2
PALM WY NW **35** H22
PALMER RD NE **29** AN21
PANAMOUNT BLVD NW ..**5** AC7
  CL NW.............**5** AE7
  CL NW 100, 200......**5** AE7
  CR NW **5** AF8
  CT NW 100, 200......**5** AD7
  DR NW **5** AE7
  GDN NW **5** AD6
  GN NW **5** AF7
  GT NW **5** AC8
  200...............**5** AD8
  HL NW **5** AD6
  HTS NW **5** AD8
  LK NW **5** AE7
  LN NW **5** AD7
  MS NW **5** AF8
  PK NW **5** AE7
  PL NW 100 ....**5** AD7
  200...............**5** AD7
  RS NW **5** AD6
  SQ NW **5** AD7
PANATELLA BLVD NW ...**5** AC6
  CIR NW **5** AE6
  CL NW.............**5** AE5
  CT NW 100 ....**5** AE5
  200, 300, 400 ......**5** AE6
  500...............**5** AF5
  DR NW **5** AE5
  GT NW **5** AF5
  LN NW **5** AE5
  PK NW 100, 200, 300 ..**5** AF4
  400, 500 ....**5** AF5
  PL NW 100 ....**5** AE5
  200..........**5** AE6, 5 AF5
  TER NW, VW NW.....**5** AE5
  WY NW **5** AE5
PANORAMA BY *(SPNG)* ..**99** D2
  HTS NW **4** X4
  RD NW **4** X7
  RDG *(SPNG)* **99** D2
PANORAMA HILLS
  BLVD NW **5** AC7
  BY NW 100, 200......**5** AC9
  CIR NW **5** AC9
  CL NW.............**5** AD9
  CM NW, CR NW......**5** AE8
  CT NW **5** AD9
  CV NW **5** AF8
  DR NW **5** AC8
  GDN NW **15** AD10
  GN NW **5** AD9
  GT NW **5** AC9
  GV NW **5** AD9
  HE NW **5** AD8
  HTS NW **5** AB8
  LD NW **5** AC8
  LK NW **5** AB8
  LN NW **5** AF8
  LN NW 100, 200 .....**5** AD8
  MR NW **5** AD8
  MS NW **5** AC9

PK NW, PL NW........**5** AE9
PT NW **5** AC9
RD NW **5** AE8
RS NW **5** AC8
SQ NW **5** AD8
TER NW 100, 200, 300...**5** AC8
VW NW **5** AC9
WY NW **5** AE8
PARADISE LN *(CHST)* ...**80** A5
  RD *(CHST)* **80** B5
PARK AV SW **59** AE41
  AV *(BNF)* **21** C8
  CR NE **51** AK31
  LN SW **59** AD38
  PL *(B CK)* **33** F8
  PT *(B CK)* **33** F8
  RD SE **50** AD36
  RD *(STMR)* **112** F7
PARK ESTATES DR SE ...**91** AI63
  PL SE..............**91** AJ63
PARKDALE BLVD NW.....**47** U31
  CR NW.............**47** V31
PARKGLEN CR SE **92** AL64
  PL SE 100, 200 ......**92** AL64
  RD SE **92** AL64
PARKHILL PL SW **59** AG40
  ST NW **59** AG40
PARKLAND BLVD SE **91** AK63
  CR SE **91** AK63
  GN SE **83** AK62
  HL SE **92** AL64
  PL SE **91** AK63
  RS SE, WY SE **91** AK64
PARKLANE DR *(STMR)* ..**112** E7
  PL, WY *(STMR)* **112** E7
PARKRIDGE CR SE **92** AM65
  DR SE, GN SE **92** AM66
  HL SE **92** AM65
  PL SE 100 ....**92** AM65
  200..............**92** AM66
  RD SE, RS SE **92** AM66
  VW SE, WY SE **92** AM65
PARKSIDE CR SE **91** AK63
  DR SE **91** AJ63
  GN SE **91** AK64
  PL SE, WY SE **91** AK63
PARKVALLEY DR SE **92** AL65
  GT SE, PL SE, RD SE ..**92** AL65
  WY SE **92** AL66
PARKVIEW CR SE **91** AK64
  CR SE *(B DMD)* **106** H3
  EST *(STMR)* **112** F6
  GN SE **91** AK64
  PL SE 100, 200 ......**92** AL66
  PL SE *(B DMD)* **106** H3
  WY SE **92** AL64
PARKVISTA CR SE **92** AL66
  PL SE..............**92** AL66
PARKWOOD CL SE **91** AJ63
  CR *(STMR)* **112** F7
  DR SE **91** AJ63
  PL SE 100, 200 ......**91** AJ63
  PL *(STMR)* **112** F7
  RS SE **83** AK62
  WY SE **83** AJ62
PARTRIDGE BY *(SPNG)* ..**99** F2
  CT, PL *(SPNG)* **99** F2
PASADENA GDN NE **44** AZ27
  GN NE.............**44** BA26
PASSCHENDAELE AV SW..**58** Y42
  RD SW **58** Y42
PATINA CT SW **46** P30
  DR SW **46** O30
  GN SW 100, 200......**46** P30
  HL SW, LN SW **46** P30
  PK SW **46** P32
  PL SW 400 ....**46** P30
  500..............**46** Q31
  PT SW, RS SW, TER SW **46** P31
  VL SW **46** P31
PATRICIAN ST *(CAN)* ...**101** B5
PATRICK AV SW **46** N29
  ST SW **46** N29
  VW SW **46** O29
PATTERSON BLVD SW ...**46** P29
  BY SW **46** P29
  CL SW.............**46** N28
  CR SW **46** P29
  DR SW, GN SW **46** O29
  GT SW **46** N30
  GV SW **46** N28
  HL SW **46** N30
  MS SW **46** O30
  MT SW 100, 200......**46** O30
  PK SW, PL SW **46** O29
  PT SW **46** N29
  RD *(OKS)* **107** C5
  RS SW **46** O30
  VW SW **46** N30
PATTON CT SW 100 ....**74** AB53
  200..............**74** AB54
  PL SW 100 ....**74** AB53
  RD SW **74** AB54
PEAKS DR *(CAN)* **101** C7
PEGASUS RD NE **30** AO22
  WY NE **30** AO22
PEIGAN TR SE *(4100)* ...**61** AQ41
PEKISKO RD *(H RV)* ...**109** B5
PENBROOKE CL SE **54** AY34
  CR SE **54** AZ33

DR SE **54** AY34
PL SE, WY SE **54** AZ34
RD SE, WY SE **54** AY34
PENEDO CR SE........**54** AY35
  PL SE, WY SE **54** AY35
PENMEADOWS CL SE ...**53** AX34
  PL SE, RD SE **53** AW34
PENNSBURG DR SE **53** AX35
  PL SE **53** AX36
  RD SE **53** AX36
  WY SE **53** AX35
PENNSYLVANIA RD SE ..**53** AW32
PENRITH CR SE **53** AX35
  PL SE **53** AX35
PENSACOLA CL SE **53** AW36
  CR SE, WK SE, WY SE **53** AW35
PENSDALE CR SE **53** AX34
  RD SE **53** AW35
PENSVILLE CL SE **54** AY34
  RD SE **54** AY33
PENSWOOD PL SE......**54** AZ33
  RD SE **54** AZ33
  WY SE **54** AY33
PENWORTH CL SE **53** AX34
  CR SE **53** AX34
  DR SE, GN SE, PL SE ..**53** AX33
  RD SE **53** AX33
  RS SE **53** AW33
  WY SE **53** AX33
PHAIR AV NE..........**51** AL31
PIKA PL *(BNF)* **21** E4
PINE AV *(B CK)* **33** G6
  PL SW **47** U34
  PL *(CRS)* **8** F1
  RD *(STMR)* **112** E9
  WY NW **35** H23
PINE CREEK RD *(H PT)* ..**115** B1
PINEBROOK CL NE **44** AY27
  PL NE **44** AY27
  WY *(SPNG)* **99** H6
PINECLIFF CL NE **44** AZ27
  DR NE **44** AZ26
  GV NE **44** AZ27
  RD NE **44** AY26
  WY NE **44** AZ26
PINECONE LN *(SPNG)* ...**99** J6
PINECREST CR NE **43** AX29
  RD NE **43** AX29
PINEGREEN CL NE **43** AW29
  PL NE **43** AX29
PINEGROVE CL NE **44** AY28
PINEHILL PL NE **44** AY28
  RD NE **44** AY28
PINEHURST CL *(H PT)* ..**115** C1
  DR *(H PT)* **115** C1
PINELAND BY NE **44** AY26
  CL NE **44** AY27
  PL NE 100, 200, 300...**44** AY26
  RD NE **44** AY26
PINELORE PL NE **44** AY27
PINEMEADOW PL NE ...**44** AY26
  RD NE **44** AY26
PINEMILL MS NE 100 ...**43** AX27
  200..............**43** AX27
  RD NE, WY NE......**43** AX27
PINEMONT BY NE **43** AW28
  GT NE, PL NE, RD NE .**43** AW28
PINEPOINT DR NE **43** AX28
  PL NE 100, 200......**43** AX28
  RD NE **43** AX28
PINERIDGE RD NE **44** AY28
  WY *(SPNG)* **99** H6
PINESET PL NE 100 ....**43** AW28
  200, 300..........**43** AW28
PINESIDE PL NE **43** AX28
PINESON PL NE **44** AY27
PINESTREAM PL NE **43** AX26
  PL NE 100..........**43** AX26
  300..............**43** AW26
PINETOWN PL NE **43** AW27
  200..............**43** AW27
PINETREE BY NE 100...**44** AZ29
  200..............**44** AZ28
  CR NE **44** AZ29
  DR *(SPNG)* **99** H6
  PL NE **44** AZ28
  RD NE **44** AZ28
PINEWIND CL NE **43** AX26
  RD NE **43** AX26
PINEWOOD CR *(CAN)* ..**101** C3
  DR SE **62** AS37
PINNACLE RIDGE
  DR *(SPNG)* **99** G3
  PL 100, 200, 300 *(SPNG)* ..**99** G3
  400 *(SPNG)* **99** G3
PINTA GDN NE **51** AK33
PIONEER DR *(IRR)* **111** C4
  RD *(CAN)* **101** F5
PITT AV SE **59** AG39
PLAINSVIEW RD *(STMR)*..**112** F6
PLUM TREE PL SW **47** V35
POINT DR NE **47** S30
POINT McKAY CR NW ...**47** S30
  CT NW, GDN NW **47** T31
  GV NW **47** T30
  RD NW **47** T31
  TER NW **47** U31
POLAR AV *(H RV)* **109** E4
POPE AV *(COCR)* **103** F5
POPLAR RD SW **47** U34

ST NW.............**35** H23
POPULAR AV *(OKS)* ...**107** D6
PORCPINE PL *(BNF)* ...**21** E3
PORTLAND ST SE **60** AK37
POWELL ST *(COCR)* ...**103** F4
PREMIER WY SW **59** AB39
PRENDERGAST PL *(CAN)* .**101** B6
PRESTWICK AV SE **97** AV64
  BLVD SE **97** AV64
  BY SE **97** AV63
  CIR SE **97** AU64
  CL SE **97** AU63
  CL SE 100, 200, 300 .**97** AU63
  CM SE **97** AU64
  CR SE **97** AV64
  CT SE **97** AW63
  CV SE **95** AT65
  DR SE **97** AU64
  GDN SE **97** AV65
  GN SE **97** AV65
  GT SE **97** AW63
  GV SE **97** AV63
  HE SE **95** AT64
  HTS SE **97** AV63
  LD SE **97** AU65
  LK SE **97** AU63
  LN SE **97** AV64
  MR SE **97** AU63
  MS SE 100, 200 .....**95** AT64
  PK SE **97** AU63
  PL SE **97** AW63
  PR SE **97** AU63
  PT SE 100, 200......**95** AT63
  RD SE **97** AU65
  ROW SE **97** AV65
  RS SE **97** AV64
  ST SE, TER SE **97** AU63
  TER SE 100, 200, 300 .**95** AT63
  VL SE **97** AV63
  WY SE **97** AV64
PRESTWICK ACRES
  LN SE **97** AW64
PRESTWICK ESTATE
  GT SE **97** AU64
  LK SE, WY SE **97** AU64
PRESTWICK POND
  TER SE **97** AU65
PRINCETON WY SW **50** AE32
  WY SW **50** AE32
PROMENADE PK SE **97** AV66
  WY SE **97** AV66
PROMINENCE HL SW ...**46** O31
  HTS SW **46** P31
  PH SW **46** P30
  PK SW **46** O30
  PT SW **46** P30
  RS SW **46** O31
  VW SW **46** P31
  WY SW **46** P30
PROSPECT AV SW **59** AB37
  CL *(CAN)* **101** C6
  CT, HTS *(CAN)* **101** C6
PUMP HILL BY SW **74** AA54
  CL SW.............**74** AA53
  CR SW **74** AA54
  DR SW **74** Z53
  GDN SW 100, 200, 300..**74** Z53
  GN SW, GT SW **74** AA54
  LD SW **74** Z52
  MS SW, PL SW **74** Z54
  RD SW, RS SW **74** AA54
  VW SW **74** AA54
  WY SW **74** Z53
PUMP VALLEY CT SW ..**74** AB53
PUMPHOUSE AV SW ...**49** Z34
  RD SW **49** Z34
PUMPMEADOW CR SW .**74** AA53
  PL SW.............**74** AA53
PUMPRIDGE PL SW 100 .**74** AA53
  300..............**74** AA53

Q

QUALICUM BEACH
  BY *(CHST)* **80** B8
QUEBEC WY SE **59** AB38
QUEEN ALEXANDRA
  CL SE **83** AK61
  RD SE, WY SE **84** AL60
QUEEN ANNE CL SE ...**84** AN61
  PL SE 100, 200......**84** AN60
  RD SE **84** AN60
  WY SE **84** AN59
QUEEN CHARLOTTE
  DR SE **84** AM61
  GT SE **84** AM60
  PL SE, RD SE, WY SE .**84** AM61
QUEEN ISABELLA CL SE .**84** AL61
QUEEN TAMARA PL SE .**84** AM60
  RD SE **84** AM60
  WY SE **84** AM59
QUEENSLAND CIR SE ...**84** AL59
  DR SE **84** AM60
  GT SE, HL SE, ...**84** AL61
  PL SE 100, 200......**84** AL60

300 . . . . 84 AM60
400 . . . . 84 AM61
500, 600 . . . . . . 84 AM61
RD SE, RS SE 84 AL61
QUEENSTON GDN SE . . 84 AN61
HTS SE, TER NE . . . 84 AN61
QUENTIN AV SW 58 Y42
CT SW, PL SW, ST SW . 58 Y42
QUESNAY WOOD DR SW 58 W42
QUIGLEY CL 100 (COCR). . 103 A4
200 (COCR) . . . 103 A4
DR (COCR) 103 B4

R

RABBIT ST (BNF) 21 D4
RADCLIFFE BY SE . . . 52 AS34
CL SE 52 AS33
CR SE 52 AR33
CT SE, DR SE . . . 52 AR34
PL SE 100 . . . . 52 AQ34
200 . . . . . . 52 AR34
RD SE 52 AR34
RADFORD RD NE . . . 51 AI30
RADISSON DR SE . . . 52 AR35
RADLEY PL SE 100 . . . 52 AS33
200 . . . . . . 52 AS33
WY SE 52 AS33
RADNOR AV NE . . . 51 AJ30
RAE CR SE 52 AR35
RAILWAY AV (AIR) . . . 113 C4
AV (BNF) 21 C5
AV (CAN) 101 C3
AV (LNG) 88 B8
CR (LNG) 88 D8
GT (AIR) 113 C4
ST SE 68 AJ47
ST (AIR) 113 D4
ST (COCR) 103 E4
ST (CRS) 8 F3
ST (H RV) 109 D6
ST N (OKS) 107 D6
ST S (OKS) 107 C6
RAINBOW AV (BNF) . . . 21 C8
BY (CHST) 80 A4
RD (CHST) 80 A5
RAMSAY ST SE 51 AI37
RANCH RD (OKS) . . . 107 G3
RANCH ESTATES
BY NW 100 . . . . 24 O16
200, 300, 400 . . . 12 O15
500 . . . . . . 12 P15
600 . . . . . . 24 P16
PL NW 100, 200, 300 . . 24 P17
400 . . . . . . 24 P17
500, 600, 700. . . . 24 P16
800 . . . . . . 24 O16
900 . . . . . . 24 O16
1000 . . . . . . 24 P16
RD NW 12 O15
RANCH GLEN DR NW . . 24 M17
PL NW 100, 200, 300 . . 24 M17
400 . . . . . . 24 M17
RANCHE RD (COCR). . . . 103 E2
RANCHERO BY NW . . . 24 M16
DR NW, GN NW. . . . 24 M16
PL NW 100, 200 . . . 12 N15
RD NW 24 N16
RS NW 24 N16
RANCHLANDS BLVD NW . . 11 L15
BY NW 24 M16
CR NW 23 L16
CT NW 100, 200, 300 . . 23 L16
GV NW 24 M16
PL NW, RD NW, WY NW 23 L16
RANCHRIDGE BY NW 100. 12 N15
200, 300, 400 . . . 24 O16
CR NW 24 O16
CT NW 100, 200 . . . 24 N16
300 . . . . . . 12 N15
400, 500, 600 . . . 24 N16
DR NW 12 N15
PL NW 24 N16
RD NW 24 O16
WY NW 24 N16
RANCHVIEW CIR NW . . . 24 N17
CR NW 24 O18
CT NW 100 . . . . 24 O17
200, 300, 400 . . . 24 O18
500 . . . . . . 24 O18
DR NW 24 O17
LK NW 24 O17
MS NW 100 . . . . 24 P17
200 . . . . . . 24 O17
300 . . . . . . 24 O16
PL NW 100, 200, 300 . . 24 N18
400, 500 . . . . 24 N17
RD NW, TER NW . . . 24 N17
RANGE CR NW 24 M15
DR NW, GDN NW . . . 24 M15
GN NW 24 M15
PL NW, WY NW . . . 24 M15
RAVENNA AV SW . . . 57 T43
RAVINE DR (H PT) . . . 115 E2

RAY McBRIDE ST (CAN) . . 101 C2
RAYMOND CL (T VAL) . . 105 B5
RAYNARD CR SE 52 AR34
READER CR NE 51 AJ30
REDWOOD CR SE . . . 62 AR37
REDWOOD MEADOWS
CL (RED) 33 E3
CT (RED) 33 D3
DR (RED) 33 C4
REFLECTION CV (EV) . . 115 E8
REGAL CR NE 51 AI30
PK NE 100, 200, 300 . . 51 AK31
400, 500, 600 . . 51 AK30
REGENT CR NE 51 AI30
REMINGTON RD NE . . . 51 AJ30
RENFREW DR NE . . . 51 AJ29
RESEARCH PL NW . . . 38 V25
RD NW 38 U24
WY NW 38 V25
RETREAT LN (COCR) . . . 103 J2
RD (COCR) 103 F3
RICHARD CT SW 57 V43
PL SW 57 V43
RD SW, WY SW . . . 57 V44
RICHARDSON LK SW . . . 57 V41
RD SW 57 U42
ST SW 65 T44
WY SW 57 U42
RICHELIEU CT SW . . . 57 U42
RICHLAND RD NE . . . 51 AK30
RICHMOND
RD SW (1800-4900) . . 56 Q41
RD SW (5400-6000). . . 56 P41
RIDDELL PL SE 52 AR35
RIDEAU CL (AIR) 113 D5
PL SW 59 AE39
RD SW 59 AE39
RIDGE RD SW. 59 AC39
RD (CAN) 101 G5
RD (STMR) 112 E8
RIDGE POINTE DR (H PT) . 115 E1
RIDGEBROOK DR (AIR) . . 113 D5
RIDGEGATE WY (AIR) . . 113 D4
RIEL PL SE 52 AR36
RILEY PL (H RV) 109 E4
ST (H RV) 109 E4
RIVER AV (COCR) . . . 103 F5
DR N (B CK) . . . 33 G7
DR S (B CK) . . . 33 G7
RD (CAN) 101 C4
RIVER HEIGHTS
DR (COCR) 103 E8
RS (COCR) 103 E8
RIVER RIDGE CL (SPNG) . . 99 E5
DR, PT (SPNG) . . . 99 E5
RIVER ROCK CIR SE . . . 76 AO54
CR SE 76 AP53
CT SE 76 AP53
GN SE 76 AP52
MR SE, PL SE . . . 76 AO54
RD SE, WY SE . . . 76 AO53
RIVERBEND DR SE . . . 76 AM50
GT SE 76 AN51
RIVERBIRCH BY SE . . . 76 AN51
CR SE 76 AN51
CT SE 76 AM50
PL SE 76 AM50
RD SE 76 AM50
RIVERBROOK CT SE . . . 76 AM51
PL SE, RD SE, WY SE . 76 AM50
RIVERCREST CIR SE . . . 76 AO50
CL SE 69 AO50
CR SE 76 AP51
DR SE 76 AN51
PL SE 76 AP51
VL SE 76 AO51
WY SE 76 AO51
RIVERCROFT CL SE. . . . 76 AO51
RIVERDALE AV SW . . . 59 AC41
RIVERFRONT AV SW . . . 50 AF33
RIVERGLEN CL (CAN) . . 76 AO51
CR SE, DR SE. . . . 76 AN51
PK SE 76 AO52
PL SE 100 . . . . 76 AN51
200 . . . . . . 76 AO51
RD SE, WY SE . . . 76 AN52
RIVERGREEN CR SE . . . 76 AM51
PL SE 100, 200 . . . 76 AM51
RIVERSIDE BLVD (H RV) . 109 A4
BY SE 100 . . . . 76 AL51
200 . . . . . . 76 AL51
BY (H RV) 109 A3
CIR SE 68 AL50
CL SE 76 AM51
CR SE. 76 AM50
CR (H RV) 109 A3
CT (H RV) 109 A4
DR (H RV) 109 B3
DR (OKS) 107 B6
GDN (H RV) 109 A3
GN (H RV) 109 A4
GT (OKS) 107 B6
MS SE 100 . . . . 68 AL50
200 . . . . . . 68 AL50
PL SE 69 AM49
PL (COCR) 103 D6
PL (H RV) 109 A4
RD SE 76 AM50
RD (H RV) 109 A2
WY SE 68 AL50

WY (OKS) 107 B6
RIVERSTONE CL SE . . . 76 AP51
CR SE, CT SE. . . . 76 AO52
CV SE 100, 200. . . . 76 AP52
DR (CAN) 101 F5
PL SE 76 AO51
RD SE 76 AP51
RIVERVALLEY CR SE . . . 76 AM52
DR SE 76 AM52
PL SE 76 AM51
RIVERVIEW BY SE . . . 76 AM51
CIR SE 76 AM53
CIR (COCR) 103 E6
CL SE 76 AM53
CL (COCR) 103 E6
CT SE 76 AM51
CT (BNF) 21 D7
CT (COCR) 103 E7
DR SE 76 AL52
DR (COCR) 103 E6
GDN SE 76 AM53
GN 100 (COCR) . . . 103 E6
200, 300, 400 (COCR) 103 E7
MS SE 76 AM52
PK SE 76 AM52
PL SE 100, 200, 300. . 76 AN53
400 . . . . . . 76 AM54
500, 600, 700 . . . 76 AN54
800, 900 . . . . 76 AM54
PL (CAN) 101 C4
PT SE 76 AM52
TER SE 76 AN53
RIVERWOOD CIR SE . . . 76 AM52
CL SE 76 AO52
CR SE, CT SE. . . . 76 AN53
MR SE 76 AO53
ROBERT RD NE. . . . 51 AK30
ST (T VAL) 105 B5
ROBINSON DR (OKS) . . 107 D4
RD (SPNG) 99 F4
ROBSON CR SE 52 AR36
ROCKBLUFF CL NW . . . 9 D10
PL NW 9 D9
ROCKBOROUGH GN NW 100 9 F8
200 . . . . . . 9 F9
PK NW 9 F8
ROCKCLIFF BY NW. . . . 9 E9
BY NW 100 . . . . 9 E10
ROCKMONT CT NW . . . 9 D7
ROCKPOINT CV NW . . . 9 E9
ROCKY RIDGE BLVD NW . . 9 D9
BY NW. 9 F11
BY NW 100, 200, 300 . 9 F11
400, 500. . . . 9 E10
CIR NW 9 E10
CL NW. 9 D10
CL NW 100 . . . . 9 D10
200 . . . . . . 9 D10
CR NW 9 F9
CT NW 100, 200 . . . 9 E10
CV NW 100, 200, 300 . 9 F10
400 . . . . . . 9 D10
DR NW 9 D10
GDN NW 9 F11
GN NW, GT NW, HE NW . 9 E10
HE NW 100 . . . . 9 E10
HTS NW, LD NW . . . 9 F10
MS NW 100. . . . 9 E11
200, 300. . . . 9 F10
PL NW 9 F9
PT NW 100 . . . . 9 F10
RD NW 10 G12
SQ NW 9 E11
VL NW 9 E11
VW NW 200, 300 . . . 9 E11
400, 500, 600 . . . 9 D10
ROCKY SPRING CIR NW . . 9 D8
GN NW 9 C9
GT NW 9 D8
ROCKY VISTA CIR NW . . 9 F12
DR NW. 9 F11
GDN NW 9 E11
PK NW, TER NW . . . 9 F12
ROCKYLEDGE CR NW . . 9 D10
RS NW, ST NW. . . . 9 D9
TER NW 9 D9
VW NW 22 D11
ROCKYVALE DR NW . . . 9 E9
ROCKYVALLEY DR NW . . 9 C9
ROCKYWOOD CIR NW . . 9 E9
PK NW 9 D9
ROLLING RANGE
DR (COCR) 103 C8
EST (COCR) 103 D8
PL (COCR) 103 D9
ROSE NW 35 H23
ROSEHILL DR NW . . . 39 AB27
ROSELAKE ST NW . . . 39 AB27
ROSELAWN CR NW . . . 39 AB27
PL NW 39 AB27
ROSERY DR NW 39 AC27
PL NW 39 AB27
ROSETREE CR NW. . . . 39 AC26
RD NW 39 AC26
ROSEVALE DR NW . . . 39 AB26
ROSEVIEW DR NW . . . 39 AB26
ROSEWOOD DR (SPNG). . 99 F4
RD NW 39 AC26
ROSS AV (COCR) . . . 103 F5
PL (CRS) 8 F3

RD NW 39 AB29
ST (CRS) 8 F3
ROSSBURN CR SW . . . 47 S34
ROSSCARROCK GT SW . . 47 T34
ROSSDALE RD SW . . . 47 S34
ROSSMERE RD SW . . . 47 S34
ROSSMOUNT RD SW. . . 47 T34
ROULEAU CR SE 52 AR36
ROWLAND LN (OKS) . . . 107 G4
ROWLEY CL (T VAL). . . 105 B5
ROXBORO RD SW . . . 59 AF38
ROXBORO GLEN RD SW. 59 AF39
ROYAL AV SW 59 AC37
AV (T VAL) 105 B4
BY NW 100 . . . . 10 G12
200 . . . . . . 10 G12
300, 400 . . . . 10 H12
CT NW 300 . . . . 10 H12
500, 600, 700 . . . 10 H12
800 . . . . . . 10 H12
MR NW, RD NW. . . . 10 G12
ROYAL ABBEY CT NW 100 10 G10
200 . . . . . . 10 G10
RS NW 10 G10
ROYAL BIRCH BLVD NW. . 10 H10
BY NW 100, 200, 300. . 10 I10
CIR NW 10 I10
CL NW. 10 J10
CR NW, GDN NW. . . . 10 H10
GN NW 10 H10
GT NW 10 I10
GV NW 10 J11
HE NW 100 . . . . 10 I10
200 . . . . . . 10 J9
HL NW 10 I10
HTS NW 10 H10
LD NW 10 I10
MR NW 10 J10
MS NW 100, 200 . . . 10 I10
PL NW 100 . . . . 10 I11
200 . . . . . . 10 I10
PT NW. 10 H11
RD NW, RS NW. . . . 10 I10
ST NW 10 I10
TER NW 10 J9
VW NW 100. . . . 10 J11
200, 300. . . . 10 J10
WY NW. 10 I9
ROYAL BIRKDALE BY NW. 10 H10
CR NW, CT NW . . . 10 I10
DR NW 10 H9
ROYAL CREST BY NW 100 10 H12
200 . . . . . . 10 H11
300, 400, 500 . . . 10 J11
CT NW 10 J11
PL NW 200. . . . 10 J11
PT NW. 10 J11
TER NW, VW NW. . . 10 H11
WY NW 10 H11
ROYAL ELM NW 10 G11
DR NW, MS NW. . . . 10 G11
RD NW 10 G11
WY NW 10 G11
ROYAL HIGHLAND CT NW 10 G10
RD NW 10 G10
ROYAL OAK BLVD NW . . 10 G10
BY NW 100 . . . . 10 H9
200 . . . . . . 10 H8
CAPE NW 10 G9
CIR NW, CM NW . . . 10 G9
CR NW 10 H10
CT NW 100, 200 . . . 10 G8
CV NW 10 G9
DR NW 10 G12, 10 I10
GDN NW 10 G8
GN NW 10 H9
GT NW 10 G8
GV NW 10 G9
HTS NW 10 G9
LK NW 10 G9
MR NW 10 I9
MS NW 100, 200, 300 . . 10 H9
PL NW 100 . . . . 10 H9
200 . . . . . . 10 H10
PT NW. 10 G9
TER NW 10 I9
VW NW 10 H9
WY NW 10 G9
ROYAL RIDGE HL NW . . 10 I11
MR NW 10 H11
MS NW 10 H11
MT NW 10 I11
RS NW 10 H11
TR NW 10 I11
ROYALITE WY (T VAL) . . 105 D5
ROYALVIEW CR NW . . . 10 G12
RUMMEL PL (CAN) . . . 101 B6
RUNDLE AV (BNF) . . . 21 D8
CR NE 51 AJ30
CR (CAN) 101 B5
DR (CAN) 101 C5
PL (AIR) 113 D5
PT (CAN) 101 B5
RUNDLE PLANT LN (CAN) 101 B6
RUNDLECAIRN GT NE. . . 43 AV28
PL NE 43 AV29
RD NE 43 AV29
RS NE, WY NE . . . 43 AV28
RUNDLEFIELD CL NE. . . 43 AU28
CR NE 43 AU28

RD NE 43 AU29
RUNDLEHILL DR NE 43 AU27
PL NE, RD NE, WY NE . 43 AU27
RUNDLEHORN CIR NE . . . 42 AS28
CR NE 43 AV28
DR NE (3700-5200) . . 43 AT28
DR NE (5300-6300) . . 43 AT28
LN NE 43 AV27
TER NE 42 AS28
RUNDLELAWN CL NE . . . 43 AT26
CT NE 43 AT26
GN NE 43 AT27
PK NE 43 AU27
PL NE 43 AT27
RD NE 43 AT26
WY NE 43 AT27
RUNDLEMERE BY NE . . . 43 AT27
PL NE 43 AT28
RD NE 43 AT27
RUNDLERIDGE CL NE . . 43 AT28
DR NE, PL NE 42 AS28
RD NE 43 AT29
WY NE 43 AT28
RUNDLESIDE CR NE . . . 43 AU26
DR NE 43 AU26
RUNDLESON PL NE 100 . 43 AT26
200 . . . . 43 AT26
300, 400 . . . . 43 AU26
RD NE 42 AS26
WY NE 43 AT26
RUNDLEVIEW CL NE . . . 43 AV26
DR NE 43 AV26
DR (CAN) 101 B5
RD NE 43 AV26
RUNDLEVILLE DR NE . . 43 AU27
PL NE 100, 200, 300 . 43 AT27
400 . . . . 43 AU27
500, 600 . . . . 43 AT27
RUNDLEWOOD BY NE . . 43 AV27
CL NE, DR NE 43 AU28
LN NE, PL NE 43 AV27
RD NE 43 AU28
RUPERT RD NE 51 AK30
RUSSEL RD NE 51 AK29
RUSSET RD NE 51 AJ29
RUTLAND RD SW 57 V40

S

SABLE DR SE 62 AR37
SABRINA BY SW 100 . . . . 74 AE56
200, 300 . . . . 74 AE56
RD SW 74 AC56
WY SW 74 AD57
SACKVILLE DR SW 74 AB56
PL SW 74 AD56
SACRAMENTO DR SW . . . 74 AD54
SADDLE RIDGE CL NE . . 19 AX13
DR NE 19 AX13
WY NE 19 AX14
SADDLEBACK RD NE . . . 19 AX14
SADDLECREEK CR NE . . 19 AW14
CT NE 100, 200 . . . . . 19 AW15
CV NE 19 AW15
GT NE 19 AW15
PT NE 100, 200, 300 . . 19 AX15
TER NE 19 AX15
WY NE 19 AW15
SADDLECREST BLVD NE 20 AY12
CL NE 20 AY13
PK NE, PL NE 20 AY13
SADDLEFIELD CR NE . . . 20 AZ14
DR NE 20 AZ14
PL NE 100, 200 . . . . . 20 AZ15
RD NE 20 AZ14
SADDLEHORN CL NE . . . 19 AX13
CR NE, DR NE 19 AX14
SADDLELAND CL NE . . . 20 AZ13
CR NE 20 AZ13
CT NE, DR NE 20 AY13
WY NE 20 AZ14
SADDLEMEAD CL NE . . . 20 AY13
GN NE 20 AY13
RD NE, WY NE 20 AY14
SADDLEMONT BLVD NE . 20 AY15
CL NE 20 AY15
CR NE 20 AZ15
GV NE, MR NE, RD NE . 20 AZ14
WY NE 20 AY15
SADDLETOWNE CIR NE . 19 AX15
SADDLETREE CL NE . . . 19 AW13
DR NE 19 AW14
SAGE WY NE 35 H22
SAGE HILL DR NW 3 U4
GDN NW 3 U4
ST ANDREWS PL NW . . . 48 W29
ST GEORGE'S DR NE . . 51 AL33
ST JULIEN DR SW 58 Y41
RD (BNF) 21 E6
WY (BNF) 21 E6
ST MONICA AV SE 51 AL35
ST MORITZ DR SW 45 I36
PL SW 45 I36
SAIT WY NW 49 AB30
SALEM AV SW 48 Y36

SALINA ST SW 74 AC55
SALISBURY AV SE 51 AI36
ST SE 51 AI36
SAM AV (T VAL) 105 B4
SAMIS RD NE 50 AG32
SAN DIEGO CR NE 44 AZ23
GN NE 44 BA22
MR NE, PL NE 44 BA23
WY NE 44 BA22
SAN FERNANDO CR NE . 44 BA23
PL NE 100 . . . . 44 BB24
200 . . . . 44 BB23
SANCTUARY RD SE 61 AO38
SANDALWOOD CL NW. . 15 AA11
CT NW, GT NW. 15 Z11
HTS NW 15 Z11
PL NW 100, 200 . . . . . 15 AA11
SANDARAC CIR NW 15 AA13
DR NW 15 Z11
PL NW 100 . . . . 15 AA13
200 . . . . 15 AB13
RD NW, VL NW 15 AB13
WY NW 15 AB13
SANDERLING CL NW . . . 15 AC11
CT NW 15 AC11
DR NW, HL NW 15 AB11
PL NW 100, 200 . . . . . 15 AC12
300 . . . . 15 AC11
RD NW 15 AB11
RS NW 15 AC11
WY NW 15 AB11
SANDHURST AV SW 48 X35
SANDPIPER CIR NW . . . 15 AB12
CT NW, GT NW. 15 AA12
LK NW, LN NW 15 AB12
LN (CHST) 80 C9
MS NW 15 AB12
PL NW 100 . . . . 15 AA12
200 . . . . 15 AB12
RD NW 15 AA12
RS NW 15 AB11
WY NW 15 AA11
SANDRINGHAM CL NW . 15 AA12
CT NW 100. . . . . 15 AA13
200 . . . . 15 AA13
300 . . . . 15 AA13
PL NW 100, 200, 300 . . 15 Z12
400, 500. . . . . . . 15 Z12
600, 700. . . . . . . 15 Z13
RD NW, WY NW 15 Z13
SANDSTONE CR (AIR) . . 113 E5
CT NW 15 AB13
CT (OKS) 107 B5
DR NW 15 AA12
DR (OKS) 107 B5
GT (OKS) 107 B5
HL NW 15 AB13
MS (OKS) 107 B5
PL NW 100 . . . . 15 AB13
200 . . . . 15 AB13
PL (OKS) 107 B5
PT (OKS) 107 B5
RD NW 15 AB13
RS NW 15 AB13
TER (CAN) 101 G6
WY NW 15 AB12
SANDSTONE RIDGE
CR (OKS) 107 B5
SANDY BEACH CV (CHST) . 80 B7
SANTA MARIA GDN NE . 51 AK33
SANTANA BY NW 100. . . 15 AC12
200, 300 . . . . 15 AC12
CR NW 15 AC12
CT NW 100. . . . . 15 AC12
HL NW, MR NW 15 AC12
MS NW 100, 200 . . . . . 15 AC12
300 . . . . 15 AC11
PL NW 100, 300 . . . . . 15 AC12
RD NW 15 AC12
SARATOGA CL NE 44 BA23
PL NE 100, 200. . . . . . 44 BA23
SARCEE RD SW 57 U42
TR NW 13 Q11, 24 O18
TR NW (1800-8000). . . 36 O28
TR SW 46 Q35, 56 Q42
SASKATCHEWAN ST (CRS) . 8 F2
SAXON PL SW 74 AB55
SAXONY LN (H RV) 109 B5
SCANDIA BY NW 100 . . . 23 H17
200, 300, 400 . . . 23 I18
HL NW, PT NW. 23 I18
RS NW 23 H18
SCANLON BY NW 23 I16
GN NW 23 H15
GT NW, HL NW 23 H16
PL NW 23 I15
SCARBORO AV SW 48 Z35
SCARPE DR SW 58 Y41
SCENIC GDN SW 23 J16
GN NW, PL NW, RD NW. 23 J17
RS NW, WY NW 23 J17
SCENIC ACRES BLVD NW . 23 I17
DR NW 23 I18
GT NW 23 J18
LK NW 23 H16
TER NW 23 J18
SCENIC BOW PL NW 100. 23 J21
200 . . . . 23 I21
RD NW 23 I21
SCENIC COVE BY NW . . 23 J16

CIR NW 23 K16
CT NW, DR NW. 23 J16
PL NW 23 K16
SCENIC GLEN BY NW 100. 23 J17
200 . . . . 23 I17
300 . . . . 23 J16
CL NW 23 I17
CR NW, GT NW, MS NW 23 J18
PL NW 100. . . . . 23 J18
200, 300 . . . . 23 J17
SCENIC HILL CL NW . . . 23 H17
SCENIC PARK CR NW . . 23 I17
GT NW 23 I19
PL NW 100, 200 . . . . . 23 I17
SCENIC RIDGE CR NW . . 23 I19
CT NW 23 I19
GN NW 23 I19
GT NW 23 I18
PL NW 23 I19
WY NW 23 I18
SCENIC VIEW BY NW 100. . 23 I15
200 . . . . 23 I15
300 . . . . 11 I14
400 . . . . 23 H15
CL NW, GT NW. 23 H15
SCEPTRE CL NW. 23 H17
CT NW 100. . . . . 23 H16
200, 300 . . . . 23 H17
SCHILLER BY NW 100 . . 23 H17
CR NW 23 H17
PL NW 100, 200 . . . . . 23 H17
SCHOONER CL NW 23 H16
CV NW 100, 200 . . . . . 23 H16
300 . . . . 23 G16
400 . . . . 23 H16
500 . . . . 23 G16
600, 700 . . . . 23 H16
LD NW 23 H15
LD NW 100, 200, 300 . . 23 H15
400, 500 . . . . 23 G15
SCHUBERT GT NW. 23 H15
HL NW 23 H14
PL NW 100 . . . . 23 H15
200, 300 . . . . 23 H14
400 . . . . 23 H14
500 . . . . 23 H14
600, 700 . . . . 23 G15
800 . . . . 23 H15
SCIMITAR BY NW 100 . . 23 J18
200 . . . . 23 J19
300 . . . . 23 I19
400 . . . . 23 J19
500 . . . . 23 J19
600 . . . . 23 J19
700 . . . . 23 J19
800. . . . . 22 B19
CIR NW, CT NW. 23 J19
HE NW 23 J19
HE NW 100 . . . . 23 J19
200 . . . . 23 I19
LD NW, PT NW. 23 J19
RS NW 23 J19
VW NW 23 I19
SCOTIA BY NW 23 I15
LD NW 11 J15
PT NW 23 I15
PT NW 100, 200, 300 . . 23 I15
SCOTLAND ST SW 48 Z35
SCRIPPS LD NW 23 H16
SCURFIELD DR NW 23 H15
PL NW 100, 200 . . . . . 23 I16
WY NW. 23 I16
SEATTLE DR SW 74 AD54
SELKIRK DR SW 74 AB54
SEMINARY DR (COCR) . . 103 D1
RDG, VW (COCR) 103 D1
SENLAC ST SW 48 Z36
SETTLER WY (CAN) 101 F4
SEYMOUR AV SW 74 AD55
SHAGANAPPI TR NW . . . 13 U9
TR NW 26 U18, 37 S28
TR NW (3500-6100) . . 37 S24
SHALOM WY SE. 91 AF68
SHAMROCK AV SW 74 AD56
PL SW 74 AD56
SHANNON AV SW 90 AB67
CIR SW 90 AC66
CL SW 90 AD67
CM SW 90 AB67
CR SW, CT SW, DR SW 90 AC67
GDN SW 90 AA67
GN SW 90 AC66
HL SW 90 AB66
LK SW, MR SW 90 AB67
MS SW 100, 200 . . . . . 90 AC67
PL SW. 90 AC66
RD SW 90 AB67
SQ SW 90 AB66
SQ SW 100, 200. . . . . . 90 AB66
300, 400 . . . . 90 AA66
TER SW 90 AB66
WY SW 90 AC67
SHANNON ESTATES
TER SW 90 AA67
SHANTARA GV (SPNG) 99 G2
SHANTZ CR (CRS) 8 F3
SHARON AV SW 49 AA35
SHAW RD SE 82 AE64
SHAWBROOKE BY SW . 90 AB68
CIR SW, CL SW 90 AB68

CR SW 90 AB67
CT SW 90 AB66
DR SW 90 AC68
GN SW 90 AB67
MR SW 90 AA67
PK SW 90 AA67
PL SW, RD SW. 90 AB67
RS SW 90 AB67
SHAWCLIFFE BY SW. . . 90 AD67
CIR SW . . . . , 90 AD67
CT SW 90 AE66
GN SW 90 AE66
GT SW, PL SW 90 AE67
RD SW 90 AE66
SHAWFIELD BY SW . . . 90 AD68
CT SW 90 AC68
DR SW 90 AD68
GT SW 90 AD68
PL SW 90 AD68
RD SW 90 AC69
WY SW 90 AD68
SHAWGLEN CT SW 90 AE68
PL SW, RD SW, RS SW 90 AE68
WY SW 90 AE68
SHAWINIGAN
CT SW 100, 200 . . . . . 90 AD66
DR SW 90 AC66
LN SW 90 AC66
PL SW 100, 200 . . . . . 90 AD68
300 . . . . 90 AC68
RD SW 90 AC68
RS SW 90 AC68
WY SW 90 AC68
SHAWMEADOWS BY SW 90 AE67
CL SW. 90 AE66
CR SW, GT SW, PL SW 90 AE67
RD SW 90 AE68
RS SW 90 AD67
SHAWNEE BY SW 82 AC63
CL SW 82 AC63
CT SW 82 AD63
DR SW 82 AB62
GDN SW 100 . . . . 82 AB62
200 . . . . 82 AB63
300 . . . . 82 AB62
GT SW 82 AE64
GV SW 82 AB64
LK SW 82 AC64
MR SW 100, 200 . . . . . 82 AC64
300 . . . . 82 AB64
MS SW, PL SW 82 AD63
RD SW 82 AD64
RS SW 82 AD63
VW SW 82 AC64
WY SW 82 AB64
SHAWNESSY AL SE. . . . 91 AF66
BLVD SW 90 AA66
DR SW 90 AD66
TER SW 90 AE67
SHAWVILLE BLVD SE . . 91 AG69
GT SE 90 AE70
LK SE 91 AF69
RD SE 91 AG69
RS SE 91 AF68
WY SE 91 AF69
SHEEP RIVER BLVD (OKS) 107 A6
BY (OKS) 107 B7
CL (OKS) 107 A7
CR, CT (OKS) 107 A6
DR (OKS) 107 A7
GN, GT, HE (OKS) 107 A6
HL, HTS (OKS) 107 A6
LK, LN, MS (OKS) 107 A7
PL (OKS) 107 B7
PT (OKS) 107 A7
TER (OKS) 107 A6
SHELBOURNE ST SW . . 48 Z35
SHELDON PL NW 37 R26
SHELLIAN LN (CAN) 101 C7
SHEPARD PL SE 77 AR53
RD SE 77 AQ51
SHEPPARD RD (H RV) . . 109 B5
RD SE 90 AF71
SHERIFF KING PL SE. . . 93 AQ72
RD SE 74 AD54
SHERMAN AV SW 74 AD54
SHERWOOD BLVD NW . . 3 R5
CIR NW 3 S6
CM NW 3 S7
CT NW 3 T6
CV NW 3 S7
GDN NW 3 T6
GN NW, GV NW 3 T7
HE NW 3 T7
HL NW 3 T7
LD NW, PT NW, RS NW . 3 T7
TER NW, VW NW 3 T7
WY NW 3 T6
SHILLINGTON CR SW . . 74 AD55
SHORT RD NW 36 O27
SIBBALD ST (COCR) . . . 103 F5
SIDNEY ST (CAN) 101 D4
SIDON CR SW 56 O39
SIENNA BY SW. 56 P39
SIENNA HEIGHTS
HL SW 100 . . . . 56 O38
200, 300, 400 . . . 56 O38
WY SW 56 O38
SIENNA HILLS CT SW . . 56 P39
DR SW, GT SW. 56 P39
LK SW 56 O39

PL SW 56 P39
TER SW 100 . . . . 56 P39
  200 . . . . 56 O39
VW SW 56 O39
SIENNA PARK BY SW 100. 56 N38
  200 . . . . 56 O39
  300 . . . . 56 O39
CR SW 56 N38
CT SW 200 . . . . 56 N39
DR SW 56 N39
GDN SW 100, 200 . . . . 56 O39
GN SW, GV SW 56 N39
HE SW 100, 200 . . . . . 56 N38
LK SW 56 N38
PL SW 56 N39
TER SW, VW SW 56 N39
SIENNA RIDGE BY SW . . 56 O39
  LD SW 56 O39
SIERRA CR SW 74 AD55
SIERRA MADRE CR SW . . 56 O42
CT SW 100, 200, 300 . . 56 O42
  400, 500, 600 . . . . 56 O43
  700, 800 . . . . 56 O42
SIERRA MORENA
BLVD SW 56 N41
CIR SW 56 O41
CL SW 56 O42
CT SW 100, 200, 300 . . 56 O40
  400, 500 . . . . 56 N40
  600, 700, 800 . . . . 56 N41
  900 . . . . 56 N41
  1000, 1100 . . . . . . 56 N42
GDN SW 56 N42
GN SW 56 N40
GN SW 100, 200, 300. . . 56 N40
GV SW 56 N41
LD SW 56 M42
MS SW 56 O42
PK SW 56 N40
PL SW 100, 200, 300 . . 56 O41
  400 . . . . 56 O41
  500 . . . . 56 N41
  600, 700, 800 . . . . 56 O41
  900 . . . . 56 O41
RD SW 56 N40
TER SW 100, 200, 300. . 56 O40
VL SW 56 O41
WY SW 56 N40
SIERRA NEVADA CL SW . 56 N42
GN SW 56 N42
PL SW 100, 200, 300 . . 56 N42
RS SW, WY SW 56 N42
SIERRA VISTA BY SW 100 56 O40
  200 . . . . 56 O40
CIR SW 56 N40
CL SW 56 O40
TER SW 56 N41
TER SW 100, 200 . . . . 56 N41
SIFTON BLVD SW 59 AB40
SIGNAL HILL BY SW . . . 56 P38
CIR SW 56 Q38
CT SW 100, 200 . . . . . 56 P38
  300 . . . . 56 Q39
CTR SW 56 P41
DR SW 56 N38
GN SW 56 Q38
HTS SW 56 Q38
MS SW 56 P39
PL SW 100, 200, 300 . . 56 Q39
  400 . . . . 56 Q39
PT SW 56 P40
PT SW 100, 200 . . . . . 56 P40
  300 . . . . 56 O40
TER SW 56 O40
SW SW, WY SW 56 P39
SIGNAL RIDGE CT SW . . 56 P38
HTS SW 56 O38
LK SW, PL SW, VW SW 56 P38
SIGNATURE CL SW 56 P37
CT SW 100 . . . . 56 O37
  300 . . . . 56 O37
HTS SW 56 O37
LK SW 56 O37
MR SW 46 P36
MS SW 56 P37
PK SW 46 Q36
PL SW 56 P37
PT SW 56 O37
PT SW 100, 200 . . . . . 56 O37
RS SW 56 P37
TER SW 100, 200 . . . . 56 P37
VL SW 46 P36
WY SW 56 O37
SIKOME CIR SE 92 AN69
RD SE 92 AM69
SILVER BIRCH WY NW . . 35 I23
SILVER BROOK DR NW . . 24 M19
RD NW, WY NW 24 N19
SILVER CREEK BLVD (AIR)113 D2
DR (AIR) 113 C1
MR NW 23 K18
MS NW 100. . . . . 23 K19
  200. . . . . 23 K18
PL NW 23 K18
SILVER CREST CR NW . . 23 L20
DR NW 24 M20
RD NW 23 L20
SILVER HILL CR NW 23 L19
PL NW 23 K19

RD NW 23 L19
WY NW 23 K19
SILVER MEAD BY NW . . 24 M19
CL NW 24 M19
CR NW, RD NW 23 L19
SILVER RIDGE CL NW . . 24 M20
CR NW 23 L20
CT NW 24 M18
DR NW 23 L20
GN NW 23 L19
PL NW 23 L20
RD NW 24 M18
RS NW 23 L18
WY NW 23 L19
SILVER SPRINGS
BLVD NW 23 K17
CR NW 24 N18
DR NW 24 N19
GN NW 24 M18
GT NW 24 N20
HL NW 24 N19
MR NW 24 N20
MS NW, PL NW 24 N18
RD NW 23 J19
RS NW 24 M18
WY NW 24 N18
WY (AIR) 113 C1
SILVER VALLEY BLVD NW. 23 J20
BY NW 23 J19
DR NW, PL NW. 23 K20
RD NW, RS NW. 23 J20
SILVERCREEK CL NW . . 23 K17
CR NW 23 J18
DR NW, GN NW 23 K18
WY NW 23 J18
SILVERDALE CR NW 24 N21
DR NW 24 N21
PL NW 24 N20
RD NW 24 N21
SILVERGROVE BY NW . . 23 L17
CL NW, CR NW. 23 K17
CT NW 23 L17
DR NW 23 K18
GDN NW, GN NW 23 L17
HL NW 23 L17
MR NW, MS NW, PL NW 23 L17
PL NW 100 . . . . 24 M17
  200, 300 . . . . 23 L17
RD NW 23 K17
RS NW 23 L17
WY NW 23 K17
SILVERSTONE BY NW . . 24 M17
MR NW 24 M18
MS NW 24 N18
PL NW 24 M18
RD NW 24 M17
SILVERTHORN DR NW . . 23 K18
RD NW, WY NW 23 K18
SILVERTIP CL (CAN) . . . 101 F5
PT, RD (CAN) 101 F3
RDG (CAN) 101 F2
TR (CAN) 101 E3
SILVERVIEW DR NW 24 M21
PL NW 24 N22
RD NW, WY NW 24 N21
SIMCOE BLVD SW 56 O37
BY SW 56 N37
CIR SW 56 O37
CL SW, CR SW, GT SW . 56 N37
LK SW, MS SW 56 N37
PL SW 46 N36
RD SW, RS SW, TER SW56 N37
VW SW 100, 200 . . . . . 56 N38
SIMCREST GV SW 56 N38
HTS SW 100, 200. . . 56 O38
MR SW 56 O37
PT SW 56 O38
SIMONS CR NW 27 AE20
RD NW 27 AD20
SINAI AV SW 66 W44
ST SW 66 W44
SINCLAIR CR SW 74 AB54
SIROCCO DR SW 56 N38
PL SW 56 Q37
SKYLINE CR NE 28 AI21
WY NE. 29 AJ21
SLATER RD (STMR) 112 E9
SLEIGH DR (RED) 33 F1
SLOCAN RD SW 74 AB55
SLOPES DR SW 55 H39
GV SW, PT SW, RD SW. 55 H38
SLOPEVIEW DR SW. 55 G37
SMED LN SE 71 AW46
SMITH AV (CRS) 8 F3
ST (AIR) 113 E3
SNOWBERRY CIR (EV) . . 115 D8
GT (EV) 115 D8
PL, PT, VW (EV) 115 D8
SNOWDON CR SW 74 AC54
SOLACE RIDGE PL (SPNG) 98 F3
SOMERCREST CIR SW . . 90 AD69
CL SW, GDN SW. 90 AC69
GV SW 90 AC69
MR SW 90 AD69
ST SW 90 AB69
SOMERGLEN CL SW . . . 90 AD70
CM SW 90 AC70
CR SW 90 AE70
CT SW, CV SW. 90 AE71
HE SW 90 AD71

PK SW, PL SW 90 AE70
RD SW 90 AE71
WY SW 90 AC70
SOMERSET CIR SW. . . . 90 AD70
CL SW 90 AD69
CR SW 90 AC70
CT SW 90 AD70
DR SW 90 AC70
GT SW 90 AE70
MR SW 90 AC70
PK SW 90 AC69
SQ SW 90 AD70
WY SW 90 AC69
SOMERSIDE BY SW . . . 90 AB70
CL SW 90 AB69
CM SW 90 AB68
CR SW 90 AB69
DR SW 90 AB69
GN SW 100. . . . . 90 AB68
  200 . . . . 90 AA68
GV SW, MR SW 90 AB69
PK SW 90 AA68
PL SW 90 AB69
SOMERVALE CL SW . . . 90 AE69
CT SW 90 AF70
DR SW, GN SW 90 AE69
LK SW 90 AE69
PK SW, PL SW 90 AE69
PT SW 90 AF70
VW SW 90 AF70
SOMME AV SW 58 Y40
BLVD SW, MR SW. 58 Y40
SONORA AV SW 48 Z35
SORREL MS SW 58 Y40
PL SW 74 AD50
SOUTHAMPTON DR SW . 74 AB56
SOUTHBOW PL SW 74 AB55
SOUTHCREEK PL (AIR) . . 113 E6
SOUTHDALE BY SW . . . 74 AB56
CL SW 74 AC57
CR SW, PL SW, RD SW 74 AB56
SOUTHGLEN DR SW 74 AC56
PL SW 74 AC56
SOUTHLAND CIR SW . . . 74 AC53
CR SW 74 AC54
DR SE 75 AF54
DR SW (500-900) 74 AC54
DR SW (1400-3200) . . 73 V55
GN SW 74 AD54
SOUTHMOUNT PL SW . . 74 AD56
SOUTHPORT LN SW 74 AE54
RD SW, WY SW 74 AE55
SOUTHRIDGE DR (OKS) . 107 C7
SOUTHWOOD DR SE . . 62 AR37
RD (T VAL) 105 C7
SOVEREIGN CR SW 48 X35
SPADINA DR SW 74 AB55
SPILLER RD SE 60 AI38
RD SE (1900-2000) . . 51 AJ37
SPOKANE ST SW 74 AB54
SPRAY AV (BNF) 21 D7
SPRAY LAKES RD (CAN). 101 A5
SPRING CR SW 55 L41
CR (BNF) 21 D8
MS SW 55 L41
VW SW 55 L41
SPRING BOK AV SW . . . 57 T43
SPRING CREEK CR (CAN). 101 C3
SPRING GATE EST (SPNG). 99 E4
SPRING GROVE CR (AIR) . 113 F6
SPRING HAVEN CL (AIR) . 113 F6
CR (AIR) 113 F6
CT 100, 200, 300 (AIR) . 113 F5
  400 (AIR) 113 F5
  500, 600, 700 (AIR) . 113 F6
  800, 900 (AIR) 113 F6
MS, RD (AIR) 113 F6
SPRING MEADOWS
LN (SPNG) 99 E3
SPRING RIDGE EST (SPNG) 99 G3
SPRING VALLEY CL SW . 55 K39
LN SW 55 L39
MS SW 55 L39
TER SW 55 L38
VW SW 55 L39
WY SW 55 L39
SPRING VILLAGE LN SW . 56 M40
SPRING WILLOW CT SW . 55 K38
DR SW 55 L38
PL SW, RDG SW. 55 K37
SPRINGBANK BLVD SW . 55 K40
BY SW 56 M40
CR SW 55 L40
CT SW 55 L41
DR SW 55 K40
GT SW 56 M40
MDWS (SPNG) 99 B2
MS SW 56 M40
MT SW 56 M40
PL SW 100, 200, 300 . . 55 K41
  400 . . . . 55 K40
RD (SPNG) 99 D2
RS SW 55 K40
TER SW 56 M41
VW SW 55 K40
WY SW 55 K40
SPRINGBLUFF BLVD SW . 55 L40
BY SW, HTS SW, LN SW 55 L40
SPRINGBOROUGH
BLVD SW 56 M37
CR SW, GN SW 55 L37

GT SW, PT SW, WY SW 56 M37
SPRINGDALE CIR (AIR) . . 113 G5
CT (AIR) 113 F5
GT (AIR) 113 G5
SPRINGFIELD PL SW . . . 74 AB55
SPRINGHILL CR SW 55 K39
SPRINGLAND WY (SPNG) . 99 H3
SPRINGLAND MANOR
CR (SPNG) 99 H3
DR (SPNG) 99 H3
SPRINGMERE CL (CHST) . 80 A6
DR, LK (CHST) 80 A6
MS 100, 200 (CHST) . . 80 A6
PL 100, 200 (CHST) . . 80 A6
RD, WY (CHST) 80 A6
SPRINGS CR (AIR) 113 F6
CT (AIR) 113 G6
PL 100, 200, 300 (AIR). 113 F6
SPRINGSHIRE PL (SPNG) . 99 E4
SPRINGSIDE ST SW (SPNG)99 F3
SPRINGWOOD CR (AIR) . 113 F6
DR SW 74 AB54
PL SW 74 AB54
SPRUCE AV (B CK) 33 G7
CTR SW 47 V34
DR SW (3300-3700) . . 47 U33
DR SW (3800-5000) . . 47 R33
LN (STMR) 112 F9
ST (BNF) 21 E4
WY NW 35 H23
SPRUCE BANK CR SW . . 47 U32
SPRUCE GROVE PL (CHST) 80 A5
SPRUCE MEADOWS TR S 89 W71
WY SW 90 AB73
SPRUCE PARK DR (STMR) 112 F9
SPRUCEGROVE CR (AIR) . 113 F6
GT, WY (AIR) 113 F6
SPUCE MEADOWS DR . . 90 AB72
SPYHILL CR NW 28 AF20
RD NW 28 AF20
SQUIRREL CR (CAN) . . . 101 A5
ST (BNF) 21 C5
STAFFORD PL (CRS) . . . 8 F2
ST (CRS) 8 F2
STAMPEDE TR SE 60 AH37
STANLEY AV (OKS) 107 E6
CR SW 59 AE43
DR SW, PL SW 59 AF42
RD SW 59 AF43
STATE RD SW 48 Y35
STEELE AV SW 57 T43
STEPHEN AV SW 49 AD34
STERLING SPRINGS
CR (SPNG) 99 E4
STEVENS ST (CRS) 8 F2
STEWART GN SW 56 P41
RD (AIR) 113 J4
STIMSON RD (H RV) . . . 109 B5
STOCKTON AV (OKS) . . . 107 E7
PT (OKS) 107 E6
STONECREEK PL (CAN) . 101 F2
RD (CAN) 101 F2
STONEGATE CL (AIR) . . . 113 F1
CR, DR (AIR) 113 F1
PL 100 (AIR) 113 F1
  200 (AIR) 113 F2
RD, RS, WY (AIR) 113 D1
STONEHAVEN RD SW. . 74 AC56
STONEHILL DR NE 7 AO7
GT NE 7 AP7
STONEPINE CV (EV) . . . 115 C7
DR, GT (EV) 115 D7
STONEY TR NE 5 AF3
TR NW . 10 K10, 11 H13, 23 G15
TR NW 3 V8, 5 AF3
TR SW . 35 H29, 35 H25, 45 G36
STORYBOOK GDN NW. . . 11 L15
TER NW 100, 200 . . . . 11 L15
STRABANE PL SW 46 P33
STRADBROOKE PL SW . . 46 O35
RS SW, WY SW 46 O35
STRADDOCK CR SW 46 N33
TER SW 46 N33
STRADWICK PL SW 46 P33
PT SW, RS SW, WY SW. 46 P33
STRANDELL CR SW 46 O33
STRANRAER PL SW 46 P33
STRASBOURG BY SW . . 46 O35
GN SW 46 O35
STRATFORD PL SW 46 O33
STRATHAM BY SW 46 P35
STRATHAVEN
BY 100 (STMR) 112 G4
  200, 300 (STMR) . . 46 N34
CIR SW 46 N34
CR (STMR) 112 G4
DR (STMR) 112 F5
GT SW 46 O34
HTS (STMR) 112 G4
MS SW 46 N34
STRATHBURY BY SW 100. 46 O33
  200 . . . . 46 O33
CIR SW, GT SW, PL SW 46 O33
RS SW. 46 O33
STRATHCAIRN PL SW . . 46 O33
STRATHCANNA CT SW . . 46 O35
STRATHCLAIR PL SW . . . 46 O35
RS SW. 46 O33
STRATHCONA BLVD SW . 46 N34
BY SW. 46 O33

BY *(STMR)* 112 F4
CL SW 46 Q34
CL *(STMR)* 112 F4
CR SW 46 Q34
DR SW 45 J33
GT *(STMR)* 112 F4
HL SW 46 Q33
MS SW 100 . . . . 46 O34
200 . . . . 46 P34
300, 400 . . . . 46 O34
500 . . . . 46 P34
PL SW 46 P34
PL *(STMR)* 112 F4
RD SW 46 O34
RD *(STMR)* 112 F4
ST SW 65 R45
ST *(CRS)* 8 F2
TER *(STMR)* 112 F4
WY *(STMR)* 112 F4
STRATHLEA CL SW . . 46 N34
STRATHEARN CR SW . . 46 Q34
GDN SW 46 Q35
PL SW 100 . . . . 46 Q35
RS SW 46 Q35
STRATHFORD
BLVD *(STMR)* 112 F5
BY 100, 200 *(STMR)* . . . 112 F4
300, 400 *(STMR)* . . . 112 F4
CL, CR, GLEN *(STMR)* . . 112 F4
PL *(STMR)* 112 F4
STRATHLEA AV SW . . 45 J33
CL SW, CM SW 45 J33
CR SW, CT SW, GN SW . 45 K33
GT SW, GV SW 45 J33
MR SW 45 K33
PL SW 45 L33
STRATHLORNE BY SW . 46 P35
CR SW, MS SW 46 P35
STRATHMORE LAKES
BY *(STMR)* 112 C8
CR, WY *(STMR)* 112 C7
STRATHRIDGE BY SW . 46 M34
CL SW 46 N33
CR SW 46 M33
CT SW 45 L33
GDN SW 46 M33
GT SW 46 N33
GV SW, HTS SW 45 L33
LN SW 46 N34
PK SW, PL SW 46 M33
PL SW 100, 200 . . . . . . 46 M33
WY SW 46 M33
STRATHROY BY SW . . 46 P33
STRATHWOOD BY SW . 46 O33
STRATTON CR SW . . . 46 O34
CT SW 46 O34
PK SW, PL SW, TER SW . 46 P34
STRATTON HILL BY SW . 46 O34
RS SW 46 O34
STRAVANAN BY SW 100 . 46 P33
200, 300 . . . . 46 P33
STRICKLAND BY SW 100 . 46 O35
200 . . . . 46 O35
SUDBURY AV SW . . . 48 Z35
SUFFOLK ST SW 48 Y36
SULLIVAN RD *(H RV)* . 109 B5
SULPHER CT *(BNF)* . . 21 C8
SUMAC RD NW 48 Y30
SUMMER ST SW 58 AA36
SUMMERFIELD
BLVD *(AIR)* 113 E6
CL, RD *(AIR)* 113 E6
SUMMERWOOD
PL 100 *(AIR)* 113 D6
200, 300 *(AIR)* 113 E6
400, 500 *(AIR)* 113 E6
RD *(AIR)* 113 E6
SUMMIT ST SW 48 Y36
SUMMIT POINTE
DR *(H PT)* 115 E1
SUN CANYON CR SE . 92 AL68
LK SE 91 AK68
PK SE 92 AL68
WY SE 91 AK68
SUN HARBOUR CL SE . 92 AL70
CR SE, GN SE, PL SE . . 92 AL70
RD SE 92 AL69
WY SE 91 AK70
SUN VALLEY BLVD SE . 91 AG68
DR SE 91 AJ68
SUNBANK CT SE 91 AI68
LN SE 91 AH69
PL SE, RD SE 91 AI68
WY SE 91 AH68
SUNCASTLE BY SE . . 91 AJ69
CR SE 91 AK69
DR SE 91 AJ69
GT SE, PL SE, RD SE . . 91 AJ69
SUNCREST WY SE . . . 91 AI69
SUNDANCE CT *(BNF)* . 21 B8
PL *(AIR)* 113 E6
RD *(BNF)* 21 B7
SUNDERLAND AV SW . 48 Y36
SUNDOWN CL SE . . . 91 AH70
GN SE 91 AI70
LK SE 91 AI70
MR SE 91 AI71
PL SE 100. . . . . 91 AI70
RD SE 91 AI70
WY SE 91 AH70

SUNHAVEN BY SE 100 . . 91 AK69
200 . . . . 91 AK68
CL SE 91 AK69
CT SE, LK SE 91 AJ68
PL SE, RD SE 91 AK68
WY SE 91 AJ68
SUNHURST CR SE . . . 91 AJ68
CT SE, PL SE 91 AJ68
RD SE 91 AI68
RS SE 91 AJ68
SUNLAKE CIR SE 91 AI70
CL SE 91 AI70
GDN SE, LK SE 91 AI70
MR SE 91 AI70
RD SE 91 AI71
ST SE 91 AI70
WY SE 91 AI70
SUNMEADOWS CR SE . 91 AJ71
CT SE 91 AJ71
PL SE 91 AJ71
RD SE 91 AI71
SUNMILLS CT SE 91 AI69
DR SE, GN SE 91 AI69
PL SE 100, 200 . . . . . . 91 AI68
SUNMOUNT BY SE 100 . 91 AK68
200 . . . . 91 AK68
CL SE, CR SE 91 AJ67
CT SE 91 AI68
GDN SE 91 AI67
GN SE 91 AJ67
PL SE 100 . . . . 91 AJ67
200 . . . . 91 AJ68
RD SE 91 AK68
RS SE 91 AJ67
SUNNY HILL LN NW . . 50 AE31
SUNNYSIDE PL *(AIR)* . 113 E6
SUNPARK DR SE 91 AH69
GT SE, PLAZA SE 91 AH68
SUNRIDGE BLVD NE . . 42 AP27
CL *(AIR)* 113 D2
CR, PL *(AIR)* 113 D2
WY NE 42 AP27
SUNRISE CIR SE 92 AL69
CL *(H RV)* 109 H4
CR SE 92 AL69
GT SE, LK SE 92 AL69
LOOP *(H RV)* 109 H5
SUNSET AV SW 48 Y35
BLVD *(T VAL)* 105 B5
CL SE 91 AK70
CR SE 91 AJ70
CR *(OKS)* 107 C4
CV SE 91 AJ70
DR *(T VAL)* 105 A4
PL SE 100 . . . . 91 AJ70
200 . . . . 91 AJ70
PL 100 *(OKS)* 107 C4
200 *(OKS)* 107 C4
300 *(OKS)* 107 D4
WY SE 91 AJ70
WY *(H RV)* 109 E4
SUNSHINE CL *(H RV)* . 109 G4
CT, PL *(H RV)* 109 G4
TR *(H RV)* 109 G5
WY *(H RV)* 109 G4
SUNTERRA BLVD *(COCR)* . 103 E3
HTS *(COCR)* 103 F3
RD, VW *(COCR)* 103 E3
SUNTERRA RIDGE
PL *(COCR)* 103 E3
SUNTREE LN *(OKS)* . . 107 C4
PL 100, 200, 300 *(OKS)* . 107 C4
400 *(OKS)* 107 C4
500 *(OKS)* 107 C5
SUNVALE CR SE 91 AH69
CT SE 91 AH70
DR SE 91 AH70
MS SE 91 AI69
PL SE, RD SE 91 AH69
SUNVISTA CL SE 91 AK70
CR SE 91 AK71
CT SE 100. . . . . 91 AK71
200 . . . . 92 AL71
PL SE, RD SE 91 AK70
WY SE 91 AK71
SUNWOOD GT SE . . . 92 AL70
PK SE 91 AK70
PL SE 92 AL70
RD SE, WY SE 91 AK70
SUPERIOR AV SW . . . 48 Z35
SURREY ST SW 48 Y35
SUSSEX CR SW 74 AC54
SWEET WATER PL *(EV)* . 115 C8
SYDENHAM RD SW . . 59 AC37
SYDNEY DR SW 74 AC55
SYLVAN PL *(AIR)* . . . 113 E6
SYLVESTER CR SW . . 74 AC55
SYMONS VALLEY PKWY NW 3 R4
RD NW 3 V1

T

TACHE AV NW 28 AF19
TALON AV NW 59 AC38
TAMARAC CR SW 47 U34

TANNER CL *(AIR)* . . . 113 G4
DR *(AIR)* 113 G5
TARACOVE CR NE . . . 32 AY16
GT NE 32 AY16
LD NE 100 . . . . 32 AY16
200 . . . . 32 AY17
PL NE 100, 200 . . . . . . 32 AY16
RD NE 32 AZ17
WY NE 32 AZ16
TARACOVE ESTATE
DR NE 32 AZ16
TARADALE CL NE 32 AY18
DR NE 32 AY18
TARAGLEN CT NE . . . 32 AZ18
PL NE, RD NE 32 AZ18
TARALEA BY NE 32 AZ17
CIR NE 32 AZ17
CR NE, GDN NE
GN NE 32 AY17
MR NE, PK NE 32 AZ17
PL NE, WY NE 32 AY17
TARARIDGE CIR NE . . 32 AY18
CL NE 32 AZ18
CT NE, DR NE, PL NE . 32 AY18
TARAVISTA CR NE . . . 32 BA17
CT NE 32 BA17
DR NE 32 AY16
GDN NE 32 BA17
MS NE 32 BA18
ST NE 32 AZ17
WY NE 32 BA17
TARAWOOD CL NE . . 32 AZ16
GV NE 20 AZ15
LN NE 20 AY15
PL NE 100, 200 . . . . . . 20 AZ15
RD NE 20 AY15
TARINGTON CL NE . . . 32 BA18
CT NE 32 BB17
GDN NE, GN NE 32 BA18
LD NE, LK NE 32 BB17
MR NE 32 BB18
PK NE 32 BA18
PL NE 32 BB17
RD NE 32 BA18
WY NE 32 BB17
TAUNTON RD NW . . . 28 AF22
TAVENDER RD NW . . . 27 AE19
TAYLOR CR NE 28 AG20
WY *(AIR)* 113 G5
TEAKWOOD AV SE . . 62 AS37
TECUMSEH RD SW . . 48 Y36
TEMPLE CL NE 43 AW25
DR NE 43 AW23
PL NE, WY NE 43 AW25
TEMPLEBOW PL NE 100 . 43 AX22
200, 300 . . . . 43 AX22
RD NE 43 AX23
WY NE 43 AX23
TEMPLEBY CL NE . . . 44 AY23
CR NE 44 AY22
DR NE 44 AY22
GT NE 44 AY23
LN NE 44 AY22
PL NE 100, 200, 300. . 44 AY22
400 . . . . 44 AY23
500 . . . . 44 AY22
RD NE 44 AY22
WY NE 44 AZ23
TEMPLEGREEN BY NE. . 44 AY24
DR NE 44 AY24
PL NE, RD NE 44 AY24
TEMPLEHILL BY NE . . 43 AX24
CR NE, DR NE, PL NE . 43 AX24
RD NE 43 AX24
TEMPLEMONT CIR NE . 43 AW23
DR NE 43 AW23
LN NE 44 AW22
PL NE 100 . . . . 43 AW23
200, 300 . . . . 43 AW23
RD NE 43 AW22
WY NE 43 AX22
TEMPLERIDGE BY NE . 43 AX24
CL NE, CR NE 43 AX23
PL NE, WY NE 43 AX24
TEMPLESIDE BY NE . . 43 AX25
CIR NE, GT NE, PL NE . 43 AX25
RD NE 43 AX25
TEMPLESON CR NE . . 44 AZ24
GT NE 44 AZ23
PL NE 44 AZ24
RD NE, WY NE 44 AZ24
TEMPLETON BY NE . . 44 AY25
CIR NE 44 AY25
GT NE 44 AY25
PL NE, RD NE 44 AY25
TEMPLEVALE DR NE . . 44 AY23
GT NE 44 AY23
PL NE 100, 200. . . . . . 44 AY24
300 . . . . 44 AY24
TEMPLEVIEW DR NE . . 44 AY25
GT NE 44 AY25
PL NE 100, 200. . . . . . 44 AY25
WY NE 44 AY25
TEMPLEWOOD DR NE . 43 AW23
MS NE 43 AW23
PL NE 100, 200, 300 . . 43 AW23
400 . . . . 43 AW24
RD NE 43 AW24
TERRACE PL *(CAN)* . . 101 F4

TERRY RD NW 27 AE21
THACKER ST SW 65 S44
THAMES CL NW. 27 AD20
PL NW 27 AD19
THEODORE PL NW . . . 27 AD19
THISTLE BY *(STMR)* . . 112 E6
PL NE 28 AG19
WY *(STMR)* 112 E6
THOMAS DR *(STMR)* . 112 E5
PL *(STMR)* 112 E7
ST NE 28 AG21
ST *(LNG)* 88 C7
THOMSON AV NE 51 AL32
THORBURN DR *(AIR)* . 113 G5
THORNABY CR NW . . . 27 AE19
RD NW 27 AE19
WY NW 27 AD19
THORNBANK DR NW. . 28 AF19
THORNBIRD RD *(AIR)* . 113 H5
RS, WY *(AIR)* 113 H5
THORNBRIAR GN *(STMR)* . 112 E6
RD NW 28 AF22
THORNBURN DR NW. . 28 AF19
PL *(STMR)* 112 E6
RD *(STMR)* 112 E6
THORNCLIFFE CR NW . 28 AF20
DR NW 28 AF19
THORNCREST RD NE . 28 AG22
RD NW 28 AF21
THORNDALE CL *(AIR)* . 113 G5
PL NW 28 AF21
PL *(STMR)* 112 E6
RD NW 28 AF19
THORNEYCROFT DR NW 27 AD20
THORNFIELD CL *(AIR)* . 113 H4
PL *(AIR)* 113 H4
THORNHILL DR NW. . . 27 AD21
PL NW 27 AE21
THORNLEE CR NW . . . 27 AD21
THORNLEIGH CL *(AIR)* . 113 H5
WY *(AIR)* 113 H6
THORNTON RD NW . . 28 AF20
THORNWOOD CL NW . 27 AD19
PL NW 27 AD19
THORSON CR *(OKS)* . 107 D4
PL *(OKS)* 107 D4
THREE SISTERS DR *(CAN)* 101 C6
TILLER PL *(AIR)* 113 G5
TIMBERSTONE CT *(SPNG)* . 99 F2
TIPPING CL *(AIR)* . . . 113 G5
TIPTON PL NW 27 AE20
RD NW 27 AE20
TOKI RD *(COCR)* 103 B6
TONGUE RD *(H RV)* . . 109 B6
TONGUE CREEK
RD *(H RV)* 109 A1
TORONTO CR NW . . . 48 W30
TORRICE AV SW 65 T44
TOUCHWOOD DR NW. . 27 AE19
TOURNAMENT LN SW. . 89 Z72
TOWER LANE DR *(AIR)* . 113 D4
TOWER'S TR *(COCR)* . 103 C6
TOWNSEND ST NE . . . 51 AK32
TRAFFORD CR NW . . . 40 AE22
DR NW 27 AE21
PL NW 40 AD22
TRANS CANADA HWY . . 35 I24
HWY *(9700-12100)* . . . 34 A24
HWY *(CAN)* 101 E24
TRAP RD *(H RV)* 109 B5
TRAPPER RS *(CAN)* . . 101 F5
TRASIMENE CR SW . . 58 W41
TRAVIS CR NE 28 AG21
PL NE 28 AH21
ST NE 28 AH21
TRAVOIS CR NW 28 AF19
PL NW 28 AF19
TREGILLUS ST NW . . 28 AF19
TRELLE DR NE 28 AG22
TREMBLANT PL SW 100 . 55 I37
200 . . . . 55 I37
WY SW 55 I37
TROLLINGER ST NE . . 28 AG20
TSUU T'INA DR *(RED)* . 33 C4
TUCKER RD *(AIR)* . . . 113 G4
TUFFY'S HAVEN *(STMR)* . 112 E6
TUNNEL MOUNTAIN
DR *(BNF)* 21 F5
RD *(BNF)* 21 E5
TURNER DR *(T VAL)* . . 105 B6
GT *(T VAL)* 105 B6
TUSCANY BLVD NW . . 22 D15
CT NW 22 C15
DR NW 22 D15
HL NW 22 E15
VILLAGE NW 22 E14
WY NW 22 D14
TUSCANY ESTATES
CL NW 22 D15
CR NW, DR NW, PT NW 22 D15
RS NW, TER NW 22 D15
TUSCANY GLEN GN NW . 22 D15
GT NW, PK NW, PL NW. 22 D1
RD NW, WY NW 22 D15
TUSCANY HILLS BY NW . 22 F15
CIR NW, CL NW 22 E15
CR NW, MS NW 22 E15
PK NW 22 E15
PT NW 22 F15
RD NW 22 E15

TER NW, WY NW 22 E16
TUSCANY MEADOWS
BY NW 22 E17
CL NW, CM NW 22 E17
CR NW 22 E18
CT NW 22 E17
DR NW, HE NW 22 E18
HTS NW 22 F16
MS NW 100 . . . . 22 F16
200 . . . . 22 F17
PL NW 22 F17
TUSCANY RAVINE BY NW 22 F17
CL NW, CR NW, CT NW . 22 F18
LD NW 22 F17
MR NW 22 F18
MS NW 22 F18
PT NW 22 F19
RD NW 22 F17
TER NW, VW NW 22 F18
TUSCANY RIDGE BY NW . 22 D14
CL NW 22 D14
CR NW 22 D14
GN NW 22 D15
HTS NW, MS NW 22 C14
PK NW, PL NW 22 D16
TER NW 22 C15
VW NW 22 D15
TUSCANY SPRINGS
BLVD NW 22 F15
BY NW 22 E12
CIR NW 22 E13
GDN NW 22 F13
GN NW 22 F12
GV NW, HL NW 22 D13
HTS NW 22 E12
LD NW, PK NW 22 E13
PL NW 9 F12
RD NW, RS NW 22 E13
TER NW 22 E13
WY NW 22 E13
TUSCANY VALLEY DR NW 22 D13
GN NW 22 D13
GT NW 22 E14
HL NW, HTS NW 22 D14
LN NW, PK NW, RS NW . 22 E14
VW NW 22 E14
WY NW 22 E15
TUSCANY VISTA CR NW . 22 C16
CT NW 22 C16
PT NW 22 C16
RD NW 22 C17
TUSCARORA CIR NW . . 22 F14
CL NW 22 F15
CR NW, HTS NW 22 F14
MR NW 22 F14
MS NW, PL NW 22 E15
PT NW 22 E15
VW NW 22 F14
WY NW 22 F14
TUSSLEWOOD BY NW . . 22 E12
DR NW 22 C12
GV NW 22 D12
HTS NW 22 D12
TER NW 100, 200, 300 . 22 D12
VW NW 22 E12
TWEED ST NE 28 AG19
TWELVE MILE COULEE
RD NW (7070-10440) . . 22 C17
RD NW (11000) 9 C10
TWO PINE DR (B CK) . . 33 F6
TYE ST NW 48 Y29

U

UDELL RD NW 38 V28
ULM ST (LNG) 88 D8
ULRICH RD NW 38 U28
ULSTER RD NW 38 W28
ULYSSES ST NW 38 U28
UMBER PL NW 38 U29
UNDERHILL DR NW . . . 38 U28
PL NW 38 U27
UNDERWOOD PL NW . . 38 U28
UNGAVA RD NW 38 U28
UNITY PL NW 38 U28
UNIVERSITY CT NW . . . 38 V27
CT NW 100, 200 . . . . . 38 V27
300 . . . . 38 V26
400 . . . . 38 V27
DR NW 38 W28
GT NW 38 W28
PL NW 38 W28
WY NW 38 W28
UNWIN RD NW 38 W28
UPLANDS PL NW 38 U28
RDG (SPNG) 99 G2
WY (SPNG) 99 G2
UPPER PL NW 38 V27
UPTON PL NW 38 U28
URALTA RD NW 38 V28
URBANA RD NW 38 V28
URQUHART RD NW . . . 38 W28
URSENBACH RD NW . . 38 U28
USHER RD NW 38 V27
UTAH CR NW 38 U29

DR NW 38 U28
PL NW 38 V29
UXBRIDGE DR NW 38 U28

V

VAL GARDENA BLVD SW . 55 J37
VW SW 55 J37
VALDES PL NW 38 U24
VALENCIA PL NW 25 Q21
RD NW 25 Q21
VALENTINE CR SE 53 AW36
VALHALLA CR NW 25 Q21
PL NW 37 R23
VALIANT DR NW 37 Q23
PL NW 37 R23
VALLANCE CR NW 25 R22
VALLEY TR (T VAL) . . . 105 C5
VALLEY BROOK CIR NW . 34 F23
CT NW, 200 . . . . 34 F23
VALLEY CREEK BY NW . 34 B23
CR NW 34 B23
PL NW 100 . . . . 34 C22
RD NW 34 C22
VALLEY CREST CL NW . 34 A23
CT NW 100, 200, 300 . . 34 B22
GDN NW, RS NW 34 A23
VALLEY GLEN BY NW 100 . 34 F22
200 . . . . 34 F22
HTS NW 34 F22
VALLEY MEADOW CL NW . 34 E23
CR NW, GDN NW 34 E23
VALLEY PONDS CR NW . 34 C24
PL NW 34 D23
WY NW 34 C23
VALLEY RIDGE BLVD NW . 34 C22
CT NW 100, 200 . . . . . 34 D22
DR NW 34 D23
GN NW 34 C22
HTS NW 34 D23
PK NW 34 C21
PL NE (B DMD) 106 H2
PT NW 34 D22
VALLEY SPRINGS RD NW . 34 E22
TER NW 100, 200, 300 . 34 E22
VALLEY STREAM CIR NW . 34 B23
CL NW, MR NW, PL NW . 34 B23
VALLEY WOODS LD NW . 34 B21
PL NW 100 . . . . 34 B21
200, 300 . . . . 34 B21
WY NW 34 B21
VALLEYVIEW PK SE . . . 61 AQ39
RD NE 41 AM28
VALOIS AV SW 59 AC39
VAN HORNE CR NE . . . 41 AM28
VANCE PL NW 37 T23
VANCOUVER CR NW . . 37 T23
VANDALE PL NW 37 R24
VANDERGRIFT CR NW . . 37 S24
PL (LNG) 88 C7
VANDOOS CR NW 25 S21
PL NW, RD NW 25 S21
VL NW 37 S22
VANDYKE PL NW 37 S24
RD NW 37 R23
VANGUARD PL NW . . . 37 S22
RD NW 25 R22
VANSTONE CR NW . . . 37 S22
RD NW 25 R21
VANTAGE BY NW 37 R23
CR NW, RD NW 37 R23
VANTAGE RIDGE
EST (SPNG) 99 A3
VARAL PL NW 37 T25
RD NW 37 T25
VARANGER PL NW . . . 37 Q25
VARBAY PL NW 37 T24
VARBOW PL NW 37 T25
VARBROOK PL NW . . . 38 U25
VARCOURT PL NW . . . 37 Q24
VARCOVE PL NW 37 T24
VARCREST PL NW 38 U24
VARDANA PL NW 37 T24
RD NW 37 T24
VARDELL PL NW 38 U24
RD NW 37 T24
VARLEY DR NW 37 T26
VARMOOR PL NW 38 U25
RD NW 37 T25
VARNA CR NW 37 Q25
PL NW 37 Q25
VARSCLIFF PL NW . . . 37 Q24
CR NW 100, 200 . . . . . 37 Q23
DR NW, GN NW 37 Q23
LN NW 37 S23
PL NW, RD NW 37 P23
VARSCONNA PL NW . . 37 T25
VARSDALE PL NW 37 R24
VARSFIELD PL NW . . . 37 R24
VARSHAVEN PL NW . . 37 T24
VARSITY CL NW 37 P23
VARSITY ESTATES
BY NW 100 . . . . 25 P20

200, 300, 400. . . . 25 P21
500. . . . . 25 P21
CL NW 25 P19
CR NW 25 O19
CT NW 25 Q20
DR NW 25 O19
GDN NW 25 Q20
GN NW 25 O21
GV NW, LK NW 25 O21
MS NW, 100, 200 . . . . 25 Q20
300 . . . . 25 O19
PK NW 25 Q21
PL NW 100 . . . . 25 P20
200, 300, 400. . . . 25 P20
500, 600 . . . . 25 O19
700, 800 . . . . 25 O20
900, 1000 . . . . . . 25 Q21
RD NW 25 P21
RS NW 25 Q21
TER NW 100, 200, 300 . 25 P19
VW NW 25 P19
VARSITY GREEN
BY NW 100 . . . . 25 Q22
200 . . . . 25 Q22
VARSITY RIDGE GT NW . 25 Q21
TER NW 25 Q22
VARSLEA PL NW 37 T24
VARSPLAIN PL NW . . . 37 T24
VARSTON PL NW 37 T25
VARSVILLE PL NW 38 U25
VARTOWN PL NW 37 T25
VARVIEW PL NW 37 Q24
VARWOOD PL NW 37 T24
VAUGHAN ST NE 41 AM28
VAUXHALL CR NW . . . 37 S24
VEGAS RD NW 37 T23
VEINER ST NE 41 AN28
VENTURA LN NE 41 AN27
PL NE, RD NE 42 AO27
TER NE 41 AN28
WY NE 42 AO27
VERCHERES ST SW . . . 59 AB39
VERDUN PL NW 37 S23
VERMILION LAKES
RD (BNF) 21 A4
VERMILLION ST NE . . . 41 AN28
VERNON PL NW 38 U24
VERONA DR NW 37 S22
VERONICA PL NW 25 Q22
RD NW 25 R22
VERULUM PL NW 37 R24
VETERANS WY NW . . . 47 T30
VICARY PL NW 37 Q24
VICEROY DR NW 25 R22
PL NW 25 R22
VICTORIA CR NW 38 Y28
VICTORIA BEACH
BY (CHST) 80 B7
VIENNA DR NW 25 R21
VILLA CR NW 38 U23
VILLAGE AV (OKS) 107 B7
GDN SW 46 Q31
HTS SW 46 P31
LN (OKS) 107 B7
MS SW 46 Q31
TER SW 46 Q31
VIMY WY SW 58 Y41
VINCENT DR NW 37 T24
PL NW 37 T23
VIRGINIA DR NW 37 S22
ST (AIR) 113 E3
VISCOUNT DR NW 37 S23
VISSAR CR NW 37 T23
VISSER PL (OKS) 107 D5
WY (OKS) 107 D5
VISTA CR NE 41 AM28
RD NE, ST NE 41 AM28
VOYAGEUR DR NW . . . 37 S22

W

WADDY LN (STMR) . . . 112 D7
WAINWRIGHT PL SE . . . 75 AF54
RD SE 75 AF54
WAKEFIELD DR SW . . . 46 Q35
WALDRON AV (OKS) . . 107 D4
PL (OKS) 107 D4
WALES GN (LNG) 112 D7
WALNUT DR SW 47 S32
WALROND RD SE 75 AI54
WANETA CR SE 75 AF55
WAPITI CL (CAN) 101 F4
DR SE 75 AF55
WARREN RD SE 75 AG54
WARWICK DR SW 47 R33
WASCANA CR SE 75 AG55
RD SE 75 AG55
WASKATENAU CR SW . . 47 R36
WATERLOO DR SW . . . 47 T33
WATERSTONE CR (AIR) . 113 E6
GT (AIR) 113 E6
PL 100, 200, 300 (AIR). . 113 E6
WATSON RD SE 75 AG55
WAVERLEY DR SW . . . 47 R33

WEDDENBURN RD SE . . 75 AF54
WEDGEWOOD DR SW . . 47 T33
WELCH CR (OKS) 107 E5
PL 100 (OKS) 107 E5
200 (OKS) 107 D5
WELLINGTON CV (STMR) . 112 D8
PL SW 47 T33
WELSHIMER CR (LNG) . . 88 E6
WENSTROM CR (LNG) . . 88 E7
WENTWORTH AV SW . . 45 I31
CIR SW, CL SW 45 J32
CR SW 45 H31
CR (OKS) 107 D5
CV SW 45 J32
DR SW 45 I32
GDN SW, GN SW 45 K32
GT SW 45 K32
GV SW 45 I32
HE SW 45 H31
HTS SW 45 I31
LK SW 45 J32
MR SW 45 J32
MS SW 45 J32
PK SW 100, 200 . . . . . 45 K31
PL SW 100, 200. . . . . 45 L32
300, 400, 500 . . . 45 K32
600, 700, 800 . . . 45 K32
PT SW 100, 200 . . . . . 45 I31
RD SW 45 K32
RS SW 45 J31
VW SW 45 I32
WY SW 45 K32
WEST AARSBY RD (COCR) 103 C4
WEST ANDISON
CL 103 C4
WEST BARRET PL (COCR). 103 C4
WEST BEYNON RS (COCR) 103 C3
WEST BLUFF BY (SPNG) . 99 H4
CT, DR, PL (SPNG) . . . 99 H3
RD (SPNG) 99 G3
RDG (SPNG) 99 G4
WEST BOOTHBY
CR (COCR) 103 C4
WEST BROATCH
PL (COCR) 103 B4
WEST CAMPUS BLVD NW . 37 T26
DR NW. 37 T27
WY NW 37 T28
WEST CEDAR PL SW . . 45 L30
PT SW 45 L31
RS SW 46 M31
WEST CHAPMAN
PL (COCR) 103 C4
WEST CHESTERMERE
DR (CHST) 80 B8
WEST COPITHORNE
PL (COCR) 103 C4
WEST CREEK BLVD (CHST) 80 A7
BY 100, 200, 300 (CHST) . 80 A7
400 (CHST) 80 A7
CIR, CL, CL (CHST) . . . 80 A7
CR (CHST) 80 A7
CV 100, 200 (CHST) . . . 80 A7
DR, GLEN
MDWS (CHST) 80 A7
POND, PT, SP (CHST) . 80 A7
SP 100, 200 (CHST) . . . 80 A7
WEST EDGE RD (COCR) . 103 B4
WEST GISSING
RD (COCR) 103 C3
WEST GLEN CR SW . . . 47 R35
WEST HALL PL (COCR) . 103 B4
WEST HOWES PL (COCR) . 103 C4
WEST KERFOOT
PL (COCR) 103 C4
WEST LAKEVIEW
CIR (CHST) 80 B7
CL (CHST) 80 B8
CR (CHST) 80 B7
DR (CHST) 80 A7
PL (CHST) 80 B8
PS (CHST) 80 B7
PT (CHST) 80 B8
WEST MacKAY CR (COCR) 103 C4
WEST McDOUGAL
RD (COCR) 103 C3
WEST McGONIGLE
PL (COCR) 103 C3
WEST McMANUS
RD (COCR) 103 C4
WEST MEADOWS
CT (SPNG) 99 D7
DR (SPNG) 99 H4
EST (SPNG) 99 D7
PL SW 45 L30
PL (SPNG) 99 D7
WEST MITFORD
CR (COCR) 103 B4
WEST MOORE PL (COCR) . 103 B4
WEST MURPHY PL (COCR) 103 C4
WEST PARK DR (CHST) . 80 B3
PL (COCR) 103 C4
WEST PINE RD (STMR) . 112 C8
WEST RANCH PL SW 100 . 45 L30
200, 300 . . . . 45 L30
RD SW 45 L30
WEST RIDGE RD (STMR) . 112 C8
WEST RIDGE PARK
LN (SPNG) 99 H4
WEST SIDE DR (COCR) . 103 C4

WEST SPICER PL *(COCR)* . 103 C3
WEST SPRINGS CL SW . . 36 M29
CT SW 46 M30
GT SW 36 M29
PL SW, RD SW 46 M30
WY SW 46 N30
WEST TERRACE
BY 100 *(COCR)* 103 B4
200 *(COCR)* 103 B4
CL, CR *(COCR)* 103 B4
DR *(COCR)* 103 A4
PL 100, 200, 300 *(COCR)* 103 A4
PT *(COCR)* 103 A4
PT 100 *(COCR)* 103 A4
200 *(COCR)* 103 A4
RD, RS *(COCR)* 103 A4
WY *(COCR)* 103 B4
WEST TOWER PL *(COCR)* . 103 B4
WEST VALLEY RD SW . . 34 E24
WEST WOOD RD *(SPNG)* . . 99 H4
WESTCHESTER
BLVD 80 B8
BY *(CHST)* 80 B9
CV, GT, KEY *(CHST)* . . 80 B8
RD *(STMR)* 112 D8
WY *(CHST)* 80 B9
WESTDALE ST *(STMR)* . . 112 D7
WESTERN DR *(CRS)* 8 E4
WESTFALL CR *(OKS)* . . . 107 C8
DR, GN *(OKS)* 107 C8
WESTLAKE CIR *(STMR)* . 112 D8
GLEN, MS *(STMR)* . . . 112 C8
RD *(STMR)* 112 D8
WESTLAND GT *(OKS)* . . 107 B8
RD *(OKS)* 107 B7
ST *(OKS)* 107 B8
WESTMINSTER DR SW . . 47 R34
PL SW 47 R34
WESTMOUNT BLVD NW. 49 AA33
DR 112 C8
RD NW 48 Y33
RD *(STMR)* 112 C8
WESTON CT SW 35 L29
DR SW, GN SW 45 L30
MR SW, PK SW, PL SW . 35 L29
RS SW 45 L30
WY SW 35 L29
WESTOVER DR SW 47 R34
WESTPOINT BY SW 46 M31
CT SW, GDN SW 46 M30
PL SW, WY SW 46 M31
WESTRIDGE CL *(OKS)* . . 107 B8
CR SW 45 L31
CR *(OKS)* 107 B8
DR *(OKS)* 107 B7
GN, RD, RS *(OKS)* . . . 107 B8
WESTROCK RD *(COCR)* . 103 C5
WESTVIEW DR SW 46 Q33
EST *(SPNG)* 99 B3
PL *(STMR)* 112 D7
ST *(STMR)* 112 D7
WESTWINDS DR NE . . . 34 AT21
WESTWOOD CR SW 46 Q34
DR SW 46 Q35
TER SW 47 S35
WHEATLAND AV SW . . . 47 R35
GN *(STMR)* 112 D7
PL *(STMR)* 112 D7
TR *(STMR)* 112 D9
WHEELER PL *(STMR)* . . 112 D7
ST *(STMR)* 112 D7
WHISKEY JACK CR *(BNF)*. . 21 D4
WHISPERING WATER
BEND *(EV)* 115 D7
HOLLOW, TR, WY *(EV)* . 115 D7
WHISPERING WOODS
TER *(EV)* 115 D8
WHITAKER BY NE 43 AT24
CL NE 42 AS24
CT NE 43 AT24
WHITE AV *(B CK)* 33 F8
CR *(B CK)* 33 G8
PL *(B CK)* 33 F8
WHITE OAK CR SW 47 R32
WHITE PINE WY NW 35 I23
WHITEBOW PL NE 43 AV22
WHITEFIELD CL NE 43 AT24
CR NE 43 AU23
DR NE, PL NE 43 AT24
WHITEGLEN CL NE 43 AV24
RD NE 42 AS23
WHITEHAVEN CR NE . . . 43 AT22
RD NE 42 AS24
WHITEHILL GT NE 43 AV23
PL NE 100 . . . . 43 AU23
200, 300, 400 . . . . 43 AU22
500 . . . . 43 AU22
WY NE 43 AU23
WHITEHORN CR NE 43 AU25
DR NE 43 AU25
PL NE 100 . . . . 43 AU24
200, 300, 400 . . . . 43 AU24
RD NE 43 AT24
WY NE 43 AU24
WHITELAND BY NE 43 AW22
DR NE 43 AV23
GT NE 43 AV22
WHITEMONT DR NE 43 AV22
PL NE 43 AV22

WHITERAM CL NE 43 AT23
CT NE 43 AT24
GT NE 43 AT24
HL NE 43 AT24
MS NE, PL NE, WY NE. 43 AT23
WHITERIDGE CR NE . . . 43 AV23
PL NE 43 AV23
PL NE 100, 200. . . . . . 43 AV24
RD NE, WY NE 43 AV23
WHITESIDE CR NE 43 AV24
RD NE 43 AV24
WHITESTONE CR NE. . . 43 AV25
RD NE, WY NE 43 AV25
WHITEVIEW BY NE 43 AV25
CL NE 43 AV25
PL NE 43 AV25
RD NE 43 AV25
WHITEWOOD BY NE . . . 43 AV23
PL NE 100, 200. . . . . . 43 AV23
RD NE 43 AV23
WHITFIELD AV *(CRS)* 8 F2
WHITLOCK CL NE 43 AU25
PL NE 100, 200. . . . . . 43 AU25
WY NE 43 AU22
WHITLOW CL NE 43 AU22
PL NE 43 AU23
WHITMAN CL NE 42 AS25
CR NE 42 AS25
PL NE 100, 200, 300. . 43 AT25
WHITMIRE BY NE 42 AS24
RD NE, VL NE. 42 AS24
WHITNEL CL NE 43 AT25
CT NE 43 AU25
PL NE 43 AT25
WHITNEY CR SE 75 AF54
ST *(LNG)* 88 D8
WHITWORTH PL NE 43 AT22
RD NE 42 AS23
WY NE 42 AS22
WILCOX ST SE 75 AI57
WILD ROSE DR *(SPNG)*. . 99 H4
WILDE RD SE 75 AG54
WILDERNESS DR SE . . . 75 AH56
PL SE 75 AG56
WILDFLOWER CR *(STMR)*. 112 B8
CV, RD *(STMR)* 112 B8
WILDWOOD DR SW 47 S31
WILKES RD SE 75 AH57
WILKINSON PL SE 75 AH57
WILLACY DR SE 75 AI57
WILLAMETTE DR SE 75 AI57
WILLAMINA CR SE 75 AH57
WILLARD RD SE 75 AI57
WILLESDEN DR SE 75 AI57
WILLIAM ST SE 51 AJ36
ST *(CAN)* 101 D4
ST *(COCR)* 103 F4
ST *(T VAL)* 105 B4
WILLIAMS PL *(B CK)* . . . 33 E7
WILLINGDON BLVD SE . . 75 AG57
WILLOUGHBY CR SE . . . 75 AH57
WILLOW CR SW 47 U33
DR *(STMR)* 112 D7
WY NW 35 H23
WILLOW BEND PL SE . . . 75 AH55
WILLOW BROOK BY *(AIR)* 113 C2
CL 100, 200 *(AIR)* 113 C2
300, 400 *(AIR)* . . . 113 C2
CR *(AIR)* 113 D3
DR SE 75 AH55
DR *(AIR)* 113 C2
GT *(AIR)* 113 C3
PL *(AIR)* 113 C2
WILLOW GROVE CR SE . 75 AH55
WILLOW PARK DR SE . . . 75 AF55
GN SE 75 AG56
PL SE 75 AH55
WILLOW RIDGE
BLVD SW *(B DMD)* . . . 106 G4
PL SE 75 AF55
RD SE 75 AF55
WY SW *(B DMD)*. . . . 106 G4
WILLOWBURN DR SE . . . 75 AI55
WILLOWCREST RD SW . . 75 AH55
WILLOWDALE CR SE . . . 75 AH54
WILLOWFERN DR SE . . . 75 AJ56
WILLOWGLEN PL SE . . . 75 AI55
WILLOWGREEN DR SE . . 75 AI55
WILLOWIND PL SE 75 AI55
WILLOWISP RD SE 75 AJ56
WILLOWMERE CL *(CHST)*. 80 A5
WY *(CHST)* 80 A6
WILLOWVIEW RD SE . . . 75 AI55
WILMER RD SE 75 AH57
WILSHIRE PL SW 47 T33
WILSON PL *(CAN)* 101 B5
RD SE 75 AH57
RD *(LNG)* 88 C6
ST *(OKS)* 107 C5
WY *(CAN)* 101 B7
WILTON PL SE 75 AH54
WILVERSIDE WY SE . . . 75 AH56
WIMBLEDON CR SE 47 R32
DR SW 47 R31
WINCHESTER CR SW. . . 47 R35
WINDERMERE
BLVD *(CHST)* 80 B5
DR *(CHST)* 80 A5

RD SW 47 R33
WINDING RIVER PT *(EV)*. 115 E7
RS, WY *(EV)* 115 E7
WINDSOR AV *(T VAL)* . . 105 A4
CR SW 67 AD44
PL *(STMR)* 112 D7
ST NW 48 W29
WINSLOW CR SW 46 Q33
WINSTON DR SW 46 Q34
WINTER HTS SW 35 J27
WINTERBOURNE CR SE. 75 AH55
WINTERGREEN RD *(B CK)* . 33 G6
WINTERS WY *(OKS)* . . . 107 G3
WOLF CL *(RED)* 33 D3
CR *(RED)* 33 D3
CT *(RED)* 33 E3
DR *(RED)* 33 C4
ST *(BNF)* 21 C5
WOLFE ST SW 59 AB38
WOLFWILLOW LN *(EV)* . 115 D9
PT *(EV)* 115 D9
RDG *(EV)* 115 D9
WY *(EV)* 115 E9
WOLVERINE ST *(BNF)* . . . 21 E6
WOOD CR SW 82 AA59
WOOD CREST CL SW . . . 81 Y61
PL SW 100, 200. . . . . . 81 Y61
WY SW 81 Z60
WOOD OAK PL SW 81 Y61
WY SW 81 Z60
WOOD VALLEY
BY SW 100 . . . . 81 U60
200, 300 . . . . 81 U60
CT SW 100 . . . . 81 V61
200 . . . . 81 U61
DR SW 81 U60
GT SW 81 U61
MS SW 81 V60
PL SW 100, 200, 300 . . 81 V60
RD SW 81 U60
RS SW 81 U61
WOOD WILLOW BY SW. . 81 Z61
CL SW 81 Z61
GT SW 81 Z60
PL SW 81 Z61
WY SW 81 X62
WOODACRES CR SW . . . 81 X61
CT SW, DR SW. 81 X61
PL SW, RD SW 81 W61
WOODBEND RD SE 75 AH55
WY *(OKS)* 107 C7
WOODBINE BLVD SW . . . 81 V60
WOODBOROUGH CR SW . 81 V58
PL SW, RD SW 81 V59
TER SW 81 V58
WOODBRIAR CIR SW. . . 81 U59
GT SW, PL SW 81 U59
PL SW 100, 200, 300 . . 81 U59
400, 500, 600 . . . . 81 U59
700 . . . . 81 U59
WOODBROOK CL SW . . . 73 V57
CT SW, GN SW. 81 V58
MS SW 100, 200, 300 . . 81 V58
PL SW 81 U58
RD SW 81 V58
WY SW 81 V58
WOODBURN CR *(OKS)* . 107 C7
WOODCROFT PL SW . . . 81 Z59
WOODFERN CT SW 81 W58
DR SW 81 W58
PL SW 100, 200. . . . . . 73 W57
RD SW 81 W59
RS SW, WY SW. 81 W58
WOODFIELD CL SW 81 W60
CR SW 81 W61
CT SW 81 W61
DR SW, GN SW. 81 W60
PL SW 81 W60
200, 300 . . . . 81 X60
RD SW 81 W60
WY SW 81 W60
WOODFORD CL SW 81 W58
CR SW 73 X57
CT SW 81 X58
DR SW 81 W58
PL SW 73 W57
WOODGATE BY SW 82 AA60
CL SW 82 AA60
RD *(OKS)* 107 C7
WOODGLEN CIR SW . . . 81 X59
CL SW 81 W58
CR SW, CT SW 81 W59
GT SW 81 X59
GV SW 81 W59
MS SW 81 X58
PL SW 100, 200, 300 . . 81 X59
400 . . . . 81 X59
PL *(OKS)* 107 C7
RD SW 81 X59
RS SW 81 X58
WY SW 81 W58
WOODGREEN CR SW. . . 81 Z60
DR SW 81 Z60
PL SW 82 AA60
WOODGROVE BY *(OKS)*. 107 D7
CR SW 82 AA60
WOODHAVEN BY SW 100. 81 V61
200, 300, 400 . . . 81 V61
500. . . . . 81 V62

CR SW 81 V61
DR *(OKS)* 107 C7
MR SW 81 W61
PL SW 100, 200 . . . . . 81 V61
300, 400 . . . . . . 81 W61
RD SW 81 V61
VW SW 81 W61
WOODHILL CT SW 81 Y60
PL SW, RD SW. 81 Y60
WOODLAND CR SE 75 AH54
WOODLARK DR SW 47 S31
WOODMARK CR SW. . . . 81 W59
PL SW 81 W58
WOODMEADOW CL SW . 81 Z59
WOODMONT CR SW 81 V60
CT SW 100, 200. . . . . . 81 W60
DR SW 81 V59
GN SW 81 V59
GT SW, PL SW 81 V60
RS SW 81 V60
TER SW 81 V59
WY SW 81 V59
WOODPARK AV SW 81 W61
BLVD SW 81 W61
BY SW 100 . . . . 81 X58
200 . . . . 81 X58
CIR SW 81 X58
CL SW 81 X58
CR SW 81 Z58
CT SW 100, 200, 300 . . 81 X58
GN SW 100 . . . . 81 X58
200 . . . . 81 Y58
300. . . . . 81 Y58
LK SW 81 Y58
PL SW 100, 200. . . . . . 81 Z58
300, 400. . . . . . 81 Z59
RD SW 81 Z59
TER SW 100, 200 . . . . . 81 Y58
WY SW 81 Z59
WOODPATH RD SW 81 V61
TER SW 81 U61
WOODRIDGE CL SW . . . 81 Z61
DR SW 81 Y61
PL SW 100 . . . . 81 Y61
200, 300 . . . . 81 Y61
TER SW 81 Y61
WOODROW PL *(OKS)* . . 107 C7
WOODSIDE BLVD *(AIR)* . 113 B2
BY SW 100 . . . . 81 Y60
200 . . . . 81 Y61
300. . . . . 81 Y61
BY *(AIR)* 113 A2
CIR SW 81 Y60
CIR *(AIR)* 113 B2
CL *(AIR)* 113 B3
CR *(AIR)* 113 C2
CT *(AIR)* 113 A2
DR *(AIR)* 113 B3
GT SW 81 Y60
GT *(AIR)* 113 C3
LK *(AIR)* 113 C2
LN *(AIR)* 113 C2
LN *(CAN)* 101 B3
MS *(AIR)* 113 C2
PK *(AIR)* 113 B2
PL SW 81 Y60
PL 100 *(AIR)* 113 C3
200 *(AIR)* 113 C3
PL *(OKS)* 107 C7
RD SW 81 Y60
RD *(AIR)* 113 C3
RS *(AIR)* 113 B2
WY *(AIR)* 113 C2
WOODSMAN LN SW. . . . 81 W59
WOODSTOCK PL SW 100 . 81 Y59
200. . . . . 81 Y59
RD SW, WY SW 81 Y59
WOODSWORTH RD SE. . 75 AI54
WOODVALE BY SW 100 . 81 Y60
200. . . . . 81 Y60
CR SW 81 X60
RD SW 81 X60
WOODVIEW BY SW 100 . 81 Z59
BY *(OKS)* 107 D7
CR SW 81 Y59
CT SW, DR SW 81 Y59
PL SW 100 . . . . 81 Y59
RD SW 81 Y59
TER SW 81 X59
WORCESTER DR SW . . . 47 R33

XYZ

YANKEE VALLEY RD *(AIR)* 113 G1
RD *(AIR)* 113 F7
YOHO TINDA RD *(B CK)* . . 33 G6
YPRES GN SW. 58 Y41
WY SW 58 Y41
ZOO RD NE 51 AK34